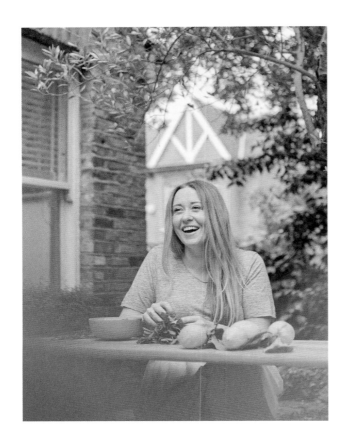

Anna Jones is a cook, writer, and stylist, the voice of modern vegetarian cooking, and the author of the bestselling *A Modern Way to Eat*, *A Modern Way to Cook*, and *The Modern Cook's Year*, which won the Guild of Food Writers Cookery Book Award 2018 and *Observer Food Monthly*'s Best Cookbook 2018. Her books have been nominated for the James Beard, Fortnum & Mason, and André Simon awards and have been widely acclaimed across the media as books of the year. Anna's books have been translated into six languages. She writes a weekly, well-loved column for the *Guardian*. Anna believes in putting vegetables at the center of the table and the unbridled joy of cooking and eating. She lives in Hackney, East London, with her husband and young son.

The Modern Cook's Year

Anna Jones

More than 250 vibrant vegetarian recipes
to see you through the seasons

Photographs by Ana Cuba

Abrams
New York

For Mum and Dad
Your kindness and love are limitless.
Parents and humans don't come better.

And in memory of Laura Plane,
a shining beacon to how life should be
lived. Your unstoppable kindness, grace,
and sense of fun sparkle on.

Editor: Laura Dozier
Design Manager: Deb Wood/Liam Flanagan
Production Manager: Kathleen Gaffney

Library of Congress Control Number: 2018945587

ISBN: 978-1-4197-3615-5

First published in Great Britain in 2017 by 4th Estate,
an imprint of HarperCollins Publishers

Text copyright © 2017 Anna Jones

Photography copyright © 2017 Ana Cuba

Design by Jonathan Pelham

Art direction by Rachel Vere

Printed and bound in China

10 9 8 7 6 5 4 3 2 1

Abrams books are available at special discounts when
purchased in quantity for premiums and promotions as
well as fundraising or educational use. Special editions
can also be created to specification. For details, contact
specialsales@abramsbooks.com or the address below.

Abrams® is a registered trademark of Harry N. Abrams, Inc.

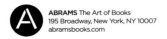

ABRAMS The Art of Books
195 Broadway, New York, NY 10007
abramsbooks.com

Introduction

There is something so joyful about eating food at its very best. Damsons as the nights draw in, apricots when the nights are at their longest, watermelon on a searing hot day, squash at Halloween. It is about an ingredient at its peak, the apex of its flavor, but more than that it's about a time, a place, and the memories of summers, Christmases, and days past that are wrapped up in every bite of food we eat.

In London, where I live, the ebb and flow of the year is so apparent, the seasons come and go with force, and how we eat changes dramatically. As a young chef, learning to cook with the seasons was truly the most miraculous discovery. Every Saturday would start with strong coffee alongside almost every London chef at Borough market. Then I'd walk over to Tony Booth's veg stall, smell peaches, squeeze tomatoes, bite sharp little apples. It reconnected me with nature, with what was growing.

For me, a year divided into four seasons feels too vague. Anyone who has stepped into a greengrocer on the winter side of spring and then again at the summer's end will tell you that the two are very different. There are so many more subtleties to what's growing than spring, summer, autumn and winter. It's this rhythm, this relationship with nature, that I encourage you to foster. No June is the same, ramps will fill the hedgerows up at different times each year, the French apricots will arrive a few weeks later. The seasons are a useful tool but our eyes and taste buds should be our guide. This book is written in six chapters, which roughly knit together two months at a time, but let your senses, and the fruits and vegetables you find at your market, lead you. As each year comes and goes I am led to cook dishes at slightly different times and find that the very best day for an ingredient does vary. With this in mind I encourage you not to think too rigidly about the seasons and the chapters of this book, use the produce on your doorstep to make the food that you feel like eating. If that's macaroni cheese in July, so be it. The pages of this book are intended as a guide; you are the cook and the eater.

As much as the ripeness and readiness of an ingredient and how it is cooked are important, the feeling at a certain time of year can inform how I cook too. A cool green salad eaten outside with little fuss suits the hot impatience of summer, a bowl of soup eaten with a spoon from a cushion balanced on a lap is homey, comforting, and grounding like autumn. A just-warm salad of freshly podded peas, fava beans, and the first asparagus echoes the promise, the smell of freshly mown grass, the verdant green of spring. It's my desire as a cook to feel and allow others to share these emotions, to punctuate the year with the memorable meals I have loved again and again, to nourish those I love with more than the flavor of food.

With that in mind, I have included milestones and things I do at different times of year here too, from making wreaths at Christmas to resetting my culinary clock in spring. I hope they help to weave a picture of the year.

The techniques I lean on in the kitchen change too as the year unfolds. In winter, my heavy cast-iron pots never leave the stovetop, always full of soup or a vegetable braise. In spring, vegetables that are tender and fresh need only a lick of heat from a hot frying pan. In summer, I use my mandoline most, to finely slice fennel and zucchini, for grilling and for raw salads. The dishes, the way I cook, and the time I want to spend doing it change as dramatically as the contents of my fruit bowl and fridge.

While summer cooking tends to be the quickest I am somewhat of an impatient cook all year round. There are odd days when I linger in the kitchen but most often I cook dinner for my husband, my son, and myself in under an hour, and those are the kind of recipes you will find in this book. A few use quite a lot of ingredients, for layering flavor and texture, which I feel is such an important part of cooking vegetables. I work with a palette of ingredients throughout the recipes in this book, so I hope that if you do invest in something new you will find lots of ideas for cooking with it in these pages.

Eating with the seasons naturally leads us to putting vegetables at the center of our tables. This is how I eat every day and increasingly how many of us are eating. In the five years since I started writing my first book, the food landscape of how we eat has changed dramatically for the better. Vegetable-focused meals a few nights a week have become the norm for many, and for that I am deeply grateful. We have damaged this planet—there have been decades of misuse—and eating mostly vegetables, and shopping and eating in season and locally, are huge personal steps we can take in a better direction.

I have wherever possible tried to include vegan alternatives in lots of recipes; my brother and sister are both vegan so I cook this way often. For me it's also important not to rely too heavily on dairy and eggs; while I do include good organic versions in my diet, I make sure a few meals each week are completely egg- and dairy-free, helping further reduce our load on the world around us.

The U.K. is a small country, so when I think about seasonal eating I include Amalfi lemons, apricots from Provence, rice from Puglia. While I shop as locally as possible and my focus is on British produce, when I need to, I lean on our European friends and their incredible offerings. Never has it been more important to foster the links that food creates, the trade it encourages, and the barriers it breaks down.

A note on shopping

I long for a vegetable garden and to grow what I eat, but that's not my reality just now; I shop for all my food (with the exception of a little foraging). The bulk of what I buy is from local shops and our excellent farmers' market, topped off with the odd supermarket delivery for bulky things and dry goods.

My weekly trip to the market is my connection with nature, with food at its source. Seeing the first zucchini appear or the array of apples in autumn is my connection with the earth. Of course, I walk in the parks and escape to the sea often, but in the city it's this trip that connects me with nature, with a place in time. I don't need to be told when asparagus is in season anymore; having cooked for years I know when it will arrive but I still go, I still walk the stalls, even if there is little to buy and my fridge is full. It grounds me, reminds me of the wonder of food, and the weeks I can't make it I miss it.

I know the reality for many is that their shopping is done at a supermarket or online, and for a few months when my son was small, so was mine (and our local shops are less than a five-minute walk away). Supermarkets are getting better at stocking and championing seasonal, local produce, so it is absolutely possible to eat seasonally and shop there. If you aren't in tune with the season, perhaps remind yourself of what's growing and good to eat now before you shop: look at labels, buy local if you can. Even if sometimes it costs a little more, it will without doubt taste superior. The more we buy ethical, local, and seasonal produce from our supermarkets, the more they will stock, so with each purchase you are making a change.

Also, my friends across the Atlantic need not worry—changes to this edition have been made to ensure that each recipe can be made in the United States using local ingredients.

Start of the year

Best of the season
  Kale
  Leeks
  Rutabaga
  Purple-sprouting broccoli
  Savoy cabbage
  Brussels sprouts
  Radicchio
  Winter citrus
  Pomegranate
  Hothouse rhubarb

Flowers
  Mimosa
  Hellebores
  Magnolia
  Anemone

Grapefruit with honey and cilantro-seed toasted oats

I eat fruit for breakfast every, day but at the start of the year I find my fruit bowl a little empty. We eat pears, apples, pomegranates, and, when they arrive, blood oranges, but it's not the offering of spring or summer and I get a bit bored. That's when I turn back to grapefruit. I ate it growing up, an inch of sugar as a roof, with a special serrated spoon to scoop out each segment. This is now a breakfast we eat on repeat. It feels grown-up and delicate but requires little more than a few minutes at the stove.

Cilantro seeds (also known as coriander seeds) find their way into many sweet things as well as savory in my kitchen these days, their lemony character a perfect pep to a bright bit of winter citrus. This is as good at the end of a meal as for breakfast.

Peel and segment or slice your grapefruit, taking care to get rid of any big pieces of bitter pith. If you have any pieces of grapefruit peel with juicy flesh attached, keep them to use in the syrup. Bash the cilantro seeds in a mortar with pestle, spice grinder, or mixing bowl with rolling pin until they have broken down a little and smell fragrant.

Put a small pan over a medium heat, add the cilantro seeds, and toast them for a minute until they smell toasty and more fragrant. Take the pan off the heat and add 2 tablespoons of cold water and the honey, then squeeze in the juice from any of the bits of grapefruit peel you have saved. Put the pan back over the heat and simmer for a minute or so until the liquid all bubbles down into a thick syrup.

In another pan, melt the butter until it's foamy, then add the oats and toast, stirring them all the time until they are buttery brown and smelling great. Add the vanilla paste and stir for another minute or so.

Put the grapefruit slices on two plates, pour over the warm syrup, and top with the yogurt and oats and a little more honey, if you like things sweet.

SERVES 2

2 grapefruits

½ teaspoon cilantro (coriander) seeds

2 tablespoons honey or agave nectar, plus more to finish

1 teaspoon butter

4 tablespoons rolled oats

1 teaspoon vanilla paste

⅓ cup (100 g) plain yogurt (I use coconut yogurt)

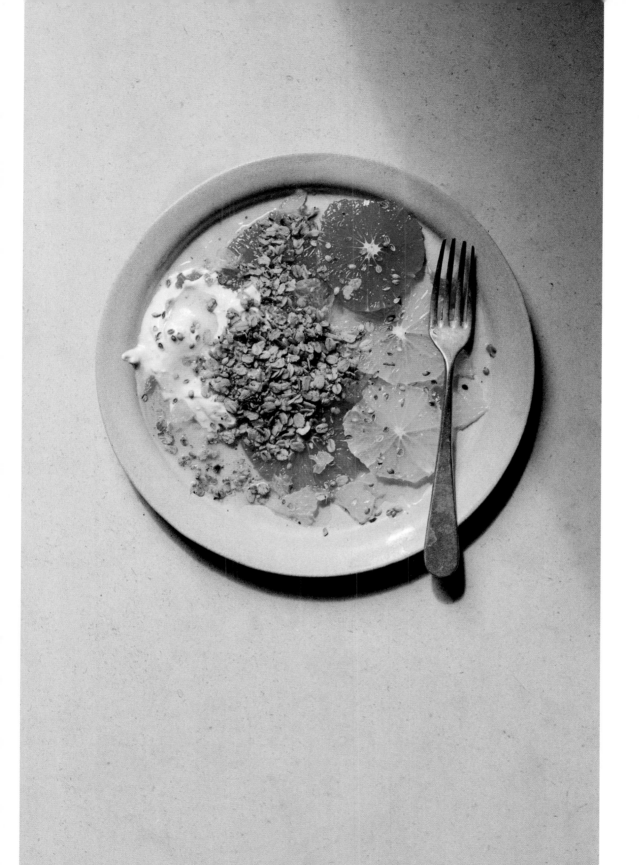

Saffron breakfast kheer

Kheer is an Indian rice pudding eaten on high holy days and at feasts. It is a calming mix of gentle spice, milk, and rice, which I find especially good to eat at breakfast time. There is nothing more nourishing to my mind than milk and rice together—easy to eat and cleansing in the best possible sense of the word. I make a double batch of this and reheat it with a little extra milk on the following days; sometimes it's dessert too. Kheer is used in the Ayurvedic tradition to balance the system during the winter; the sweet cinnamon helps digestion, and the warmth of the rice and milk protects against any wintery cold.

I use brown rice here but white rice would be just as delicious. I suggest soaking the rice overnight—it is a two-minute job and will vastly speed up the cooking process. If you don't remember to do it overnight, then soaking it as long as you can will be OK. If saffron is a bridge too far for breakfast, then you can just leave it out; the other spices will hold up.

SERVES 4

1 cup (150 g) long-grain brown rice

¾ cup (100 g) cashew nuts

⅓ cup (50 g) blanched almonds

4½ cups (1 L) almond milk (I use unsweetened)

6 cardamom pods

⅔ cup (100 g) raisins (I use golden ones)

¼ teaspoon ground ginger

a pinch of saffron threads, soaked in 3½ tablespoons (50 ml) boiling water (optional)

1 small cinnamon stick

2 tablespoons golden honey

TO SERVE

the zest of 1 unwaxed lime

a small handful of toasted coconut flakes

Soak the rice in one bowl and the cashews and almonds in another in cold water for at least 30 minutes but ideally overnight.

In the morning, drain the rice and put it into a saucepan with the milk and 2 cups (500 ml) of cold water and bring to a simmer. Cook for 20 minutes at a gentle bubble until the rice has puffed up and the liquid is beginning to thicken.

Meanwhile, drain the nuts and finely chop them—you can do this in a food processor if you like. Bash the cardamom pods in a mortar with pestle, spice grinder, or mixing bowl with rolling pin and remove the fragrant seeds, then discard the pods and grind the seeds until you have a powder.

After 20 minutes add the nuts, raisins, spices, and honey to the rice and cook for another 15 minutes until thick and creamy, somewhere between rice pudding and porridge. You want to reach the sweet spot where the rice is soft, with very little bite, and the kheer is creamy but not too thick. If it looks like it is thickening too fast, turn the heat down and add a little boiling water from the kettle. Serve spooned into bowls with the lime zest and coconut flakes on top; if you have a sweet tooth, you could add a little extra honey on top.

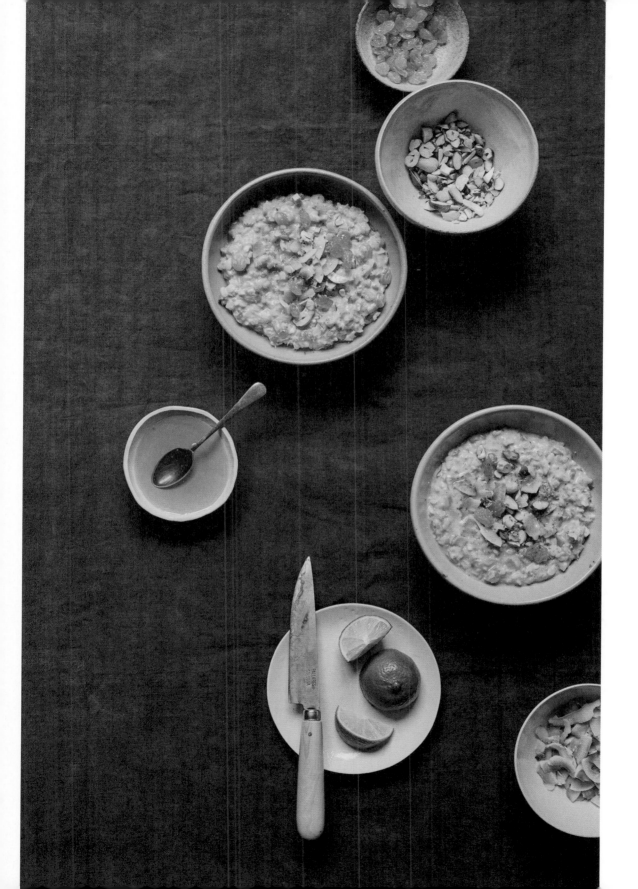

Baked apple porridge with maple butter

The snap of cold that comes at the start of the year is perfect porridge weather. I've never understood those who eat it like clockwork, regardless of the temperature. I love the warmth of it on a cold day, a bowl in my hands like a morning hot-water bottle, the quick but nourishing time spent stirring at the stove a welcome interruption to the busy rush of the morning and a few minutes to let my mind wander at the start of the day.

This porridge is a bit different in that it is baked so the edges crisp and the starry apple slices on top soften and brown. I top it with a maple cream so good it's hard not to spoon it all straight from the dish before the porridge is ready. It takes a little longer to make than a regular porridge—it's a weekend one.

I make it to feed a crowd, or on a Sunday with intentional leftovers so that I know we have a good breakfast in the fridge to start the week. This keeps well in the fridge for a few days, and any extra can be reheated with a little extra milk in a small pan. I make a big batch of spice mix, which I keep in a jar and add to my stovetop porridge throughout the week too (this makes more than you'll need for the baked porridge, but if you prefer you could add a pinch of each spice to the recipe rather than making a large batch). I make this without dairy, using almond milk and coconut oil, as that's how I like to eat it, but regular milk and butter work just as well.

SERVES 6

FOR THE SPICE MIX

2 tablespoons ground cardamom

2 tablespoons ground ginger

½ teaspoon ground nutmeg

½ teaspoon ground cloves

½ teaspoon ground cinnamon

coconut oil or butter

3 large apples

1 unwaxed lemon

2 cups (200 g) rolled oats

1½ teaspoons baking powder

¼ teaspoon fine sea salt

1 cup (100 g) nuts, toasted and chopped (I use pecans and hazelnuts)

3 cups (750 ml) almond milk

½ cup (125 ml) pure maple syrup, plus extra for drizzling

FOR THE MAPLE CREAM

2 tablespoons nut butter (I use cashew)

2 tablespoons maple syrup

4 tablespoons almond milk

a tiny pinch of fine sea salt

a drop of vanilla extract or paste

Make the spice mix first by stirring the spices together in a small jar, then set aside.

Preheat the oven to 400°F (210°C). Grease an 8-inch (20-cm) square ovenproof dish with coconut oil.

Grate two of the apples. Turn the last apple on its side and slice it very thinly, so that you get a lovely star pattern. Grate the zest from half the lemon to use later, then cut the lemon in half and squeeze the juice from one half over the sliced apple to stop it from browning. →

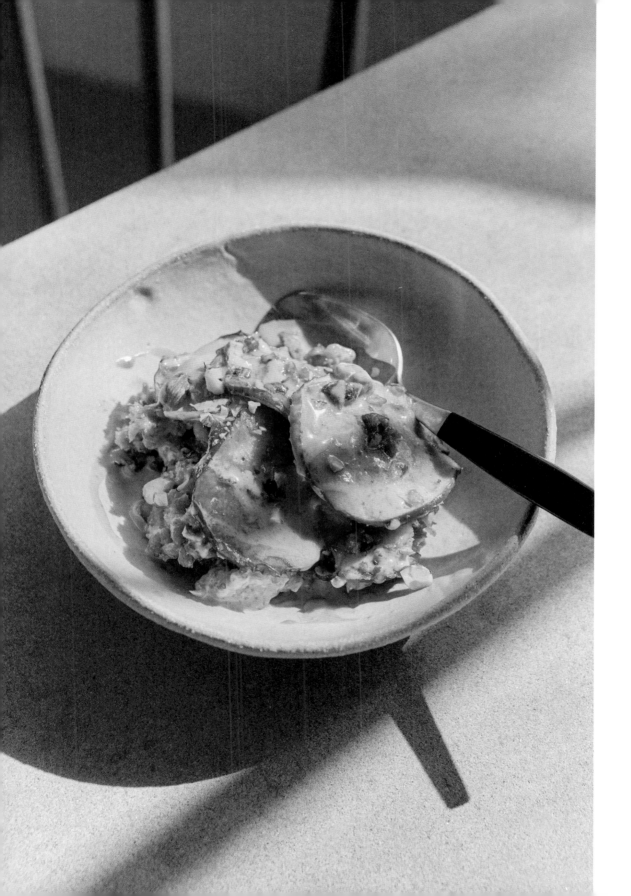

In a large bowl, combine the oats, baking powder, salt, 1 teaspoon of the spice mix, the grated apple, and most of the chopped nuts (saving a small handful for the topping). Stir to combine. In a pitcher or separate bowl, mix the milk with the maple syrup, the juice of the remaining half lemon, and the reserved zest.

Pour the oat and apple mixture into the greased dish, pour over the milk and maple syrup mixture, arrange the sliced apples on top, and drizzle over a little maple syrup. Dot the top of the oats with butter or little dollops of coconut oil. Bake for 25 to 30 minutes, or until the top of the porridge is golden brown and all the liquid has been absorbed.

While the porridge bakes, make the maple cream. In a medium bowl, whisk together the nut butter, maple syrup, milk, salt, and vanilla. You are looking for something totally smooth and pourable. If the mixture seems too thick, add a little more milk.

Serve the baked porridge hot, spooned into bowls with the maple cream for pouring over.

Lentils on toast

Beans on toast is a meal I proudly eat, along with many of the greatest cooks and chefs I know. If you are not familiar with them, I mean Heinz baked beans from a can, haricot beans in a sweet tomato sauce, on hot, well-buttered toast with lots of black pepper. I am sure the childhood comfort of it is as nourishing as the actual food on the plate. These yogurt-spiked lentils are something I have taken to making as an alternative to beans when we want something quick without a trip to the store, but that feels a bit more put together. The lentils are warming and filling and have a depth of flavor that would make you think they'd taken much longer than five minutes.

This recipe is intended to be made from fridge and store-cupboard staples, so the herbs are optional—if you have some in the fridge or on the windowsill, all the better. The same goes for the cheese; I always have a piece of Parmesan in the top of my fridge, but pretty much any hard cheese would work here.

First, toast your nuts in a dry pan over a medium heat until they smell toasty and are beginning to brown. Once toasted, pour them into a bowl and when they are cool enough to handle, chop or crumble them.

Meanwhile, put the pan back over a medium heat and add a good glug of oil and the garlic. Sizzle until the edges of the garlic are beginning to brown, then add the lentils and their liquid (if you are using home-cooked lentils you'll need about ⅝ cup (150 ml) of their cooking liquid) along with the vinegar and honey. Cook for about 5 minutes, until all the liquid has been absorbed.

Now add a pinch of salt and a good grind of pepper to the lentils along with a good drizzle of olive oil. Taste and add more salt, honey, pepper, or vinegar if needed. Once they taste great, take them off the heat and stir in the yogurt.

Drizzle olive oil over hot toast and serve the lentils piled on top with the herbs, nuts, and a good grating of cheese. Any leftover lentils can be eaten hot or cold and will keep for 3 to 4 days in the fridge.

SERVES 2

½ cup (50 g) nuts (I like walnuts or almonds)

olive oil

1 clove of garlic, thinly sliced

1 × 14-ounce (400-g) can of green lentils (or 1 cup/250 g home-cooked, see page 461)

1 tablespoon red wine vinegar

a squeeze of golden honey

sea salt and freshly ground black pepper

4 tablespoons thick Greek yogurt

TO SERVE

a few slices of good toast

a small bunch of soft herbs (basil, parsley, dill, tarragon), leaves picked and roughly chopped

a little grated Parmesean or other hard cheese (I use a vegetarian/rennet-free one)

Cooking with grace

I have spent time in ashrams and been to more yoga classes than I can remember. When I was pregnant I became really interested in the power of the mind and hypnotherapy. All of these things—meditation, yoga, and positive thinking—are tools I use in my life to make it happier and better. And the more I have delved into how to keep my life as happy, free of stress, and joyful as possible, the more I know that my kitchen is where I find my calm space. Not every night. Some nights I clatter around, throwing things in a pan with very little grace, and the result, while usually edible, is never repeated. But I know that the kitchen can be a transformative place, and that goes for anyone—you don't need to consider yourself a cook.

When I center myself and take in every little nuance of what's going on, cooking becomes my solace, my meditation. Whether it's the pleasing glide of my favorite potato peeler, taking in the intoxicating perfume of a bunch of mint or basil, or the searing splattering of juice that sprays up when I cut into a lemon, noticing these moments connects me with my food and reminds me of the wonder of where it has come from. Cooking is an offering: to me, to my body, and to those I love—the people I cook for. And it is healing, not just through the nourishment it provides but in the very act and process of doing something physical and practical. It calms my mind and allows me to focus on just one thing.

A big part of this grounding, nourishing practice has been lost in cooking. Sure, we all know that making a loaf of bread, or jarring up some jam from heavy-laden fruit trees will give us a deep sense of satisfaction. But

I think that our everyday cooking can be as much an act of meditation, escape, and dare I say it, mindfulness. This may be nothing new, and it is by no means groundbreaking information, but if, like me, you tend to get caught up in the day-to-day of life, let this be my encouragement to you to remember that even the simplest of tasks in the kitchen can be something to embrace and delight in.

I truly believe that when we cook the emotions, thoughts, and feelings of the cook get translated into the food. That may sound a little far out, but having cooked thousands of dishes, I know that when I'm paying close attention to what I am doing, giving each task and ingredient the reverence it deserves, the food tastes infinitely better. Equally, sometimes I throw everything in a pan with a million other things going on as that's all I can manage, and when I do, I don't give myself a hard time.

For me, focusing on how I cook means turning off other things like TV or music, following each task with dedication, taking as much care as I have time to do. To appreciate and even, if I don't sound like too much of a hippie, marvel at my ingredients, our natural treasures. Make sure you take time to smell, taste, and immerse yourself in the amazing process of cooking, and then finish it by putting the food on each plate with care if you can. When I cook like this I find it soothing and rewarding, and everything I cook tastes better.

Our state of mind as we eat has a huge effect on how we digest our food and how we take in the nutrients and energy from it. Stress and anxiety around food and eating is something I try to avoid in my recipes and in my kitchen. I truly believe that a pizza and a beer enjoyed in good spirits, slowly and calmly with friends, can be as nourishing as endless green smoothies, which are inhaled on the run or sipped while reading emails at our desks with no real thought about the true meaning of nourishment. We've lost the connection with how we eat our food, the emotions going on around eating, and the sense of offering that comes with feeding ourselves. I don't manage it every time I eat, but a couple of seconds to slow down and be thankful for the food on my plate before diving in seems to set a good tone for the meal and often allows me to appreciate the flavors, textures, and sensations a little more.

A few observations on cooking and eating mindfully and with grace

— Turn off music, radio, and phones, if you can, so that you can focus on all the sensations of cooking.

— Try to notice the little things—the color change in the skin of a peach, the tiny pores on the skin of an orange, the condensation on the lid of a pan.

— Notice the sounds—the sizzle of frying, the bubbling of a pot. These tell you as much about what you are cooking and where you are in the process as anything you can see.

— Follow the process with all your senses, smell the changes as ingredients are added, feel how a mixture firms up as you stir it, notice the change in color as you fry or blanch. And notice how you feel, whether ingredients or smells bring up memories or emotions.

— Try to keep your attention totally focused on your food; and if your mind wanders, don't worry: Just bring it back to the food.

— Tune in to even the most mundane parts of the job—peeling carrots, picking herbs—immersing yourself totally in the detail of each task will allow you to switch off from other pressures.

Broken eggs with Lacinato kale, ricotta, and chickpeas

Broken eggs are somewhere between scrambled and poached eggs. They cook gently in the pan with a couple of turns of the spoon, then finish their cooking at the table. A heavy or cast-iron frying pan is great here, as it holds on to the heat better.

I first ate eggs like this at Raw Duck, a favorite breakfast spot near where I live. Cooking eggs this way means the last bit of cooking is controlled at the table, which means no overcooked, rubbery eggs, and that you can spoon them out when they are cooked just as you like, leaving some in the pan for people who like their eggs less runny.

You can use kale or any greens you have, and any other beans would work in place of the chickpeas—if they are home-cooked, so much the better. A scattering of toasted almonds or hazelnuts or even dukkah would be welcome here too.

Strip the leaves from the Lacinato kale, shredding any larger ones. Finely chop the stalks, discarding any really thick sinewy ones.

SERVES 4

1 head of Lacinato kale (about 300 g)

olive oil

1 × 14-ounce (400 g) can of chickpeas, drained (or about 1 cup/250 g home-cooked, see page 461)

1 clove of garlic, thinly sliced

1 red chile, finely chopped

the juice of 1 unwaxed lemon and the zest from half

sea salt and freshly ground black pepper

a good grating of nutmeg

6 medium organic eggs

⅓ cup (100 g) ricotta or thick Greek yogurt

4 rounds of toast or toasted flatbread (see page 456), to serve

Heat a heavy, ideally cast-iron, medium frying pan (about 11 inches/ 28 cm) over medium heat. Add a little olive oil, then the chickpeas, cook for a couple of minutes to crisp a little, then add the chopped Lacinato kale stalks, garlic, and chile. Cook for another few minutes until the stalks are tender and the garlic has started to brown, then add the leaves. Add the lemon juice, zest, a good pinch of salt and pepper, and the nutmeg, then cook for 4 to 5 minutes, until the Lacinato kale leaves have softened.

Next, break each egg into a bowl and get your flatbread or toast ready. Spoon the ricotta into the pan, dotting it around, then pour the eggs one by one gently on top of the Lacinato kale mixture. Keep the pan over the heat and gently stir the eggs a couple of times, just to break them a little. You want the whites and yolks to stay separate: Don't mix them together as you would with scrambled eggs. Quickly take the pan off the heat and carry it to the table along with a wooden spoon; the residual heat of the pan will continue to cook the eggs. Use the wooden spoon and continue to stir until the eggs are set to your liking. (I like mine to be soft and curdy.) Serve right away with charred flatbread or toast.

Twice-baked potato skins with crispy buffalo chickpeas

These double-baked potato skins bring back childhood memories of American diners, but rather than the inch-deep cheese, these are piled high with spicy baked chickpeas, which pick up a pleasing crunch in the oven, and a grown-up "sour cream" dip. I make the dip using cashews, which I blitz to a cream, but you can use yogurt instead of the cashews if you'd prefer. I serve these with a salad for dinner, but they would be great as a party snack if you used smaller potatoes. Kids love them if you go easy on the spice.

——————————————

Preheat the oven to 395°F (180°C). Set two oven racks in the middle of the oven. Wash and dry the potatoes, prick with a fork and rub with a little olive oil, then sprinkle over some salt and rub in with your hands. Place the potatoes directly on the top oven rack. Bake them until they feel tender and the skin is crisp, about 1 to 1½ hours.

While the potatoes are baking, get on with the chickpeas. Heat a pan over medium heat. Pour in a little olive oil, add the onion, and cook for 10 minutes, until soft, then add the celery, paprika, cumin, and garlic and cook for another 10 to 15 minutes, until soft and sticky.

Add the chickpeas, tomatoes, and chile and stir again. Season with a little salt and pepper and cook for another 10 minutes, until the tomatoes have thickened and it has all come together nicely. While the chickpeas are cooking, make the dip. If you are using the cashews, drain them and put them into a blender with 5 tablespoons of cold water and blitz until very smooth, then mix with the other ingredients. If using yogurt, simply mix everything together.

Once the potatoes are baked and cool enough for you to handle them, cut them in half lengthwise. Lay the halves on a baking sheet. Scoop out a couple of tablespoons of potato from each half, season the inside of the potato with salt, and drizzle with olive oil.

Save the scooped-out potato for another meal. Divide the chickpeas between the potatoes and bake in the oven for another 10 minutes so that the chickpeas crisp a little. Serve each potato topped with the parsley and celery leaves and the dip.

SERVES 4

4 medium baking potatoes

olive oil

sea salt

1 red onion, finely chopped

1 stalk of celery, finely chopped (reserving the inner leaves)

1 teaspoon smoked sweet paprika

1 teaspoon cumin seeds

1 clove of garlic, finely chopped

2 × 14-ounce (400-g) cans of chickpeas or other white beans, drained (or 2 cups/ 500 g home-cooked chickpeas, see page 461)

¾ cup (200 ml) passata, or canned crushed tomatoes, puréed then strained to remove seeds

a pinch of red pepper flakes (I use a generous pinch of a mild Turkish variety called pul biber or Aleppo pepper)

a small bunch of flat-leaf parsley, leaves picked

FOR THE DIP

¾ cup (100 g) cashew nuts, soaked in cold water for about an hour, or ⅝ cup (150 ml) thick Greek yogurt

the zest and juice of 1 unwaxed lemon

a small bunch of chives, chopped

Caper, herb, and egg flatbread

This recipe is really quick to make and is one of the most flavorful fast lunches I know. Corn tortillas crisped and filled with egg, herbs, and some punch from capers and cornichons; it's a recipe that crosses continents, but that's often how I cook. It's as quick as making a sandwich, and while we eat this all year round, it's something I make most often in the winter, when I want food from the stovetop and warmth. It is loosely based on a much-cooked recipe from my friend Heidi Swanson.

This recipe serves two as a lunch or light dinner, but scale it up as you need. For the herbs I use dill and basil, but mint, tarragon, parsley, and chives would all work too. I buy large 100 percent corn tortillas online from a good Mexican supplier; the standard ones found in grocery stores just aren't the same. Flour tortillas will work well here too.

SERVES 2 AS A LIGHT MEAL

⅔ cup (200 g) thick Greek yogurt

1 unwaxed lemon

sea salt and freshly ground black pepper

2 avocados

2 organic eggs

olive oil

2 medium corn or flour tortillas or wraps (about 5 inches/12 cm)

a few sprigs of soft herbs (see note above), chopped

2 tablespoons small capers

a few cornichons, roughly chopped

¼ cup (25 g) freshly grated Parmesan (I use a vegetarian/rennet-free one)

First, in a bowl mix the yogurt with the grated zest and juice of half the lemon, a pinch of sea salt and a good grind of black pepper.

Cut the avocados into quarters and remove the pits, then cut each one down to the skin in thin slices. Squeeze over the juice from the remaining lemon half and set aside. Beat the eggs in a little cup with a pinch of salt.

It's best to cook the tortillas one by one. Heat a frying pan big enough to fit your tortilla over medium heat. Add a tiny splash of olive oil, then add half the eggs and let it set into a kind of pancake for 10 to 15 seconds. Working quickly, place a tortilla on top of the egg; you want the egg to be a bit runny so that it will attach itself to the tortilla as it sets. When the egg has set, use a spatula to turn the whole thing over, sprinkle over half the herbs, half the capers and cornichons, and half the cheese. Cook until the cheese has melted. Repeat this process for the second tortilla.

To serve, fold the tortillas in half and top with the yogurt and slices of the avocado. To make a meal of them, serve with a little lemon-dressed green salad.

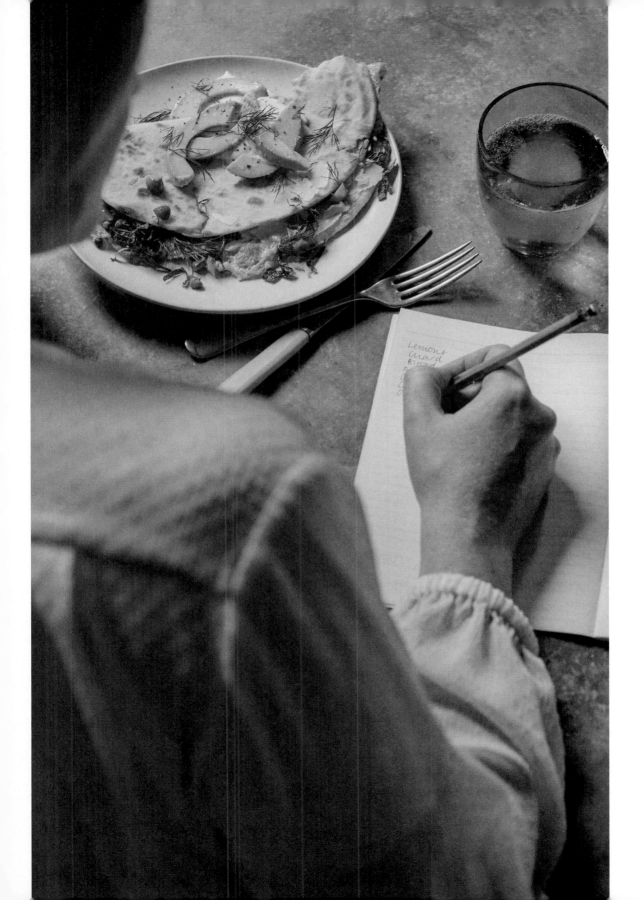

Beet and mustard-seed fritters with cardamom yogurt

This time of year gets a tough write-up; gray, dark, and rainy, and yes, sometimes it is. But my kitchen is filled with arguably the most colorful produce of the year: blood oranges, pink radicchio, and creamy Castelfranco radicchio, splattered with pink like a Jackson Pollock painting. There is so much deep red, orange, pink, and scarlet.

Beets too, in all their colors: neon yellow, bright burnt orange, candy-cane stripes, and of course, the deep magenta of the red beets. You can use any beets you like for these spiced fritters; I often make them with ready-cooked ones.

Vegans can add some extra flour and a tablespoon of chia seeds mixed with 3 tablespoons of water in place of the egg, and use coconut yogurt.

SERVES 4

1 × 14-ounce (400 g) can or jar of chickpeas, drained (or 1 cup/250 g home-cooked, see page 461)

coconut or ground nut oil

2 teaspoons mustard seeds

2 teaspoons cumin seeds

9 ounces (250 g) cooked beet, peeled

2 tablespoons chopped cilantro

2 scallions, chopped

the zest and juice of ½ an unwaxed lemon

1 organic egg

sea salt and freshly ground black pepper

FOR THE YOGURT SAUCE

2 cardamom pods

½ cup (150 g) thick Greek yogurt

the zest and juice of ½ an unwaxed lemon

sea salt

TO SERVE (OPTIONAL)

chapatis or flatbread (see page 456)

a few handfuls of salad greens

First, put two-thirds of the chickpeas into a food processor and pulse until you have a rough paste. Roughly squash the remainder with a fork so they break into smaller pieces.

Next, make the yogurt sauce. Bash the cardamom pods to remove the seeds, then lightly toast the seeds in a dry frying pan over medium heat. Grind in a mortar with pestle, spice grinder, or mixing bowl with rolling pin until you have a fine powder. Transfer this to a bowl, add the yogurt, lemon zest and juice, and a good pinch of salt to taste. Stir well and put to one side.

Put the frying pan back on the heat, add a splash of oil, then add the mustard and cumin seeds. When the mustard seeds begin to pop and start to smell more fragrant, pour them into a mixing bowl.

Grate the beets using a coarse grater, then squeeze the beet to remove excess liquid and transfer to a mixing bowl with the seeds. Add the other fritter ingredients, season with salt and pepper, and mix well. Using the palms of your hands, take heaping tablespoons of the mixture and shape into small fritters (about 12). Put a little oil into a large frying pan and place over medium heat. Fry some of the fritters for 2 to 3 minutes on each side, until golden brown. Transfer to a plate lined with a paper towel and repeat with the rest.

Serve warm with the cardamom yogurt, some salad greens, and chapatis or flatbread.

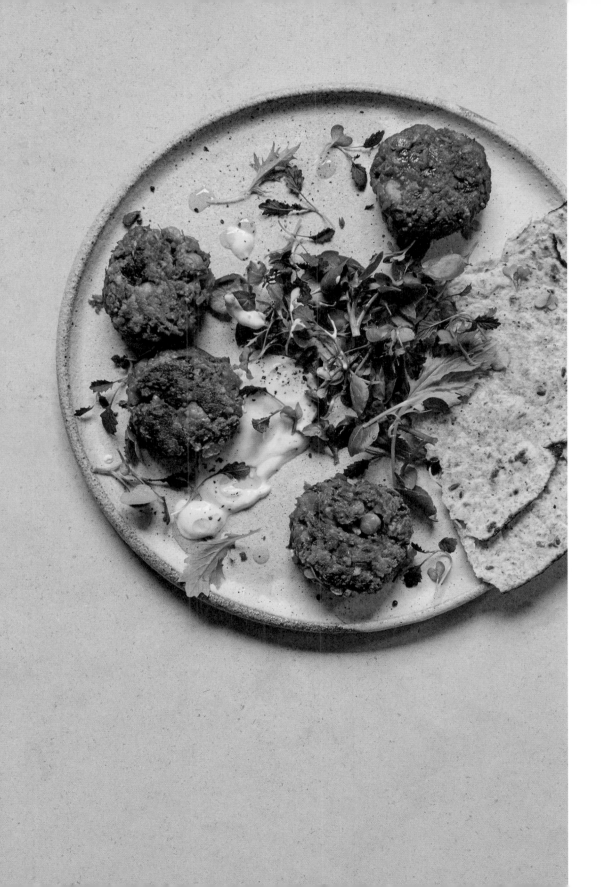

Gentle potato chowder
with toasted chile oil

This soup is like yin and yang: a very gentle, warming potato chowder, cooked in milk, with lentils for sustenance, that I top with a searing chile and toasted almond oil. The oil sits on top of the white soup like lava, a serious punch of toasty fire. It's one of the most comforting soups and warms you right down to your toes.

I use ancho chile flakes. Ancho is a lot milder and has a more rounded, complex, dried-fruit flavor than the supermarket red pepper flakes, which can just add heat, so if you are using those I would suggest a teaspoon, unless you like things very hot. The chile oil makes more oil than you need but keeps for months. It can be made in the time it takes to simmer the soup, but store-bought chile oil can stand in.

Fill and boil a kettle. In a medium to large pot, melt the butter over medium heat. Add the leeks with a pinch of salt, lower the heat, and cook, stirring occasionally, until they are soft and sweet; this should take about 10 minutes.

Stir in the flour and allow to cook for another minute or so to get rid of the raw flour flavor. Gradually add 2½ cups (600 ml) of hot water from the kettle, a bit at a time, then add the stock powder or cube. Add the potatoes and bring the mixture to a simmer. Cook until the potatoes are cooked through, which should take about 25 minutes, making sure you stir the soup from time to time to keep it from sticking.

Meanwhile, make the oil. Put the chiles, red pepper flakes, and garlic into a food processor and pulse until fine, then add the almonds, a good pinch of salt and a generous amount of black pepper. Pulse again, put into a small saucepan with the oil, and cook slowly for 10 minutes or so, until everything is toasted and golden, then remove from the heat and set aside. The oil can be used warm (not hot) on your soup. The leftovers should be left to cool completely, then stored in a jar in the fridge for up to 3 months.

Back to the soup. Add the milk to the pot, stir in the lentils, and heat until the milk is just simmering. Serve the soup ladled into deep bowls, topped with a slick of the chile oil.

SERVES 4

2 tablespoons unsalted butter or coconut oil

2 leeks, washed, trimmed and cut into ½-inch- (1-cm-) thick rounds

sea salt

2 tablespoons flour (I use spelt)

1 tablespoon vegetable stock powder or 1 stock cube

6 cups (800 g) baking potatoes, peeled and cut into rough chunks

1¼ cups (300 ml) whole milk or soy milk

1 × 14-ounce (400-g) can of green lentils, drained (or 1 cup/250 g home-cooked, see page 461)

FOR THE CHILE OIL

2 red chiles

1 teaspoon to 1 tablespoon red pepper flakes (see note above)

2 cloves of garlic

1 heaping tablespoon almonds

sea salt and freshly ground black pepper

¾ cup (200 ml) mild-flavored oil (light olive or canola)

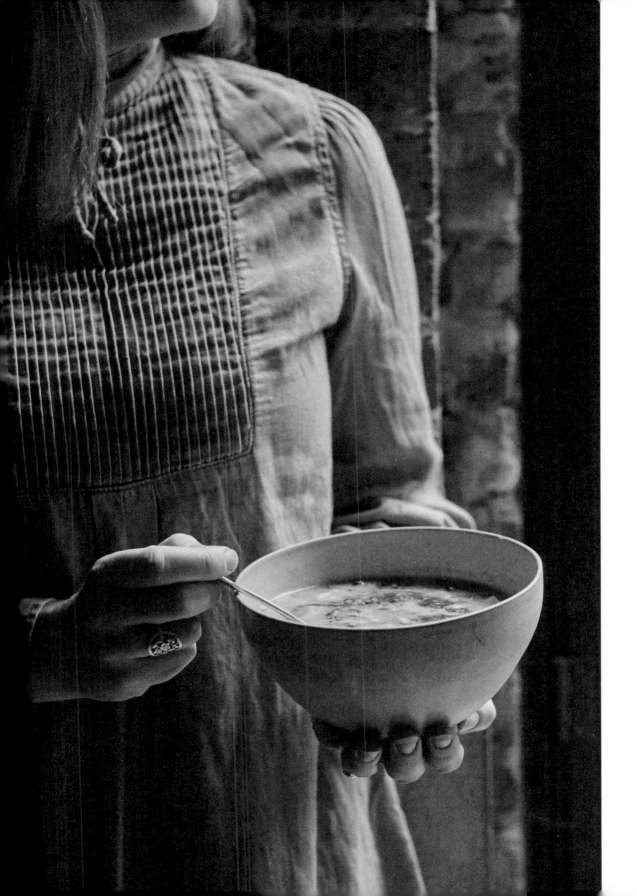

Kimchi and miso noodle soup

SERVES 4

3 cups (200 g) Asian mushrooms (enoki, shimeji, shiitake, oyster)

1 tablespoon tamari or soy sauce, plus a little extra to season and serve

juice of ½ a lemon

2 tablespoons golden honey or agave nectar

3 cups (250 g) soba noodles (I use 100 percent buckwheat ones)

3 tablespoons sesame oil

sea salt

6 scallions, trimmed and finely chopped

a small thumb-size piece of ginger, peeled and grated

1 teaspoon gochujang paste or red pepper flakes

4 cloves of garlic, thinly sliced

3½–5 ounces (100–150 g) cabbage kimchi, (see page 68) drained

3 cups (250 g) purple sprouting broccoli, woody ends removed and cut into thumb-length pieces

3 tablespoons miso paste (I use a brown rice one)

9 ounces (250 g) extra-firm tofu

TO SERVE

sesame seeds

squeeze of lemon or lime

some cilantro or shiso leaves (optional)

I make kimchi purely so that I can make this soup. It is clean-tasting and enlivening, nicely sharp with spice and the mellow, vinegary punch of the kimchi. I don't care much for kimchi on its own (my husband, John, eats it by the jar), but I do think that it is an incredible ingredient to use as a flavorful base for stews, in dressings, and in wraps and sandwiches. The amount of kimchi that you use is quite dependent on how strong it is. My homemade one (on page 68) is quite mellow but store-bought ones can be much more potent, so taste it first and use your tastebuds as a guide, adding more if you need.

I cook with miso a lot, and it happens to be really good for you too. I learned recently that if you heat it too much it loses a lot of its goodness, so now, when I can, I mix it with a little of the liquid I am adding it to, then stir it in at the end like a seasoning and don't cook it for ages.

I have used gochujang paste here, which is a fermented chile paste from Korea with complex flavors. It's getting easier to find and it does add an extra edge to the soup. If you can't get the paste, dried chile works just fine. Do be careful to check the paste's ingredients list, as some varieties contain ingredients I'd rather not eat!

First, put your mushrooms into a bowl with the tamari, lemon juice and 1 tablespoon of the honey, and put to one side to marinate for at least 15 minutes.

Cook the soba noodles according to the packet instructions. Drain and run under cold water, then toss in 1 tablespoon of the sesame oil.

Heat the remaining 2 tablespoons of oil in a large soup pan over medium to high heat. Once the mushrooms have had their marinating time, drain them but keep the marinade. Add the mushrooms to the pan in a single layer with a pinch of salt (you can do this in batches if you need to). Cook until the mushrooms are golden where they meet the pan, then toss and keep cooking until the mushrooms are deeply browned all over—this should take 5 minutes or so. Remove from the pan and set aside. →

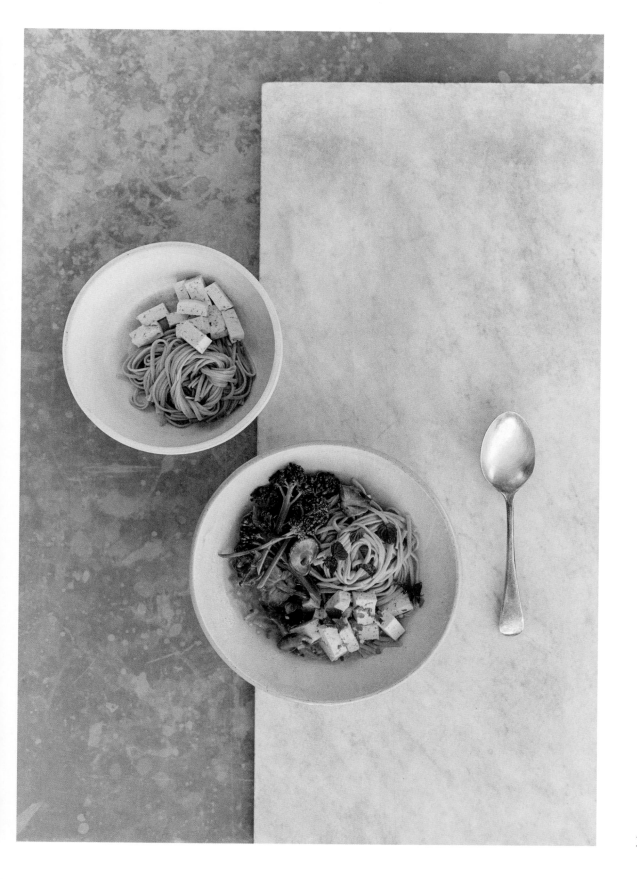

Fill and boil the kettle. Put the empty pan back over medium heat, add the scallions and sauté for a few minutes before adding the ginger and gochujang paste. After another minute or so, add the garlic and the drained kimchi. Sizzle until the garlic is starting to brown around the edges. Add 5 cups (1¼ liters) of water from the kettle along with the remaining tablespoon of honey and bring to a boil. Now, add the broccoli and simmer for 1 minute, or just until the broccoli becomes bright green.

Remove the soup from the heat. Place the miso in a small bowl and whisk it with a splash of the broth to thin it out. Stir the thinned miso into the soup. Taste your soup; you really need to get the balance right here. If the broth tastes a bit flat, you might need more salt or miso, or a splash of soy sauce.

Just before serving, cut the tofu into little ¾-inch (2-cm) pieces—you'll have about 1 cup—and drizzle it with the reserved marinade from the mushrooms.

To serve, divide the noodles among four bowls and ladle over the soup. Top with the tofu, mushrooms, and a sprinkle of sesame seeds. Finish with more soy if you like, a squeeze of lemon or lime, and the shiso or cilantro leaves if using.

Green peppercorn and lemongrass coconut broth

This is what we eat when we feel like the cold has got the better of us. It's packed with immune-system-boosting turmeric, ginger, and garlic to fight off colds, and some fiery green chile to blow away cobwebs. I use green peppercorns too, as I love the grassy punch they give; seek out the fresh ones on tiny branches if you can, but if not the brined ones in jars will do just fine. The paste can be made in advance or in a double batch and the leftovers will keep in the fridge for a few days and in the freezer for a couple of months.

Gently melt the coconut oil in a pan over low heat—you don't want to heat it, just melt it. Put the ginger, garlic, and chile (the amount you use and whether you keep the seeds in depends on how hot you like things) into your food processor with the scallions, almost all of the cilantro, and the mint leaves (reserve a few leaves for serving). Add the coconut oil, then blitz for 30 seconds, or until you have a smooth, deep green paste.

Place a deep, medium-size pan over medium heat and add the herb paste, stirring it for a minute while it warms. Stir in the turmeric, peppercorns, both cans of coconut milk, the juice of one of the limes, the stock powder, and the tamari. Fill one of the cans one and a half times with hot water from the kettle and add the water to the pan.

Using a rolling pin or pestle, smash the lemongrass so that it splinters but remains together, then tuck it into the pan. Bring the liquid to a boil, then lower the heat and leave to simmer, bubbling gently.

Fill and boil a kettle. Meanwhile, slice the squash as thinly as you can and add this to the pan too. Place the noodles in a heatproof bowl and pour over enough of the boiling water from the kettle to cover them.

Once the squash is cooked through, add the greens to the soup and allow the liquid to come to a simmer again. Check the seasoning of the soup, adding the coconut sugar if it needs some sweetness and more lime and salt as needed. Drain the noodles, then divide them among four deep soup bowls. Ladle over the soup and vegetables, adding a generous squeeze of lime juice and, if you like, a few of the reserved cilantro and mint leaves.

SERVES 4

4 tablespoons coconut oil

a thumb-size piece of ginger (about ½ cup/50 g), peeled and roughly chopped

2 cloves of garlic, peeled

1–2 small green chiles, stalks removed

4 scallions, trimmed and roughly chopped

a small bunch of cilantro (leaves and stalks)

a few sprigs of mint, leaves only

1 heaping teaspoon ground turmeric or a small thumb of fresh, grated

15 fresh or brined green peppercorns (see note above)

2 × 13.5-ounce (400-ml) cans of coconut milk

2 limes

1 tablespoon vegetable stock powder or ½ a stock cube

1 tablespoon tamari or soy sauce

1 stalk of lemongrass

½ a medium butternut squash, deseeded and peeled

4 ounces (100 g) thin vermicelli brown rice noodles

5 cups (100 g) shredded spinach or winter greens

1 tablespoon coconut sugar or honey

Not-chicken soup

This is a soup for the soul; chicken soup without the chicken and with no apology. It's the get-well soup I have been searching for, to cure whatever ails you, whether that's a cold or a broken heart. As gentle and as nourishing as they come, the soup has a base of slow-cooked sweet fennel and leek, layered with old friends celery and carrot, with a pep of ginger and lemon, and warmth from a generous amount of white pepper. Crisp little pieces of tofu top the broth, sticky from a minute or two in a pan, with some soy and a sprinkling of seasoning.

The seasoning, nutritional yeast, adds depth and umami and tastes much more complex and gentle than its ungenerous name suggests (though it is a great source of elusive B vitamins for vegetarians and vegans). If you don't have it the soup will still be delicious without. Be sure to save the fronds from your fennel and leaves from your celery for finishing it prettily.

SERVES 4

olive oil

1 onion, finely sliced

1 leek, finely sliced

3 bulbs of fennel, trimmed and finely sliced, fronds reserved

3 stalks of celery, chopped into ½-inch (1-cm) pieces, leaves reserved

1 carrot, peeled and chopped into rough ½-inch (1-cm) pieces

8 cloves of garlic, very thinly sliced

a small thumb-size piece of ginger, peeled and grated

1 lemon

1 teaspoon whole white peppercorns, plus more to taste

sea salt

½ cup (50 g) small pasta or broken-up spaghetti pieces

extra-virgin olive oil, to serve

FOR THE TOFU

7 ounces (200 g) firm tofu, sliced roughly into 1½-inch (1-cm) sticks (¾ cup)

3 tablespoons soy sauce

1 heaping teaspoon nutritional yeast

olive oil, for frying

Pour a little olive oil into a large soup pot and place over medium heat. Add the onion, leek, fennel, celery, and carrot, turn the heat down low, and cook gently for 20 to 30 minutes, until everything is very soft and sweet, without browning too much. Add a splash of water if it looks like anything is going to stick.

Add the garlic and ginger, cook for another couple of minutes, then squeeze in the lemon and add the peppercorns. Add 8 cups (2 liters) of cold water (or you can use vegetable stock) and a good pinch of sea salt. Bring to the boil and simmer for 20 to 30 minutes.

Once the soup is nearly ready, toss the tofu in 2 tablespoons of the soy sauce. Heat a pan with a little olive oil, fry the tofu over a medium to high heat until crisp then add the final tablespoon of soy sauce and toss quickly—the soy should stick to the tofu and give it a rich stickiness. Remove from the heat, add the nutritional yeast, and toss again.

Add the broken pasta to the soup and cook for another 8 minutes (or as long as your pasta takes). Taste and add more salt or water or even a squeeze more lemon. Ladle into shallow bowls, top with the tofu, some fennel fronds and celery leaves, and a good drizzle of olive oil.

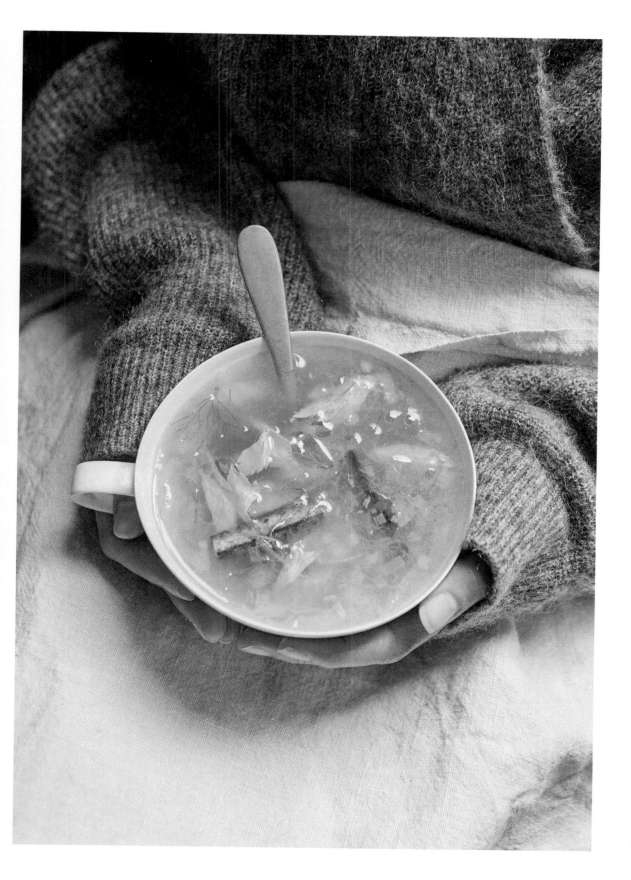

Soups: a flavor map

1 Create the base layer	2 Choose an herb	3 Choose a spice	4 Choose the main body of your soup
1 onion or leek, finely chopped	a few sprigs of thyme	cumin seeds	butternut squash
+	a couple of sprigs of rosemary	cilantro (coriander) seeds	sweet potato
2 stalks of celery, trimmed and finely chopped	10 sage leaves	3 cardamom pods (remember to take the seeds out before you blend)	peas
+	3 bay leaves	½ cinnamon stick	celeriac
2 carrots, roughly chopped	a few sprigs of oregano	mustard seeds	parsnips
	the stalks from a bunch of basil	smoked paprika	tomatoes
	the stalks from a bunch of cilantro	black pepper	carrots
		red pepper flakes	broccoli
			cauliflower
Sweat all three in a little olive oil over medium heat until soft and sweet.	Add the herb and sizzle for a couple of minutes to release its flavor.	Add 1 tablespoon, or the quantity suggested, and sizzle for a minute or two.	Add your main vegetable (about 1¾ to 2¼ pounds/ 800 g to 1 kg), peeled and chopped if needed, and enough hot stock to cover. Simmer for 40 minutes.

5	6	7
Choose a backup flavor	**How to make it more substantial**	**Finish your soup**

broccoli	cooked quinoa	roasted seeds
peas	drained canned beans	yogurt
fava beans	cooked amaranth	tahini
artichokes	cooked brown rice	toasted nuts
asparagus	torn-up bread	quick croutons
spinach (add at the end)	broken-up noodles	chopped soft herbs
	small or smashed pasta	herb oil

Add a couple of handfuls of washed, podded or chopped vegetables and simmer for 5 more minutes.	This is optional. If using, add a couple of handfuls just before your soup is ready, warm through (make sure it's cooked if it's noodles or pasta), and blitz if you like.	Top with one or two of these options and a drizzle of olive oil.

Pomelo and peanut winter noodles with carrot and coconut dressing

SERVES 2 AS A MAIN MEAL,
4 AS PART OF A MEAL

sea salt

8 ounces (200 g) soba
    noodles

1⅓ cups (200 g) shelled
    edamame (fresh or frozen)

½ a medium pomelo

2 big handfuls of watercress
    or other peppery leaves

⅔ cup (100 g) unsalted
    peanuts, toasted

a small bunch of cilantro,
    leaves picked

FOR THE DRESSING

3½ tablespoons (50 ml)
    full-fat coconut milk

a generous pinch of ground
    turmeric

a large thumb-size piece of
    ginger, peeled and grated

1 carrot, peeled

1 green chile

2 tablespoons extra-virgin
    olive oil

1 tablespoon toasted sesame
    oil

1 tablespoon maple syrup

2 tablespoons brown rice
    vinegar

1 shallot, peeled and roughly
    chopped

Cheerful and layered with flavor, this is a bright bowl that makes the most of January citrus. I use pomelo, but you can use another citrus if pomelo is hard to come by; clementines and blood oranges are both great. The carrot and coconut milk dressing makes more than you will need, which is intentional, as it's easier to make in a big batch and I love having it in the fridge to use through the week. I have made suggestions on how else to use it (opposite), but if you'd prefer not to have extra, halve the ingredients.

I use 100 percent buckwheat soba noodles, as I love their super-savory note, but any noodles you like would work here. If you are using soba, be careful not to overcook them, and be quick to refresh them in cold water so that they don't stick together.

Bring a large pot of well-salted water to a boil and cook the noodles according to the packet instructions. When the noodles are nearly cooked, add the edamame to the pot for a quick swim. Remove from the heat, drain, rinse with cold water to stop the cooking, and shake off as much water as possible.

Meanwhile, make your dressing. Put the coconut milk, turmeric, ginger, carrot, chile, olive oil, sesame oil, maple syrup, brown rice vinegar, shallot, and some salt into a blender and blend until very smooth. Taste and adjust, if needed, with more salt or vinegar, or any other ingredient you think might need a little boost.

Cut the peel from the pomelo and use your knife to slice between the membrane to cut it into segments, removing as much of the pith as you can.

Transfer the noodles and edamame to a large serving bowl, add a few tablespoons of the dressing, and toss well. The noodles really absorb the sauce, so start by adding a couple of tablespoons at a time, then mix and add more if needed, as you don't want to drown them. Finish with the watercress, peanuts, pomelo, and cilantro, and toss everything together gently.

How to use your dressing

- Add to grated winter root vegetables with rounds of citrus and some toasted seeds

- Use it to finish a bowl of simple steamed rice and green veg and top with a few toasted nuts

- Use it to finish some flash-fried tofu and serve with rice noodles and some greens

- Toss a packet of feta cheese in a little of the dressing, then roast for 25 minutes until golden and toss with a salad of leaves or grains

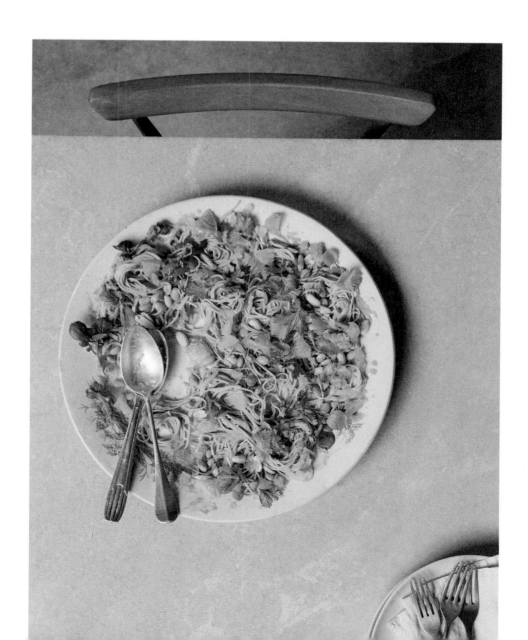

Turmeric and coconut-baked aloo gobi

SERVES 4

1 large head cauliflower or
  2 small ones

sea salt

1¼ pounds (600 g) potatoes

4 tablespoons coconut oil

a thumb-size piece of ginger,
  peeled

4 green chiles

4 cloves of garlic, crushed

1 tablespoon black mustard
  seeds

2 teaspoons ground turmeric

1 × 14.5-ounce (400-ml) can
  of coconut milk

freshly ground black pepper

1 unwaxed lemon, cut in half

TO SERVE

thick Greek or coconut yogurt

almonds

a small bunch of cilantro,
  leaves picked

There is something grand and celebratory about roasting a vegetable whole. It becomes a centerpiece, which is something I think people look for in vegetable-centered cooking. The food I make most nights celebrates vegetables in some way, but cooking them whole like this takes a cauliflower one step further: golden and crackled, its color intensified, in all its glory as nature intended.

Whole roasted cauliflower is something that has been finding its way onto restaurant menus the last couple of years, partly due to the cauliflower renaissance spearheaded by vegetable magician Yotam Ottolenghi. Burnished and browned, a whole cauliflower is such a pleasing thing to put in the middle of the table, with a sharp knife for everyone to cut brave wedges for themselves and uncover the buttery clean white inside, a sharp contrast to the crisp and highly flavored outside.

This is my favorite way to eat cauliflower: the sweet note of coconut milk, the punch of ginger and green chile, the earthiness of mustard seeds, and the clean spiced note of turmeric are perfect sidekicks to the neutral-flavored, buttery roasted cauliflower. I add some halved potatoes to the pan to absorb the coconut and lemon goodness. There are few things that are as friendly in the way they soak up flavor as a cauliflower.

Preheat the oven to 425°F (220°C). Fill and boil water in the kettle.

Using a pair of scissors, cut the large leaves and stalks away from the cauliflower. You can leave the little leaves close to the florets—they will get nice and crispy when roasted. Turn the cauliflower upside down and, using a small paring knife, carefully cut a hole in the middle of the stalk, so that it cooks evenly. Take a pan big enough to hold the cauliflower, half fill it with water from the kettle, and bring it to a boil. Season the water with salt, then immerse the cauliflower and simmer for 6 minutes. Drain the water, put the lid back on, and leave the cauliflower to steam in the residual heat for another 10 minutes. Meanwhile, cut the potatoes into ¾-inch (2-cm) pieces, leaving the skin on. →

Cauliflower rice with eggs and green chutney

SERVES 4

FOR THE CHUTNEY

a large bunch of cilantro

2 green chiles

a few sprigs of mint

juice of 1 lime

3½ tablespoons (50 g) coconut cream

½ teaspoon golden honey

1 tablespoon peanut oil or mild olive oil

FOR THE REST

6–7 cups (800 g–1 kg) cauliflower

coconut oil

6 scallions, peeled and finely sliced

a thumb-size piece of ginger, peeled

1 teaspoon ground turmeric

sea salt

1 head of chard or other winter greens, stalks finely sliced, leaves roughly shredded

1 lemon

3½ tablespoons (50 g) coconut cream

4 organic eggs

1 tablespoon nigella seeds

⅔ cup (100 g) roasted unsalted peanuts, roughly chopped

I make this because I love it. It's quick and can be eaten from the bowl. Our weeknight dinners, and even dishes on restaurant menus, have more and more become a collection of elements eaten from a bowl. Often, though, when I eat them outside of my kitchen I find they lack a cohesiveness—they need something to bring them together as a whole. That's where a chutney or pesto comes in.

Here I use a quick, zippy chutney of green chiles, cilantro, and mint, with coconut backing them all up. This is my guess at a chutney made by a friend's mum, a great Gujarati cook, that we enthusiastically pile on everything we eat when we are at her house. I haven't had the nerve to ask for the recipe, as it seems a proud inherited family one; I hope this does it justice.

———————————

First, make your chutney. Put half the cilantro (reserving the rest for later) into a food processor with all the other ingredients and blitz until grassy green and smooth, adding a little water as you go if it looks too dry. You are looking for a spoonable consistency, a little thinner than a pesto.

Take the leaves and gnarly root off your cauliflower and chop it into big pieces, using the stalks too. Put them into the food processor and pulse until you have a rice-like texture. You could also use the coarse side of a box grater.

Put your largest frying pan over high heat (if you don't have a nice big one, two smaller ones will work). Add a large pour of coconut oil along with the scallions. Cook for 5 minutes, until soft, stirring from time to time.

Meanwhile, grate the ginger and finely chop the stalks of the remaining cilantro, keeping the leaves for later. Once the scallion is soft, add the ginger and turmeric and cook for a couple of minutes, then season well with salt.

Turn the heat right up. Add the cauliflower rice and cook, stirring every couple of minutes to make sure all the rice gets a little browned on the bottom of the pan; this will take about 10 minutes. →

Meanwhile, heat another pan over medium heat and add a teaspoon of coconut oil. Add the shredded greens, a little splash of water, a tiny squeeze of lemon juice and a good pinch of salt. Once the water has evaporated and the greens are wilted, take the pan off the heat and cover to keep warm.

Once the edges of the cauliflower rice have nicely browned, squeeze over the rest of the lemon juice and pour in the coconut cream. Cook until it has all been absorbed by the rice and there is a slightly caramelly smell. Push the rice to one side of the pan and spoon the greens to the other.

Put the pan that had the greens in back over the heat and add another teaspoon of coconut oil, then crack in the eggs and cook over medium to high heat, until the edges are crispy and the yolks are just cooked. Sprinkle the eggs with the nigella seeds and take off the heat.

Serve the cauliflower rice in bowls, topped with the greens, chutney, peanuts, crispy eggs, and with the rest of the cilantro leaves for sprinkling over the top.

Ways to use this chutney

- Next to any curry or dhal

- To marinate paneer or tofu before frying or baking

- Diluted with a little oil and used to dress a simple salad of grated carrots and shredded cabbage, topped with toasted cashews

- On top of scrambled eggs

- Mashed into some avocado for an Indian riff on guacamole

- To add some punch to some roasted beets

- Mixed with oil and a little lemon or lime juice as a dressing for any grain or rice salad

Golden miso potato salad

Potatoes are pretty magical in all their forms: the crispy-edged golden brown crunch of a roastie; cloud-like mash; a little new potato, boiled and tossed with grassy green herbs, good oil, and flaky salt.... This warm potato salad has become a household staple, a dinner for cold nights and wet homecomings: bolstering, full of flavor and comfort. I bake the potatoes in miso until deeply golden brown, then slather them in a tomato and ginger dressing before mixing them with lentils and toasted almonds. A complete meal.

Although new potatoes aren't around yet, I find this recipe works well with smaller potatoes, so I buy them from the loose bin and pick out the smallest ones I can find. If yours are big, you might want to cut them in half or quarters.

―――――――――――――――――

Preheat the oven to 425°F (220°C).

Rinse the potatoes, scrubbing off any gnarly bits, and dry well. Mix the miso and olive oil with 1 tablespoon of water. Put the potatoes on a baking sheet, add the miso mixture, and toss well to coat.

Put the garlic cloves into the baking sheet as well. Roast the potatoes until they are fluffy inside and golden outside, this should take 25 to 35 minutes depending on the size of your potatoes.

Meanwhile, make your dressing. Combine the sun-dried tomatoes and their oil with the lime zest and juice and the ginger, and mix well.

Remove the potatoes from the oven and spoon out the garlic cloves. Squeeze the softened cloves from their papery outsides, mash them, and add them to the dressing.

Tumble the potatoes into a large bowl, add the lentils and the dressing, and toss together. Top with the almonds and tear over the basil.

SERVES 4

2 pounds (1 kg) small
   potatoes

2 teaspoons white miso paste

2 tablespoons olive oil

the cloves from 1 head of
   garlic, skin on

1 × 14.5-ounce (400-g) can of
   Puy lentils or 250 g home-
   cooked (see page 461),
   drained

¾ cup (100 g) almonds, skin
   on, toasted and sliced

a handful of basil, leaves
   picked

FOR THE DRESSING

2 tablespoons sun-dried
   tomatoes in olive
   oil, chopped, plus
   2 tablespoons of their oil

the zest and juice of
   1 unwaxed lime

a thumb-size piece of ginger,
   peeled and finely chopped

39

Roasted savoy squash with Cheddar and rye

In the colder months of the year I find it all too easy to lean on Asian, Indian or Mexican flavors to perk me up and create a bit of excitement when the offerings of the season have become a bit monotonous. But truthfully it's at this time of year I want simple British flavors most, and this salad sings with them. The sometimes forgotten savoy cabbage is roasted into crisp-edged wedges, more pleasing to me than the now ever-present roasted broccoli or kale, and paired with plump roasted squash, caraway seeds, a rye crumb, and a mustard-spiked dressing, all finished with a crumble of sharp Cheddar (though vegans can happily leave this out). This dish is so rooted in time and place, and that's when eating and cooking feels best to me.

SERVES 4

1 small delicata or butternut squash (about 1 pound/500 g)

1 savoy cabbage (about 14 ounces/400 g), tough outer leaves removed

sea salt and freshly ground black pepper

olive oil

1 teaspoon caraway seeds

2 thin slices rye bread

2 tablespoons baby capers, drained

3½ ounces (100 g) good sharp Cheddar, crumbled (1 cup)

FOR THE DRESSING

1 tablespoon whole-wheat mustard

1 teaspoon honey

1 tablespoon cider vinegar

3 tablespoons good extra-virgin olive or canola oil

Preheat the oven 425°F (220°C).

Halve and deseed the squash and cut into wedges ¾ inch (2 cm) thick. Cut your cabbage into eight chunky wedges. Place them both on a large baking sheet and sprinkle with a good amount of salt and pepper. Add a good drizzle of oil and the caraway seeds and roast in the hot oven for 35 minutes until the squash is soft and cooked through and the cabbage is golden and crisp and charred at the edges.

Meanwhile, put the rye bread into a food processor and blitz until you have rough bread crumbs—you still want a good bit of texture here. Put the crumbs on a baking sheet with a drizzle of olive oil, a good pinch of salt, a generous grind of black pepper, and the capers. Toast in the hot oven for 5 minutes, until the crumbs smell toasty and have a pleasing crunch, being careful not to burn them—with the dark color of the rye bread it can be easy to overcook them.

Mix the dressing ingredients, season well, and put to one side.

When the cabbage and squash are cooked, take them out of the oven and pour onto a platter with the Cheddar. Drizzle generously with the dressing, mix well, then scatter over the rye crumbs and take to the table.

Toasted quinoa, roast brassicas, and spiced green-herb smash

There is something about the burnished edges of a vegetable, especially brassicas, which suit the darker nights and more complex flavors I love. These roasted florets sit next to some lemon-scented toasted quinoa and are topped with a Yemeni herb and spice smash called skhug. It's good stirred into hummus, to finish a soup or mixed with oil to dress a salad.

SERVES 4–6

1 small head of broccoli (about 14 ounces/400 g)

1 small cauliflower (about 14 ounces/400 g)

a pinch of red pepper flakes

1 teaspoon cumin seeds

sea salt

a good drizzle of olive oil

1½ cups (250 g) quinoa

1 unwaxed lemon

½ a vegetable stock cube or 1 teaspoon of vegetable stock powder

1 cup (100 g) almonds, skin on, toasted and roughly chopped

FOR THE HERB SMASH

a large bunch of cilantro

the juice of 2 lemons

1 clove of garlic, roughly chopped

1–2 green chiles (depending on how hot you like things), roughly chopped

1 teaspoon cumin seeds

½ teaspoon ground cardamom (or the crushed seeds from 5 pods)

a pinch of ground cloves

2 tablespoons extra-virgin olive oil

Preheat your oven to 395°F (180°C).

Roughly chop your broccoli and cauliflower into small florets, about 1 inch (2–3 cm), and the stalks and root into thin slices. You want to cut your cauliflower a little smaller than the broccoli as it cooks a little slower. Place it all on a baking sheet with the red pepper flakes, cumin seeds, and a good pinch of salt. Drizzle with the olive oil and roast in the hot oven for 20 to 25 minutes.

Next, cook the quinoa for a couple of minutes in a large dry saucepan over medium heat, letting it crackle and toast. This will give it a deep nutty flavor. Once it is beginning to smell fragrant, cut the lemon in half, place both halves in the pan, and quickly pour over 2½ cups (600 ml) of water. Crumble in the stock cube and bring the liquid to the boil, then reduce the heat and simmer for about 15 minutes, until most of the water has been absorbed. Top off with more boiling water, if needed, as you go.

To make the herb smash, put all the cilantro, including the stalks, the juice of one of the lemons, and the other ingredients into a food processor, along with 2 tablespoons of cold water and blend on a high speed to make a smooth grassy-green sauce. Taste and adjust the seasoning as necessary, adding more lemon, garlic, or oil as you see fit. (Any leftovers can be stored in the fridge for up to one week.)

Once the brassicas are roasted and the quinoa is cooked, pour them all into a bowl and pour over one-third of the dressing. Scatter over half the almonds, mix well, and finish with the rest of the almonds and a good squeeze more of lemon.

Little pea and white-bean polpette

This recipe is made out of stuff I always have on hand in the cupboard, freezer, and fridge. It's at this time of year that I rely on these staples: Frozen peas and preserved lemons add a flash of green and some freshness, an interruption from the root vegetables and grains while we wait for the fresh green march of spring. I make a batch of these and turn them into a few meals: served with a grain and greens for dinner, in a wrap with some pickles, or with spaghetti and a spiced tomato sauce (see page 362). I add a little Parmesan to balance the flavor here, but vegans can use nutritional yeast.

_____

Preheat the oven to 395°F (200°C) if you are baking your polpette.

To make the salsa, roughly chop together all the ingredients except the oil. Put in a bowl and add the oil little by little, stirring well. Taste as you go—you may not need all the oil.

Put the onion into your food processor with the garlic, cilantro seeds, and red pepper flakes and pulse until the onion is finely chopped. Heat a frying pan, add 3 tablespoons of olive oil, and fry the onion mixture gently until it's soft and fragrant. Next, add the rest of the polpette ingredients to the food processor with a good grind of black pepper and mix until the beans have been mashed and everything has come together.

Shape the polpette. Wet your hands and roll into balls using roughly a tablespoon of mixture for each one (you should get about 18), then place on a baking sheet. If you are baking them, drizzle the balls with a little olive oil and bake in the oven for 20 to 25 minutes, or until golden. To cook them in a frying pan, chill them for at least 20 minutes, then simply fry them in a little olive oil over medium heat for 10 to 15 minutes, turning every few minutes. Serve with the salsa verde.

If you are freezing the polpette, cook them for a few minutes less, then let them cool completely (they firm up as they cool down). Transfer to containers or bags and freeze.

FOR THE CUPBOARD SALSA VERDE

a small bunch of flat-leaf parsley

2 tablespoons capers, drained

1 tablespoon cornichons, drained

2 sun-dried tomatoes, drained

the zest of 1 unwaxed lemon

10 tablespoons extra-virgin olive oil

FOR THE POLPETTE

1 red onion, peeled and roughly chopped

2 cloves of garlic, peeled

2 teaspoons cilantro (coriander) seeds

a generous pinch of red pepper flakes

olive oil

1 × 10.5-ounce (300 g) bag of frozen peas

1 × 14.5-ounce (400 g) can of white beans (or 1 cup/250 g home-cooked, see page 461), drained

½ cup (50 g) bread crumbs or roughly blitzed oats

½ a preserved lemon, flesh removed and discarded, peel finely chopped

1 teaspoon flaky sea salt

the zest of 1 unwaxed lemon

4 sun-dried tomatoes

½ cup (50 g) freshly grated Parmesan (I use a vegetarian/rennet-free one) or 1 tablespoon nutritional yeast

freshly ground black pepper

Spelt with pickled pears and pink leaves

This warm winter salad has everything going for it. It's the prettiest of salads, with gentle off-white celeriac and caramel-colored spelt offset by the dusky rose of pink radicchio and the Expressionist pink and cream splatter of Castelfranco lettuce. If you haven't guessed already, I love these bitter lettuces; they cheer up my January table and happily, they are now much more widely available, though a few heads of chicory would do fine in their place. Be careful not to use overripe pears; you need them to be a little on the firm side so they hold their shape as they cook.

Put 4 tablespoons of the vinegar, the black peppercorns, sugar, and salt into a saucepan with ½ cup (100 ml) of water and bring to the boil. Meanwhile, peel the pears, halve them, and scoop out the cores with a teaspoon. Lower the pears into the pickling liquid, lower the heat, and leave to cook until tender (about 10 minutes). Remove from the heat, cover with a lid, and let rest.

Preheat the oven to 395°F (180°C). Roast the celeriac in the oven on a baking sheet, with a little oil, for 20 minutes. Mix the honey with the miso and mustard. After 20 minutes, take the sheet out of the oven and add 1 tablespoon of the miso mixture, toss with the celeriac, then return to the oven for another 5 to 10 minutes, until crispy and golden.

Meanwhile, cook the spelt. Bring a pan of salted water to a boil, then add the spelt and cook for 20 to 25 minutes, or until cooked through and tender. Mix the remaining miso mixture with the remaining tablespoon of vinegar and the olive oil, drain the spelt, and toss in the dressing.

Once everything else is ready, tear all the leaves from your bitter lettuces and lay on plates. Top with the spelt, celeriac, and the pickled pears and crumble over the cheese.

SERVES 4

- 5 tablespoons white wine vinegar
- ½ teaspoon black peppercorns
- 2 tablespoons superfine or caster sugar
- a generous pinch of flaky sea salt
- 4 just-ripe pears
- 3 cups (400 g) celeriac or parsnip, peeled and cut into ¾-inch (2-cm) pieces
- 1 tablespoon golden honey
- 1 tablespoon white miso paste
- 2 tablespoons whole-wheat mustard
- 1 cup (200 g) pearled spelt berries
- 1 tablespoon extra-virgin olive oil
- 2 heads of Castelfranco, radicchio, or other bitter salad leaves (see note above)
- ⅓ cup (50 g) blue cheese

Quick carrot dhal

SERVES 4

2 cloves of garlic

1 green chile

a thumb-size piece of fresh
ginger, peeled

1 red onion, peeled

coconut or vegetable oil

1 teaspoon cumin seeds

1 teaspoon cilantro
(coriander) seeds

1 teaspoon black mustard
seeds

1 teaspoon ground turmeric

1 teaspoon ground cinnamon

1 cup (200 g) red lentils

1 × 13.5-ounce (400-ml) can
of coconut milk

2½ cups (600 ml) vegetable
stock

6 carrots, peeled

2 large handfuls of spinach

juice of 1 lemon

FOR THE PICKLE

a thumb-size piece of fresh
ginger, peeled

1 green chile

1 unwaxed lemon

2 handfuls of radishes

1 tablespoon nigella seeds

1 tablespoon white wine
vinegar

honey or agave nectar

a bunch of cilantro, chopped

sea salt

TO SERVE

plain yogurt

cooked brown basmati rice

a few poppadoms

This dhal has its roots in South India. It comes together quickly but has rich layers of flavor that might lead you to think it had spent hours on the stovetop—curry leaves, pops of mustard seeds, warming cinnamon, all the things I love in a dhal.

The turmeric and carrots make this a vibrant sunny-hued bowl, and on top lies a color pop of sweet-shop pink radish pickle. I serve it with poppadoms scrunched into shards over the top for a welcome bit of crunch. We have dhal in some form or another at least once a week, and this is one I keep coming back to. If you really wanted to speed things up, you could do all your grating in the food processor.

Finely grate the garlic, chile, and ginger (I use a sharp Microplane grater; if your grater isn't quite up to the job, finely chop them), then coarsely grate the red onion. Put a large saucepan over medium heat, add a little oil and everything you have grated, and cook for 10 minutes until soft and sweet.

Pound the cumin and cilantro seeds a bit in a mortar with pestle, spice grinder, or mixing bowl with rolling pin, then add to the pan with the other spices and cook for a couple of minutes to toast and release their oils. Add the lentils, coconut milk, and stock to the pan and bring to a simmer, then turn the heat down and bubble for 25 to 30 minutes. Meanwhile, grate all the carrots and add those too.

While that is cooking make a little pickle to go on top. Finely grate the ginger, chile, and the zest of the lemon into a bowl, then use a coarser grater to grate the radishes into the bowl. Add the nigella seeds, vinegar, a squeeze of honey, half the cilantro, a good pinch of salt and mix well.

To finish your dhal, take it off the heat, then stir in the spinach and allow it to wilt a little, stirring in the other half of the cilantro and the juice of the lemon too. Pile into bowls and top with the radish pickle, spoonfuls of yogurt, and brown basmati rice. At the table, crumble over your poppadoms.

Beet, rhubarb, and potato gratin

This might just get the all-time gratin crown. There's gentle comfort from the potatoes and cream, with an unexpected pop of sweet acidity from the rhubarb, a foil for the unrepentant earthiness of the beets. The lively warmth of the pink peppercorns tops things off. It's a pretty beautiful-looking dishful too; there are some amazing colors at play: whites, neon pinks, magenta, and the dots of fluorescent pink peppercorns—you'd struggle to find one pinker.

I tend not to cook with a lot of dairy but here I make an exception, using the best I can get my hands on. Vegans might try this with almond or oat milk, or even some vegetable stock in place of the creams. I make the stock for this with about half the powder or stock cubes that the packet suggests, so the flavor of the stock doesn't overwhelm; if you have homemade stock (see page 460), all the better.

Preheat the oven to 395°F (200°C). Butter a large gratin dish.

Peel the potatoes and slice them very finely—a mandoline or the fine slicer attachment on a food processor is the best way to do this; just watch your fingers if you're using a mandoline. Cut the beets into fine slices as well—they don't have to quite be as thin, so you could cut them with a knife.

Put the stock and both the creams into a large saucepan, along with the bay leaves and 1 teaspoon of the peppercorns. Bring the liquid to just under a boil, then take off the heat and leave to sit for 30 minutes or so. Remove the bay leaves, leaving the peppercorns in, then bring the liquid to just below a simmer. Add the sliced potatoes and cook gently for 5 minutes.

Remove from the heat, season really well with salt and pepper, and spoon half the potatoes into the gratin dish. Put half the beets and rhubarb on top, seasoning as you go, then top with the rest of the potatoes and their cream, followed by the rest of the beets.

Roughly bash the remaining pink peppercorns in a mortar with pestle, spice grinder, or mixing bowl with rolling pin and sprinkle on the gratin. Bake for 1 hour, or until the vegetables are completely tender. Cover the top with foil after about 45 minutes if it looks like it is becoming too dark.

SERVES 4–6

butter, for greasing

2 pounds (1 kg) potatoes, preferably waxy ones, such as Yukon Gold or red gold

16 ounces (500 g) cooked beets (the ones in vacuum packs or home-cooked), peeled

1¼ cups (300 ml) weak vegetable stock (see note above)

1¼ cups (300 ml) heavy cream

⅝ cup (150 ml) sour cream

2 bay leaves

2 teaspoons pink peppercorns or ½ teaspoon black peppercorns

sea salt and freshly ground black pepper

2 cups (200 g) forced rhubarb, thinly sliced

Butter bean stew with kale and sticky blood oranges

This is a seriously comforting bowl. Sweet spiced beans, burnished blood oranges, and the bright green goodness of kale, all topped off with a hazelnut and sesame seed crunch; full of flavor and texture. It's quick but nourishing, with the satisfying depth of a pot that's been very slowly ticking away on the stove for hours.

SERVES 4

olive oil

3 cloves of garlic, finely sliced

1 × 14.5-ounce (400-g) can of chopped tomatoes

2 bay leaves

a small bunch of thyme (4 or 5 stalks)

sea salt

1 red onion, finely chopped

2 × 14.5-ounce (400 g) jars or cans of butter beans, drained (or 1 cup/250 g home-cooked beans, see page 461)

2 blood oranges, or regular oranges, peeled and sliced

1 tablespoon sherry vinegar

1 teaspoon honey

10½ ounces (300 g) curly kale, leaves pulled away from the stalks and roughly torn (4½ cups)

¾ cup (100 g) hazelnuts

2 tablespoons sesame seeds

the zest of 1 unwaxed lemon

1 tablespoon sumac

feta or goat cheese, to serve (optional)

Fill and boil water in the kettle. First put a little olive oil into a pan, add 2 cloves of the garlic and fry for a minute or two, then add the tomatoes, herbs, and a good pinch of sea salt and simmer for 10 minutes.

Meanwhile, heat a frying pan over medium heat, add a little oil, then add the onion and the other garlic clove, and cook for 10 minutes, until soft and sweet. Add the butter beans to the tomatoes, then half fill the tomato can with hot water from the kettle, add this too and simmer for 10 minutes.

Once the onions are cooked, add the blood oranges, sherry vinegar, and honey to the frying pan and cook for 3 to 4 minutes, until the orange slices are starting to caramelize and catch around the edges. Add the kale, put a lid on the pan, turn the heat down, and cook until wilted, about 8 minutes. Meanwhile, roughly chop the hazelnuts and mix with the sesame seeds, the lemon zest, and 2 tablespoons of olive oil. Fry in a pan over medium heat for 2 to 3 minutes, until crisp and starting to toast brown.

By now the bean mixture should be nicely reduced. Remove the thyme and the bay leaves, season, and add a good drizzle of olive oil.

Serve the beans topped with the kale and oranges and a good sprinkling of the hazelnuts, sumac, and sesame seeds. Crumble a bit of feta or goat cheese over the top if you like too.

One-pan squash, caper, and kale pasta

This may not be for traditionalists, but I think this way of cooking pasta is clever—the starch from the pasta water comes together to make a velvety, creamy sauce that you wouldn't get if they were cooked separately. I'm not suggesting all pasta be cooked this way, but when a quick dinner is needed this is where I look.

You can swap in any pasta that cooks in about 8 minutes. I've gone for a whole-wheat rigatoni here, but I've had success with quinoa and corn pasta too. I use delicata squash, but you could use butternut squash instead—the skin is tougher, so it's best to peel it.

Halve the squash and scoop out the seeds, then thinly slice the squash halves into half moons about 2 inches (5 cm) thick. Strip the kale leaves from their stalks and roughly tear any big pieces. Finely slice the stalks, discarding any particularly sinewy ones.

Heat a tablespoon of the olive oil in a large shallow pan over medium heat and add the squash with a generous pinch of flaky sea salt. Cook the squash in the pan for about 10 minutes, stirring every couple of minutes, so that the pieces of squash start to catch and brown at the edges. Fill the kettle with water and put it on to boil.

Once the squash has had its 10 minutes, add the garlic and kale stalks and stir for a minute or so before adding the pasta, lemon zest, lentils, red pepper flakes, stock cube, and 4½ cups (1 liter) of water from the kettle. Cover with a lid and cook over medium heat for 6 minutes.

Next, remove the lid and add the kale leaves and capers. Cover with the lid for a couple more minutes, until the kale is starting to wilt and turn bright green. If your pasta is a little dry, you can add a tiny bit more water, about ½ cup (100 ml). Remove the lid and simmer for another 2 to 3 minutes, until the water has been absorbed, then take the pan off the heat and stir in the remaining tablespoon of olive oil and half the Parmesan. Taste and add a little more salt if needed, then let sit for a minute or so before piling into bowls and topping with a good grating of the remaining Parmesan.

SERVES 4

1 small delicata squash (about 14 ounces/400 g)

4 cups (250 g) roughly torn curly kale leaves, stalks reserved

2 tablespoons good olive oil

flaky sea salt

3 cloves of garlic, finely chopped

12 ounces (350 g) pasta (I use whole-wheat rigatoni or penne)

the zest of 2 unwaxed lemons

½ × 14.5-ounce (400-g) can of green lentils, drained

a pinch of red pepper flakes

½ a vegetable stock cube or 1 teaspoon vegetable stock powder

2 tablespoons baby capers, drained

½ cup (50 g) Parmesan (I use a vegetarian/rennet-free one)

Flatbreads: a flavor map

Flatbreads or quesadillas are a weekly quick lunch or dinner in our house. They require little more than a few minutes' attention, one bowl, and a pan, and with a few salad leaves or a bit of mashed avocado they make a perfect too-lazy-to-cook lunch or dinner.

I make quesadillas a bit differently, leaving the seriously cheese-laden ones to fond childhood memory. Instead, I use vegetables, pulses, herbs and even eggs to make textured fillings with pops of flavor that move from Mexico to Italy, France, Morocco, and back again. In fact, quesadillas are really just sandwiched flatbread, which in some form or another you'll find in almost every culture. I use seeded tortillas, piadina flatbread (see page 316 for my Quick squash piadina recipe), or large corn tortillas; all are easy to come across in good supermarkets these days, though for the really good, pure corn ones, you might need to order them online.

We make armies of them when we have a crowd to feed, as they are the perfect vehicle for dipping, a great snack with a cold beer in hand, and are pretty fuss-free. A flatbread or quesadilla allows you to play around and use what you have to hand. It's important to fill them with something that will bind the two sides together—some cheese, egg, or soft mashed vegetables or beans are ideal.

1
___

Choose
your vehicle:
you'll need a pair of
one of the following

seeded tortillas

whole-wheat tortillas

corn tortillas
(see page 18)

piadina flatbread

Turkish flatbread
(see page 456)

2
___

Create the base:
something soft or melty
to help the tortillas
stick together

mashed butter beans

mashed black beans

grated Cheddar

1 organic egg
(see Caper, herb, and egg
flatbread on page 18)

torn mozzarella

mashed chickpeas

grated and sautéed
zucchini

3
Add backup:
another soft texture
to add interest

|

sautéed grated
sweet potato

|

sautéed grated squash

|

chopped roasted
red peppers

|

chopped cherry
tomatoes

|

grated carrot

|

grated beets

|

sautéed shredded
greens or kale

|

a crumbling of feta

↓

4
Choose a top
flavor note:
(one or two of these)

|

finely chopped
scallions

|

chopped red chile

|

baby capers

|

chopped pitted olives

|

smoky chipotle paste

|

finely chopped red onion

|

a spice mix (garam
masala, zatar, etc.)

|

a grating of lemon
or lime zest

↓

5
Add a
soft herb:
some freshness

|

cilantro

|

mint

|

basil

|

parsley

|

dill

↓

6
Serve with
something
to dip:

|

guacamole

|

salsa

|

tahini and yogurt dip

|

smashed peas with
mint and lemon

|

hummus

Take an ovenproof dish or pan (that can go on the stovetop as well) large enough to hold the cauliflower. Spoon in the coconut oil, and grate the ginger into the oil. Finely chop the chiles, discarding the seeds if you wish, then add them to the pan. Add the garlic, then place over medium heat and let the spices and aromatics cook for a few minutes, until fragrant. Stir in the mustard seeds and continue cooking until the garlic has softened, then add the turmeric and a big pinch of salt.

Pour the coconut milk into the spice mixture, stir well, and season with a little black pepper. When the milk starts to bubble gently, turn off the heat, place the drained cauliflower in the dish, then baste it with the coconut-spice mixture. Throw the lemon halves into the side of the dish too, then scatter the potatoes around; they will sit in the coconut milk.

Bake the cauliflower, basting it occasionally with the spiced sauce in the dish, for 40 to 45 minutes. You want it to brown a little on top. To test if the cauliflower is cooked, insert a small sharp knife into the middle—it should be really tender and the potatoes and cauliflower should have soaked up most of the sauce. Once it's perfect, take it out of the oven and transfer to a serving dish, then squeeze over the roasted lemons. Serve in the middle of the table, with little bowls of yogurt, almonds, and cilantro for sprinkling on top.

Whole-wheat spelt, date, and molasses scones

These are not scones to keep in a tin but scones to eat warm, with salted butter and tea. These are everything I want from something baked on a cold day: rounded deep sweetness from molasses, caramel notes from the dates, and maltiness from the spelt.

I have intentionally made them in quite a small batch; they are very quick to whip up and taste much more decadent than their ingredients might suggest. You can use whatever black tea you like here—I love the bergamot kick of Earl Grey, brewed strong, but I can imagine a smoky lapsang souchong might be amazing.

Preheat the oven to 395°F (200°C). Line a baking sheet with parchment paper.

Soak the dates in the hot tea for 15 minutes, until the tea has cooled a little. Mix together the flour, baking powder, allspice, and salt with your fingertips, then add the butter until the mix looks like bread crumbs. You could also do this by pulsing it in a food processor.

Drain, then roughly chop the dates and add them to the mix, along with the molasses and buttermilk. Mix slowly and lightly until the mixture forms a soft but not too sticky dough. Shape into a rough round ball, place on your prepared baking sheet, and use a knife to score across the top to mark out 6 portions, stopping before the knife reaches the baking sheet; it should look a bit like a loaf of soda bread.

Mix the egg and milk for the glaze with a pinch of salt and brush it over the top, then sprinkle with the oats, pressing them into the dough lightly to stick them down.

Bake for 15 minutes, then turn the baking sheet and reduce the heat to 360°F (180°C) and continue to bake for about 10 more minutes, until the top is a dark golden brown and when you turn the scone over and tap it, it sounds hollow. Serve warm from the oven and break up as required. The scones are very good with the curd on page 66.

MAKES 6

1 cup (125 g) pitted dates

5 fluid ounces (150 ml) freshly brewed strong black or Earl Grey tea

1 cup (125 g) whole-wheat spelt flour

2 teaspoons baking powder

¼ teaspoon ground allspice

¼ teaspoon flaky sea salt

2 tablespoons (30 g) cold unsalted butter, cubed

1 tablespoon molasses

⅓ cup (75 g) buttermilk or thin natural yogurt

FOR THE GLAZE

1 organic or free-range egg

1 tablespoon milk

a pinch of sea salt

a handful of rolled oats

Brewing your own kombucha

We have been drinking kombucha for years, mostly when I have traveled to visit my sister in L.A. where it seems to be as available as water. When I started drinking it every day I noticed really positive changes in how I was feeling. Back home I have found it harder to get my hands on and it's very expensive, so I started brewing it myself. I am sure it has helped us ward off a few winter colds.

Kombucha is a drink that's been around for thousands of years. It's a sweet fermented green or black tea with a bubbly character that I think is totally delicious. Kombucha has been widely praised as being good for you, as it contains digestion-supporting probiotic enzymes that lots of us are lacking in our diets. It supports the healthy bacteria in our guts and can help improve our digestion and how we absorb the nutrients from our food. By making kombucha yourself, it will be completely raw (some commercial ones are pasteurized) so it has maximum health benefits; you can also control the fizziness and how long it's brewed to your taste.

The first thing I will say is that I'm not an expert; brewing kombucha is a huge topic and there are books and blogs entirely devoted to the subject. The brewing process is pretty simple: all you need is a bit of time, food (sugar), and good bacteria to create the brew (the scoby). Outlined below is how I brew mine, and so far it's been very successful. Before I started I was quite daunted by the process, but after you've done it once you'll get into the rhythm and it becomes really easy. Before you brew I recommend you read this explanation a couple of times; it may look like a lot of information, but if you have a level of understanding it makes the process easier and quicker.

The scoby

The scoby, which stands for Symbiotic Culture of Bacteria and Yeast, is what you will need to ferment your tea. A scoby is a very strange-looking thing that I am weirdly fascinated by; it is like a big rubbery pancake. You can buy scobys online, but as they are live they multiply, so there are lots out in the world waiting for owners. A kombucha-brewing friend will have one or a quick search on the internet will probably unearth one for free.

The water

Filtered or at the very least boiled water is essential for kombucha brewing, as some of the chemicals in tap water can affect the fermentation process.

The tea

You can use black or green tea, but I prefer the flavor of my kombucha when it's made with green and it will be lower in caffeine. Flavored and herbal teas don't work, as I discovered when I tried to make a batch with Earl Grey; it's best to add any flavors after brewing. The caffeine in kombucha contains only about a third of that in brewed tea.

The sugar

The scoby and the fermentation are fed with sugar. It may seem like you are adding a lot of sugar, but during the brewing process it will turn from a very sweet tea into something far less so.

The alcohol

While your kombucha is brewing, it will contain a very small amount of alcohol, about 0.5 percent. It's all part of the fermentation process, but it's something to bear in mind if people are sensitive to alcohol, and I certainly wouldn't give kombucha to children.

The equipment

— 1 large or a couple of smaller teapots or pitchers to brew your tea

— 1 × 5- to 7-quart (5- to 6-liter) jar or kombucha crock (mine has a tap at the bottom)

— a clean piece of tea towel or muslin to cover

— a piece of string or a rubber band

— a funnel

— 4 × 4½-cup (1-liter) bottles to store your finished kombucha

The ingredients

— 1 scoby

— 2 cups (500 ml) premade kombucha tea (store-bought or from your last batch)

— 1 cup (250 g) sugar (I use superfine or caster sugar)

— 4 quarts (4 liters) filtered or boiled water

— 2 heaping tablespoons green or black tea

The method

First brew your tea. Bring your preboiled or filtered water to a boil and pour it over the tea leaves of your choice; I do this in a couple of teapots and measuring pitchers. Let it steep for 20 to 30 minutes, so it's good and strong.

Add the sugar, stir to dissolve, then allow the tea to cool. This step is important, as the scoby will die if it's too hot.

Remove any metal jewelery and from this point on don't use any metal sieves or spoons, as they react with the scoby. Get the jar or crock you are using for the brewing and pour in the premade kombucha. Add the cooled tea, then carefully place the scoby on top of the mixture. Cover the jar with a piece of fabric and secure it with string or a rubber band. A paper towel would also work; you just want air to be able to pass into the jar. Place the kombucha container in a place where it will not be disturbed, out of direct sunlight. I leave mine on my work surface where I can keep an eye on it.

The fermentation can take anywhere from 7 to 14 days, depending on the heat of the room, the scoby, and how you like your kombucha. The longer you leave it, the more acidic it will become. During the brewing process it's normal to see things happening in the brew: the scoby moving, bubbles of air. After a few days the surface of the tea will start to look opaque—this is your new scoby forming and a very good sign. →

57

How long to brew?

After it's been brewing for about a week I start to taste mine every day (remembering to use a nonmetal spoon). If you like a sweeter drink, you may want to bottle yours now, if you like things more tart, perhaps wait a full 14 days.

Once your kombucha tastes good to you, you can bottle it. Lift the scoby into a bowl or rimmed plate (remembering to keep any metal away). Divide your kombucha among the 1-liter bottles (a funnel is useful here), saving 2 cups (500 ml) for your next batch. Once the kombucha is bottled, you can start from the beginning on your next batch.

Once bottled you have a few options:

— Store it in the fridge and drink it as is (it keeps for several months).

— Flavor your kombucha. I find the best way to do this is using freshly squeezed or juiced fruits (I've found sweeter ones, such as strawberry, mango, peach, plum, pear, guava, and watermelon work best). You'll need about 2½ cups (600 ml), so about 10 tablespoons (150 ml) per bottle, but you can adjust this to your own taste based on the sweetness of the fruit. Sometimes I add spices too: For each bottle I add a teaspoon of grated fresh turmeric or ginger, some bashed cardamom seeds, a few rose petals, or even fennel seeds. Now you can either put this straight into the fridge or do a second fermentation.

— Ferment it a second time in the bottle to make it bubbly. I always do this, as I love the Champagne-like bubbles. Seal the bottles and keep them on the work surface. It's really important to open the bottles every day to let the air out so the tops don't pop off (this is called burping). At the same time, I taste for fizziness and when it's nicely bubbly (usually 2 to 3 days) I put it in the fridge to store.

Taking time off

You might want to take a break from brewing. To pause the process, take the scoby out of the jar, separate the new scoby (the baby) from the original one (the mother) and put them into separate glass jars with enough of your brewed kombucha to cover. Place in the fridge and seal, remembering that nothing can come into contact with metal. They will keep like this in the fridge for at least a few months. When you are ready to brew again bring the scoby to room temperature and start the process above, adding all the liquid you stored the scoby in too. If you are organized you can plan your second fermentation to finish on the day you go away.

Basic dos and don'ts

— Ideally use filtered but at the very least boiled water to brew.

— Avoid using any metal during the brewing process; take any rings off when you handle the scoby.

— Use real sugar. Honey and other natural sweeteners don't work as well; I've tried.

— Use green or black tea; I use loose-leaf organic. Flavored and herbal teas don't work.

— Wash your hands before handling the scoby, being sure to wash off any soap residue.

— I wash my equipment every couple of brews using hot water and vinegar (not soap).

— Make sure the brew is covered at all times, to prevent flies getting in.

— If you see mold or anything unsavory on the scoby, discard everything and start again.

— While I brew with green tea the most, every 5 brews or so I use black tea, as it helps the scoby stay healthy; I don't understand why, but it works.

— If I have a bad batch I brew the next batch a little sweeter and use black tea; it usually solves the problem.

— As you brew each batch, a new scoby will form on the top of your kombucha; this means it's a good healthy brew and it's a good sign. When you go to make another batch, you can separate the old scoby (the mother) and the new one (the baby) and make an additional batch. Give the old scoby away or keep it in the fridge; I tend to separate my scobys every few batches. If you have too many to find a use for, they can be composted.

Resources

There are some amazing expert resources online; you can get very specific answers to any kombucha problem in great detail. My favorite is culturesforhealth.com.

Super-chocolate tiffin bites

These little chocolate bites were born of two childhood obsessions: Terry's Chocolate Orange bars and chocolate tiffin. I love both but the super-sweet versions I lapped up as a kid now make me a bit crazy, so I came up with these. I make them in batches and keep them on hand for that time of day when I need something sweet. Sure, they have a bit of sugar, but I find the nuts and seeds balance out the hit of sweetness. They are spiked with orange zest, salt, and vanilla. I'm always a bit happier after one of these.

You can mix up the nuts and fruit you use here. I imagine any citrus zest, sweet spice, or even a hit of red pepper flakes would work well. I use little silicone molds that double for freezing curry pastes, pestos, and even baby food. You could also make this mixture into a bark if you prefer by just pouring the chocolate onto a baking sheet lined with parchment paper and sprinkling over the toppings.

Preheat your oven to 395°F (200°C).

Break your chocolate into small pieces (this will help it melt evenly) and put it into a small heatproof bowl that fits neatly over a saucepan. Put a couple of inches of boiling water in the pan, put your chocolate on top, and leave to melt.

Roughly chop your almonds and put on a baking sheet with the pumpkin and sesame seeds. Toast in the hot oven for about 4 minutes—you want the almonds to be just toasted but still a little white and buttery inside—then remove from the oven and pour into a bowl.

Once the chocolate is melted, add the coconut oil and stir until this has melted and is incorporated, then add the vanilla, orange zest, and salt and mix gently. If you don't have molds and are making the tiffin on a baking sheet, pour it into a baking sheet lined with parchment paper, then scatter over the toasted nuts and seeds and the raisins. If using molds, add the toasted nuts and seeds and raisins to the mixture and gently stir again. Pour into molds and leave to set.

Once set, turn the tiffin bites out of the molds. Store in a sealed container where they will keep for up to 2 weeks.

MAKES ABOUT 20

14 ounces (400 g) dark chocolate (at least 70% cocoa solids)

1 cup (100 g) almonds, skin on

½ cup (75 g) pumpkin seeds

2 tablespoons sesame seeds

1 tablespoon coconut oil

1 teaspoon vanilla paste

the zest of 2 unwaxed oranges

a good pinch of flaky sea salt

½ cup (75 g) raisins

Brownie energy bites with maple-pumpkin praline

I am something of a snacker. I marvel at people who stop at three meals a day. Since becoming a mum, I have had less time to cook than ever before, but it has been really important that I feed myself well. In the kitchen, this has put the spotlight on one-pan dinners prepared during Dylan's nap, meals that can be cooked with one hand, and ready-to-go bites of energy that perk me up when dinner seems a long way away.

Half truffle and half brownie, of all the things I have tried, these have been the quickest to leave the jar. Covering these little bites in chocolate takes a little longer and can be skipped, but I welcome any opportunity to pretend I am in a chocolate factory. I use raw cacao powder here as I prefer its deep, pure chocolate flavor (its health benefits are well reported too). If you're using standard dates, soak them in boiling water for 10 minutes first.

MAKES ABOUT 30

1½ cups (200 g) pecans

¾ cup (100 g) cashews

4 tablespoons raw cacao or cocoa powder

1 teaspoon vanilla paste

½ teaspoon fine sea salt

½ teaspoon ground cinnamon

1¼ cups (175 g) pitted Medjool dates

1 tablespoon coconut oil

FOR THE PUMPKIN AND MAPLE PRALINE

⅓ cup (50 g) pumpkin seeds

a pinch of flaky sea salt

1 tablespoon maple syrup

FOR THE CHOCOLATE COATING

3 tablespoons coconut oil

2 tablespoons raw cacao or cocoa powder

1 teaspoon maple syrup

In the bowl of a food processor, pulse the pecans and cashews until you have a rough powder. Add the cacao, vanilla, sea salt, and cinnamon. Pulse to mix evenly. Add the dates and coconut oil and blitz, scraping down the sides of the bowl here and there. The mixture should ball up, appear glossy, and come together in your fingers; if it's still a little powdery, add a teaspoon of water and blitz again until it comes together but is not too sticky and wet.

Scoop out the mixture in heaping teaspoon-size bites and roughly roll into balls. Put on a baking sheet lined with parchment paper and chill in the fridge for at least 20 minutes. Make the praline by toasting the seeds in a frying pan until they start to pop, then add the salt and maple syrup and toss well. Allow to cook for 1 minute, then pour on a plate. Once cool, roughly chop.

Make the chocolate coating. In a small saucepan, combine all the ingredients and whisk over low heat until it thickens slightly, taking care it doesn't stick on the bottom. Set aside to cool. Dip the bites into the coating, turning with two forks to cover. Put on a baking sheet, top with a little praline and leave to set. Store in the fridge until you're ready to eat them—they will keep for a week or so.

Chocolate and blood orange freezer cake

This is a no-cook cake, raw, in fact, if you are into that kind of thing; I use the freezer to set the cake instead of the oven. These cakes are sometimes called ice-box cakes, which I think sounds quite magical. It's the kind of dessert I like to eat in January.

I use a raw cashew butter here, which I buy from the supermarket, though if I have time I make it at home, as the flavor is gentler than the toasted nut butters you can buy and it has notes of white chocolate. Any more subtly flavored nut butter would work here.

SERVES 6–8

FOR THE CRUST

¼ cup (25 g) cashews

coconut oil, for greasing

¾ cup (120 g) pitted Medjool dates

1 teaspoon vanilla extract

1 tablespoon raw cacao or cocoa powder

a generous pinch of flaky sea salt

½ cup (120 g) nut butter (I use a raw cashew butter, see note above)

¾ cup (125 g) whole buckwheat

FOR THE FILLING

⅔ cup (70 g) cashew nuts

⅓ cup (50 g) pitted Medjool dates

a good pinch of salt

3 medium ripe peeled bananas

the seeds from 1 vanilla pod or 1 teaspoon vanilla paste

⅓ cup (70 g) coconut oil, melted

the zest and juice of 1 unwaxed blood orange

3 passion fruits, cut in half

TO FINISH

3 blood oranges

1½ ounces (40 g) dark chocolate (70% cocoa solids)

First, soak both the cashews for the filling and for the crust in separate bowls of cold water for 3 to 4 hours if you have time: If not, then soak them in warm water for 30 minutes. Grease the bottom of a 9-inch (22-cm) loose-bottomed tart pan with coconut oil and put to one side.

Next make the crust. In a food processor, blitz the ¼ cup (25 g) of soaked, drained cashews and the dates until they have broken down into tiny pieces and start to come together in a ball. Add the vanilla, cacao, salt, and nut butter and blitz until combined. Then add the buckwheat and blitz until the buckwheat has broken down a bit and the crust dough comes together in your fingers when pinched. Put the crust mixture into the middle of the greased pan and use your fingers to push it out to the edges and up the sides of the pan, then put it into the freezer to set for at least 3 hours.

Next, make the filling. Put the soaked, drained cashews into a blender with the dates, salt, bananas, and vanilla and blitz until completely smooth. Pour in the melted coconut oil, then add the orange zest and blitz again. Pour two-thirds into the chilled crust.

Scrape the seeds from the passion fruits into a sieve resting over a bowl. Use the back of a spoon to push the juice through, add this to the remaining banana mixture in the blender, and add the juice of the blood orange, then pour this layer over the banana one. Smooth everything over with a spatula and put the crust back in the freezer for 30 minutes to firm up, though it can happily sit there for much longer.

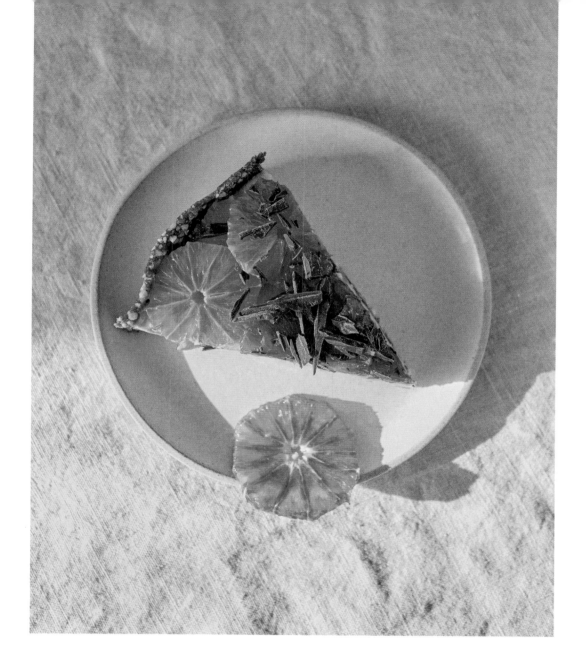

To finish, take the tart out of the freezer about an hour before you want to eat. Cut the peel off the blood oranges and slice the flesh into thin rounds. Break the chocolate into shards.

Once the cake is thawed enough that the filling is beginning to soften, arrange the blood oranges and chocolate on top prettily and pat yourself on the back. Any leftovers can be stored in the freezer for up to 2 weeks.

Grapefruit and honey curd

I feel sorry for grapefruit. I think it's been pushed to the sidelines in favor of its more approachable (clementines) or glamorous (blood orange) cousins. I love them—not just the pink ones, I love the straight-up yellow ones I ate as a kid. You could use either here. This curd is exactly what I want to spread on a piece of toast or to top a bowl of yogurt year-round, but, especially when it's still dark, it sings of the sunshine where these sunny fruits were grown, and the ginger and honey add even more cheer.

Making curd is not for anyone impatient: It's a slow meditative stir that makes the best, smoothest curd. You'll feel like it's never going to thicken, but have faith, it will—it always does. If you get overexcited and turn up the heat too much it will become grainy. If it does, you can press it through a sieve to resurrect it, but the joy comes from the slow stirring. Any citrus can be swapped in for the grapefruit here: Just adjust the level of honey a little depending on whether the fruits are sweeter or more acidic.

MAKES A DECENT JARFUL

1 cup (250 ml) freshly squeezed grapefruit juice

a small thumb-size piece of ginger, peeled and grated

5 tablespoons unsalted butter, at room temperature

¼ cup (60 ml) golden honey

2 large organic egg yolks

2 large organic eggs

a good pinch of flaky sea salt

the juice of ½ a lemon

Put the grapefruit juice and ginger in a small saucepan, bring it to a simmer, and leave it to reduce to about ⅝ cup (150 ml). Let it cool a bit, then strain through a sieve.

Cream the butter in a medium heatproof mixing bowl. Add the honey and beat until fluffy and light. Add the egg yolks, and then the eggs, one at a time, beating well to incorporate each one before you add the next. Stir in the salt, then gradually add the reduced grapefruit and lemon juice.

Rinse out the small saucepan you used earlier and fill it one-third full with water. Bring to a simmer and place your bowl of curd on top of it. Stir constantly and heat the curd slowly. This step usually takes me about 20 minutes. Pull the curd from the heat when it is just thick enough to coat your spoon; it will thicken as it cools.

There's no need to strain the curd, unless it has some lumps. And you can keep it refrigerated for up to 2 weeks, or up to a month in the freezer.

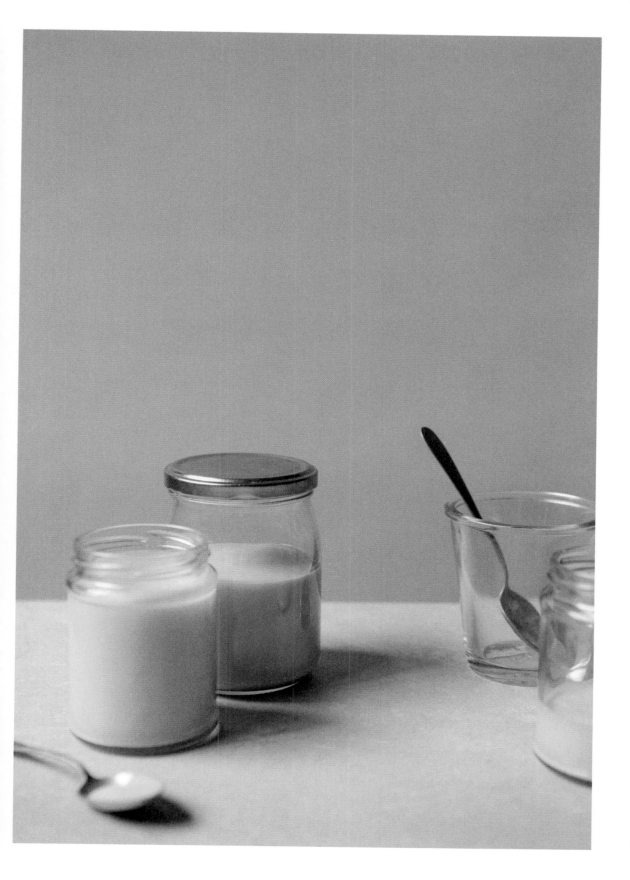

Apple and white miso kimchi

This is a gentle kimchi; the apple, radish, and white miso mellow the chile and sharpness that comes from the fermentation. Fermented foods contain beneficial bacteria, which is important because we need a diverse population of bacteria in our gut for optimal health; I do notice the difference when I include some fermented foods in my diet (see "Brewing your own kombucha" on page 56).

Make sure you use a pure sea salt, as iodized sea salt will prevent this fermenting properly. Check the heat of your chiles, as they vary so much. I use one to two, depending on their heat, for a medium-hot kimchi, but if you like things hot you can use a few more. The amount of time it will take for your kimchi to ferment will depend on two things: the air temperature and the humidity. How fermented you like your kimchi is a very personal thing—I like mine fermented for about two weeks in the winter and only a few days in the summer.

MAKES 4 JARS

1 Chinese leaf cabbage (about 2 pounds/850 g)

4 scallions

2 tablespoons good sea salt

1 daikon or kohlrabi (about 8 ounces/200 g), or 8 ounces (200 g) radishes

2 firm green apples

2 teaspoons white miso paste

1 clove of garlic, finely sliced

2–4 red chiles, finely chopped (with seeds)

a thumb-size piece of ginger, peeled and finely chopped

Coarsely shred the cabbage into ¾-inch- (2-cm-) thick pieces, finely slice the scallions, and put them both into your biggest bowl with the salt. Scrunch with your hands for 5 minutes, until the cabbage has released a lot of water, then leave it for 2 hours to release all its water, massaging it another couple of times to help this process.

Meanwhile, peel the daikon and cut it into thin ⅜-inch- (1-cm-) long matchsticks. Cut the apples into pieces about the same size—you can leave the skin on.

Mix the miso with the garlic, chiles, ginger, and 2 tablespoons of cold water. Once the cabbage has had its 2 hours, add the daikon, apple, and miso garlic paste to the bowl of cabbage and its water.

Put the kimchi and the liquid it sits in into a large jar or fermenting pot, taking care to pack the vegetables down firmly under the liquid so that no bits of vegetable are poking out, there are no air pockets, and there are a few inches of space at the top of the jar for the air to escape.

Cover the jar loosely with a lid, or, if you would prefer to close the lid to keep the smell in, make sure you open it up every day to let the air out. Leave the kimchi on your work surface for 2 to 3 days, checking every day to see how it tastes. This winter I fermented mine in a cool cupboard for about 2 weeks. Once it tastes good to you, put it in the fridge, where it will keep for several months.

Ways to use your kimchi

- In the kimchi soup on page 24

- In a toasted sandwich with a good sharp Cheddar

- In the bao on page 410

- As a pickle on the side of your favorite bowl of noodles

- Wrapped into summer rolls

- To top some sriracha-spiked avocado on toast

- Chopped finely and mixed with oil and lemon for a punchy dressing for a grain

- As a base for a quick fried rice

- Added to the end of a stir-fry

- Fried in a pan before you add some eggs and scramble them

Tonics and teas for cold days

These are the things I make when winter sets in and coughs and colds strike; when we are cold to the bones or feeling a little depleted. I don't intend these recipes to be medicine. I have no proof that they work, but they make me and my family feel better. Perhaps it's just the act of making something to nurture us, perhaps it's the ingredients; whatever it is, I keep making them.

Turmeric, ginger, and black pepper tea to warm

For two cups, grate about a tablespoon of ginger into a teapot. Squeeze in the juice of 1 to 2 lemons (depending on their size), add half a teaspoon of ground turmeric or about a tablespoon of fresh grated turmeric, a tiny pinch of red pepper flakes and a good few grinds of black pepper, then pour in 2½ cups (600 ml) of hot water. Allow it to cool a little before sweetening with a little honey (I use the raw stuff for maximum goodness); this will make sure the amazing properties of the honey aren't killed by the boiling water.

Magic golden turmeric honey paste for colds

Mix 2 tablespoons of ground turmeric, or a small thumb of the freshly grated root, with 1 tablespoon of ground black pepper. Melt, then cool 2 tablespoons of coconut oil. Add to the bowl and mix well, then stir in 2 tablespoons of honey—raw is best. You can either eat this from the spoon or stir into hot water or warmed milk—I like oat milk.

Carrot, ginger, and red chile juice to lift and enliven

For one glass, peel 6 carrots and a thumb of ginger. Cut the green stalk off 1 chile, and if you like things hot, keep the seeds in; if not, then remove. Put it all though a juicer and serve over ice. If you like, you can gently warm this juice, though don't heat it too much or let it boil.

Kombucha and kefir (page 56)

These are great things to drink when you are feeling under the weather. I mix some turmeric and lemon into my kombucha and stir some of the golden paste above into my morning kefir. Both support healthy bacteria so are particularly great to drink if you are taking antibiotics.

Cinnamon and cardamom for sore throats

Mix 1 tablespoon of ground cinnamon and the bashed seeds of a cardamon pod with 1 tablespoon of golden honey and 1 of melted, cooled coconut oil. Store in a glass jar at room temperature, and take a teaspoon whenever you have a tickle in your throat.

Vilcabamba cold cure

A lady made this cold cure for me on a trip to Ecuador and it worked. Juice 6 oranges into a small saucepan, add the juice of 1 lemon and 1 cinnamon stick. Warm to almost boiling, then leave for 10 minutes to steep. Once cooled, add a little honey if you like.

Lemongrass and three-chile tea

For two cups, roughly chop a good thumb of ginger, bash 2 lemongrass stalks, and add to a pan with 1 red chile, 1 green chile and a pinch of red pepper flakes. Add 1 liter of water and bring to a boil, then turn the heat down and simmer for 30 minutes, until it has a deep aromatic flavor. Now you can add a black or green tea bag and steep for 5 minutes before drinking. Sweeten with honey to taste.

Not-chicken soup (page 28)

Ginger shots for the brave

Use your juicer to juice enough ginger to make about 2 tablespoons of juice. Just knock it back and wait 10 minutes before drinking any water.

Garlic shots for the braver

Stick with me here. This doesn't taste great but I am sure it's helped me stave off a cold more than a few times. Finely chop 1 clove of garlic, put it into a small glass with 3 tablespoons of cold water, take a deep breath, and knock it back. Don't chew it. It might make you feel a little weird, but don't be tempted to drink water for about 10 minutes.

Herald of spring

Best of the season

    Ramps

    Sorrel

    Lovage

    Butter lettuce

    Early spring herbs

    Dandelion

    Radishes

    Watercress

    Celeriac

    Morels

    Broccoli

    Kale

    Hothouse rhubarb

Flowers

    Narcissus and daffodils

    Lily of the valley

    Sweet peas

    Ranunculus

Salted maple buckwheat and seed granola

This isn't strictly a seasonal recipe, but I have included it here as the first light mornings and brighter days mark a transition at our breakfast table, from toast and porridge, to breakfasts that are lighter and not necessarily warm (though on cooler days this does work very well on top of porridge or even with a little warm almond milk).

Buckwheat might not be something you have bought before; if not, I think you should give it a try. It adds a brilliant crunch to this granola and some good morning energy, though if you like, you could swap it for the same volume of quinoa flakes or rye flakes.

This recipe allows for some gentle swaps: seeds for nuts, perhaps a little cinnamon and nutmeg as you see fit. I make mine with a little dried fruit–apricots, cherries, and dried peaches and pears are all favorites. How I eat this changes with the seasons–with poached rhubarb and yogurt in spring, strawberries and rosewater in summer, orchard fruits in autumn.

MAKES 1 VERY LARGE JAR, 10–15 SERVINGS

2 cups (220 g) oats

1 cup (280 g) buckwheat

1 cup (200 g) pumpkin seeds

½ cup (100 g) sesame seeds

½ cup (100 g) sunflower seeds

¾ cup (200 ml) maple syrup

the seeds from 1 vanilla pod or 1 tablespoon vanilla paste

2 tablespoons mild olive or coconut oil (melted)

a big pinch of flaky sea salt

½ cup (150 g) dried fruit (I use golden raisins)

Preheat your oven to 395°F (200°C). Put the oats, buckwheat, and seeds into a large mixing bowl. Mix the maple syrup, vanilla seeds or paste, oil, and salt in a pitcher or bowl, then pour it over the oats and stir to make sure everything is well coated.

Divide the mixture between two baking sheets, spreading it out well to make sure that it's even. Put the baking sheets in the oven for 15 minutes. After 15 minutes, take the baking sheets out and give everything a good stir, then put them back into the oven, with the one that was on the top shelf on the bottom this time, and cook for another 15 minutes.

Remove the baking sheets again and stir in your dried fruit, then put them back in the oven for 10 minutes (if you add the fruit any sooner it will burn). Take the granola out of the oven. Everything should be deeply golden and crisp by now, and your house should smell like a bakery.

Allow the granola to cool completely before storing in an airtight jar or container, where it will keep for up to a month.

Black bean and tofu scramble

I first ate tofu scramble years ago on a trip to California, and it's been a weekend staple ever since. This is a brunch dish in our house, but it would work for any meal. Tofu has a pleasing bounciness that is suited to cooking this way; it soaks up the flavors—here big, brave notes of smoked paprika, garlic, and the deeply savory, almost inky, black beans.

The tofu I use here is neither the silken stuff nor the firm stuff. It's usually just labeled as tofu in water; it crumbles nicely in your fingers when you break it up. I always try to buy the best tofu I can: Most supermarkets stock good organic varieties these days.

SERVES 4

2 ripe avocados

2 unwaxed limes

sea salt and freshly ground black pepper

9 ounces (250 g) cherry tomatoes, roughly chopped

2 red chiles, finely chopped

olive oil

6 scallions, finely sliced

2 cloves of garlic, finely sliced

a small bunch of cilantro, leaves picked, stalks finely chopped

1 teaspoon hot smoked paprika

1 × 14-ounce (400-g) can of black beans, drained (or 1 cup/250 g home-cooked, see page 461)

14 ounces (400 g) tofu (see note above), crumbled into bite-sized pieces

4 flour or corn tortillas

First, mash the avocados with the zest of one of the limes and half its juice and a little salt and pepper.

Mix the tomatoes with the chiles, a good pinch of salt and pepper, and squeeze over the juice of the other lime half.

Heat a frying pan over medium heat and add a little oil. Add the scallions, garlic, and chopped cilantro stalks. Cook for around 2 minutes, or until the edges of the garlic are beginning to brown. Add the smoked paprika and a little more salt and pepper, then cook for another minute.

Add the black beans to the pan and fry them for around 2 minutes, or until they have dried out a little. Add the crumbled tofu, turn the heat up, and cook until the tofu has begun to brown a little, which will take about 4 minutes. Make sure you keep stirring so that it doesn't stick. Take off the heat and season well with salt and pepper.

Warm or toast the tortillas: I do this by holding them over the gas flame on my stovetop for 30 seconds or so on each side, turning them with tongs, but you could also warm yours in a dry frying pan. Wrap them in foil and put them in a low oven to keep warm, if you need to.

Pile the tofu mixture onto the toasted tortillas, with a little chile and the cilantro leaves strewn over, and serve with the avocado and tomatoes for spooning on top.

Avocado and cardamom smoothie

This smoothie is driven more by the mood of the season than by the ingredients that are listed. It's what I want for breakfast when the mornings get a bit more cheerful. It's a meeting of two things I love: avocados and cardamom. I often add a handful of kale or other dark leaves to give it an extra punch of green too. If you'd like something even more sustaining, you could add a handful of oats or quinoa flakes and a little more water. I had a smoothie like this in a café in L.A. and it was topped with a slick of buttery olive oil. I loved the combination; I realize it's not for everyone, but do give it a try if you are curious. It's delicious. A high-speed blender works best here; if you don't have one you might want to use some apple juice instead of a whole apple, and ground cardamom instead of the pods.

Bash the cardamom pods to get the seeds out and put them into a dry pan over medium heat. Toast for a few minutes until they smell fragrant.

Put the seeds into a blender, add the rest of the ingredients, and whizz until you have a silky-smooth pale green smoothie. Pour into two glasses.

MAKES 2

4 cardamom pods

the juice and zest of 1 unwaxed lime

1 green apple

1 ripe avocado, peeled and stoned

1 cup (250 ml) milk (I use unsweetened almond)

1 tablespoon golden honey

1 cup (250 ml) cold water

8 ice cubes

Sunny egg muffins

If there is a recipe that makes more of an egg, I have yet to find it—a whole egg hidden inside a muffin, the yolk still runny. These are based on a muffin I ate at a brilliant bakery in the Mission District of San Francisco called Craftsman and Wolves. It's the perfect breakfast muffin: a little bite from polenta, a hit of red pepper flakes, some brightness from the dill. They also travel well to a picnic, though be sure to eat them straight from the oven if you want a runny yolk, as the yolk will set a little as they sit.

This is a recipe that you will need to follow closely if you are after a runny egg. If you can't get buttermilk easily, yogurt thinned down with a splash of milk will work too. You will need to use a deep, nonstick jumbo muffin pan.

MAKES 6 LARGE MUFFINS

8 medium organic eggs, at room temperature

¾ cup (100 g) fine polenta

1⅓ cups (180 g) white spelt flour

1 teaspoon flaky sea salt

1 tablespoon baking powder

½ cup (50 g) coarsely grated sharp Cheddar

4 scallions, finely sliced

a small bunch of dill, finely chopped

¼ teaspoon red pepper flakes

1 cup (240 ml) buttermilk

6 tablespoons (90 ml) olive oil, plus a little extra for greasing

First, boil your eggs. Have ready a bowl of iced water. Bring a large pan of water to a rapid boil and lower in 6 of the eggs. Boil for exactly 4 minutes, not a second more. Remove from the pan and immerse in the ice-cold water, then chill in the fridge for at least 30 minutes.

Meanwhile, get your muffin mix ready. In one bowl, mix together the polenta, flour, salt, baking powder, cheese, scallions, dill, and red pepper flakes and whisk with a balloon whisk to break up any lumps of baking powder.

In a separate pitcher or bowl, mix together the buttermilk, olive oil, and remaining 2 eggs.

When you're ready to bake the muffins, preheat the oven to 395°F (200°C). Grease 6 molds of a deep muffin pan with a little oil. Get your eggs out of the fridge and peel them really, really carefully, putting them on a couple of sheets of paper towels to keep them from rolling away.

Pour the buttermilk mixture into the flour and stir gently. Don't overmix, or the muffins will be tough; a few lumps are fine. Spoon a couple of tablespoons of the muffin batter into the bottom of each muffin mold, then very gently put an egg on top. Carefully add the rest of the batter so that you don't squash the egg, and immediately bake for 20 minutes, not a second longer.

Remove the muffins from the oven, take each one carefully out of its mold and place on a cooling rack. Using a sharp knife, cut right through the middle of the muffin and pat yourself on the back for achieving a perfectly soft yolk.

Ramps and yogurt baked eggs

In early spring ramps lines our hedgerows, paths, and parks. You can smell it a mile away, so it's pretty easy to be sure you have the right stuff. It's a great place to start gathering your own food—there is a satisfaction from picking something from the wild which would have otherwise gone unloved. While the leaves will smell very garlicky in the hedgerows as you pick them, they will mellow as they cook, so don't worry.

That said, you don't have to use ramps here. If you can get your hands on some, great; if not, you can add a little more arugula and a clove of finely chopped garlic. It won't taste exactly the same, but will still be delicious.

Preheat the oven to 340°F (170°C). Wash the ramps and the arugula and place them in a 9-inch (23-cm) ovenproof frying pan with a drizzle of oil. Add some salt and cook over medium heat for about 5 minutes, or until the arugula has wilted and most of the liquid has evaporated. Strain the liquid from the leaves in a sieve set over the sink, pushing down to remove as much of the water as possible, then put them back into the pan. Grate over half of the lemon zest.

Make four deep indentations in the arugula mix, and crack an egg into each little hole. Place in the oven for 7 to 10 minutes, or until the egg whites set. Meanwhile, mix the yogurt with the other half of the lemon zest and some salt and pepper.

Heat about 3 tablespoons of oil in a frying pan until it's good and hot but not smoking, line a plate with paper towels, then add the sage leaves to the pan. Cook for a few seconds until they are crisp, then scoop out with a slotted spoon and drain on the paper. Using the same pan, add the sesame seeds to the sage oil for 30 to 45 seconds, until they turn a deep golden color. Scoop them out onto a separate paper towel.

Once the eggs are done, take them out of the oven and spoon over half the yogurt mixture (leaving the rest for the table). Top with the fried sage, the toasted sesame seeds, and a sprinkling of pul biber, and serve with flatbread or good sourdough.

SERVES 2

⅓ cup (50 g) ramps

3 cups (150 g) arugula

sea salt

olive oil

1 unwaxed lemon

4 organic eggs

½ cup (100 g) Greek yogurt

freshly ground black pepper

12 sage leaves

¼ cup (30 g) sesame seeds

a pinch of pul biber (Aleppo pepper) or red pepper flakes

flatbread (see page 456) or sourdough bread, to serve

Breakfast cake

One day I thought if I could make a cake with all the things I usually eat for breakfast, then it would be completely legitimate to eat cake for breakfast on a regular basis. Life has been much better ever since.

This is a shallow cake that is best cooked in a pan, then spooned out into a bowl and topped with more yogurt and berries, though as it cools it firms up, and any leftovers can be sliced and warmed in the oven.

During early spring, seasonal fruit is in short supply, so I reach into my freezer for bags of blueberries, blackberries, and dark cherries, which see us through until the first strawberries find their way to us. Rice flour works well here in place of the whole-wheat if you want to make it gluten free. Aquafaba (which, if you've not come across it, is the liquid from cooking chickpeas that miraculously whips up like egg whites) works in place of the eggs (I used ½ cup/135 ml of aquafaba made to the instructions on page 459) and coconut or oat yogurt works well too for vegans.

SERVES 6

½ cup (100 g) coconut oil or olive oil, plus extra for greasing

1 cup (250 g) plain yogurt, plus extra to serve

10 tablespoons (150 ml) golden honey or maple syrup

2 firm, crisp apples, roughly grated

the zest of 1 unwaxed lemon

3 organic eggs, separated

1⅛ cup (100 g) rolled oats

1 cup (100 g) ground almonds

⅓ cup (50 g) whole-wheat flour

1 teaspoon baking powder

sea salt

1⅓ cups (200 g) frozen berries, plus extra to serve

Preheat your oven to 375°F (190°C). If you are using coconut oil, gently melt it and allow it to cool. In a bowl, mix the yogurt with the honey, and add the apples and the lemon zest. Add the cooled coconut oil or olive oil. Add the egg yolks to the yogurt mixture.

Put the oats in a food processor and blitz until you have a scruffy flour, then pour into a bowl and add the almonds, whole-wheat flour, and baking powder and whisk to get rid of any lumps of baking powder.

Add the dry ingredients to the yogurt mixture and mix to combine everything. Whisk the egg whites with a pinch of salt until they form soft peaks, then gently fold them into the batter with a spatula or large spoon. You want to incorporate as much air as you can here to make the cake light and fluffy, so try not to mix more than you need to.

Rub a 9-inch (23-cm) ovenproof frying pan with oil and warm it over medium heat for a minute or two so the base of the cake crisps up nicely. Take it off the heat and pour the cake batter into the pan (I use an ovenproof frying pan here, but you could use a similar-size cake pan instead. If you're using a cake pan, pour the batter in without heating it on the stovetop).

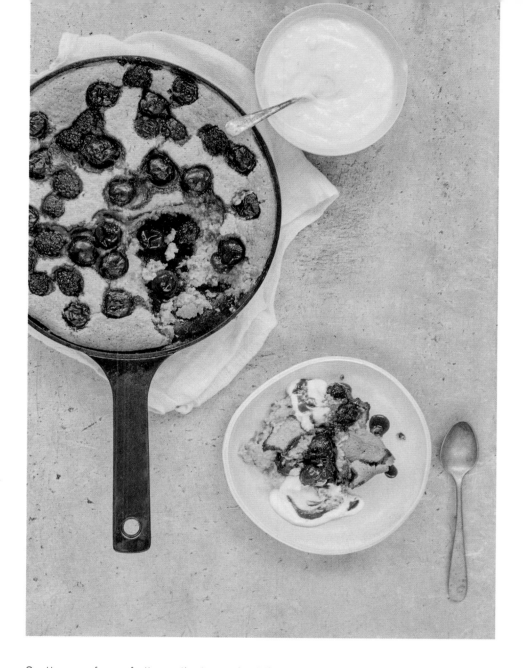

Scatter your frozen fruit over the top and put the pan into the hot oven for 45 to 50 minutes, until the cake is golden and a skewer inserted into the cake comes out almost clean. If you are using a cast-iron pan, the cake will continue to cook as it sits, so you can afford a few minutes less.

Serve in the middle of the table, with more yogurt and some more berries if you like.

On juicing

Juices are pure, alive and potent essences. Juicing brings out the purity of an ingredient with unmatched vibrancy. While I do like to juice fruit and vegetables to drink, that usually only happens when I feel like a reset (see page 96) or if I am under the weather. More often than not I will eat my fruit, as I like the texture and it feels like more of a meal somehow. But recently I have been looking at juicing as a much wider culinary tool, as it can be an interesting way to think about flavor and cooking. I've been using my juicer to juice stray bunches of herbs, ginger, celery, fennel, and even nuts and oats into milk, enhancing the use of what can sometimes be quite a bulky piece of kitchen equipment.

Juicing is a great way of extending the life of leftover vegetables or the end of a bunch of herbs. While I like to use the juices fresh when I can, they can also be frozen—I use an ice-cube tray. Savory juices can be added to soups, stews, even risottos; those made with fruit can be added to drinks like ice cubes to flavor water or to add punch to a smoothie.

Some people are put off juicing as they think that cleaning a juicer is a bit of a pain, and that is partially true, though it only takes a few minutes—not much longer than say, a food processor. The amount of juice you get will depend on how powerful your juicer is, so it's worth investing in a decent one.

Herbs and aromatics

Ginger
A 9-ounce (250 g) hand of ginger makes about 7 fluid ounces (200 ml) of juice.
Freezes well; good added to dipping sauces, broths, and teas (see cold cures on page 70).

Cilantro
A large bunch makes about 3 fluid ounces (100 ml) of juice.
Good juiced with green chile; add to yogurt, mashed avocado, or salsas.

Dill
A large bunch makes about 2 fluid ounces (60 ml) of juice.
Stir into yogurt, whisk with eggs for an omelette, add to cold summer soups.

Parsley
A large bunch makes about 2½ fluid ounces (80 ml) of juice.
Add to stocks, risotto, dressings, or pour over tomato salads (see page 170).

Basil
A very large bunch makes about 2½ fluid ounces (80 ml) of juice.
Add to dressings, cooked pasta, tomato salads, mozzarella, or to finish soups, stews, and risotto.

Savory

Cucumber
1 large cucumber makes about 1 cup (250 ml) of juice (no need to peel).
Add to cold soups or drinks in summer; freeze for gin and tonics.

Beets
4 large beets make about 1 cup (250 ml) juice.
Use it in the beet pasta on page 200 instead of the grated beet.

Carrot
1 pound (500 g) of carrots makes about 1 cup (250 ml) of juice (no need to peel).
Use as the base for a soup or stew, to finish pasta, add to dressings (see page 32).

Fennel
1 large bulb makes about 1 cup (250 ml) of juice.
Add to broths, use in place of stock, add to dressings and juices.

Celery
1 head of celery makes about 13½ fluid ounces (400 ml) of juice.
Add to broths, use in place of stock, add to dressings and juices.

Kale
2 large heads of kale or Lacinato kale make about 1 cup (250 ml) of juice.
Add to soups, broths, and juices.

Fruit

I like citrus in winter and more vibrant juices combined with veg in the summer. Here are a few combinations, listed with the main ingredient first to the smallest amount needed at the end, which is more of an accent.

— Grapefruit, lemon, ginger

— Pear, apple, kale, ginger

— Cucumber, apple, lettuce, flat-leaf parsley

— Carrot, celery, ginger, lemon, cayenne pepper

Nuts and grains

Almonds
Soak 1 cup of raw almonds in water overnight, drain, add 3 cups of water, and juice. Add a touch of vanilla and a pinch of salt. Season the leftover meal and use like nut butter.

Pistachios
Soak 1 cup of unsalted shelled pistachios in water overnight, drain, add 3 cups of water, and juice. I like this as it is. Season the leftover meal and use like nut butter.

Hazelnuts
Soak 1 cup of raw hazelnuts in water overnight, drain, add 3 cups of water, and juice. I add a pinch of salt. Season the leftover meal and use like nut butter.

Oats
Soak 1 cup of rolled oats in water overnight, drain, add 3 cups of water, and juice. Great for adding to coffee.

Creamy cannellini and sorrel on toast

This time of year brings one of my favorite things: sorrel. It's the perfect blend of verdant green herb and zesty lemon all in one succulent little leaf. It is such an underused herb, probably because it can be hard to get a hold of. If you can find it, sorrel's lemony tart liveliness makes your mouth water like no other food I know. And if there were ever an herb to get our palates excited for spring, it's this one.

This is a quick riff on the creamy Italian-style cannellini beans I learned to make under some great Italian cooks as a young chef. As this is a speedy recipe, I have suggested you use a can of beans, but even better would be some home-cooked beans. Whatever you use, the beans will be delicious, scented with bay leaves, and good olive oil, and topped with a crown of green sorrel.

Blot the cannellini beans dry on a paper towel–lined plate.

In a 9-inch (23-cm) frying pan, heat half the olive oil over medium heat and add the bay leaves. Fry them for 1 to 2 minutes, until the leaves blister and start to release their oils. Turn the heat down and add the beans along with a pinch of salt and pepper. Leave the beans cooking over low heat for 10 to 15 minutes, stirring occasionally.

While the beans are cooking, heat a griddle over medium-high heat for couple of minutes. When the pan is really hot and nearly smoking, place the bread in it and char for 2 to 3 minutes on each side, so you end up with smoky black stripes. Remove from the pan and place on warm plates.

Put the sorrel into a bowl with the orange juice and scrunch with your hands to break it down a little and soften the leaves.

Remove the bay leaves from the beans and crush half the beans with the back of a wooden spoon, so you're left with a creamy, but still textured, beany mash. Pile the beans on the warm toast and top with the sorrel, the remaining olive oil, and a sprinkle of salt and pepper.

SERVES 2

1 × 14.5-ounce (400-g) can of cannellini beans, drained

4 tablespoons good olive oil

2 bay leaves

sea salt and freshly ground black pepper

2 chunky slices of sourdough or other good bread

1¾-ounce (50-g) bunch of sorrel, washed well

the juice of 1 unwaxed orange

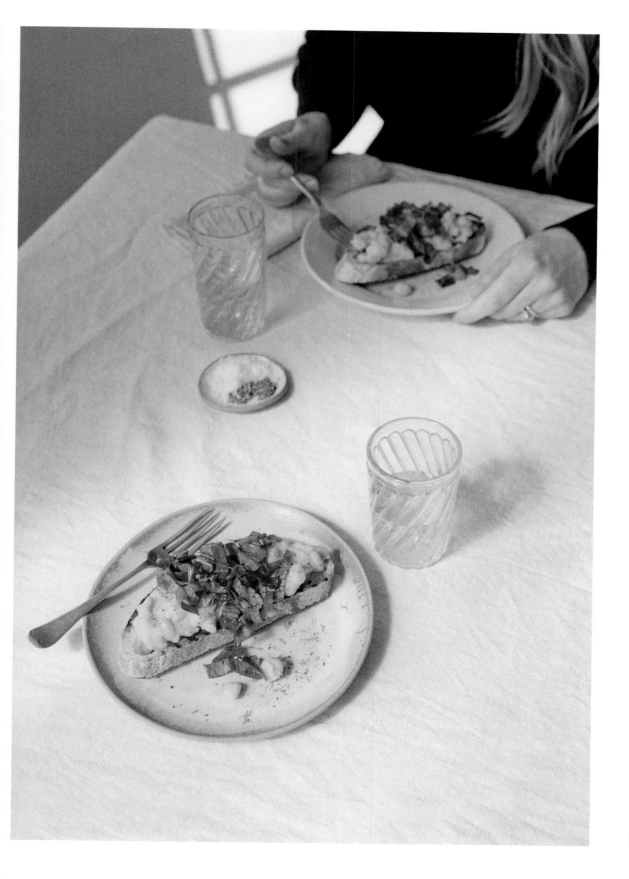

Sesame and green olive bars

My new addiction. I was skeptical about a savory snack bar, but these are as moreish as they are balanced: salty olives and nori (sheets of dried seaweed used to wrap sushi), buttery sesame seeds, toasted oats, crunchy puffed rice, and a hint of sweetness. If you are struggling to find brown rice syrup, you could use golden honey, but they won't set quite as firm, so be sure to store the bars in the fridge. This is a recipe from my column in the *Guardian*; I have made them so many times since it was printed, so I felt I had to include it here.

MAKES ABOUT 16 BARS

2 sheets of nori

2¾ cups (150 g) rolled oats

1 cup (150 g) olives, pitted and roughly chopped

1¼ cups (30 g) walnuts, toasted and finely chopped

4 tablespoons sesame seeds

1¼ cups (30 g) unsweetened puffed rice cereal

2 tablespoons chia seeds

a small pinch of red pepper flakes (optional)

¾ cup (300 g) brown rice syrup

½ cup (100 g) coconut oil, plus extra for greasing

Preheat the oven to 395°F (200°C). Put the nori sheets on one baking sheet and the oats on another. Bake for 3 to 5 minutes, or until the sheet has darkened a little and crumbles easily in your hand and the oats smell toasty.

Grease a 8-by-12-inch (20-by-30-cm) baking sheet with coconut oil. Mix all the dry ingredients, including the olives, together in a large bowl and set aside.

Combine the rice syrup and coconut oil in a small saucepan over medium heat. Stir for a minute or two until it melts and thickens a little—this will take about 4 minutes. Pour the coconut oil mixture over the oat mixture and stir until everything is well mixed.

Spread the mixture on the baking sheet and press down firmly; this will help your bars stick together. Chill for a few hours before cutting into bars. I go for about 16, but you could make them bigger or smaller as you wish. They will keep in the fridge for up to a week.

Green ramps and Puy lentil soup

In ramps season, I pick loads and make it into this pesto (no extra garlic added), which can be kept under a slick of olive oil in the fridge for weeks or in the freezer for much longer. Ramps has a strong taste when it's raw, but that mellows when you cook it. If you can't get your hands on it, a finely chopped clove of garlic and some spinach will stand in; there is no need to soak the garlic or spinach.

First soak the lentils in boiling water for 10 minutes; this will help speed up the cooking time and make them softer. Drain the lentils and put them into a large deep saucepan with 3 cups (750 ml) of cold water and simmer until they are cooked and soft but not falling apart—this should take between 20 and 25 minutes.

Put another pan over medium heat, add a little oil and then the shallot, fennel, celery, and your root vegetable. Add a good pinch of salt, then cook for 10 minutes, until soft and sweet.

Meanwhile, toast the hazelnuts in a dry pan until golden brown. Once they are nicely toasted, take off the heat. Grate in the lemon zest and add 2 tablespoons of olive oil, then put the pan back on the heat for a minute or so until you hear a sizzle. Transfer to a bowl to cool. Once cool, roughly chop.

Fill the kettle with water and boil. Once the vegetables and the lentils are cooked, stir the vegetables into the lentils and add 2 cups (500 ml) of hot water from the kettle. Leave to simmer at a very low heat.

Put the ramps into a bowl, cover with boiling water and leave for a minute, then scoop out with a slotted spoon. Squeeze out any excess water, then put into a food processor with a tablespoon of oil and enough cold water (about 2 tablespoons) to purée it.

Stir the spinach and ramps purée into the soup. Serve with the lemon hazelnuts, a little more olive oil, and garlic flowers, if you have them.

SERVES 4

1 cup (200 g) dried Puy lentils

good olive oil

1 banana shallot, finely chopped

1 bulb of fennel, finely chopped

2 stalks of celery, finely chopped

½ cup rutabaga, parsnips, or carrots, finely chopped

sea salt

⅓ cup (50 g) hazelnuts

1 unwaxed lemon

a good bunch of ramps (about 2 ounces/50 g)

a bunch of young spinach or other greens (about 2 ounces/50 g)

garlic flowers, to serve (optional)

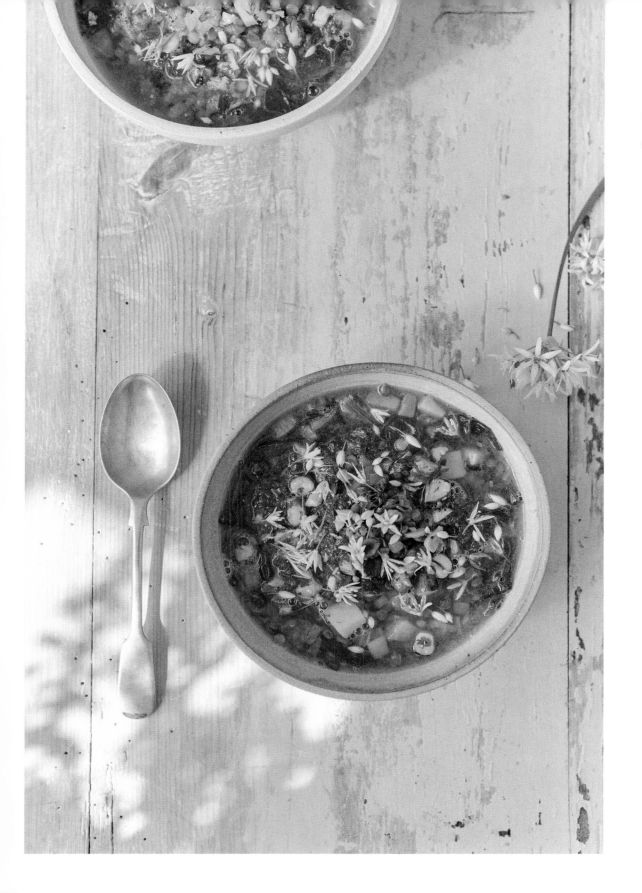

Citrus and lemongrass broth

This time of year feels right for eating crisp, clean food. This gentle broth is as much flavored with lemon and orange as it is with the aromatic lemongrass; the flavor is subtle and delicate, and that's the idea.

The soup is restorative and warming, as well as lifting and enlivening, making it perfect to ward off a cold, a chill in the air from the change of season, or just to eat for a brightening lunch or supper. Such is my love for the gentle citrus notes of this broth, I am pretty sure I could eat this soup every day from April to September.

I keep this very simple, with just noodles, clean tofu, and broth, but if you like you could add some more veg: shredded greens, sugar snaps, peas, and broccoli would all work well.

Put 8 cups (2 liters) of water into a pan and bring it to boil. Once boiling, add the lemongrass, lime leaves, ginger, shallots, and cilantro seeds. Bring to a boil again, then turn down to a simmer and cook for 30 minutes. You can cook it for a bit longer if you'd like a really intense flavor.

Strain the soup, using a large sieve over a big mixing bowl and a spoon to push down on the aromatics to get maximum flavor from them, then pour the liquid back into the saucepan.

Next, add the juice of the oranges and the lemon, watching out for seeds, and stir in the miso and a little salt, to taste. The broth will keep like this for 4 to 5 days and freezes well.

When you are ready to eat, warm your broth. Pile your noodles into bowls, topping with the herbs and tofu. Ladle the citrus broth over, and serve steaming.

SERVES 4

4 stalks of lemongrass, bashed

4 lime leaves

a thumb-size piece of ginger, peeled and grated

2 shallots, peeled and roughly chopped

1 tablespoon cilantro (coriander) seeds

the juice of 2 oranges or mandarins

the juice of 1 lemon

2 tablespoons white miso paste

sea salt

TO SERVE

1½ cups (200 g) cooked noodles (I use buckwheat)

a small bunch of basil, leaves picked

a small bunch of cilantro, leaves picked

a few chives, chopped, or a pinch of chive cress

7 ounces (200 g) firm tofu, chopped into small pieces (¾ cup)

Three-day reset

Spring holds promise. To me, it feels like the true start of the year, when everything is waking from its winter sleep; when the first green shoots, leaves, and vegetables show their heads. It is rebirth, reawakening, resetting. So it's at this time of year that I often feel like it's time for a reset. Let me be very clear here—this is not a detox. On the whole I don't believe in them—they make me hungry and angry and longing for endless slices of bread or corner-shop chocolate bars. But what I do find helpful is resetting my eating clock. In fact, my whole journey into eating vegetarian food and, in turn, writing these books came out of one such reset.

Like anyone else, I get into patterns and habits with food; some good, some bad, driven as much by emotion as nutrition, so I do a reset to help me connect with what I am eating again. It breaks the habits I have fallen into and allows me to reconsider why I am eating, when I am eating, and what really feels good for me and my body. When we eat we are voting for how we want to look, think, and feel, but it's this very simple connection that can be lost in the day-to-day of life. By eating mindfully for a few days, I find I can reconnect.

I know it's time for me to reset when I move to viewing food as fuel; when I lose a bit of that magical connection with food; when I slice into a beet or a blood orange and I fail to be awed by it; when I feel a bit jaded and can't come up with ideas for dinner; or I can't work out what I want to eat, what it is I fancy.

So every so often, and always at the beginning of spring, I make space over a few days to simplify things, to eat food wholly centered on fruits and vegetables. This doesn't mean "boring;" it's food that's delicious and filling and that I am still excited about eating: juices, smoothies, soups, and stews; if the odd square of chocolate creeps in, that's OK.

Reset advice

— Fill your fridge with seasonal fruits and vegetables.

— Eat only when you are hungry; listen to your body.

— I would suggest a smoothie for breakfast and soup for lunch and dinner (or one of the recipes I've suggested below) with some snacks in between. If you are really hungry, add some cooked brown rice or soba noodles.

— I snack on a piece of fruit or some chopped-up veg.

— Avoid caffeine (herbal teas are fine).

— Drink lots of water: 8 cups (2 liters) a day at the least.

— On waking: drink hot water with lemon.

— For breakfast: a smoothie or juice, or, if you are hungry, kheer (see page 8).

— Snack: a piece of fruit or carrot sticks, or a cup of miso soup.

— Lunch: a bowl of soup or salad.

— Snack: herbal tea.

— Dinner: a bowl of soup.

There are a number of recipes in this book that would be suitable for a reset. I try to avoid using too much salt or soy sauce when eating this way, so you may want to reduce them a little when cooking them, as well as leave out heavier things like the bread and pasta if I have suggested serving the recipes with these.

Breakfast

Saffron breakfast kheer (page 8).

Avocado and cardamom smoothie (page 79).

Summer morning bowl (page 232).

Cherry and almond breakfast smoothie (page 231; use frozen cherries at this time of year).

See "On juicing" (page 86).

Lunch and dinner

Kimchi and miso noodle soup (page 24).

Green peppercorn and lemongrass coconut broth (page 27).

Not-chicken soup (page 28; I do this without the tofu).

Ginger-spiked spring herb salad (page 106).

Simple yellow split pea soup with green olives (page 322).

Smacked cucumbers (page 252; go easy on the soy sauce/tamari).

Sweet potato mash with cilantro and chile (page 357; again easy on the soy sauce/tamari).

Drinks

Kombucha (page 56).

Herbal teas and infusions (page 222).

97

Gently spiced, lemon-braised root vegetables

This is a marriage of humble ingredients and a great example of how careful and considered cooking can transform them. I inherited the recipe from my friend Anna Shepherd. It's loosely Turkish in its flavor: The root vegetables are braised in olive oil, spices, and lemon juice, which bring a really generous sweetness to the vegetables and coat the couscous in the most delicious kind of warm dressing.

I make this during the hungry gap—that little bit of time when the spoils of spring haven't yet arrived and the stores of winter are dwindling. The freshness of the lemon and the bright herbs elevate this to something suited to the first days of spring, but it's still warming and hearty.

Pul biber is a milder Turkish chile flake, somewhere between chile and red pepper. The grocery stores near where I live are full of it, but if you can't get your hands on it a pinch of regular red pepper flakes will step in; they are much hotter, so you'll need substantially fewer. I use mograbieh—giant couscous—and choose the whole-wheat version, which you can buy in most supermarkets.

SERVES 4

¾ cup (150 g) whole-wheat giant couscous (mograbieh)

1 small rutabaga (about 18 ounces/500 g)

4 small carrots (about 11 ounces/300 g)

2 small parsnips (about 11 ounces/300 g)

6 tablespoons olive oil

½ teaspoon cayenne pepper

2 teaspoons cumin seeds, roughly bashed

2 cloves of garlic, finely chopped

the zest and juice of 2 unwaxed lemons

1 teaspoon pul biber chile flakes (see note above)

sea salt

a large bunch of dill

4 tablespoons pumpkin seeds

2 tablespoons plain yogurt

Place the giant couscous in a bowl, cover with cold water and set aside. Peel the rutabaga and roughly chop into ¾-inch (2-cm) cubes. Slice the carrots lengthways into quarters and then across the middle into eighths. Do the same with the parsnips, cutting them into smaller pieces if the parsnips are much larger than the carrots.

In a large, deep frying pan with a lid, gently heat 4 tablespoons of the olive oil, and add all the root veg. Turn the heat up to medium-high and stir for about 5 minutes, or until you can see the oil bubbling at the sides and the edges of the vegetables crisping at the bottom of the pan.

Turn the heat down to medium and add the cayenne pepper and half the cumin, the garlic, lemon juice, and 7 tablespoons (100 ml) of water. Stir to make sure the spices are lending their flavors evenly through the pan. Cover with a lid, turn the heat down again, and leave to braise for 30 to 35 minutes, until the vegetables are soft all the way through.

While the root vegetables are gently cooking, make the pul biber oil by mixing the remaining 2 tablespoons of olive oil with the pul biber and a generous pinch of salt. Pick the leaves from the bunch of dill. Fill your kettle with water and bring to a boil; drain the giant couscous.

Next, remove the lid from the pan of root vegetables and stir the couscous. Add ⅝ cup (150 ml) of water from the kettle, or just enough to cover the vegetables and couscous. Cook for another 8 minutes, or until the couscous is pillowy soft. Stir in the dill.

Meanwhile, heat a glug of oil in a small frying pan and add the pumpkin seeds and remaining cumin. Toast the seeds, stirring frequently, until they begin to pop and split a little. Stir in the lemon zest and take off the heat.

Spoon the vegetables and couscous into deep bowls and top with the yogurt, pul biber oil, and toasted pumpkin seeds.

Early spring stew with baked ricotta

SERVES 4–6

1 pound (500 g) baby new
potatoes

1 × 1-cup (250-g) tub of
ricotta

sea salt and freshly ground
black pepper

½ cup (100 ml) extra-virgin
olive oil, plus more for
cooking

2 unwaxed lemons

a large bunch of basil, leaves
picked

2 heads of small lettuce, such
as Baby Cos or Little Gem

½ teaspoon Dijon mustard

¼ teaspoon golden honey

a bunch of scallions, finely
chopped

4½ cups (1 liter) good
vegetable stock

10.5-ounce (300-g) bag
frozen fava beans or
2 pounds (900 g) fresh,
unpodded weight

½ pound (200 g) frozen peas
4 cups (600 g) fresh,
unpodded weight

a couple of bunches of soft
herbs, leaves only, roughly
chopped

This is what I make when I feel like eating something green and vibrant, but the green tide of spring hasn't yet arrived. I use frozen peas and fava beans. (I double-pod mine, which I know takes ages, so there is no need to if you are in a hurry. To double-pod the frozen ones you'll need to leave them in a bowl of boiling water for a few minutes before you can pop them out of their little pods.)

Use whatever soft green herbs you can get your hands on: I like a combination of something heady, like mint or basil, something fragrant like tarragon, and something more neutral like parsley. But you could really use any soft herb you have and this is a great way of using up the end of a few bunches. I use a generous amount of oil here, as it adds a butteriness and a peppery kick to the final dish; you can add it bit by bit and stop when it tastes good to you.

Preheat the oven to 395°F (200°C). Halve or quarter any larger potatoes and place them on a baking sheet. Make a space in the middle for the ricotta, then upturn the tub of ricotta onto the tray so that it sits in a little mound in the middle.

Season everything with salt and pepper and drizzle with a tablespoon of olive oil. Use a spoon to turn the potatoes over to make sure they are coated in the oil and seasonings, then grate over the zest of the lemons, making sure there is plenty of zest on top of the ricotta. Scatter over half the basil leaves. Put the baking sheet into the hot oven to cook for 20 minutes. →

Meanwhile, cut your lettuce into 4 wedges and put them on another baking sheet. In a small bowl, mix together the juice of half a lemon, 2 tablespoons of the olive oil, the mustard, honey, and a good pinch of salt and grind of pepper. Pour the dressing over the lettuce wedges and use your hands to coat them really well. Once the potatoes have had their 20 minutes, add the tray of lettuce to the oven and cook everything for another 15 minutes, or until the potatoes are brown and the lettuce is charred at the edges, then take them out of the oven.

Meanwhile, in a large deep saucepan with a lid, heat a little olive oil over medium heat, add the chopped scallions, and cook for a couple of minutes until brown at the edges. Add the stock and the olive oil and bring to a boil. Taste the stock, and if you think it needs it, add a little seasoning.

Add the fava beans and peas to the broth and cook for a minute or two, then stir through half the chopped herbs and take off the heat.

To serve, divide the potatoes and lettuce among four bowls, top with the broth, then break or spoon over the ricotta, the rest of the herbs, and a drizzle of oil.

Roasted root vegetables with wasted pesto

There is a movement in the food world to stop us wasting so much; a third of what we produce worldwide is thrown away, enough to feed 17 million people, and yet millions still go hungry. In the last few years I've been doing my best to tackle waste in my own kitchen.

Rigid sell-by dates and a squeamish attitude to imperfection encourage us to throw away perfectly good food: tops are cut off turnips, beets, and carrots before we have even had a chance to think of using them; imperfect melon trimmings are abandoned to make our little bowls of prechopped fruit more presentable. And that's without mentioning the fuel and water that has been used to produce and transport it all.

I have been cooking using the whole ingredient, trying not to throw any of the precious food I have bought in the trash (I hope you will excuse me a papery garlic skin). This is a pleasing pan of roasted root vegetables with a pesto made from things you'd probably usually overlook. There is little more satisfying than making something out of nothing.

Preheat the oven to 425°F (220°C).

Separate the green tops from the carrots and beets, then wash and put to the side for later.

Wash all the vegetables really well; the carrots and beets will need a particularly good scrub, as you're not going to peel them.

Cut the butternut squash in half lengthways and use a spoon to scoop out the seeds (keep these aside to use later), then slice the squash into ⅜-inch (1-cm) moon-shaped wedges.

Slice the beets into quarters or halves if they are small, and the carrots in half lengthways, or quarters if they are really big.

Place all the root vegetables on a large baking sheet and drizzle with a good glug of the oil from the olive jar. Sprinkle about 2 tablespoons of the caper brine over the vegetables—this will be your salt—then add the capers and give everything a good mix. →

SERVES 4

1 bunch of carrots with tops

1 bunch of beets with tops

1 small butternut squash

⅔ cup (100 g) whole black olives in oil, pitted

2 tablespoons baby capers in brine

1 unwaxed lemon

1 bulb of garlic

a piece of hard, white cheese (Manchego, Parmesan, Cheddar; optional)

extra-virgin olive oil

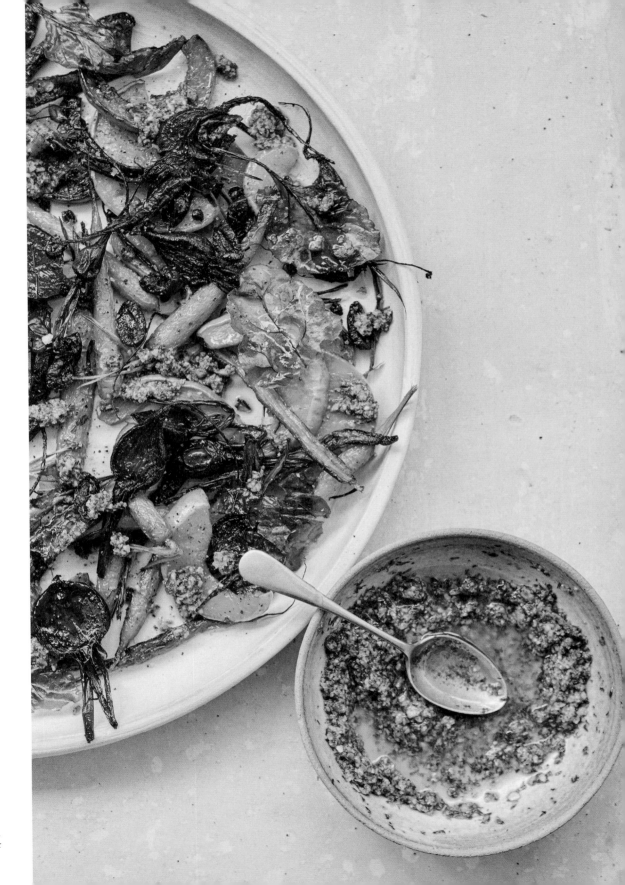

Grate over the zest of the lemon, then cut it in half and add to the baking sheet, along with the whole bulb of garlic. Bake for 30 to 40 minutes, until the vegetables are cooked through and golden around the edges.

Meanwhile, wash the squash seeds under cold running water to get rid of any fibrous bits. Coat with a little more oil from the olives, add with the olives to the baking sheet, and roast in the oven for 10 minutes, or until you can hear them pop and they look a shade darker.

Once the vegetables are cooked, remove the baking sheet from the oven, carefully spoon out the lemon and garlic to make the pesto, and put the veg back in the oven to keep them warm.

To make the pesto, squeeze the roasted garlic out of its papery skin into the bowl of a food processor. Add the roasted squash seeds, whole roasted lemon halves (picking out any seeds), and grated cheese if you're using it, and blitz to a coarse paste. Add the carrot and beet tops and about 4 tablespoons of olive oil (from the olive jar), then add a little more if you need to (alternatively, you could add a splash of water) and pulse until you have a chunky pesto. Season with a little caper brine.

Serve the roasted veg in the middle of the table, with the pesto for spooning. Freeze leftover pesto in ice cube trays for up to a few months, or keep in a jar in the fridge, covered with a thin layer of olive oil, where it will keep for up to a week.

Ginger-spiked spring herb salad

The start of April brings the first home-grown soft herbs. It feels like a shift; the deep savoriness and rich oils of the woody herbs of winter are put away for a while to make way for the verdant grassy-green herbs of spring and summer.

Here I use a mixture of the ones I have at home. Picking the leaves into a bowl is a lovely thing to do—you'll be hit by a wave of fragrance and the bowl will get prettier and prettier as you pick.

The delicate herbs could just be dressed in lemon and oil and a good pinch of salt and would still be quite some salad, but here I toss them in a ginger-spiked dressing with some tiny shards of lightly pickled cucumber and some toasted coconut. It's a light salad, great next to curries and Asian food, but I most often eat it simply, with some flatbread and thick yogurt.

SERVES 4–6

¼ a cucumber, chopped into tiny ¼-inch (½-cm) pieces

2 tablespoons white wine vinegar

the juice of 1 lemon

1 teaspoon flaky sea salt

1 teaspoon superfine or caster sugar

1 cup (50 g) raw coconut chips or ¼ cup (25 g) unsweetened desiccated coconut

5 generous handfuls of mixed soft herbs

FOR THE GINGER DRESSING

the zest and juice of 2 limes

1 green chile, finely chopped

1 shallot, finely chopped

½ teaspoon tamari or soy sauce

1 teaspoon brown rice vinegar

1 teaspoon golden honey or agave nectar

½ a small thumb-size piece of peeled ginger

1 small clove of garlic

Mix the cucumber in a bowl with the vinegar, lemon juice, salt, and sugar. Scrunch well to help begin the pickling, then cover with a plate and set to one side. Lightly toast the coconut chips in a dry frying pan over medium heat, until they begin to brown and smell toasty, then place on a plate and allow to cool.

Roughly pick the leaves from the herbs, discarding any tough stalks, and wash well in a bowl of cold water. Put into a salad spinner and spin to dry well—they'll retain more of the dressing and won't wilt immediately, which can sometimes happen when the leaves are wet.

Next, make the dressing. Mix the lime zest and juice, chile, shallot, tamari, vinegar, and honey in a bowl. Use a fine grater to grate in the ginger and garlic. Mix well with a fork and season to taste.

Drain the cucumber and pat dry with a paper towel. Toss in a large bowl with the dried herbs and dress with the ginger-spiked dressing, turning the leaves a few times to coat them evenly. Sprinkle with the coconut and serve immediately.

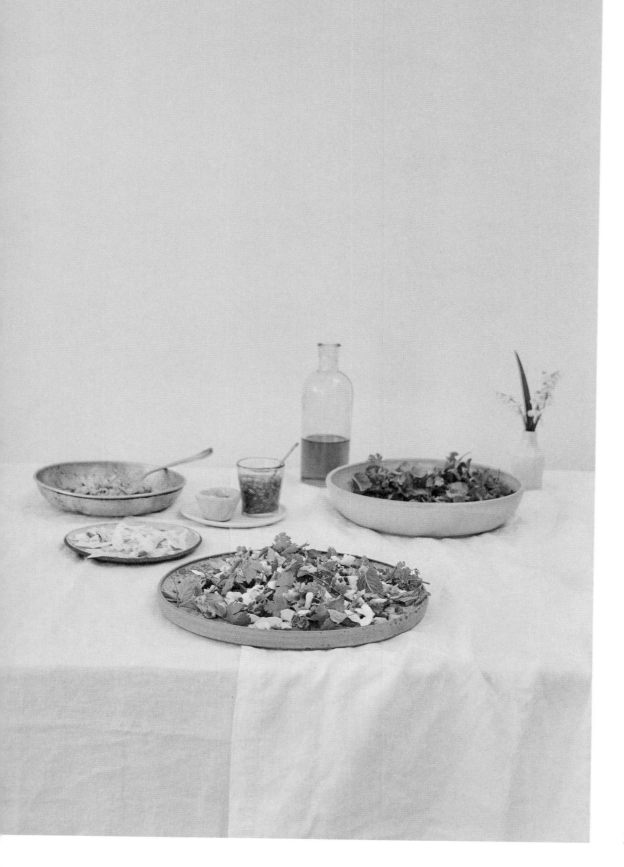

Roasted radishes with sorrel, crispy lentils, and buttermilk dressing

This is a very cheerful dinner. Radishes and potatoes are roasted in a little honey and lemon to exaggerate their sweetness, offset by the crispy roast lentils. I use my favorite spring leaf here, sorrel. Its bright lemony flavor makes you sit up when you take a mouthful. This recipe is everything I want in the winter, brightness that somehow makes your mouth water.

If you can't get hold of sorrel, scrunch a couple of handfuls of spinach together with the juice of half a lemon and roughly shred. Scatter over the top in place of the sorrel. It won't be quite as pretty, but it will taste great. Look out for the long breakfast radishes here or the unusual purple ones; they will add some extra-good looks. The flavors in the salad are subtle, so be sure to season it carefully.

Preheat the oven to 425°F (220°C). Pour the radishes and potatoes into a baking sheet with a tablespoon of the olive oil, the juice from half the lemon, the honey, and some salt.

On a separate baking sheet, mix the lentils with a generous pinch of salt, another tablespoon of olive oil, and the zest of the lemon.

Place the baking sheet with the radishes and potatoes in the oven for 30 minutes, giving it a shake once or twice during the roasting time. With 15 minutes to go, add the baking sheet with the lentils to the oven. After 15 minutes they should be crispy and beginning to blister in places, and the radishes and potatoes should be soft and brown at the edges.

Meanwhile, make the dressing by whisking the buttermilk with a good squeeze of the other half of lemon and the remaining tablespoon of olive oil. Season well with salt and pepper, taste, and add more lemon if you like and set aside.

Once the lentils and radishes have had their time, remove from the oven and mix everything in rough layers on a large platter with the sorrel, then drizzle the buttermilk dressing over the top.

SERVES 4

3½ cups (400 g) radishes, halved

14 ounces (400 g) new potatoes, halved

3 tablespoons olive oil

1 unwaxed lemon

sea salt

1 tablespoon golden honey

2 × 14.5-ounce (400-g) cans of Puy lentils, drained and dried on paper towels

3½ tablespoons (50 ml) buttermilk or thin plain yogurt

freshly ground black pepper

2 handfuls of sorrel leaves

108

Crushed new potatoes, broccoli, and blood-orange cream

This is a gentle, soothing dish. The potatoes are warm, crisp, and golden next to the bright broccoli stems, whose little treetops soak up the pale pink blood-orange cream. The garlic is sweet and subtle behind it all. I eat this for supper but also often serve it as part of a spread, as its subtle notes mean it goes well with an endless list of things.

If you are vegan you could make a cashew cream to use in place of the crème fraîche. (Soak ¼ cup/25 g of cashews in cold water for at least 2 hours, then drain and blitz with ½ cup (100 ml) of fresh cold water until you have a smooth cream—you'll need a powerful blender to get it totally smooth.)

SERVES 4

1¼ pounds (600 g) new potatoes, large ones halved

sea salt

3⅓ cups (300 g) purple sprouting broccoli

2 tablespoons olive oil

2 cloves of garlic, skin on

10 tablespoons (150 g) crème fraîche

the zest and juice of 2 unwaxed blood oranges

freshly ground pepper

⅓ cup (50 g) hazelnuts

Put the potatoes in a medium saucepan and cover with cold water. Add a generous pinch of salt and bring to boil over a high heat. Once the potatoes are boiling, let them cook for another 10 to 12 minutes, depending on the size, until a knife passes through them easily.

While the potatoes are cooking, trim the broccoli spears, cutting off any dry, tough ends and slicing any larger pieces in half lengthwise.

Remove the potatoes with a slotted spoon, leaving the pan on the heat. Place them in a bowl and cover to keep warm. Lower the broccoli into the water that the potatoes were cooking in and boil for 3 to 4 minutes, until just tender. Leave to steam dry. →

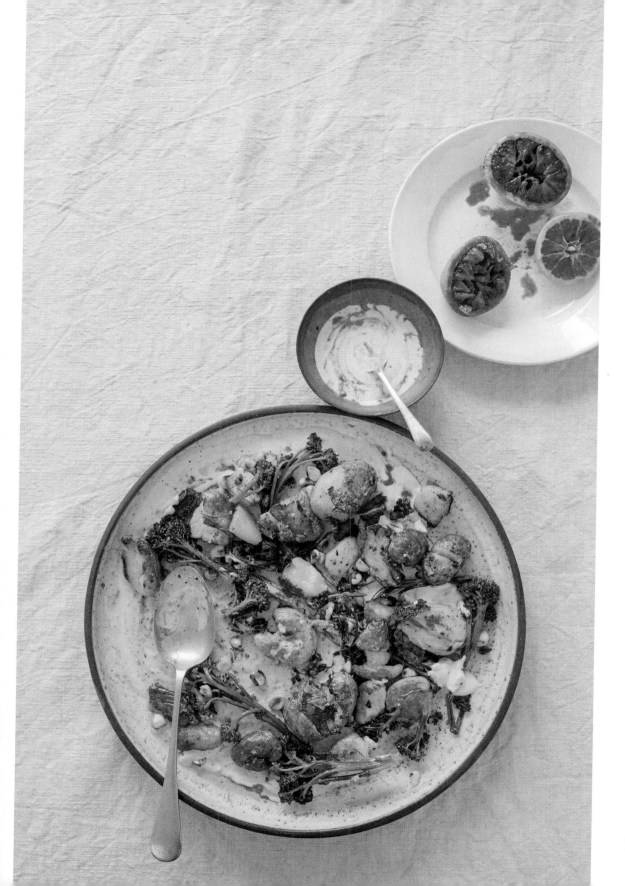

Find two frying pans in which one fits inside the other easily and heat the olive oil in the larger one over medium heat (if you don't have two frying pans, you could just roast the potatoes in the oven, at 425°F [220°C] at the beginning of the recipe and burst a few with a potato masher halfway through). Bash the garlic cloves with the side of a knife and put them into the hot oil, leave for a minute to flavor the oil, then take the garlic out and set aside. Place the potatoes in the pan and cover with the smaller pan so that the potatoes are crushed by the weight of the pan. Cook the potatoes like this in the pan for 25 minutes, turning them 2 to 3 times during the cooking process and pressing down with the back of a wooden spoon on some to help them split and crisp.

Meanwhile, mix the crème fraîche with the blood-orange zest and juice and season with salt and pepper. Toast your hazelnuts quickly in a dry pan over medium heat, until they turn from pale brown to rich golden brown, then remove and roughly chop.

Once the potatoes are crisp, split, and golden, remove them from the pan, place in a serving bowl, and put the pan back on the heat. Peel and roughly chop the cooked garlic and add it to the pan with the broccoli. Cook until the edges of the broccoli begin to crisp—this should take only a few minutes.

Pour the broccoli into the bowl, top with the blood-orange crème fraîche, and mix while everything is still warm. Scatter over the hazelnuts and serve in the middle of the table.

Pea and charred scallion fritters

These flavorful little fritters have become a favorite on my table. Scallions are something we are used to seeing year-round, but they are at their best in early spring, when they are mellow and sweet. You could use calçots (a delicious Catalonian scallion) if you make this during their short season and you can get your hands on some.

I char the scallions to give them depth and smokiness to offset the bright sweet little peas. And I serve them with a spring herb salad that is purposefully heavy on the herbs and brings an amazing fragrance to the table. The double-mint yogurt makes use of dried mint. As a rule, I prefer fresh herbs to dried, but this is an exception, in which both dried and fresh mint sing together and bring their own different notes.

Heat a griddle until very hot. Add the scallions and cook until soft all the way through and charred all over. If you don't have a griddle, you could roast them in a hot oven at 425°F (220°C) for 10 minutes.

Blanch the peas in salted boiling water until just cooked—about 30 seconds to 1 minute.

Toast the sesame seeds in a dry frying pan over medium heat until golden, then pour into a bowl to cool.

Put the white beans into a food processor with half the cooked peas and blitz until they are mashed up but not pasty—you still want a few beans to be visible. You can do this with a bit of determination and a potato masher too, if getting the food processor out is a chore. Transfer to a mixing bowl.

Roughly chop the charred scallions and place in the bowl with the rest of the peas and the flour, 2 tablespoons of the sesame seeds, the lemon zest, and mint. Season well with salt and pepper.

Mix the yogurt with the mint—dried and fresh—the zest of the lemon, and the olive oil. Season well and put into a bowl, then top with the sumac and the remaining toasted sesame seeds. →

SERVES 4

3 bunches of scallions

2¾ cups (400 g) fresh or frozen peas, podded if fresh

3 tablespoons sesame seeds

1 × 14.5-ounce (400-g) can of white beans, drained

2 tablespoons plain flour (I use spelt)

the zest of 1 unwaxed lemon

a few sprigs of mint, leaves picked and finely chopped

sea salt and freshly ground black pepper

olive oil, for frying

warm flatbread (see page 456), to serve (optional)

FOR THE MINT YOGURT

½ cup plain yogurt

2 teaspoons dried mint

a few sprigs of mint, leaves picked and finely chopped

1 unwaxed lemon

a glug of olive oil

1 teaspoon sumac

FOR THE HERB SALAD

a small bunch of dill

a small bunch of mint

a small bunch of chervil or tarragon

2 handfuls of pea shoots

113

For the salad, pick the leaves from all the herbs and mix with the pea shoots, then squeeze over the juice of half of the lemon you used in the yogurt.

Heat a frying pan over medium heat, add a covering of olive oil, and spoon heaping tablespoonfuls of the fritter mixture into the pan—the mix will make 12 heaping tablespoon-size fritters. Flatten each one a little with the back of the spoon and leave to cook for 3 to 4 minutes on each side, until golden brown. You can keep the first batch warm in a low oven while you cook the rest if all 12 don't fit in your pan.

Serve with the double-mint yogurt, herb salad, and some warm flatbread if you like.

Staffordshire oatcakes

Oatcakes are a thing of beauty. These are the famed Staffordshire version, not the crisp biscuity ones; they're more of a chewy toothsome pancake. They are sold in shops in the north of England, but it's hard to come by them where I live in London. We used to bring packs home in our suitcase from trips up north, but they are actually surprisingly easy to make; you'll need a couple of hours to let the batter rise, but the rest is very easy. The oatcakes can be made successfully with a gluten-free flour blend (if you use GF oats) and are naturally dairy free if you use oat milk, though normal milk works too.

In a small saucepan, heat the milk with 1⅔ cups (400 ml) of water until it's about body temperature, then take off the heat. Remove a couple of tablespoons of the warm liquid to a separate bowl and stir the yeast and sugar into it. Set aside for 10 minutes.

In a mixing bowl, combine the oats, flours, and salt and whisk until no lumps are visible. Once the yeast mixture is frothy, make a well in the center of the flours and pour in the yeast. Sprinkle some flour over the top. Set aside for another 10 minutes. Whisk the remaining milk and water in until you have a pourable batter that's a little thicker than a pancake batter. Cover with a damp tea towel and set aside for at least an hour, ideally two.

Heat a large frying pan with a splash of canola oil over medium heat. Give the batter a quick mix, then ladle it into the pan and tilt to ensure the base is evenly covered like a thick pancake. Cook for around 4 minutes on the first side, until it's bubbling and the color has changed from dark to a couple of shades lighter; the batter will also look dry on the top. When the sides of the oatcakes start to come away from the pan, ease a spatula around them and gingerly flip them over. Cook for another 2 minutes on the other side. Top them as you wish (see page 118 for some of my suggestions) and serve warm.

Any leftovers can be left to cool, and the oatcakes can be wrapped in waxed paper and stored in the fridge for up to 5 days or the freezer for a few months. Reheat them in a dry pan or under a hot grill for 30 seconds on each side. →

MAKES ABOUT 10

1⅔ cups (400 ml) oat milk

1¼ teaspoons (4 g) dried active yeast

½ teaspoon sugar

2½ cups (225 g) finely ground oats (or you could use oatmeal)

⅔ cup (80 g) whole-wheat spelt flour

⅔ cup (80 g) white spelt flour

½ teaspoon sea salt

Canola oil, for frying

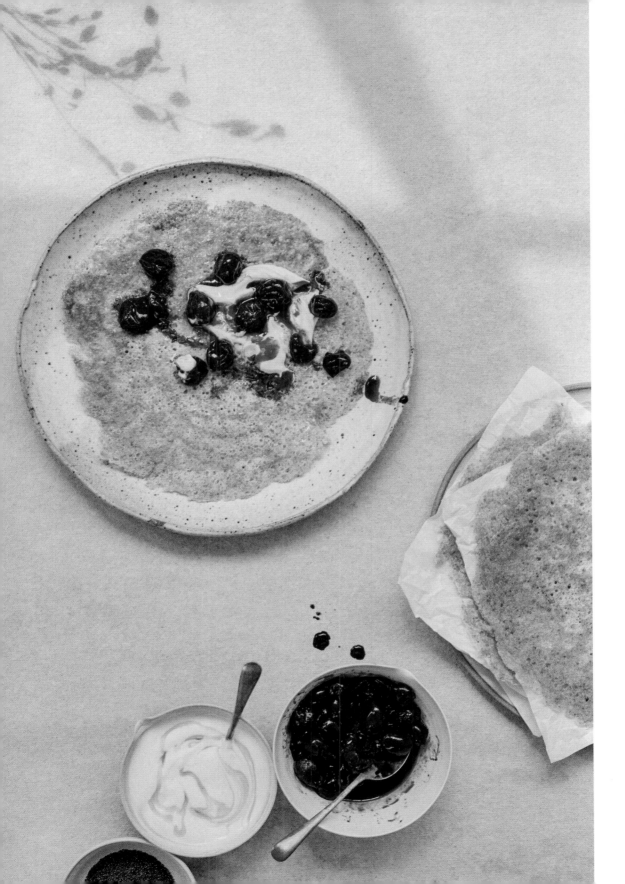

How to top your oatcakes

- Mustard, capers, and arugula (enough for 4 oatcakes)

Mix a teaspoon of whole-grain mustard with 1 cup (100 g) of grated Cheddar and 2 tablespoons of crème fraîche. Fry 4 tablespoons of capers in 2 to 3 tablespoons of olive oil until crisp, then add 2 handfuls of arugula and allow to wilt. Cover the oatcakes with the crème fraîche mixture, top with the capers and arugula and finish with a grating of lemon zest.

- Cheese and chutney

Top each oatcake with a thin spreading of chutney, then grate over some cheese and pop it under the grill to melt.

- Sunny egg florentine

Poach an egg per person; meanwhile wilt some spinach in a pan with a little cider vinegar and grated nutmeg. Top the warm oatcake with the wilted spinach and egg, and finish with a good grind of salt and pepper.

- Cherries, yogurt, and poppy seed (enough for 4 oatcakes)

Put ⅔ cup (100 g) of frozen cherries in a pan with a tiny splash of water and a teaspoon of vanilla paste and cook for 10 minutes until they are sticky and sweet. Mix ½ cup (100 g) of plain yogurt with a little honey and another teaspoon of vanilla paste. Top the oatcakes straight from the pan with the warm cherries and yogurt, and sprinkle over some poppy seeds to finish.

Spring chickpea stew with salted lemons

This is a fresh spring stew, sustaining thanks to the chickpeas, fresh with a hit of lemon, with a pleasing savoriness from the caraway and chile. Spring carrots and arugula along with the lemon lift this.

I use pumpkin seed butter here, which I keep on hand at home; it's great to use as you would a nut butter. If you can't get your hands on it, you can make your own easily by blitzing pumpkin seeds with a little canola oil and a pinch of salt.

The salted lemon recipe is my version of the quick preserved lemons from *The Modern Pantry Cookbook*; it's an easy way to make them without fuss. I have suggested you make more than you will need, as it's a very useful thing to have in the fridge. Use as you would preserved lemons: chop into dressings, toss with pasta, and flavor stews.

Heat a large saucepan over medium heat, add the carrots, onion, and garlic with a drizzle of oil and a good pinch of salt and pepper, and cook for about 10 minutes until soft and sweet.

In the meantime, make the salted lemons. Peel the zest of the lemons into long strips with a speed peeler, then put the strips in a pan with all their juice and the salt and bring to the boil. Simmer for 10 minutes, then remove from the heat and leave to cool.

Next add the caraway, red pepper flakes, thyme, tomatoes, chickpeas and their liquid, wine, and stock to the carrots and onions and simmer for 15 minutes until you have a thick well-flavored soup.

Bash the basil in a mortar with pestle, spice grinder, or mixing bowl with rolling pin, then add the pumpkin seed butter, a pinch of salt, and a squeeze of lemon juice and mix well.

When the soup is nearly done, add three of the pickled lemon pieces and simmer for another 5 minutes. Taste and adjust, adding more salt, pepper, or salted lemon as needed. Once cool, the rest of your lemons and their liquid can be kept in a jar in the fridge for months.

Once the soup is tasting great, stir in most of the arugula. Serve in bowls and top each one with a good spoonful of the pumpkin seed and basil butter. Finish with the last bit of arugula.

SERVES 4

- 2 carrots (about 10½ ounces/300 g), peeled and finely diced
- 1 red onion, finely chopped
- 3 cloves of garlic, finely chopped
- olive oil
- sea salt and freshly ground black pepper
- 1 heaping teaspoon caraway seeds
- a generous pinch of red pepper flakes
- a few sprigs of thyme
- 1 × 14.5-ounce (400-g) can of tomatoes
- 1 × 1½-pound (700-g) jar of chickpeas
- 6 ounces (175 ml) glass of white wine
- 2 cups (500 ml) good vegetable stock
- 2 big handfuls of arugula

FOR THE SALTED LEMONS

- 4 unwaxed lemons
- 1 teaspoon flaky sea salt

FOR THE HERB AND SEED BUTTER

- a bunch of basil
- 2 tablespoons pumpkin seed butter (see note above)
- the juice of 1 lemon

Easter egg and spring veg tart

This is what I have made on Easter Sunday for the past few years. The recipe makes a hero of the egg; it shows it off in all its sunny-yolked glory. As tarts go, this is quick to make—it unashamedly uses good store-bought puff pastry, though a homemade flaky pastry would certainly elevate it to another level if you had the time. It is a wash of green and yellow, using the first baby vegetables and fava beans. I make this tart all through spring and summer, varying the vegetables as different things come into season—peas and leeks one time, asparagus and fava beans the next.

Most years I have in fact made two tarts, one as the recipe reads, and a vegan version for my brother (most puff pastry is actually vegan, as it uses oil rather than butter), and I top it with a quick cashew cream (see page 110 for a quick recipe). For the nonvegans I use ready, rolled all-butter puff pastry, but if you buy a block or make your own, roll it out to just bigger than an 8½-by-11-inch piece of paper, to about the thickness of a coin.

This tart is most delicious eaten straight out of the oven, and the eggs are best cracked over just before baking, so if you want to get ahead I'd suggest making the tart and topping it with everything but the eggs and adding them just before it goes in the oven. I like to shell my fava beans, but if you buy baby ones they will be sweet and you might not need to. I serve this with a simple lemon-dressed green salad and some buttered new potatoes.

SERVES 4

5 organic eggs, from the fridge

sea salt

11¼ ounces (320 g) puff pastry (see note)

8 scallions, trimmed

6 baby zucchini, halved lengthways

freshly ground black pepper

olive oil

3½ ounces (100 g) small podded fava beans (14 ounces/400 g unpodded)

¾ cup (200 g) crème fraîche

2 tablespoons Dijon mustard

1 unwaxed lemon

TO FINISH

soft herbs (I use chives, parsley, chervil, tarragon)

toasted hazelnuts, roughly chopped

Preheat your oven to 425°F (220°C). Crack one of the eggs into a cup with a big pinch of salt, beat well, and leave to one side. Fill the kettle with water and bring to a boil.

Spread your puff pastry out on a cold baking sheet, roll the pastry out a little bigger than an 8½-by-11-inch-sized piece of paper, then trim a ⅜-inch (1-cm) strip from each side and put to one side. Working quickly, prick the base all over with a fork and lightly brush with the beaten egg. Put the trimmed pastry pieces back on the base along each edge, forming a raised edge that will keep the filling in. Egg wash the top of those too. →

Put the scallions and baby zucchini on a baking sheet, drizzle with a little olive oil, and season with salt and pepper. Bake, along with the puff pastry case, for 20 to 25 minutes, until the vegetables are golden and the pastry is really crispy.

Meanwhile, pour a little boiling water over the fava beans, allow to cool, then pop each one out of its tough outer skin, leaving the bright green bean. If you have small young fava beans, there's no need to do this—you can use them as they are.

As soon as the pastry comes out of the oven, press down the middle rectangle of the base (which will have puffed up a little), leaving yourself a nice border around the outside.

Mix the crème fraîche with the mustard and a little salt and pepper, and spread it over the crispy pastry, keeping it within the border. Arrange the zucchini and scallions over the top, then make four little spaces to crack the eggs into. Stop here if you are preparing the tart in advance, then cover and keep it in the fridge.

When you are nearly ready to eat, take the eggs out of the fridge and really carefully crack each one into a little cup. As an egg ages, some of the white turns watery and you want to lose this bit, leaving only the freshest part; it means the white will hold its shape during the cooking and won't run all over the tart. Pour the first egg into your cupped hand, with your fingers closed, and let the very watery part of the white drain off. Gently place the egg in one of the spaces, repeating with the other three, then sprinkle over the fava beans and bake for 15 to 20 minutes, until the egg whites are set and the yolks are still a little soft.

Remove the tart from the oven, grate over the zest of the lemon, and scatter over the herbs and hazelnuts.

Caper and watercress-cauliflower tart

This is a tart you could eat any day of the week. While I love a pastry tart and do eat them regularly, sometimes I want something that looks and feels as generous, without having to rely on pastry as the base. This tart uses cauliflower, almonds, and oats to make a quick case, which is much, much easier and quicker than pastry and is a much lighter load. The base won't crisp up quite like pastry, but it's baked twice, so it should be crisp on the outside and soft in the middle. I crown it with a quick ricotta, caper, and watercress topping.

———————————

Preheat the oven to 425°F (220°C) and line a baking sheet with parchment paper.

Blitz the cauliflower in a food processor until it has a fine, ricelike texture. Put it in a mixing bowl, add the ground almonds, oats, lemon zest, chopped parsley, and a good pinch of salt and pepper, and mix with your hands. Make a well in the center and add the eggs. Mix it all together, then use your hands to form it into a ball. It won't look like a traditional pastry dough: It will be a little wetter and less firm.

Rub the parchment paper with some olive oil, then put the dough in the middle of the baking sheet and use your hands to flatten it out until it is about ¼-inch (0.5-cm) thick, slightly thicker around the edges. Bake for 20 minutes, until golden all over and set into a crust.

Meanwhile, make the filling. Roughly chop the cornichons with the parsley and watercress and put them into a bowl with the capers and ricotta. Add the lemon zest, Parmesan, and artichokes, then add the beaten egg and a good pinch of salt and pepper, and mix well.

Remove the tart base from the oven and turn the oven up to 425°F (220°C). Spread the topping over the base and finish with some more Parmesan, drizzle with a little more oil, then put back into the oven for another 15 minutes to cook the filling.

Once cooked, serve with some green leaves, a drizzle more oil, and a little more Parmesan.

MAKES A LARGE TART TO SERVE 4–6

FOR THE BASE

1 medium cauliflower (about 1¾-pounds/800 g), broken into florets

1 cup (100 g) ground almonds

1 cup (100 g) rolled oats

the zest of 1 unwaxed lemon

a small bunch of flat-leaf parsley

sea salt and freshly ground black pepper

2 organic eggs, beaten

olive oil

FOR THE FILLING

5¼ ounces (150 g) cornichons

a small bunch of flat-leaf parsley

a small bunch of watercress or spinach

4 tablespoons baby capers

8¾ ounces (250 g) ricotta

the zest of 1 unwaxed lemon

a good grating of Parmesan (I use a vegetarian/rennet-free one)

7 ounces (200 g) jarred artichokes, quartered

1 organic egg, beaten

TO SERVE

a few handfuls of green leaves

Sweet potato and green chile masala dosa

SERVES 4

¾ cup (75 g) chickpea flour

½ cup (75 g) rice flour

2 green chiles, finely chopped

a small thumb-size piece of ginger, peeled and grated

1 teaspoon mustard seeds

FOR THE FILLING

3 sweet potatoes (about 1¼ pounds/600 g), peeled and cut into ¾-inch (2-cm) pieces

1 tablespoon cumin seeds

coconut oil

2 cloves of garlic, finely sliced

a large thumb-size piece of ginger, peeled and grated

4 scallions, trimmed and finely sliced

1 green chile, finely chopped

a small bunch of cilantro, leaves picked and stalks finely chopped

½ teaspoon ground turmeric

2 cups (250 g) peas (defrosted if frozen)

TO SERVE

1¾ ounces (50 g) pea shoots

2 unwaxed limes

plain yogurt

mango chutney, lime pickle or my green chutney (see page 36)

I first ate masala dosa on a trip to India years ago. We were at a faded old restaurant in the back streets of Cochin. It was breakfast time. We ordered masala dosa, and when we saw it in the waiter's hands, on its way from the ramshackle kitchen, the thin roll of lentil pancake looked longer than my arm. It teetered on a plate, comically small for it, but the pancake was so crisp, it held its shape. It looked like an impossibly huge meal, but the pancake was so light and lacy and perfect, and the mustard seed and curry leaf–seasoned potato inside so flavorsome, that we ate one each. It was the start of my first Indian adventure and a lifelong love for the food of southern India. It's hard to pick out moments that shape you, but this one definitely had a hand in shaping how I cook. This one is for you Jon Abbey; thanks for a great adventure.

This is my version of masala dosa. I use sweet potato instead of the traditional potato, and make the most of the first peas and their shoots, though if you are making this outside of pea season, then frozen ones will work well. The traditional way to make it is with rice and urud dhal, which are ground and then fermented. That makes a great dosa but isn't the most practical for a weeknight, so I use chickpea and rice flour instead, which are easy to find and work well. Sorry if it makes any traditionalists cross.

Put the flours into a food processor. Add the chile, ginger, and mustard seeds and 1 cup (250 ml) of cold water and blitz until it's a little thinner than milk, then put into a pitcher or bowl to sit for 30 minutes or so.

Steam or boil your sweet potatoes for 8 to 10 minutes until cooked through, then allow to sit and steam dry.

Heat a frying pan, add the cumin seeds, and toast for a couple of seconds, then add a tablespoon of coconut oil, the garlic, ginger, scallions, chile, cilantro stalks, and the turmeric. Cook for a minute, until the edges of the garlic begin to brown. Add the cooked sweet potatoes and fry for a few minutes until the sides begin to catch, then stir in the peas and most of the cilantro leaves (keep a few back for serving) and keep warm on a very low heat.

Put a large nonstick pan or crepe pan on the heat, rub with a little oil, then use a paper towel to wipe out any excess, keeping the paper towel for the next one. Pour one medium ladle of the batter into the pan, then lift the pan at an angle and rotate to allow the batter to flow over the surface of the pan. Cook for 30 seconds to 1 minute, until the bottom of the dosa is golden, then flip and cook for another 30 seconds. Pile on a plate with waxed paper in between each one and keep warm while you cook the remaining batter—this should make about 6 small dosas or 4 medium ones.

Pile the warm dosas with the sweet potato mixture and top with pea shoots, remaining cilantro leaves, lime for squeezing over, and yogurt and chutney.

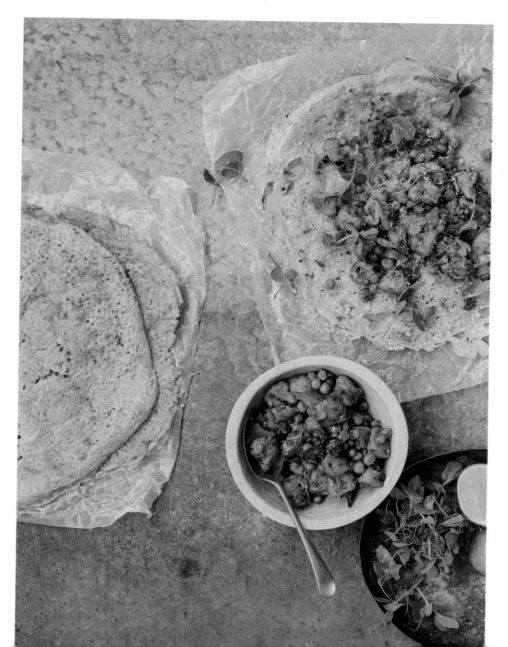

Fritters: a flavor map

Pick one thing from each column, using your tastes and instincts to guide you as to which flavors will work well. Remember to season with salt and pepper and fry gently in olive or coconut oil. Serve with a salad and rice, quinoa, or wrapped in flatbread as you see fit. These will make enough for a hearty dinner for two.

1
Choose a hero vegetable
(about 2 large handfuls, shredded or grated)

beets

parsnips

purple-sprouting broccoli

spring greens

asparagus

2
Add a pulse
(a 14.5-ounce/400-g can, drained and roughly mashed or blitzed)

chickpeas

butter beans

black beans

black-eyed peas

3
Choose one spice
(use a heaping teaspoon, roughly ground in a mortar with pestle)

cumin seeds

cilantro seeds

caraway seeds

a good pinch of red pepper flakes

a good grating of fresh nutmeg

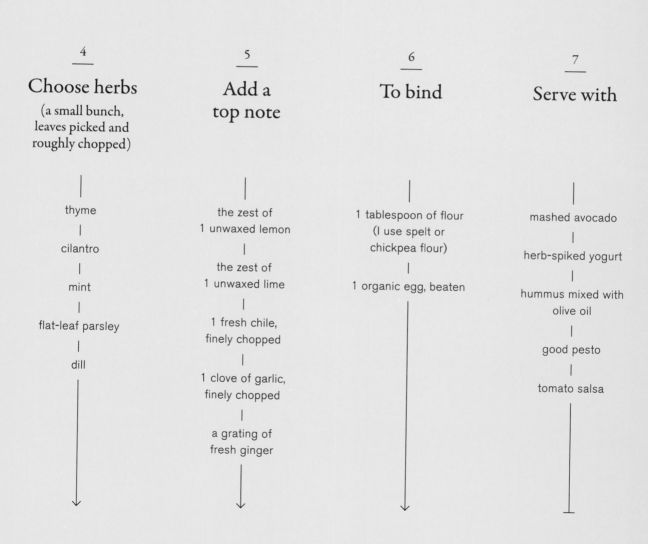

4

Choose herbs
(a small bunch,
leaves picked and
roughly chopped)

|

thyme

|

cilantro

|

mint

|

flat-leaf parsley

|

dill

5

Add a
top note

|

the zest of
1 unwaxed lemon

|

the zest of
1 unwaxed lime

|

1 fresh chile,
finely chopped

|

1 clove of garlic,
finely chopped

|

a grating of
fresh ginger

6

To bind

|

1 tablespoon of flour
(I use spelt or
chickpea flour)

|

1 organic egg, beaten

7

Serve with

|

mashed avocado

|

herb-spiked yogurt

|

hummus mixed with
olive oil

|

good pesto

|

tomato salsa

Roast leek, feta, and lemon polenta cake

Polenta in a cake is something I love: It's toothsome and textured and adds a pleasing crunch to a slice. In fact, I love polenta in all its forms—cooked with butter and Parmesan until soft and oozy like good mash, or bouncy slices of it griddled and charred. Though polenta can be a hard sell to some, I am convinced this savory cake would persuade the most committed polenta-hater. It's easier and quicker than a tart but looks just as good. For a gluten-free version, you can use gluten-free cornmeal instead of the spelt.

Preheat the oven to 425°F (220°C). Butter a loose-bottomed 9½-inch (24-cm) cake pan and line with parchment paper.

SERVES 8

4 leeks (about 5½ cups/ 500 g), cut into ⅜-inch (1 cm) slices

2 tablespoons unsalted butter, plus extra for greasing

1 cup (150 g) white spelt flour

1 cup (120 g) coarse-ground polenta

1½ teaspoons baking powder

½ teaspoon flaky sea salt

a good grinding of black pepper

2 tablespoons nigella seeds

the zest and juice of 1 unwaxed lemon

1 red chile, finely chopped

½ a bunch of thyme, leaves picked

1 cup (150 g) feta, crumbled

4 organic eggs, lightly beaten

7 tablespoons milk

¾ cup (200 g) plain yogurt

First, sauté your leeks in a tablespoon of the butter in a frying pan over medium heat until soft and sweet—this should take about 10 minutes.

Melt the remaining tablespoon of butter and use it to brush the parchment paper. Meanwhile, put the flour, polenta, baking powder, salt, pepper, and a tablespoon of the nigella seeds in a bowl and whisk to get rid of any lumps of baking powder. Add the lemon zest, red chile, and thyme leaves and crumble in the feta.

Put the juice of the lemon in a small bowl and whisk together with the eggs, milk, and yogurt.

Mix the yogurt mixture into the flour mixture until just combined (being careful not to overmix). Once the leeks are cool, stir half of them into the batter. Pour the batter into the lined cake pan and scatter the rest of the leeks on top, then sprinkle over the reserved tablespoon of nigella seeds.

Bake for 35 to 45 minutes, until the top is golden and a skewer inserted into the cake comes out clean. Leave to cool in the pan for 5 minutes, then cool on a wire rack to room temperature before slicing.

Grilled kale with honeyed tofu and shallots

Kale is not just for deep winter: It's around until early spring. There seems to be no stopping the kale renaissance of recent years; despite it being annoyingly plastered on teenage T-shirts and liberally scattered on every restaurant menu for the last couple of years, people still seem to have an appetite for it—including me. I love the frilly, minerally deep-green bunches, and this is a fresh way to eat it, grilled so it's a little smoky, offset by the honeyed tofu but still fresh thanks to some mint and lemon in a bright tahini dressing. This is a salad that will make you friends.

Be sure to use a good firm tofu here—organic is best if you can find it. Soy is one of our most processed crops, so organic is the best way to avoid GMO soy. If you are especially hungry, you could serve this with some brown rice or quinoa.

SERVES 4

2 tablespoons golden honey

1 tablespoon tamari or soy sauce

¾ cup (200 g) firm organic tofu, sliced into ⅜ inch- (1 cm-) thick sticks

olive oil

3 banana shallots, peeled and finely sliced

2 heads of kale (about 1¾ pounds/800 g), de-stalked and torn

a few sprigs of mint

½ cup (75 g) almonds, toasted

FOR THE DRESSING

½ cup (100 g) Greek yogurt

1 tablespoon light tahini

2 tablespoons olive oil

the juice of ½ lemon

sea salt and freshly ground black pepper

Mix the honey with the tamari and spoon it over the tofu, then toss everything well to coat.

Heat 2 tablespoons of oil in a frying pan over medium to low heat and slowly fry the shallots for 10 to 15 minutes, or until they are golden. Remove with a slotted spoon and leave to drain and crisp up on paper towels. Keep the pan for later.

Mix the dressing ingredients together, then season well with salt and pepper and taste, adjusting the seasoning and the amount of lemon or oil if needed—you can add a little cold water here if your dressing looks too thick.

Put a griddle on to heat up—you want it over a medium heat. Put the shallot pan back over medium heat and add the tofu. Cook until it is golden on all its edges, then take the pan off the heat and keep the tofu warm. Toss the kale in a tablespoon of olive oil and season with salt and pepper. Drizzle with 3 tablespoons of water and mix well. Put a batch of kale onto the griddle and cook for about a minute on each side until it is wilted and charred, then put in a serving bowl while you char the rest—it should take 4 to 5 minutes total.

To serve, pour the tofu and crispy shallots into the kale, add the mint and the dressing. Toss well and top with the almonds.

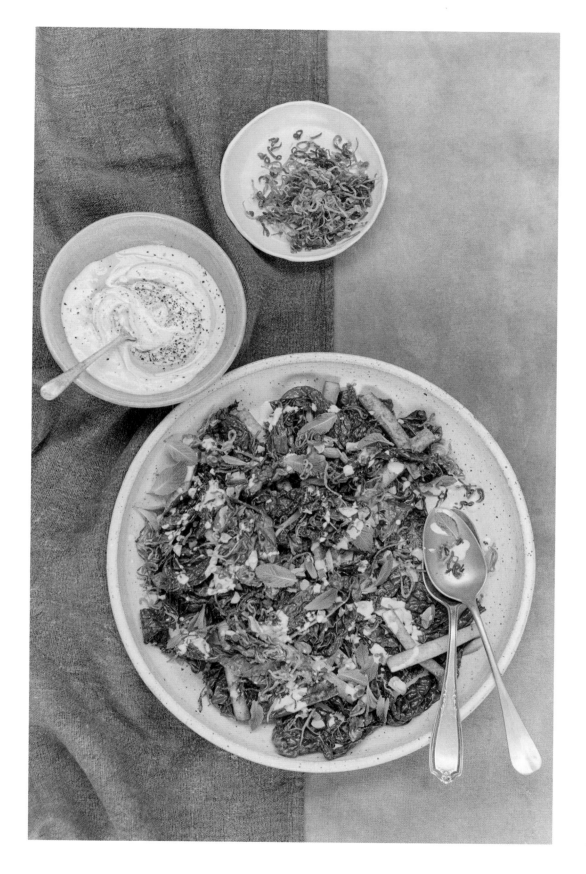

Spring green rolls with almond satay

I love these rolls—they are fresh and lively, filled with spring greens and herbs, which is the perfect way to wake up our palates after the winter root vegetables and woody herbs. They are much easier to make than you might expect and are brilliantly portable, making them a great snack for a picnic or a journey and, if you are organized, perhaps even a plane snack, though I've never quite managed it.

As the rolling takes a little while, I usually make these for a crowd; if you'd prefer to make fewer, then halve the recipe. They will keep well in the fridge too for a few days if you have leftovers.

The key here is to soak your rice papers for just the right amount of time—you want to take them out of the water while they still feel a little stiff, as they will continue to soften as they sit. I make these for parties too and cut them in half. If you can, rope a few early guests in to help with the rolling. The rolls are a great thing to make with kids too—just leave out the chiles from the dipping sauce if you are serving them to little ones.

MAKES 12–15
(TO SERVE ABOUT 6)

FOR THE TOFU

14 ounces (400 g) extra-firm tofu

2 cloves of garlic

2 teaspoons tamari or soy sauce

2 teaspoons golden honey or agave nectar

1 teaspoon of brown rice vinegar

2 tablespoons coconut oil

FOR THE ROLLS

3½ cups (200 g) spring greens

1 lime

sea salt

3½ ounces (100 g) whole-wheat rice vermicelli noodles

a small bunch of mint

a small bunch of Thai basil, washed and dried

a small bunch of cilantro, washed and dried

½ large cucumber, sliced into thin batons

a small bunch of chives, finely chopped

12–15 × 6-inch (15-cm) rice paper wrappers →

First, make a marinade for the tofu by pounding the garlic to a rough paste in a mortar with pestle. Leave to one side. Mix the tamari, honey, and vinegar and place in a bowl to one side.

Pat the tofu dry with paper towels and cut into 6 equal chunky slices. Gently toss the tofu in a bowl with the marinade and cover. Leave to one side while you make the rest of the filling for the rolls.

Peel the leaves of the spring greens away from the core and cut the core away from the middle of the leaves, leaving a thin V-shaped gap in each leaf. Layer 4 or 5 similar-sized leaves together on the cutting board and roll them up tightly into a cigar shape. Slice into thin ribbons.

Place the spring green ribbons in a large mixing bowl and squeeze over the juice from half of the lime then sprinkle over a little salt. Scrunch the leaves with your hands firmly, pushing the juice and salt into the leaves as you go. The leaves will turn a deep green and should reduce in size by about half after a couple of minutes. Cover and set to one side. →

Cook the rice noodles according to the package instructions and refresh under cold water. Drain well and set aside.

Pick the leaves from the herbs and discard the mint and basil stalks. Finely chop the cilantro stalks to add to the dipping sauce later.

Next, make the dipping sauce by whisking all the ingredients together in a bowl with a fork, then stir in the chopped cilantro stalks.

When you're ready to eat, heat the oil for the tofu in a wide frying pan over medium heat and lay out the tofu in the pan so there's no overlap. Fry on each side for 4 to 5 minutes, or until golden. Allow to cool a little, then cut into pencil-size pieces.

Mix the spring greens, noodles, cucumber, and herbs in a large bowl with 3 tablespoons of the dipping sauce.

To assemble, get all your elements together. Fill a wide shallow bowl or plate with ⅜ inch (1 cm) of warm water. Dip rice paper into the warm water for between 3 and 5 seconds—how long you need to soak it will depend a little on the brand of rice papers you use. Resist over-soaking them—even if the paper is a little bit stiff, it will continue to absorb water as you assemble the wrap.

Put the paper on a nonstick surface, like a plate or cutting board, and leave the paper to sit until just tacky. Pile all your ingredients in the center of the wrapper, keeping a couple of inches clear at the top and bottom and 1½ to 2 inches (4 to 5 cm) on each side.

Now for the rolling. Fold the top and bottom of the paper over the filling, then quickly roll the whole thing over the filling to enclose everything, tucking in as you go and keeping the roll as firm as possible. Repeat with the remaining papers and filling, then serve on platters with the rest of the dipping sauce.

FOR THE DIPPING SAUCE

4 tablespoons almond butter

4 tablespoons white miso paste

the zest of 3 unwaxed limes and the juice of 4

3 teaspoons sesame oil

a large thumb-size piece of ginger, peeled and grated

2 red chiles, finely chopped

3 tablespoons tamari or soy sauce

2 tablespoons golden honey or agave nectar

Double lime, cashew, and ginger stir-fry

John, my husband, is the king of a healthy vegetable-packed dinner. The first few months after having my son I did very little cooking, but John kept us going, cooking each night as I rocked Dylan to sleep. John makes a mean stir-fry. Somehow the word stir-fry feels a bit ungenerous; it conjures up old memories of raw chunks of red pepper and packet sauces. John's are nothing of the sort. They are fresh, filling, and always have a rainbow of veg. This is the sort of thing he makes; mine are never as good.

I use pickled ginger here, as I love the balance of sweet and tart it brings, but if you don't have it, a little more ginger will stand in, no problem. I also use short-grain brown rice, but white or brown basmati or jasmine would all work too.

SERVES 2

1 cup (200 g) rice (I use short-grain brown rice)

sea salt

4 unwaxed limes

3 tablespoons rice wine vinegar

a thumb-size piece of ginger, peeled and grated

2 tablespoons golden honey

a bunch of scallions, finely sliced

1¾ cups (200 g) radishes, cut into quarters

3⅓ cups (200 g) sugar snap peas, cut in half

a bunch of asparagus

a head of spring greens

a small bunch of cilantro

coconut oil

1 ounce (25 g) pickled ginger

2 tablespoons tamari or soy sauce

½ cup (50 g) cashews, toasted

Cook the rice in boiling salted water until cooked but with a little bite, then drain and leave to steam dry.

Meanwhile, grate the zest of 2 of the limes into a large bowl, add the juice of all 4, along with 2 tablespoons of the vinegar, the ginger, and half the honey. Add half the scallions, all the radishes, and the sugar snaps.

Snap the ends off the asparagus and trim off the tips, then cut the remaining stalks into ⅜-inch (1-cm) pieces and add these to the bowl too. Toss everything in the lime marinade to coat and leave it to sit while you get on with the rest.

Shred the spring greens finely. Pick the cilantro leaves from their stalks, finely chop the stalks, and add them to the bowl with the vegetables. Put the cilantro leaves to one side for later.

Heat a large frying pan over medium heat and add a little coconut oil. Once hot, add the cooked rice and fry for a couple of minutes so the edges begin to crisp, then add the pickled ginger and remaining tablespoon of rice wine vinegar and keep warm. →

135

Heat another large frying pan over really high heat; it is important you have a large frying pan or a wok here so that there is enough room for the liquid to evaporate from the veg and for it to cook quickly. Put the vegetables into a sieve set over another large bowl to drain their marinade, keeping the marinade for later. Add the vegetables and fry for a few minutes until they have just lost their rawness but still have some crunch. Now stir in the spring greens.

While the veg are cooking, add the tamari and remaining tablespoon of honey to the bowl of marinade and mix well. Once the veg are cooked to your liking, add the marinade and cook for about 30 seconds, until it has all evaporated. Serve in deep bowls with the ginger rice and top with the reserved scallions, a sprinkling of cilantro leaves, and the toasted cashews.

Avocado and popped-bean burritos

These are quick, fresh, spring-like burritos that I have found myself making over and over; they are loved by young and old. Making a dressing out of the avocado with loads of lime means that there will be no browning and makes these burritos quite portable, though if you plan to wrap them up for later, I'd suggest letting the beans cool before you do.

    If you want the burritos to be really sustaining, you can add some cooked rice or quinoa tossed in a little lemon or lime juice and some salt and pepper.

First, make your dressing. Place all the ingredients in a blender and blitz on a high speed until you have a smooth pale green dressing, adding a little water tablespoon by tablespoon, until the dressing is the consistency of a thick smoothie (I usually end up adding about 3 tablespoons).

Toast the pumpkin seeds in a large nonstick frying pan with the lime zest and a good pinch of salt, then transfer to a bowl for later.

Put the spinach and kale in a bowl with the lime juice and a big pinch of salt and scrunch with your hands until the kale has broken down a little—this will take about 3 to 4 minutes. Add half the avocado dressing to the bowl and mix well.

Pat the drained beans dry with paper towels. Put the frying pan back on the heat and add the olive oil. Once it's nice and hot, add the beans and cook for a couple of minutes. Once they begin to pop and blister, add the cilantro seeds and cook for another 2 minutes, until all the beans have burst and are crispy.

Toast your tortillas by warming them in a dry frying pan on a low-medium heat, or as I do, directly over the gas flame on the stovetop, turning them with tongs after a few seconds. Lay them out and divide the beans and greens among them. Top with a little more of the avocado dressing and the pumpkin seeds, then roll them up and enjoy.

SERVES 4

FOR THE DRESSING

1 ripe avocado, peeled and pitted

the zest and juice of 1 unwaxed lime

¼ teaspoon cayenne pepper

1 teaspoon golden honey

3 tablespoons olive oil

1 green chile, finely chopped

a bunch of scallions, roughly chopped

a bunch of cilantro

⅓ cup (50 g) pumpkin seeds

the zest and juice of 1 unwaxed lime

sea salt

5 cups (100 g) spinach or spring greens

2⅓ cups (150 g) curly kale leaves

4 whole-wheat seeded tortilla wraps

FOR THE POPPED BEANS

1 × 14.5-ounce (400-g) can of cannellini beans, drained

2 tablespoons olive oil

1 teaspoon cilantro (coriander) seeds

Almond satay bowl with tempeh

SERVES 4

FOR THE ALMOND SATAY

1 small red chile, roughly chopped

1 clove of garlic, roughly chopped

½ cup (125 g) almond butter

2 tablespoons tamari or soy sauce

the juice of 1 lime

2 tablespoons golden honey or agave nectar

7 tablespoons (100 ml) full-fat coconut milk

14 ounces (400 g) new potatoes

2 tablespoons coconut oil, plus a little extra

4 carrots (about 8¾ ounces/250 g), peeled into strips

a small head of spring greens, shredded

3 cups (150 g) mung bean sprouts

a bunch of cilantro, roughly chopped

sea salt

2 shallots, sliced into rings

7 ounces (200 g) tempeh, sliced into long ⅜-inch- (1-cm-) thick slices

2 tablespoons maple syrup

2 tablespoons tamari or soy sauce

lime wedges, to serve

cooked brown rice, to serve (optional)

This dressing is so good I could spoon it straight from the jar. It perks up some humble vegetables and elevates this to a seriously flavorful bowl. I use tempeh here, a fermented soy bean cake, which is as good for you as it is delicious. It can be hard to find, however, which is why I hold off from using it too much.

You can use other seasonal vegetables here: purple sprouting broccoli and asparagus when spring kicks in, tomatoes and corn in summer. Perhaps roasted root vegetables in the winter. It's a pretty versatile bowlful. Other nut butters like peanut could be used instead of almond too.

———————————

First, make the dressing. Put all the ingredients into a food processor and blend on high speed. If you are not a fan of chile, add less or deseed yours. Add a little water until the sauce is thin enough to pour, but not watery. Taste and adjust the seasoning as needed.

Have all your vegetables ready. Put a steamer over boiling water and place the potatoes inside first; cover and set a timer for 12 minutes. Once tender, remove them from the steamer, toss with a teaspoon of the coconut oil, then cover to keep warm.

Fill the steamer with the carrots and greens and cook for 2 to 4 minutes, until tender-crisp, then toss with the remaining coconut oil. In a large bowl combine all the steamed veg with the sprouts and cilantro. Sprinkle with salt and toss.

Heat a frying pan over medium heat, add a little coconut oil, and fry the shallots until crisp and golden but not burned, then drain on paper towels. Put the pan back on the heat and add the tempeh. Cook until crisp on each side, add the maple and tamari, then take off the heat.

To serve, layer everything in a bowl and top with the dressing. Serve with the lime wedges and brown rice if you are really hungry.

Bay and lemon–laced crème caramel

I can't tell you emphatically enough how much I love these. What I can tell you is that the first time I made them I ate two in succession. The lemon, vanilla, and bay are a favorite combination: The gentle herbaceous bay, lifting lemon, and warm sweetness of vanilla together is unexpected, comforting, and refreshing. You need the best full-cream milk here.

Making a caramel can put people off, but I have given easy instructions here, so don't be nervous: it's really not hard at all. Be sure to check the wobble on the baked crème caramels—you want a very light wobble in the middle; they shouldn't be liquidy. You will need six individual ramekins or ¾-cup (170-ml) dariole molds to make these.

SERVES 6

butter, for greasing

2 cups (500 ml) organic whole milk

1 unwaxed lemon

2 bay leaves

1 vanilla pod

2 medium organic eggs, plus 4 egg yolks

⅓ cup (75 g) superfine or caster sugar

FOR THE CARAMEL

¼ cup (60 g) superfine or caster sugar

⅓ cup (60 g) light muscovado sugar

the juice of 1 lemon

Preheat the oven to 340°F (170°C). Grease all the ramekins or dariole molds with butter.

Start by infusing your milk. Pour the milk into a saucepan. Peel 4 strips of zest from the lemon with a speed peeler and add to the milk with the bay. Scrape the seeds from the vanilla pod and add to the milk along with the pod. Heat gently over low heat, and when it's just under a simmer, take off the heat and allow to cool a little and infuse for 15 minutes.

Next, make the caramel by melting the superfine or caster and muscovado sugars together in a large, deep saucepan with the lemon juice and 2 tablespoons of water. Try not to it stir once it's heated (stirring will encourage the sugar to crystallize)—a gentle shake and tilt of the pan now and again will help the sugar to melt evenly.

Let the sugar mixture cook until it's bubbling, is a rich molasses color all over and smells caramell-y. It should take around 3 minutes from when it starts to bubble. If you're nervous and want to test that it's done, pour a small dot onto a cold plate, and if it sets, it's done. Pour the caramel into your greased ramekins, distributing evenly across all 6 servings, and leave to one side to set. →

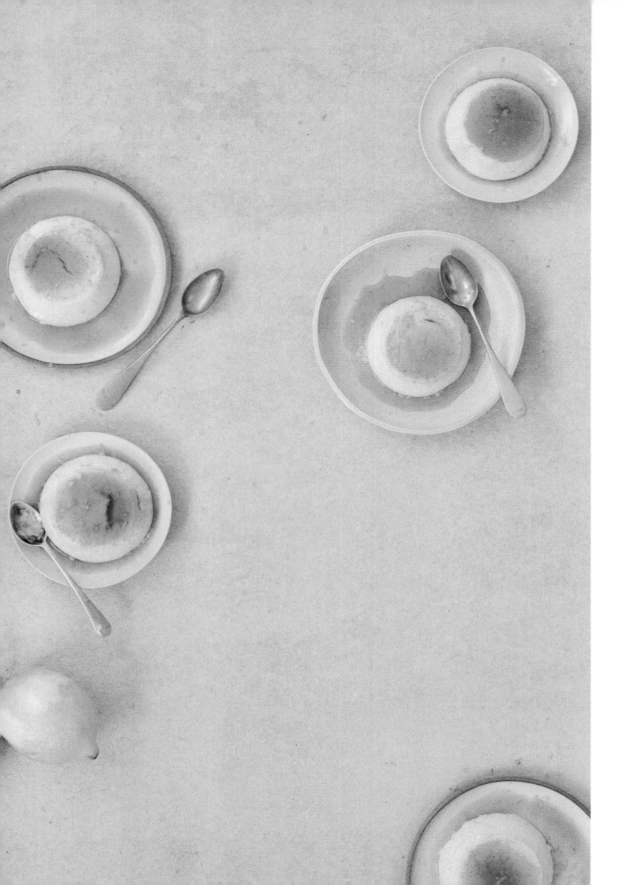

Now on to the custard. Crack the whole eggs into a mixing bowl and whisk with the yolks and superfine or caster sugar until everything is combined. Gradually add the cooled milk to the eggs and sugar, gently combining with a whisk as you go. Fill and boil water in the kettle.

Pour the mixture through a sieve into a Pyrex measuring cup, then pour into the ramekins and place them in a deep roasting pan. Cover each ramekin tightly with foil. Carefully pour the hot water from the kettle around the ramekins to about halfway up the sides.

Bake in the center of the hot oven for 15 minutes, then remove the foil and bake for another 15 to 20 minutes, until they're set with a bit of wobble still in the center. Cool on a roasting pan, then place covered in the fridge, ideally overnight, but definitely for at least 3 to 4 hours.

Remove from the fridge at least 30 minutes before you want to serve them. When you're ready, gingerly run a small offset spatula around the edge and invert each one onto a plate.

Rhubarb and rose frozen yogurt

This sweet-shop pink frozen yogurt is as cheerful as it is delicious. Thanks to the bright bubblegum color of the forced rhubarb and the gentle cloudy white of the Greek yogurt, it ends up the most beautiful tone of rosy pink. This year we ate it from good waffle cones in the garden on my birthday in early April, on one of the first warm days of the year; I couldn't have been happier. If you use outdoor rhubarb for this it will be less pink.

I infuse the rhubarb with some rose geranium leaves. I have a plant that sits on my windowsill but you may not, so you could use a couple of teaspoons of rosewater in their place. The rose geranium has a fresher, less perfumey rose note, though, so use it if you can.

Chop the rhubarb into roughly 1-inch (2.5-cm) pieces and place in a medium saucepan with the sugar, rose geranium leaves, orange zest, and a couple of tablespoons of water. Cover with a lid and place over medium heat for 3 minutes, until everything is steamy and smelling fragrant, then turn the heat down and let the pan blip away for another 7 minutes, until the rhubarb is completely soft and bright pink. Transfer to a bowl to cool for at least 20 minutes.

Once the rhubarb has cooled, remove the rose geranium leaves and mash up any big pieces of rhubarb with a fork. Stir the yogurt and salt into the rhubarb; you can leave a bit of a ripple here if you like, but I mix mine quite well.

Churn in your ice-cream maker until the frozen yogurt has thickened to a scoopable consistency. Transfer to your freezer if you like a really set frozen yogurt.

If you don't have an ice-cream maker, chill the yogurt and rhubarb mix in the fridge for at least 1 hour, then transfer to a 4½-cup (1-liter) container with a lid. Freeze for 1 hour, until its wobble is no longer visible, and beat with a whisk or fork to incorporate all the frozen pieces and ensure the frozen yogurt has an even consistency. Mix twice more over the next couple of hours, and remove from the freezer a few minutes before serving.

MAKES ABOUT 4½ CUPS (1 LITER)

1 pound (500 g) rhubarb

1 cup (200 g) superfine or caster sugar

6–8 rose geranium leaves, or 1–2 teaspoons rosewater, depending on how strong it is

the zest of 1 unwaxed orange

2¾ cups (800 g) Greek yogurt

a pinch of flaky sea salt

Lemon and cardamom upside-down cake

As far as I am concerned, there is no greater cake than a lemon cake, and this one has the crown. It's an upside-down cake with an easy candied lemon bottom, which, once cool, is turned over to become a gilded lemon roof. The lemons burnish as the cake cooks, under a crumb of almonds, polenta, and oats (so it's free of gluten, if that's something that's on your radar). The lemon comes with a backup of cardamom and vanilla, a combination that's well used in my kitchen and for very good reason.

A vegan version can be made quite successfully with aquafaba in place of the eggs (use the method on page 459). It will need 9 tablespoons (135 ml) of aquafaba. If you'd like to keep this totally gluten-free, be sure to use gluten-free oats.

Preheat your oven to 395°F (200°C). Next, grease and line a 9½-inch (24-cm) springform cake pan with waxed paper.

Put the zest and juice of 2 of the lemons in a small bowl and set aside. Next, prepare the remaining lemons for the base of the pan. Using a really sharp knife, slice the lemons into wafer-thin slices (about ¼ inch/0.5 cm is ideal). Remove any visible seeds from the slices.

Put ¼ cup (50 g) of the sugar into a medium saucepan with 3½ tablespoons (50 ml) of water and heat until the sugar has dissolved, then simmer for about 5 minutes until you have a syrup. Add the lemon slices and very gently simmer for another 10 to 15 minutes, until they are starting to turn slightly translucent, then carefully scoop them out of the syrup and put them on some parchment paper to cool so that you can handle them. Reserve any syrup for later.

Meanwhile, blitz the oats in the food processor until you have a rough, flour-like consistency.

Bash the cardamom seeds to a rough powder. Beat the canola oil and remaining sugar with a wooden spoon. Mix in the polenta, baking powder, almonds, cardamom, vanilla, eggs, ground oats, and reserved lemon juice and zest. Sprinkle over the salt and mix well again. →

SERVES 10

butter, for greasing

5 unwaxed lemons

¾ cup (175 g) superfine or caster sugar

¾ cup (75 g) rolled oats

seeds from 12 cardamom pods

10 tablespoons (150 ml) canola oil

2¾ ounces (75 g) polenta

1 teaspoon baking powder

¾ cup (75 g) ground almonds

1 teaspoon vanilla paste

3 organic eggs

a generous pinch of flaky sea salt

plain yogurt whipped with a little vanilla, to serve

Arrange the sliced citrus on the bottom of the lined cake pan, leaving some little gaps for the batter to hit the bottom of the tin, which will allow some of the steam to escape. Pour the batter on top and level it out with the back of a spoon.

Bake in the middle of the oven for 35 to 40 minutes, checking at 30 minutes and perhaps covering with foil if it looks like it's getting very brown on top. Check that it's cooked through by piercing the cake with a skewer; if it comes out clean, the cake is ready.

After the cake has cooled for about 20 minutes, remove the pan, peel away the paper and carefully upturn it on to a plate. Pour any leftover syrup from the lemons over the top. Serve with yogurt, whipped with a little vanilla.

Cheddar, turnip, and ramps scones

These might sound more wintry, but this time of the year is filled with just as many cold days as warm ones, and these warming, quick little scones are the kind of thing I make when we run out of bread, or if I want to make a bowl of soup look a bit more like a meal. These are hard to mess up, so if bread is a stretch for you, these are a better bet. I use rutabaga, as it's pretty much my favorite root vegetable through the winter: cheap, British and abundant and its season lasts a little longer than the other root vegetables—into the early spring. Parsnips, celeriac, or sweet potatoes would happily stand in.

Preheat the oven to 475°F (240°C). Put the flour, baking powder, and salt in a large mixing bowl and whisk together until smooth and well combined.

Grate in the butter, then rub it in with your fingertips until the mixture looks like fine bread crumbs.

Finely grate in all but ¼ cup (25 g) of the cheese, then add the rutabaga, ramps or chives, and the mustard and stir to combine. Mix in the milk and water until the dough just comes away from the edge of the bowl; don't handle it any more than is necessary, as this will make your scones tough.

Turn the dough out on to a very lightly floured surface and flatten into a rectangle about 1 inch (2.5 cm) high. Cut out with a fluted cutter (I use a 2½-inch/6-cm one for 16 scones), reshaping as necessary while handling the dough as little as possible.

Carefully place the rounds on a lined baking sheet and brush the tops with the egg and milk mixture. Grate the remaining cheese over the top and bake for about 12 minutes, until golden. Allow to cool slightly on a cooling rack before splitting open.

MAKES ABOUT 16

- 1¾ cups (450 g) plain spelt flour, plus a little extra to dust
- 6 teaspoons baking powder
- 1 teaspoon salt
- 7 tablespoons cold unsalted butter
- ¾ cup (100 g) Cheddar
- 2 cups (200 g) rutabaga, peeled and grated
- 1 ounce (25 g) ramps leaves or chives, finely chopped
- 1 heaping tablespoon whole-grain mustard
- ½ cup (120 ml) cold milk
- ½ cup (120 ml) cold water
- 1 organic egg, beaten with a splash of milk

First warm days

Best of the season
- Asparagus
- Garden herbs
- Radishes
- Sorrel
- Baby spinach
- Cauliflower
- Fava beans
- Peas
- Beets
- Globe artichokes
- Samphire
- Lettuce
- New potatoes
- Elderflowers
- Gooseberries
- Outdoor rhubarb
- First strawberries
- First raspberries

Flowers
- Iris
- Nigella
- Daffodils
- Cornflowers

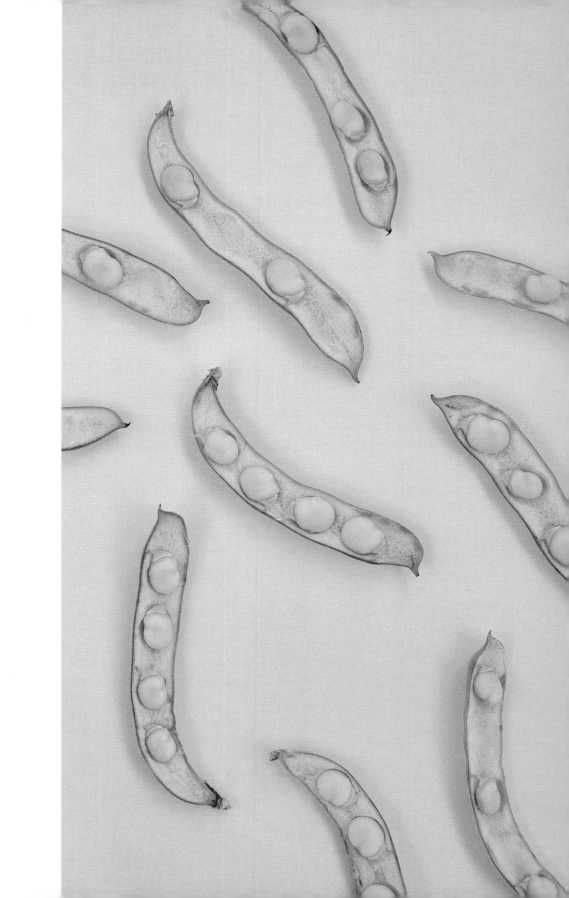

Roasted strawberry and chia breakfast bowls

I usually double this recipe and make enough for two days. The night before, stick a baking sheet of strawberries in the oven for spooning on top the next day. The syrupy roasted red strawberries take this breakfast from holier-than-thou porridge to a proper food-lover's breakfast. If you have beautifully sweet strawberries there is no need to roast them.

Chia is a funny ingredient to cook with and, quite honestly, I'm not always a fan of it, but it works here. I find it a particularly good thing to eat in the morning—it gives me lots of energy without making me feel really full like porridge can. If you are new to chia seeds, you could try starting with 2 tablespoons and 2 of rolled oats, which will make it a bit creamier.

MAKES 2 BOWLS

4 tablespoons chia seeds

1¼ cups (300 ml) almond milk (or other milk of your choosing)

a handful of strawberries

a pinch of flaky sea salt

the zest of 1 unwaxed lemon

a splash of vanilla extract

2 teaspoons maple syrup or golden honey

FOR THE ROASTED STRAWBERRIES

3½ cups (500 g) strawberries

1 tablespoon olive oil

2 teaspoons maple syrup or golden honey

a pinch of flaky sea salt

TO SERVE

toasted coconut flakes

a drizzle of maple syrup or golden honey

The night before, combine the chia seeds with the milk and stir well. Mash a handful of fresh strawberries with the salt, lemon, vanilla, and maple syrup, then stir them into the chia. Refrigerate overnight so the seeds can bloom and soften.

For the strawberries, preheat the oven to 395°F (200°C). It is important to use a baking sheet with a lip or a large baking dish to prevent the juices running off the sheet onto the bottom of your oven. If you are using a baking sheet, line it with parchment paper.

Cut the strawberries in half. Put the berries on the baking sheet and pour over the olive oil, maple syrup, and salt. Toss gently until coated.

Arrange the strawberries in a single layer and roast for about 40 minutes, just long enough for the berry juices to thicken and set slightly, but not long enough for the juices to burn. Watch the edges of the tray in particular. While still warm, scrape into a jar and put in the fridge for the morning.

Just before serving, sweeten the chia to taste with a little more maple syrup, if you like, then top with toasted coconut flakes and a spoonful of roasted strawberries.

Seeded spinach breakfast waffles

I love waffles. With their crisp checkered edges and their fluffy insides, I can't think of anything I'd rather eat for breakfast. In her book *I Remember Nothing*, Nora Ephron lists waffles, as well as the idea of waffles, as things she will miss when she dies.

The idea of waffles is usually a sweet one. One morning I realized I'd never had a savory waffle, and about an hour later the waffle iron was heating up and then the batter was being ladled in. These are the result: rich with buttermilk (or plain yogurt), buckwheat flour, cheese, and spinach. The cheese melts when it hits the waffle iron, making the most delicious crisp, cheesy exterior. I serve these with roasted tomatoes and goat cheese, but I've listed a few other options on page 158 too.

I have made a vegan version with oat milk and 1 tablespoon of chia mixed with 3 tablespoons of water in place of the egg, and leaving out the cheese (or adding a pinch of nutritional yeast); they don't puff up quite as much but are still very good. If you want a gluten-free version, you can use all buckwheat flour and skip the whole-wheat. You can also fry the batter like a pancake.

MAKES 6

olive oil

4 scallions, chopped

⅓ cups (100 g) lightly packed spinach leaves

1 red or green chile, finely chopped

2¾ cups (400 g) cherry tomatoes on the vine

sea salt and freshly ground black pepper

1 cup (130 g) buckwheat flour

½ cup (60 g) whole-wheat spelt flour

1 heaping teaspoon baking powder

2 tablespoons little seeds (I use a mixture of flax seed and poppy seed)

1½ cups (375 ml) buttermilk, kefir, or thin yogurt

1 organic egg, beaten

¾ cup (125 g) grated or crumbly Cheddar cheese, plus extra to serve

1 generous cup (125 g) soft goat cheese, to serve

Preheat your waffle maker. I use an electric one, but if you are using a stovetop iron, leave it on very low heat to warm up.

Heat a little olive oil in a frying pan over medium heat, add the scallions, and cook for a few minutes until they have started to brown, then add the spinach and cook until most of the moisture has evaporated. Stir in the chile, then put the mixture on to a cutting board to cool and put the pan back on the heat.

Add the tomatoes to the pan (you can keep them on the vine) with a good pinch of salt and pepper, and cook over high heat, letting the sides of the tomatoes brown and blister.

Meanwhile, put your flours, baking powder, seeds, and a good pinch of salt and pepper into another mixing bowl and stir with a whisk to get rid of any lumps of baking powder.

In another bowl, mix the buttermilk and egg and crumble in the Cheddar cheese. →

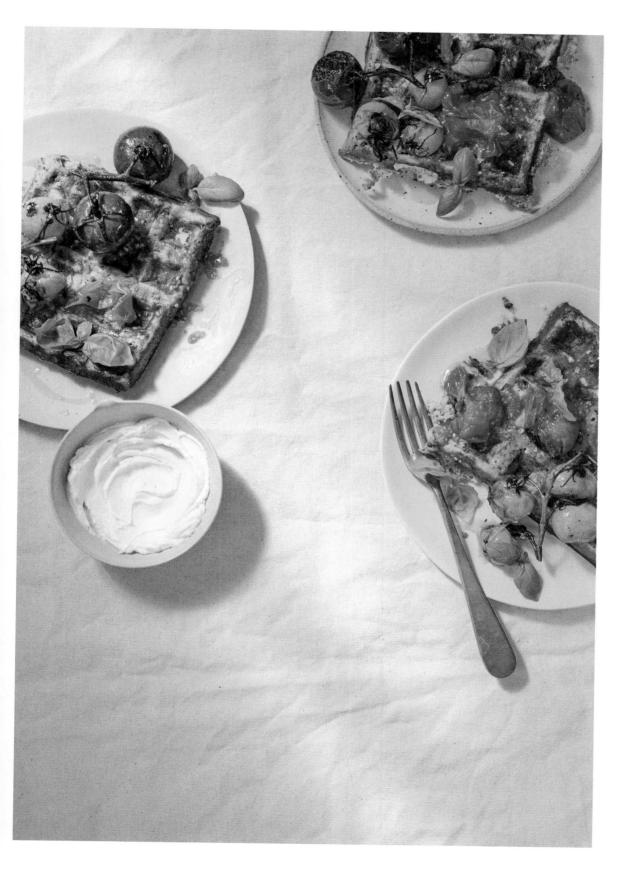

Once the spinach mixture is cool, put it into a sieve and use the back of a spoon to squeeze out any excess liquid. Then, back on the cutting board, roughly chop it.

Add the spinach to the buttermilk and egg, then mix this into the dry ingredients. Season well with salt and pepper. This is your waffle mixture.

Brush your heated waffle iron with a little olive oil and pour a small ladle (about ½ cup/125 ml) of the mixture into each of the bottom waffle wells. (Depending on the size of your waffle maker you may need to add a little more or less.) Close the waffle maker and cook the waffles for 5 to 6 minutes, until golden brown on both sides.

Serve the crisp golden waffles with the roasted tomatoes, the goat cheese and any of the other options below. These waffles freeze well and can be warmed in the oven from frozen.

Topping options

- Avocado mashed with lemon

- Crisp-edged mushrooms

- A spoonful of tomato chutney or the tomato kasundi on page 176

- Spiced refried beans

- Some leaves dressed with lemon and soft goat cheese

Zucchini skordalia

If ever there were a dip to give hummus a run for its money, it's skordalia. Traditionally, it's a Greek dish of mashed, then whipped, potato, spiked with garlic and lemon and a generous amount of olive oil. I make mine with the addition of some buttery slow-cooked zucchini, which adds to the comforting creaminess, and a little bit of veg.

My son eats hummus at almost every meal, so I was keen to find something he loved as much. This is it.

Skordalia should be absolutely smooth—use a potato ricer to mash the potatoes or push the cooked potato through a sieve with the back of a spoon.

Put the potatoes (skins on) into plenty of cold salted water and bring to a boil. Simmer for 25 to 35 minutes, depending on the size of your potatoes.

Put the zucchini in a frying pan with a good drizzle of olive oil and fry over low heat for 20 to 25 minutes, until they have broken down and are buttery and soft.

Meanwhile, chop the garlic finely, add a pinch of salt, and use the side of a knife to crush the garlic into a fine paste.

Once the potatoes are cooked, drain and leave to steam dry. When cool enough to handle, peel them, then push them through a sieve, mouli, or a potato ricer and add the garlic paste.

Once the zucchini is cooked, put it into a blender with half the oil and whizz until completely smooth—you don't want any lumps. You may need to add a little water if it needs loosening.

Bit by bit, beat the zucchini mixture, remaining oil, and lemon juice into the potato mix. Check the skordalia for salt and pepper and place in a bowl. Scatter the toasted almonds on top. Your skordalia should last for 3 to 4 days if kept covered in the fridge.

MAKES ENOUGH FOR A FEW DAYS' DIPPING

10½ ounces (300 g) new potatoes, unpeeled

sea salt

10½ ounces (300 g) zucchini, chopped into ¾-inch (2-cm) slices

9 tablespoons olive oil, plus a little extra to fry the zucchini

2 cloves of garlic

the juice of 1 small lemon

freshly ground black pepper

½ cup (50 g) almonds, toasted and finely chopped

Green baked eggs

Through the winter I make breakfast eggs in a quick, gently spiced tomato sauce, but as the sky gets brighter and the vegetables greener, this is what I make. This is a light, bright, late-spring brunch of baked eggs, slow-cooked zucchini, jarred artichokes (use fresh if you like, though—see Vignarola, page 196), sweet roasted shallots and bright greens, all doused in the sunshine mellow yellow of saffron. It goes without saying that organic, free-range eggs should be used whenever possible—the sunnier the egg, the happier the eater.

In our house some people have two eggs and some one, so the filling and cooking method is generous enough that you can add the number of eggs that suits your eaters' appetites.

SERVES 4

4–5 banana shallots

sea salt

2 tablespoons olive oil

1¼ pounds zucchini, cut into
⅜-inch (1-cm) coins

2 cloves of garlic, crushed

2 heads of spring greens,
finely sliced

4 artichoke hearts from a jar,
drained and halved

a pinch of saffron, soaked in
3½ tablespoons boiling
water

1 tablespoon cider vinegar

4–6 organic eggs, depending
on how hungry you are

TO SERVE

a small bunch of mint

a small bunch of parsley,
chopped

plain yogurt

red pepper flakes

Preheat the oven to 425°F (220°C).

Peel the shallots, then slice them into quarters from root to tip. Warm the olive oil in a heavy, shallow pan that can go in the oven. Add the shallots and a big pinch of salt and lightly brown them on both sides over medium heat.

When the shallots are soft, push them to one side, add the zucchini and garlic to the other side of the pan, and cook for a few minutes until the zucchini begin to turn golden. Depending on the size of your pan, you may need to do this in two or three batches to make sure the zucchini don't overlap as they cook.

Next, add the greens, artichokes, saffron water, cider vinegar, and another pinch of salt; cook for a minute or two until the greens have just wilted, then transfer the whole pan to the oven. Bake the vegetables for 15 minutes to allow the shallots and zucchini to roast and soften, then remove the pan from the oven.

Place the pan over medium heat for 3 minutes to simmer away any excess liquid, then make four, five, or six small, shallow hollows in the vegetables. Crack an egg into each, then return to the oven for 7 to 8 minutes, until the whites are set and the yolks are still runny.

Serve scattered with the mint leaves and parsley, a dollop of yogurt, and a sprinkle of red pepper flakes, if you like.

English garden toasts

These little toasts are a riot of color and represent all that is great about English gardens in the late spring. The first radishes, roasted until they sweeten, the sweet peas, and some allium or chive flowers, if you can get them, add some prettiness as well as a punch of flavor.

These go particularly well with a glass of ice-cold rosé outside on a warm day. I use the dip-dyed pink-and-white breakfast radishes here, but the regular round ones would work really well too. We eat this for a late evening dinner, but I'd proudly serve this as a quick starter too. They are also great at a picnic or a party; just double or triple the recipe for a crowd.

Preheat your oven to 395°F (200°C).

Put the radishes, keeping the tops intact (if you have them), on a baking sheet, drizzle with olive oil, season with salt and pepper, then roast in the oven for 20 minutes, or until the tops are crisp and the radishes have turned a softer, more mellow pink.

Fill the kettle with water and boil. Put your sliced onion in a little bowl with a good pinch of salt and the lemon juice. Scrunch it all together with your hands. Leave to one side to continue to lightly pickle.

Pour the boiling water from the kettle into a small saucepan, add a pinch of salt, and bring to a boil again. Cook the peas for a few minutes, then drain. Mash them a little with a potato masher or in a large mortar with pestle. Add the lemon zest, then a good pinch of salt and black pepper. Finely chop most of the mint (saving a few little leaves for later) and stir through the peas.

Once the radishes are roasted, toast or griddle your bread. Drizzle with a little olive oil or spread with a little salted butter. Pile the peas on the toasted bread, drain the now-bright-purple onions from their liquid, and dot on top of the peas. Crumble the goat cheese on top and scatter with radishes. Finish with the remaining mint and some allium flowers or chopped chives, if you like.

MAKES 4

a bunch of radishes

2 tablespoons olive oil

sea salt and freshly ground black pepper

1 red onion, finely sliced

the zest and juice of ½ unwaxed lemon

1⅓ cups (200 g) podded fresh peas

a small bunch of mint

4 slices of good bread, such as sourdough

salted butter (optional)

3½ ounces soft goat cheese or ricotta

a few allium flowers or chopped chives (optional)

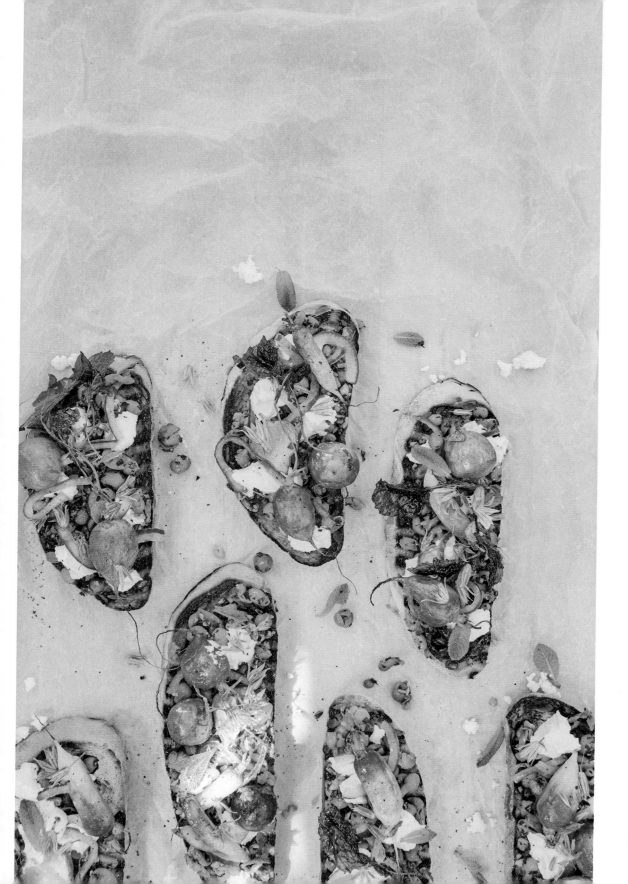

Quick tartines

"Tartine." Such a nice word, isn't it? But whatever you choose to call them—bruschetta, open sandwiches, tartines—many a memorable meal can be made by piling simple ingredients on good bread. Some of my favorite quick meals have come from moments where everything aligns: a few things pulled from the fridge and fruit bowl, then added to bread have turned out unexpectedly triumphant. Here are a few I have remembered to make again.

Honey and pecorino

set honey

good pesto

toasted almonds

arugula

shaved pecorino
   (I use a vegetarian/
   rennet-free one)

lemon juice

Cheddar club

smoked tofu

aged Cheddar

gherkins

crispy romaine lettuce

cherry tomatoes

mustard

mayonnaise

Fridge raid

hummus

harissa

black olives

sun-dried tomatoes

peppery leaves

toasted seeds

Falafel and pickles

smashed falafels

chopped caper berries

tomatoes

hummus

pickled beets

spinach

lemon juice

All green

mashed avocado

feta

cilantro

lime zest

green chile

Full of veg

mung bean sprouts

grated carrot

spinach

mashed avocado

cherry tomatoes

pumpkin seed butter (see page 119)

Asparagus

shaved raw asparagus

avocado

toasted pumpkin seeds

arugula

lemon juice

shaved Parmesan
    (I use a vegetarian/
    rennet-free one)

Beets

grated raw beets

soft goat cheese

toasted almonds

black olives

orange zest

Kale smash

sun-dried tomatoes

kale and lemon juice blitzed to paste

carrot dressed with lemon

mashed butter beans

crunchy lettuce

Asparagus and coconut soup

This is a quick and simple soup that puts asparagus at the center. The greens add a little minerally depth, and the coconut milk some gentle creaminess. I love using coconut milk in soups—it adds silkiness without having to use dairy or cream, and the coconut flavor is subtle when mixed with vegetables. This soup comes together in a very short time, so it's a great spring staple at our house.

It works really well with other green veg too as the seasons change: peas, broccoli, or zucchini. I have suggested my favorite ways to top and adapt it below.

Put a large deep pan over medium-high heat, add the butter and leek, and cook for 10 minutes, stirring, until the leeks are soft and sweet.

Next, add the asparagus, the basil stalks, and the greens and allow to cook for a minute or two, then add the coconut milk and stock and simmer until the asparagus is tender—this should take about 4 to 5 minutes.

Add the basil leaves and blitz in a blender or in the pan with an immersion blender, until the soup is completely silky smooth. Squeeze in the juice of the lemon.

Next, make any adjustments to the soup. Add more water if the soup is too thick, a pinch of salt if needed, or more lemon. Once it is tasting great, ladle it into bowls and top with one of the suggestions below.

SERVES 4

2 tablespoons butter or coconut oil

1 leek, finely chopped

3¾ cups (500 g) asparagus, trimmed and cut into ½-inch (1.5-cm) pieces

a small bunch of basil, leaves picked, stalks finely chopped

13 cups (400 g) spinach or greens

1 × 14.5-ounce (400 ml) can of coconut milk

2 cups (500 ml) vegetable stock

1 lemon

Topping ideas

- Toasted coconut flakes and a drizzle of olive oil

- Little basil leaves and a little coconut milk

- Some pan-crisped white beans and lime zest

- Some chopped mint, lemon zest, and yogurt

- Grated hard-boiled egg and some spring herbs

- Lots of toasted sesame seeds and some pan-fried tofu

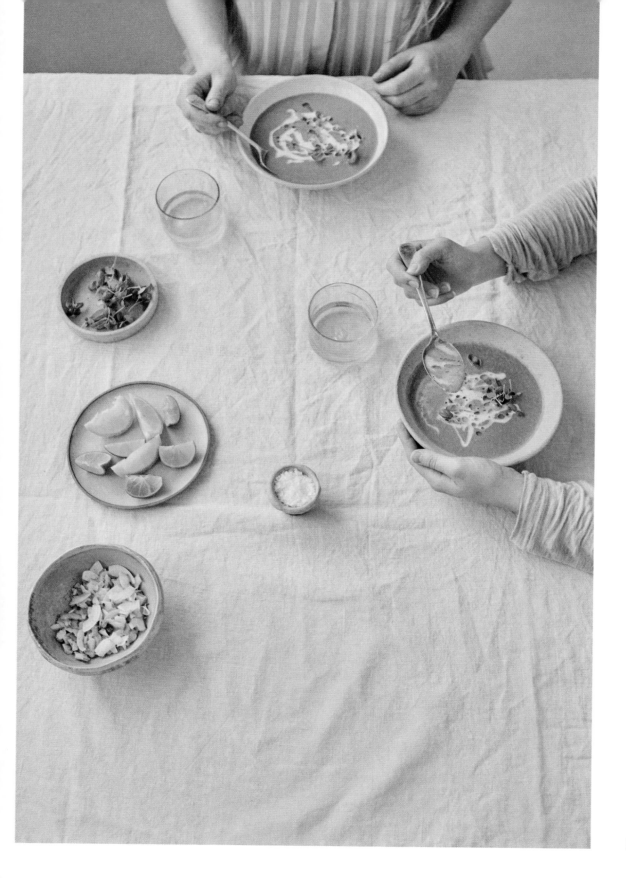

Four-herb and yogurt soup

Four soft green herbs make an appearance in this soup—dill, tarragon, cilantro, and parsley—but really any combination of your favorite soft herbs would work. This soup is light and optimistic in flavor with lemon and herbs, but backed up with butter beans and yogurt for some sustenance. The freshness of the herbs is answered by some anchoring spice: cumin, cilantro, and fennel. It's a pleasing yin and yang balance, and a great soup for filling that gap between the very cold and the warmer days. Vegans can use coconut yogurt here.

SERVES 4

olive oil

1 onion, finely chopped

2 stalks of celery, finely sliced

sea salt and freshly ground black pepper

½ a small bunch of dill

½ a small bunch of tarragon

a bunch of cilantro

a bunch of flat-leaf parsley

2 cloves of garlic, peeled and finely sliced

1 teaspoon ground cumin

1½ teaspoons cilantro (coriander) seeds

1 teaspoon fennel seeds

1 × 14.5-ounce (400-g) can of butter beans, drained

4½ cups (1 liter) weak vegetable stock

4 tablespoons Greek yogurt

the juice of 1 lemon

sumac, to serve

Heat a good glug of oil in a large saucepan over medium heat. Add the onion and celery, season with salt and pepper, and fry for about 5 minutes, stirring from time to time, until the onion is really soft and translucent. Meanwhile, separate and roughly chop the herb stalks.

Once the onions are soft and sweet, add the garlic, spices, and chopped stalks, then cook for another 2 to 3 minutes, until everything smells great.

Add the butter beans and the stock to the pan, then bring to a simmer and cook for 5 minutes.

Allow to cool a little, then blitz with an immersion blender in the pan until you have a really smooth soup. Add the yogurt and most of the herb leaves (reserving a few for garnishing the soup) and whizz again, until smooth.

Add the lemon juice and taste, adjusting the seasoning by adding more salt or pepper or lemon if you think it's needed. Ladle the soup into bowls and top with a sprinkling of sumac and a few of the reserved herbs.

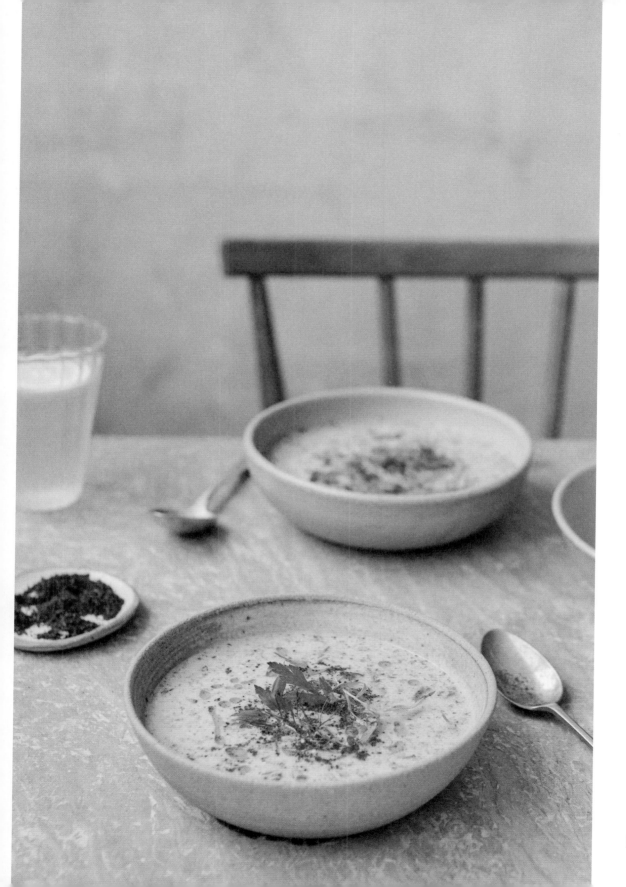

Charred zucchini with mozzarella and lovage

Zucchini starts showing up when the days get warmer, and stays around for most of the summer. I cooked this on a hot and heavy day early last year, at a supper club, and it's now a meal I regularly dream of. The sweetness of the charred zucchini paired with the cool, calm, and creamy mozzarella and the verdant hit from the lovage is pure joy. It was the brainchild of the brilliant Robbin Holmgren, the head chef at Fifteen London. I am sure his version is much fancier, but this is how I do it at home.

The lovage oil is the crowning glory and simpler than you might think, though a good pesto would work too. Any leftover oil can be kept in a jar in the fridge for a few weeks. A mixture of parsley and celery leaves will also work.

First, make the lovage oil. Fill a bowl with boiling water and another with cold. Plunge the lovage into the boiling water, scoop it out immediately, and immerse in the cold water to cool. Pat dry with paper towels; this keeps the lovage green.

Put the lovage in a food processor or blender, add the olive oil and a small pinch of salt, then blend until really smooth. Leave the food processor running for at least a couple of minutes to extract as much flavor from the lovage as possible. Pass the oil through a sieve, then transfer to a jar and set aside. Push any herb in the sieve down with a spoon to squeeze out the most flavor.

Next, heat your grill (or griddle) until it's smoking hot. While it heats up, cut your bigger zucchini into ⅜-inch (1-cm) rounds and smaller ones into long slices or just in half. Once hot, char your zucchini on both sides until nicely charred and softened a little in the middle. This will take longer on a griddle, but try not to move them around too much—otherwise, the char marks won't form in even lines. About 2 to 3 minutes each side should do the trick, even less on a grill.

Serve the charred zucchini alongside the mozzarella, torn into pieces, and finish with a little sea salt, black pepper, a drizzle of the lovage oil, and torn zucchini flowers if using.

SERVES 4

a bunch of lovage

6 tablespoons good extra-virgin olive oil

sea salt

6 zucchini (I mix yellow and green)

2 balls of buffalo mozzarella or burrata

TO FINISH (OPTIONAL)

sea salt and freshly ground black pepper

some zucchini flowers

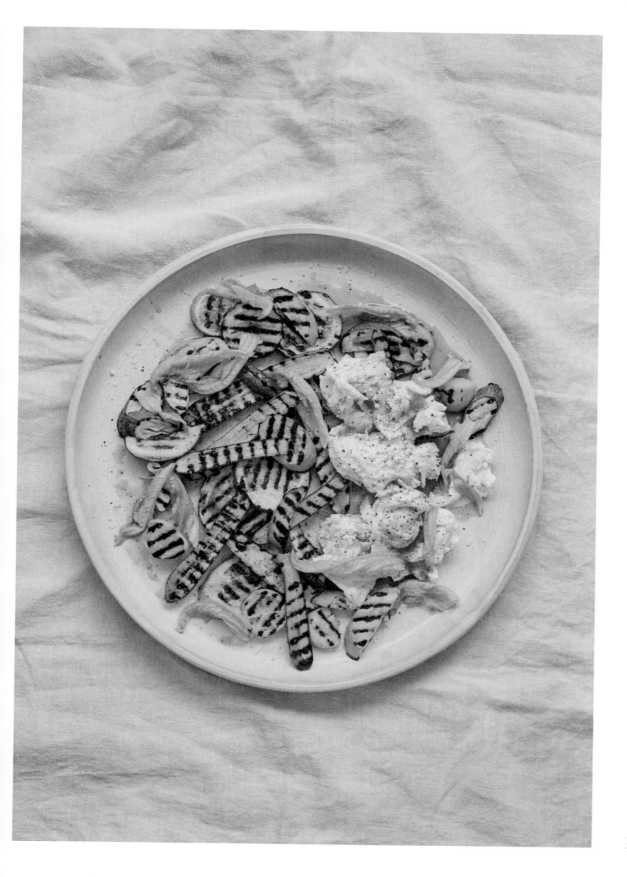

Elderflower fava bean toasts

I love elderflowers. When the floaty little blooms show up all over the parks near where I live, I know that the first days of summer are here. These toasts have a lot going on: The sweet but slightly sharp elderflower contrasts with delicate leaves (I use a mixture of arugula and pea shoots), milky burrata, and the smokiness of the charred sourdough. You can make the salad and dressing ahead of time and keep them in the fridge, but make sure you grill the toast at the last minute.

SERVES 6

a good loaf of sourdough bread

FOR THE SALAD

10½ ounces (300 g) fava beans

14 ounces (400 g) delicate salad leaves

a drizzle of good extra-virgin olive oil

1 unwaxed lemon

10½ ounces (300 g) burrata or good buffalo mozzarella

FOR THE DRESSING

3 tablespoons elderflower and rose cordial (see page 221)

1 tablespoon white wine vinegar

4 tablespoons extra-virgin olive oil

sea salt and freshly ground black pepper

TO FINISH (OPTIONAL)

some fresh elderflowers

First, blanch your fava beans in boiling water for 2 to 4 minutes, depending on their size, then drain and leave to cool. Once cool, peel the bitter skins from each one unless they are small and sweet, in which case you can leave them on.

Heat a griddle on your stovetop's highest heat.

Next, make your dressing by mixing all the ingredients in a pitcher, season well with salt and pepper and leave to one side.

Carefully pick through your salad leaves, wash and dry them well, then put them in a bowl with the fava beans.

Slice the sourdough loaf into ½-inch- (1.5-cm-) thick slices and grill them until they have nice char marks on both sides. Drizzle all the toasts with olive oil, grate over the zest of the lemon, and season well with salt. Put the toasts on a big platter or individual plates and tear over the burrata or mozzarella. Dress the leaves and fava beans with the elderflower dressing and pile on top of each toast. Finish with a scattering of confetti-like elderflowers if you like.

172

Butter lettuce and buttermilk dressing

SERVES 4

FOR THE SALAD

2 slices of sourdough bread

2 heads of butter lettuce, washed and dried

⅓ cup (50 g) almonds, skin on and chopped

FOR THE BUTTERMILK DRESSING

½ cup (125 ml) buttermilk (or see note above)

1 teaspoon golden honey

2 tablespoons extra-virgin olive oil

the zest and juice of 1 unwaxed lemon

a bunch of chives, finely chopped

sea salt and fresh ground black pepper

This is my dream salad. I crave simple butter lettuce, and there is no better way to eat it than with a buttermilk dressing. Sometimes I just cut the lettuce into wedges and pour over the dressing; other times I pick the individual leaves. This salad sits well next to pretty much anything you might eat a salad with. I serve it as a simple start to a meal sometimes, and even as a light meal through spring and summer too.

This time of year sees some of the first local lettuces appear. I would encourage you to buy them whole. I use butter here, but oakleaf, lollo rosso, frisée, or a mix of more delicate leaves would all work well too. You can use yogurt thinned with a splash of milk if you can't get your hands on buttermilk.

———————————

Heat a griddle over high heat for a few minutes to get the pan really hot. Grill the sourdough slices for a couple of minutes on each side until they are toasted and have dark char marks. Be bold here, as the charring imparts a smokiness that works as a great foil to the delicate lettuce and dressing.

Make the dressing. Whisk all the ingredients together in a pitcher or shake in a tightly sealed jam jar. Taste and add salt and pepper to season.

Quarter the lettuce, then lay on a platter and drizzle over the dressing. Tear the charred toasts into rough chunks and scatter over the lettuce, then sprinkle over the almonds. Serve immediately.

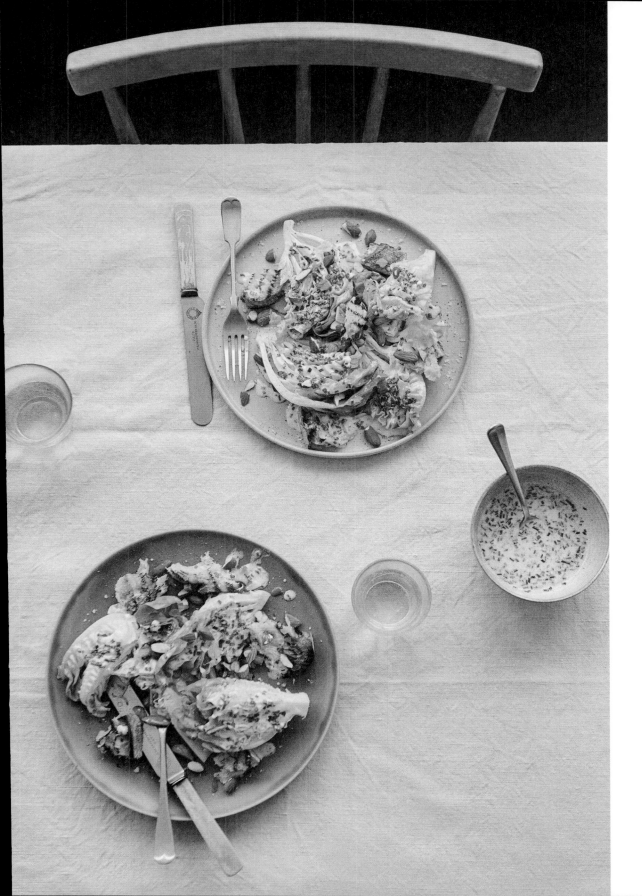

New potato tortilla with halloumi and tomato kasundi

I ate something like this at a café near where I live, then went back twice in the following weeks for the same thing, until I realized I should probably just figure out how to make it myself. It was spring, so I used new potatoes instead of the sweet potatoes the café had gone for. I have kept my tortilla pretty simple, but you could also add any other spring or summer veg that you like.

The real star here is the tomato kasundi, which is an insanely good Indian tomato relish. It is a variation of kasundi, which is originally a sauce made from fermented mustard seeds. Mine is not much like the original. This recipe makes more kasundi than you will need, so your efforts will be rewarded beyond just one dinner. I have also suggested a few favorite ways to use the kasundi you are left with. If you don't have time to make it, a good tomato relish would work.

I cook some halloumi here to sit with the tortilla. I realize I am crossing a few continents, but I don't really mind; it's a great combination.

SERVES 4

FOR THE TOMATO
KASUNDI

2 tablespoons coconut or
  olive oil

1 tablespoon black mustard
  seeds

1 teaspoon ground turmeric

a small thumb-size piece of
  ginger, peeled and grated

1 green chile, finely chopped

2 cloves of garlic, finely
  chopped

1 teaspoon cumin seeds

1 × 14.5-ounce (400-g) can of
  chopped tomatoes

1½ tablespoons light brown or
  coconut sugar

½ teaspoon flaky sea salt

2 tablespoons cider
  vinegar →

First make the kasundi. Melt the coconut oil in a large frying pan over medium heat and add the mustard seeds. Cook until they start to pop, then add the turmeric, ginger, chile, garlic, and cumin seeds. Fry for a minute, until everything smells fragrant.

Add the tomatoes, sugar, salt, and vinegar and turn the heat down. Simmer gently for 45 minutes to 1 hour, stirring occasionally. When the oil rises to the top of the pan, the kasundi is ready.

While the kasundi is gently cooking, melt the tablespoon of coconut oil in a large ovenproof frying pan (I use one that's 11 inches/ 28 cm) over medium heat and add the red onions. Cook for 6 to 8 minutes, stirring regularly, until the onions are completely soft and sweet, then add the potatoes along with the fennel seeds and a pinch of salt. →

Cook for 20 minutes, stirring from time to time, until the potatoes are soft and yielding but beginning to crisp at the edges.

Meanwhile, finely chop the cilantro stalks and add these to the pan too. After the potatoes have had their time, add the red pepper flakes, lime zest, and spinach and cook for another 2 to 3 minutes, until the spinach has completely wilted.

Beat the eggs in a small bowl with a pinch of salt and pour into the frying pan. Turn the grill on. Cook the tortilla on medium heat on the stove for 8 minutes, then place under the hot grill for another 4 minutes to finish and brown the top.

While the tortilla is cooking, fry the halloumi in a nonstick frying pan for a couple of minutes on each side, until golden brown.

Serve the tortilla in wedges, with a couple of slices of halloumi and a spoonful of tomato kasundi. Finish with the cilantro leaves and wedges of lime, and a few salad leaves if you like.

Ways to use your kasundi

- Stir it in fried rice and top with a fried egg

- In a grilled cheese sandwich

- In a wrap with falafel and salad

- Stir it in some mashed potatoes

- Use it to dress cooked green beans

1 tablespoon coconut or olive oil

2 red onions, finely sliced

1¾ pounds (800 g) new potatoes, sliced ¼ inch (0.5 cm) thick

1 teaspoon fennel seeds, roughly bashed

a few sprigs of cilantro

a pinch of red pepper flakes

the zest of 1 unwaxed lime, plus an extra lime cut into wedges

3⅓ cups (100 g) spinach

6 organic eggs

8¾ ounces (250 g) halloumi, sliced into ⅜-inch- (1-cm-) thick pieces

salad leaves, to serve (optional)

Sorrel quinoa bowl with crispy greens

This is a take on a brunch dish I ate at one of my favorite L.A. spots. It makes the most of sorrel and is fine late-spring or early-summer eating. At Sqirl they serve it with rice and make it much fancier, but this is how I make it. If you can't get sorrel, any spring herb would work: basil, dill, or lovage. The flavor will be different, but all the other elements are quite neutral here; it's the sorrel oil that does the talking, so you can confidently swap it for another herb. Vegans, try this with some pan-fried tofu (see page 28), adding a squeeze of honey to the pan just as you take it off the heat.

    I toast quinoa before I cook it, as this gives it a deeper, nutty flavor that I really love. Be sure to use a mild-flavored extra-virgin olive oil for the sorrel oil—a peppery one will overpower the lemoniness of the sorrel.

First, make the pickled radishes. Mix the radishes in a large bowl with the lemon juice, vinegar, salt, and honey and scrunch well with your hands to speed up the pickling. Place a plate over the top of the bowl and set aside.

Meanwhile, rinse the quinoa in a sieve. Fill the kettle with water and boil. Heat a pan over medium heat, add the quinoa, and cook until the residual water has evaporated and it has begun to smell toasty. Cover it with double the volume of boiling water from the kettle and add a good pinch of salt. Bring the pan to a boil over a high heat, then turn the heat down to low. Let the quinoa simmer for 15 minutes, until all the water has been absorbed and the germ comes away from the seed.

Meanwhile, make the sorrel oil by blitzing the sorrel in a blender with the olive oil and salt. Taste, and add lemon juice if you like a really punchy lemony flavor.

Bring a pot of water to a boil and lower in the eggs. Turn the heat down to a simmer and cook for 6 minutes with the lid on. →

SERVES 4

FOR THE PICKLED RADISHES

15 radishes, thinly sliced

the juice of ½ a lemon

1 tablespoon white wine vinegar

1 teaspoon fine sea salt

a squeeze of honey or maple syrup

1 cup (200 g) quinoa

4 organic eggs

olive oil

2½ cups (100 g) spring greens

⅓ cup (50 g) pumpkin seeds

a pinch of flaky sea salt

the zest of ½ an unwaxed lemon

FOR THE SORREL OIL

a large bunch of sorrel (about 1⅓ cups/50 g)

6 tablespoons mild extra-virgin olive oil

a small pinch of flaky sea salt

½ lemon (optional)

179

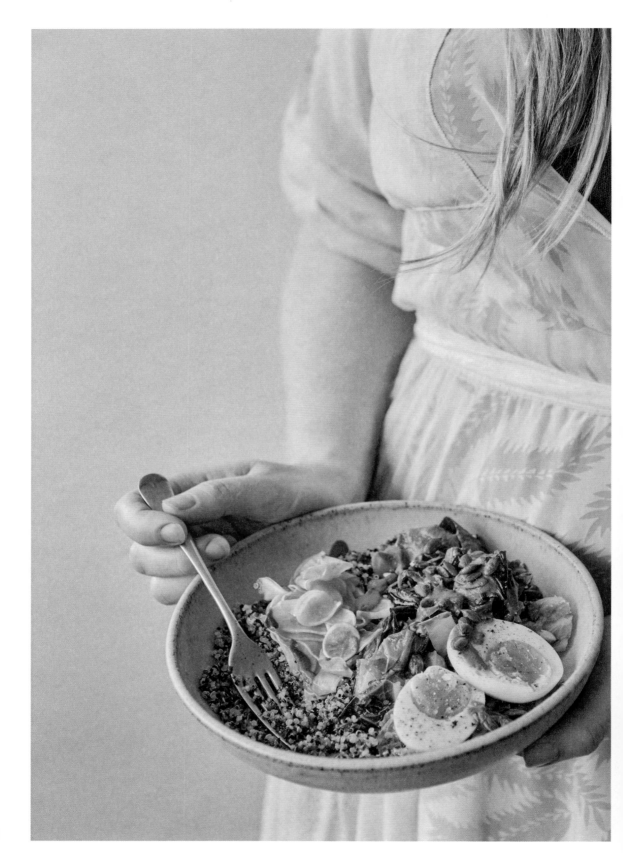

While the eggs are cooking, place a frying pan over medium heat with a little olive oil. Tear any tough stems from the greens and roughly shred them. Add to the pan along with the pumpkin seeds and a little salt and cook until the pumpkin seeds start to pop and the greens have turned a deeper green and are starting to crisp at the edges. Take the pan off the heat and stir in the lemon zest.

When the quinoa is cooked and all the liquid has evaporated, take the pan off the heat, leave covered for 5 minutes, then fluff up with a fork.

Once the eggs have had their time, remove them with a slotted spoon, tap on a hard surface to break the shells, then run them under cold water until they are cool enough to handle. Peel the shells away, then cut each one in half.

Drain the pickled radishes and roughly chop them into small pieces, about the size of the pumpkin seeds.

Divide the quinoa among four bowls and top with the greens, followed by the pickled radishes and the eggs. Spoon over the sorrel oil and serve warm.

Flash-roasted green veg

It may seem a bit unusual to roast fava beans in their pods, but do give it a try. The pods sweeten, soften, and char all at once, keeping the sweet little beans nestled safely inside, and you can eat the whole pod so nothing is wasted. I use the long, thin, pale, lime-green Turkish peppers here as they are readily available in the market near where I live, but if you can't find them, then a couple of normal green peppers, deseeded and cut into chunky strips, will do.

I like to use jarred chickpeas, as I find them to be more carefully cooked and hence more tender than canned. The pulses tend to be bigger than those in the 14.5-ounce (400 g) cans, so use about 10.5 ounces (300 g) of drained jarred chickpeas, if you can get your hands on them.

_____

SERVES 4

8 thin green Turkish peppers

4 red onions, cut into thin wedges

8 fava bean pods

4 bunches Little Gem lettuce, halved

a bunch of radishes

a bunch of scallions

sea salt and freshly ground black pepper

Turkish chile powder (pul biber)

extra-virgin olive oil

7 ounces (200 g) feta

1 × 14.5-ounce (400 g) can of chickpeas, drained

the zest and juice of 1 unwaxed lemon

a small bunch of thyme

2 cloves of garlic, finely chopped

Yogurt flatbread (see page 456)

FOR THE DRESSING

a small bunch of mint

a small bunch of dill

a small bunch of flat-leaf parsley

a splash of white wine vinegar

1 teaspoon maple syrup

Preheat your oven to 425°F (220°C).

Put all the vegetables on a baking sheet—you may need two if you have smaller ones—then season liberally with salt and pepper and sprinkle over 2 good pinches of the pul biber. Drizzle generously with olive oil and put into the very hot oven to roast for 25 minutes. You want the oven to be quite fiercely hot, so that everything will char. Turn your vegetables a couple of times while they cook.

On another baking sheet, lay the whole block of feta on one side and the chickpeas on the other. Drizzle a splash of oil over the chickpeas and toss to coat. Top the feta with a little more pul biber, half the lemon zest, and the thyme tips. Put this into the oven on the rack underneath the veg.

Meanwhile, make the dressing. Chop all the herbs and put them in a bowl with the remaining lemon zest and almost all the juice, plus 4 tablespoons of olive oil, the vinegar, and the maple syrup.

When the vegetables are nearly done, squeeze the last of the lemon juice over the top, scatter with the garlic, and return the baking sheet to the oven for a couple of minutes.

Serve the roasted vegetables, topped with chickpeas, chunks of feta, the herb dressing, and Turkish flatbread.

How to make a hearty salad

1	2	3
Start with some leaves	**Add a hero vegetable**	**Add some texture**
(2 handfuls per person)	(½ a handful per person)	(a small handful per person)

spinach	roasted squash	olive oil–baked croutons
arugula	pickled beets	mixed toasted seeds
Little Gem	seasoned tomatoes	chopped toasted nuts (see page 459)
radicchio	roasted leeks	crumbled tortilla chips
mustard leaf	avocado	sprouted lentils and beans
shredded kale	sliced radishes	pomegranate seeds
shredded spring greens	zucchini "noodles"	flash-fried bread crumbs
	grated carrots	crushed poppadoms

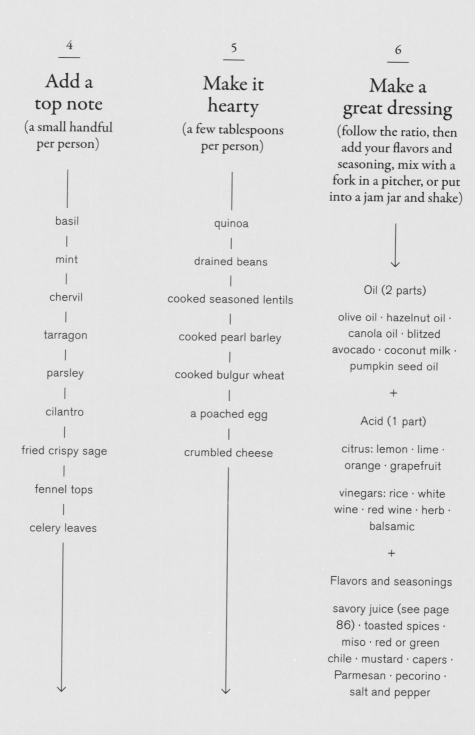

4

Add a top note

(a small handful per person)

basil

mint

chervil

tarragon

parsley

cilantro

fried crispy sage

fennel tops

celery leaves

5

Make it hearty

(a few tablespoons per person)

quinoa

drained beans

cooked seasoned lentils

cooked pearl barley

cooked bulgur wheat

a poached egg

crumbled cheese

6

Make a great dressing

(follow the ratio, then add your flavors and seasoning, mix with a fork in a pitcher, or put into a jam jar and shake)

Oil (2 parts)

olive oil · hazelnut oil · canola oil · blitzed avocado · coconut milk · pumpkin seed oil

+

Acid (1 part)

citrus: lemon · lime · orange · grapefruit

vinegars: rice · white wine · red wine · herb · balsamic

+

Flavors and seasonings

savory juice (see page 86) · toasted spices · miso · red or green chile · mustard · capers · Parmesan · pecorino · salt and pepper

185

Golden six-spice paneer with lime pickle and smashed peas

I recently developed an obsession with paneer—its calm flavor and pleasing bouncy texture, the way it softens ever so slightly when it cooks but still holds its shape. What I do struggle with, though, is buying paneer made with good organic milk; I have found only one shop that sells it, so I often make my own. It's really very easy.

What I love most about paneer is its ability to take on flavor. Here I marinate it in six spices, then dry-fry it until it's crisp and golden. It sits next to a quick pea and coconut smash and an Indian slaw mixed with a clever little lime pickle that punctuates the slaw with little sherbet lime pops. I use fresh peas here, but you could use frozen if you like. This recipe also works well on a grill if it's warm enough to eat outside.

SERVES 4

FOR THE PICKLE

2 unwaxed limes

1 tablespoon cumin seeds

1 teaspoon flaky sea salt

1 teaspoon superfine or caster sugar

FOR THE PANEER

14 ounces (400 g) paneer, sliced into ¾-inch- (2-cm-) thick slices

2 tablespoons canola or mild olive oil

1 teaspoon Kashmiri chile powder

½ teaspoon ground turmeric

1 heaping teaspoon cumin seeds, ground

1 heaping teaspoon cilantro (coriander) seeds, ground

½ teaspoon fennel seeds, ground

a good grind of black pepper

½ teaspoon flaky sea salt →

To make the pickle, lightly peel the zest from the limes in long strips with a speed peeler. Put them into a saucepan and squeeze in their juice, then add the cumin seeds, salt, and sugar. Bring to a boil over high heat, then turn the heat down to low and simmer for 10 minutes, until the strips of zest have shrunk and started to curl at the edges. Once it's had its time, take it off the heat and leave to cool.

Toss the paneer in the canola oil and all the remaining paneer ingredients and leave it to sit while you get on with a couple of other things.

While the pickle is cooking, fill the kettle with water and boil, and place the peas in a bowl. Cover them with boiling water and set aside for a few minutes. Heat a frying pan over medium heat and add a splash of oil, then the garlic, ginger, chile, and red onion, and sauté for a few minutes until everything is soft and sweet and smells fragrant. →

186

FOR THE PEA SMASH

1⅓ cups (200 g) podded
    fresh peas

canola or mild olive oil

2 cloves of garlic, finely
    chopped

a small thumb-size piece of
    ginger, peeled and grated

1 green chile, finely chopped

1 small red onion, roughly
    chopped

the zest and juice of
    1 unwaxed lime

sea salt and freshly ground
    black pepper

1¾ ounces (50 g) creamed
    coconut

FOR THE SLAW

½ spring cabbage

1 large beet (I use a pink
    candy cane one)

1 crisp red apple

2 scallions

2 tablespoons mild olive oil

the juice of 1 lemon

TO SERVE

4 rotis or chapatis

Drain the peas well and return them to the bowl, then add the onion mixture (keeping the pan to use later), the lime zest and juice, and a good pinch of salt and pepper. Crush the peas with a fork or a potato masher and grate the creamed coconut over the top. Stir the coconut through and check the seasoning. Set aside until you're ready to eat.

Next, make the slaw by removing the tough core from the cabbage (discard it). Shred the leaves finely and put them into a mixing bowl.

Peel the beet and grate it on the coarse side of a box grater, or cut it into small matchsticks and add it to the bowl. Grate the apple into the bowl, discarding the core and seeds. Slice the scallions finely and mix them through as well. Remove the pickled lime from the saucepan and chop it finely. Add this to the bowl with the oil and half the lemon juice and toss to mix well. Taste and add more salt, pepper, and lemon juice as needed.

For the paneer, put the frying pan back over medium heat and fry the slices for about 3 minutes on each side, until they are beginning to crisp and have turned a deep golden brown all over (you may need to do this in batches depending on the size of your pan).

Warm the rotis or chapatis in another dry frying pan or over an open flame, using tongs to hold them. Place bread on each plate and spread a generous layer of pea smash down the center. Put two or three pieces of crispy, spiced paneer on top and a heaping spoon of the slaw. Fold the sides over and eat while the paneer is warm.

Sri Lankan green bean and tomato curry

Where I live in London, Sri Lankan food is having its moment in the sun. There have been a flurry of restaurants opening, serving traditional Sri Lankan hoppers and egg curries. This is a curry my friend Emily told me she'd eaten on a trip to Sri Lanka. It's a great thing to make with a glut of green beans, a curry that is even better the next day. If you want a really filling curry, you could stir in some cooked lentils, sprouted mung beans, or a can of black-eyed peas just before serving.

This makes a jarful of Sri Lankan–style curry powder, which I keep on my spice shelf, where it will last for a couple of months. It is deep and smoky and uses some roasted rice too, which adds an amazing crunch, and as the spices are already toasted, you can use it to top hummus or mix it with a little olive oil for a spicy dip for bread. If it sounds like too much, you can cut the quantity in half easily. I have suggested some other ways I like to use it on page 191.

First, make the curry powder. Place the rice in a dry nonstick pan. Heat over medium heat, until the rice starts to turn light brown. Add the spices and roast them for 3 to 5 minutes, until they start to brown, toast, and become aromatic. Keep moving the pan to prevent the spices from burning. Remove from the heat and stir in the lemon zest, then leave to cool down.

Once the spices are cool, use a spice grinder (or a mortar and pestle) to grind them into a powder—you might need to do this in a few batches.

Next, on to the curry. Fry your onions in a little coconut oil until soft and sweet—it will take about 10 minutes. Once they are soft, add the garlic and turmeric and cook for another few minutes, until the garlic is starting to color a little. →

SERVES 4

FOR THE CURRY POWDER

2 tablespoons basmati rice

4 tablespoons cilantro (coriander) seeds

3 tablespoons cumin seeds

2 tablespoons black peppercorns

1 tablespoon black mustard seeds

2 teaspoons whole cloves

1 heaping teaspoon cardamom seeds (from the pods)

1 heaping teaspoon fennel seeds

the zest of 2 unwaxed lemons

2 onions, roughly chopped

coconut oil

4 cloves of garlic, finely sliced

1 heaping teaspoon ground turmeric

2 tablespoons brown mustard seeds

20 fresh curry leaves

1 pound string beans

1 × 14.5-ounce (400-ml) can of coconut milk

4 tomatoes, roughly chopped

⅔ cup (50 g) coconut flakes

the zest and juice of 1 unwaxed lime

TO SERVE

cooked basmati rice, rotis, or flatbread

189

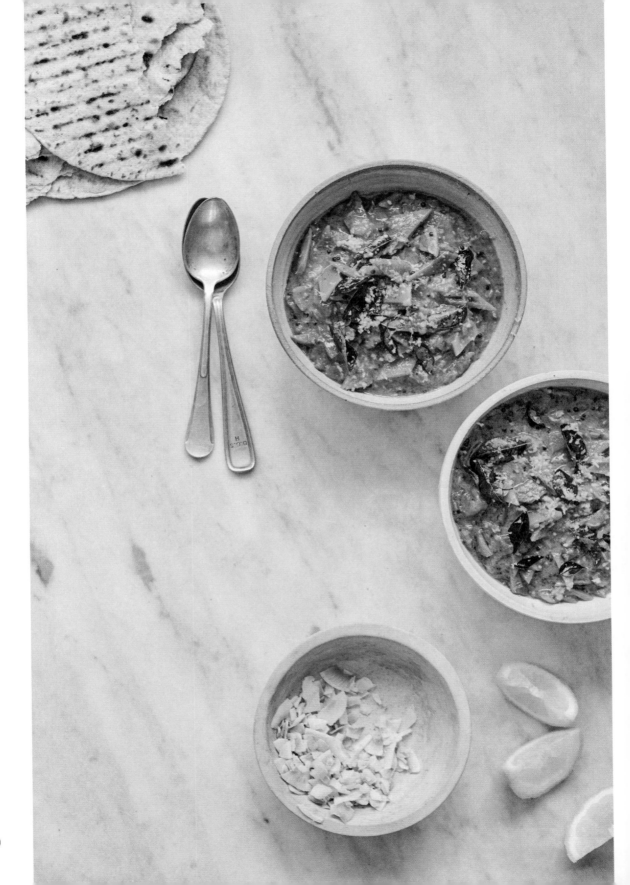

Next, add the mustard seeds and curry leaves and cook until the seeds start to pop, then take them off the heat. Add 2 tablespoons of the curry powder and stir for a minute, until it has lost its rawness. The rest can be stored in an airtight container for up to 2 months.

Meanwhile, peel the rough strings from the edges of the string beans and then chop the beans at an angle into ⅜-inch (1-cm) pieces. Add to the pan with the coconut milk and tomatoes and cook for 15 minutes, until the beans are soft.

While the curry is cooking, toast the coconut flakes in a dry frying pan until golden, then add the lime zest and a pinch of salt.

Once the curry is ready, add the lime juice and take it off the heat. Serve the curry ladled into bowls, with the coconut flakes sprinkled on top, and some rice or flatbread on the side.

Ways to use your curry powder

- as a killer base for a curry (obviously)

- to top hummus

- mixed with olive oil and garlic as a quick dip for bread or veg

- scattered over a baking sheet of veg before it goes into the oven to roast

- scattered over a cucumber and tomato salad

- tossed over some pan-fried paneer

- sprinkled on top of some lemon mashed avocado on toast

Lemon and fennel seed pizzettes

I love the combination of fennel, chile, and lemon and it's well used in my kitchen—it gives these pizzette a freshness that so suits this time of year. We are lucky enough to have a pizza oven that lives in our small garden, so when the sun is out, we make the little pizzas in there; you can mimic the effect by setting your oven to its highest heat and preheating a heavy baking sheet or pizza stone.

These little pizzette are white, so they have no tomato, just the clean, simple slices of lemon that crisp and burnish in the oven, and some milky mozzarella with a hit of fennel from the quick salt. I make these for a crowd, but you can scale the recipe back and make it for fewer without too much hassle. For the dough, I have given you two options: a slow sourdough, and a quick no-prove pizza dough that yields a result far better than the effort you have put in.

MAKES 12 SMALL PIZZAS

3 lemons, very finely sliced, ideally using a mandoline

1 tablespoon fennel seeds, smashed

a good pinch of red pepper flakes

1 tablespoon flaky sea salt

flour, for dusting

1 batch sourdough or 2 × quick pizza dough (see page 457), rested and divided into 4 balls

olive oil

3 × 5¼-ounce (150-g) balls of mozzarella, roughly torn

a large bunch of basil, leaves picked

Arugula and other salad leaves or basil leaves and edible nasturtiums (organic/nonsprayed), to finish

Preheat your oven to its highest temperature (500°F/260°C for most ovens) and put a pizza or baking stone inside if you have one. Put the lemon slices in a bowl and cover with boiling water, leave for 1 minute, then drain. Mix the fennel with the red pepper flakes and salt and put in a small bowl.

Sprinkle a little flour on the work surface. Take a ball of pizza dough and divide it into 3 pieces. Roll a small ball of dough into an oval or round, pulling and stretching the dough, until it is as large as your hand. Repeat with a few more balls, then take a break while you start topping and baking the first batch of pizzas.

Once the first bases are ready, brush each with a little olive oil, then top with a little torn mozzarella, a few lemon slices, a sprinkling of the fennel salt, and a scattering of basil leaves. Put on the hot baking stone and cook for 6 to 8 minutes, until blistering and golden. When the pizzas come out of the oven, top each one with arugula and salad leaves.

Return to the rolling when the first batch has gone into the oven and continue until all 12 pizzas have been baked.

One-pan pea, lemon, and asparagus pasta

This pasta is a complete revelation. It's been one of the most popular recipes from my *Guardian* column, so I wanted to include it here. The sauce is magically made from the pasta water and asparagus as the pasta cooks—all in one pan. No fuss, and a killer bowl of pasta.

The key to this recipe is to measure your water carefully and use the right pan: You need a large, shallow sauté pan or a casserole dish large enough to fit the pasta lying down. A large, deep frying pan or wok would work too. Keep tossing the pasta as it cooks to keep it from sticking, as there is less water than you might be used to. Make sure your pasta is a type that cooks in 8 minutes; any longer will need water and more cooking.

I use sorrel here. It's a bright green, lemony, almost juicy leaf that I love. Be sure to add it if you can get your hands on it. If not, use watercress. The flavor will be more peppery than the sprightly lemon tang of sorrel, but both work beautifully.

Fill a kettle with water and boil, and get all your ingredients and equipment together. If you are using spinach or watercress, scrunch it between your hands with a little lemon juice and a pinch of salt.

SERVES 4

3½ ounces (100 g) sorrel or watercress or spinach

2 large unwaxed lemons

14 ounces (400 g) spaghetti or linguine

14 ounces (400 g) asparagus

1 clove of garlic, thinly sliced

7 ounces (200 g) fresh podded or frozen peas

3½ fluid ounces (100 ml) olive oil

1 teaspoon flaky sea salt

a small bunch of basil or mint

1½ ounces (40 g) freshly grated Parmesan (I use a vegetarian/rennet-free one)

Put the pasta into a pan. Snap the woody ends off the asparagus and chop the stalks into ¼-inch rounds, leaving the tips intact. Put the tips to one side and throw the rounds into the pan along with the garlic and peas. Grate in the zest of both lemons and add the oil and salt. Add 4½ cups (1 liter) of boiling water, put a lid on the pan and bring to a boil. As soon as it comes to the boil, remove the lid and simmer on a high heat for 8 minutes, using a pair of tongs to turn the pasta every 30 seconds or so as it cooks.

Meanwhile, remove any big stalks from the watercress (if using). Once the pasta has had 8 minutes, take the lid off and stir in the asparagus tips, the sorrel, and the basil or mint. Squeeze in the juice of 1 lemon and simmer for a final 2 minutes.

Once almost all the water has evaporated, take the pan off the heat and leave to sit for a minute or two, so the pasta can absorb most of the remaining water and form a lemony sauce. Tangle into four bowls and top with a little Parmesan.

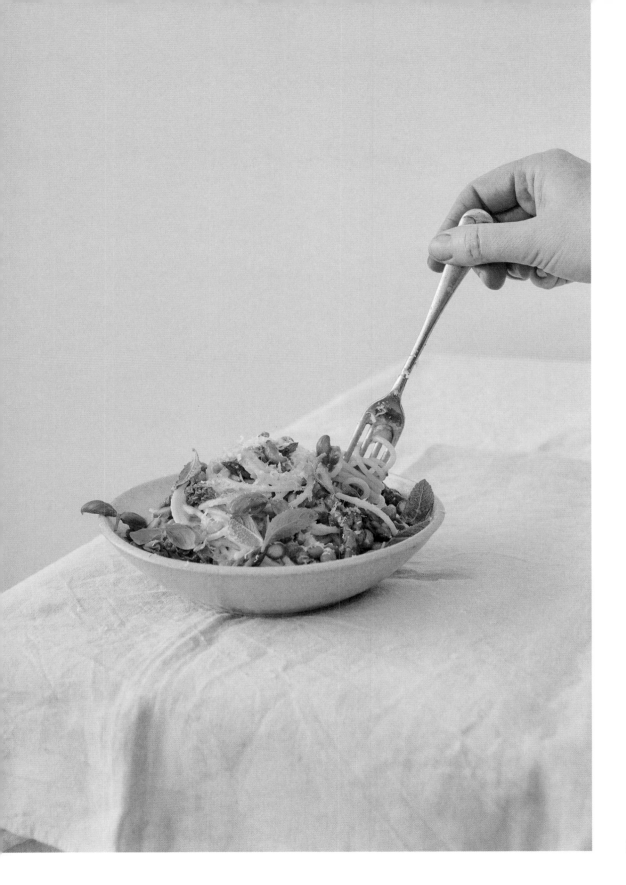

Late-spring stew of artichokes, peas, and herbs

SERVES 4

8 small violet artichokes

sea salt

12¼ ounces (350 g) podded
fresh baby fava beans

7 ounces (200 g) spinach or
chard

a few slices of good seeded
bread

extra-virgin olive oil

2 small white onions, finely
chopped

1 leek, shredded

2½ cups (350 g) podded
fresh peas

the zest and juice of
1 unwaxed lemon

1 teaspoon smoked salt

freshly ground black pepper

a small bunch of fresh
mint, leaves picked and
chopped

a small bunch of fresh flat-leaf
parsley, leaves picked and
chopped

a few chive flowers, to serve
(optional)

Vignarola is a Roman stew that is cooked in April in Rome. It uses everything that is wonderful about this season. Mine is a little different from the classic Roman version, as it is topped with some crisp seedy bread and a lot of herbs instead of the traditional crowning of prosciutto. I will probably be in trouble with purists and Italians, but this dish is so good I didn't want to stop making it when I stopped eating meat. It's a celebration of the vegetables of the hour, and the smoked salt and crisp cornered bits of bread add a depth that I think matches the classic version.

Artichokes are something I don't cook that much at home, mainly because they take quite a bit of preparing; but when I do I adore them. I use the small violet artichokes here, which are less time-consuming to prepare than their bigger cousins. If you are pushed for time, you could use some good jarred ones.

———————————————

Preheat your oven to 425°F (220°C).

First, deal with your artichokes. Put them in a large pot of cold salted water and bring to a boil. Once simmering, cook for about 10 minutes or until they are tender (check by inserting a knife into the heart to see if it is soft), then drain well and allow them to cool.

Fill the pot with 6½ cups (1.5 liters) of water, add some salt and bring to a boil. Blanch the fava beans for a minute, then remove from the water with a slotted spoon and drain. Blanch the spinach or chard until just wilted. Keep this water. If you have the patience to double-pod your fava beans, now is the time to pop them out of their tougher outer casings.

Once the artichokes are cool, peel back the outer leaves of the flower part until you reach the pale tender edible ones; if you are unsure when that is, try one—if it's good to eat and not too tough you are there. Next, use a small sharp knife to cut ½ inch (1.5 cm) off the top (this top bit can be tough), then cut the artichoke in half lengthways and use a teaspoon to scoop out the fibrous choke. Tear or cut the hearts into quarters. →

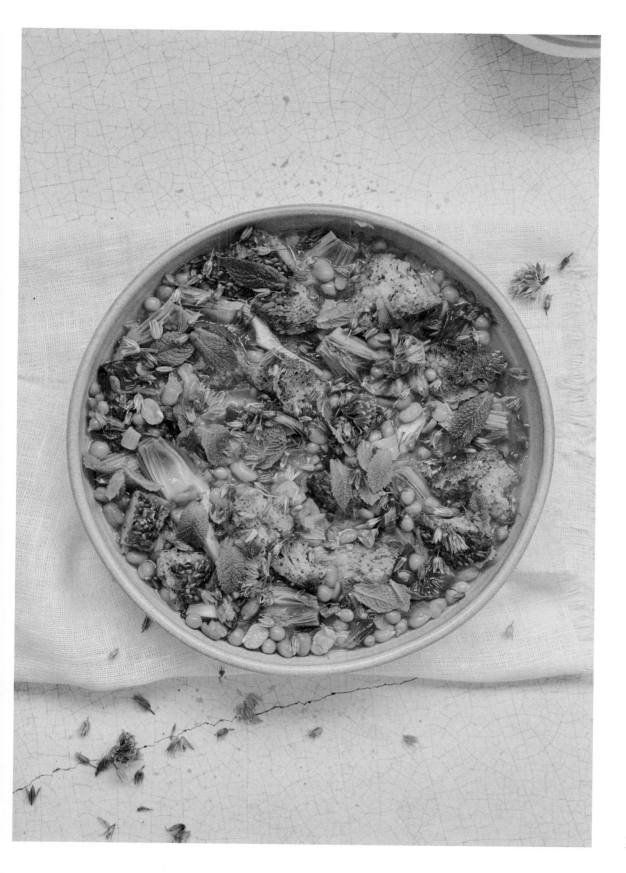

Tear the bread into coin-size pieces and lay it on a large baking sheet. Drizzle with olive oil and scatter liberally with salt, then put the sheet into the hot oven for 15 minutes for the bread to crisp up.

Heat a large saucepan (big enough to hold all the ingredients) and add a good splash of oil. Cook the onions and leek with a pinch of salt very gently for about 10 minutes, until soft, then add the reserved vegetable cooking water, along with the peas and fava beans, and bring back to a gentle simmer.

Roughly chop the spinach or chard and add to the peas with the artichokes. Bring back to a simmer and let all the vegetables stew together for about 10 minutes more.

Taste, season with the lemon zest and juice, the smoked salt and some pepper, then stir together with almost all of the chopped herbs. Serve in bowls, with a generous drizzle of olive oil, the crisped bread on top, and finally the flowers, if you are using them, as well as the remaining herbs.

Lemon, fennel seed, and potato bake

I ate this in a restaurant many years ago and have never forgotten it. It's a simple dish that uses my two favorite ingredients as its stars. I eat this with an herby salad on the side, but it would sit well next to most dinners.

It's a very flexible recipe; you can swap the fennel for other spices or woody herbs. And even add a little stock or cream before baking too, if you like.

Preheat the oven to 425°F (220°C). Slice the potatoes as finely as you can—a mandoline can help here; you want the slices to be about ⅛ inch (3 mm) thick.

Cut the top and bottom off the lemons, then slice them as finely as you can, keeping the rind on—you want the slices to be about the same thickness as the potatoes. The rind will soften and sweeten as it cooks.

Grease a medium ovenproof gratin dish with a little butter. Next, lay some potato slices in a row across the end of the dish, propped up a little by leaning them at an angle against the side of the dish. Against this row, lay a line of lemon, not as many as the potatoes, but 2 or 3 slices.

Continue with potatoes and then lemon until you have filled the dish, shuffling the potatoes back a little as you go if you need to make enough space to fit them all in.

Pour over the stock then finish with a very good seasoning of salt and pepper and scatter over the fennel seeds. Dot the top with the butter. Cover the dish with foil and scrunch the edges to seal, then put in the hot oven for around 30 minutes, until the potatoes are cooked through.

Remove the foil and continue to cook for 30 to 40 more minutes, or until the potatoes are browned and the lemons are sticky and caramelized. Serve with a zippy lemon-and–olive oil dressed salad.

SERVES 4

2½ pounds (1 kg) new potatoes, scrubbed but not peeled

2 small unwaxed lemons

3½ tablespoons (50 g) butter, plus extra to grease the dish

¾ cup hot vegetable stock

sea salt and freshly ground black pepper

1 tablespoon fennel seeds

Bright pink pasta

This is about as cheerful as dinner gets. It is super simple but will cheer up even the grayest day. Be sure to undercook your pasta in the water as it will cook for another couple of minutes with the beets, which will turn it bright fuchsia pink—nature's neon. I like to make this for kids, and my son loves to jump up into my arms and watch as the pasta starts to turn pink.

If you like, you can finish this with a crumbling of goat cheese or feta, but I like it just as it is.

First, peel and coarsely grate your beets. Fill a kettle with water and boil. Heat a frying pan over medium heat, add a drizzle of olive oil, then the beets and capers, and cook for about 7 minutes until the beets have lost their rawness and there is no liquid in the pan.

Meanwhile, fill a large pot with boiling water and add a good pinch of salt. Bring back to a boil, then add the pasta and cook for 3 minutes less than the package instructions.

Once the pasta has had its time, drain it in a colander, reserving about ⅝ cup (150 ml) of the cloudy pasta water to make your sauce. Put the pasta and the reserved water into the pan with the grated beets and simmer over a high heat for about another 3 minutes, until all the water has evaporated and the pasta has turned deep pink and is perfectly cooked.

Take the pan off the heat and add the chopped dill, then squeeze over a little lemon juice, and finish with a really generous drizzle of olive oil (more than you think you'll need) and salt and pepper.

SERVES 4

10½ ounces (300 g) raw beets

extra-virgin olive oil

2 tablespoons baby capers

sea salt

14 ounces (400 g) whole-wheat tagliatelle

a small bunch of dill

juice of 1 lemon

freshly ground black pepper

200

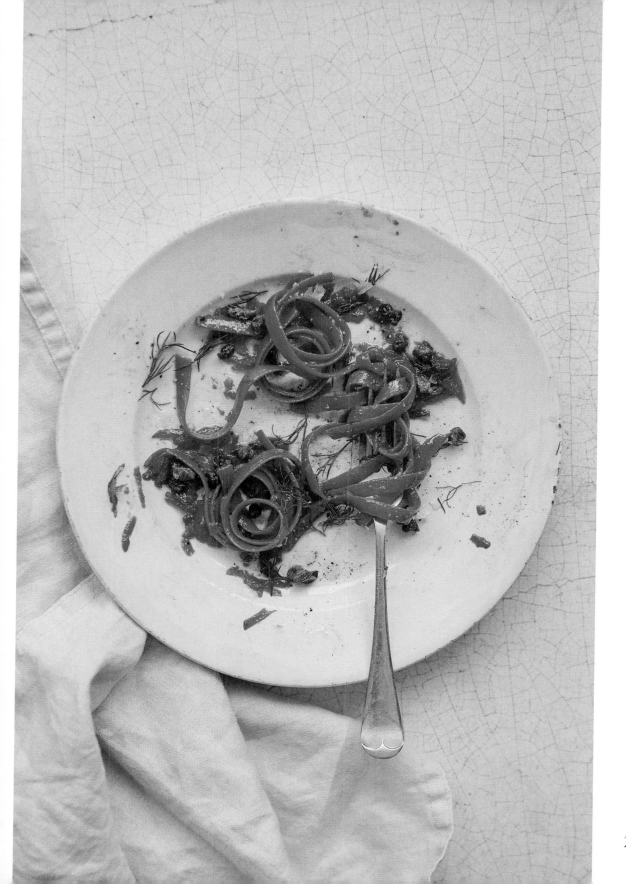

Vegetable shawarma

There is something so good about charred, soft flatbread with some cooling yogurt and warming spice. Some years ago on a trip to Granada in Spain I remember discovering their amazing shawarma stands. There is such a strong North African influence there, and the barbecue smoke and heady spices filled the streets. We sat outside and ate from our laps as we drank rosé mixed with lemonade, and ice-cold beers. For years since I have been trying to perfect a vegetable shawarma that didn't feel second best, and I think I've managed it.

I use spring carrots, little new potatoes, and asparagus, which are spiced with cumin and cilantro and charred and roasted in the oven, though on a hot day they could be blanched and then charred on a griddle or barbecue. They sit on top of warm flatbread with a very good pistachio yogurt spiked with cilantro and sweetened with a drop of maple syrup. Vegans can use coconut yogurt here to keep it free of dairy.

This dish is one I love in late spring and summer, but you can change the vegetables as they come in and out of season. Other favorite combinations are red peppers and eggplant; broccoli and string beans; beets and cauliflower. Just be clever when you chop the veg—cut the veg that will cook slowly quite small and the quicker-cooking veg a bit bigger.

SERVES 4

1 tablespoon cumin seeds

1 tablespoon cilantro (coriander) seeds

14-ounce (400-g) bunch of baby carrots, scrubbed well

olive oil

sea salt and freshly ground black pepper

8¾ ounces (250 g) new potatoes

½ a cucumber

1 lemon

7 ounces (200 g) asparagus, woody ends snapped off

4 yogurt flatbreads (see page 456) or round pitas

FOR THE HERBED PISTACHIO YOGURT

⅓ cup (100 g) Greek yogurt

1 teaspoon maple syrup

a few sprigs of cilantro, roughly chopped (stalks and all)

the zest of 1 unwaxed lemon

⅓ cup (50 g) shelled pistachios, roughly chopped

Preheat your oven to 425°F (220°C).

Bash the cumin and cilantro seeds in a mortar with pestle, spice grinder, or mixing bowl with rolling pin until roughly ground. Toss the carrots with a good drizzle of olive oil, a pinch of salt and pepper, and half the cumin and cilantro seeds. Transfer to a large baking sheet, cover with foil, and roast in the center of the oven for 10 minutes.

Meanwhile, make the herbed yogurt by mixing all the ingredients together with a pinch of salt. →

After the carrots have had their time, push them to one side of the baking sheet, quarter or halve the potatoes, and add to the other side. Drizzle over a bit more oil, and the other half of the cumin and cilantro. Toss to mix the potatoes with the spices, put the foil back on and return the baking sheet to the oven for 20 minutes.

While the potatoes are roasting, thinly slice the cucumber (I like to scoop the seeds out of the middle first), mix it with the juice from half the lemon, a good pinch of salt and pepper, and a splash of olive oil, then put to one side.

Once the potatoes have had their 20 minutes, remove the baking sheet from the oven, take off the foil, and scatter over the asparagus. Squeeze over the remaining juice of the lemon, drizzle with a little oil, and put back into the oven for 10 minutes until the asparagus are beginning to brown.

Toast or warm the flatbread. When you're ready to eat, take the baking sheet out of the oven and roughly crush the carrots with the back of a fork.

Spread some of the pistachio yogurt over half of each flatbread and add the roasted carrots, then the potatoes and asparagus. Add a generous serving of the cucumbers and fold the warm flatbreads over to envelop everything. Eat straightaway.

Farinata with slow-cooked zucchini

I have an obsession with pancakes; any opportunity to make or eat them for breakfast, lunch or dinner, and I'll take it. So I've had to expand my pancake horizons beyond the Fat Tuesday classics and the fluffy American ones. One of my favorite ways to make pancakes is with chickpea flour. All over the world chickpea (gram) flour is used to make socca, farinata, and Indian pudla. Farinata are a distinctly Italian creation.

The pancakes come together easily and quickly and can be made in advance and warmed up if that's your kind of thing. I serve them with slow-cooked zucchini—"trifolati" zucchini, to give this kind their proper name, which means cooking them slowly in olive oil and garlic. It's also used for cooking mushrooms and truffles. I love cooking zucchini this way, as it brings out a sweet buttery character that you don't get when you cook them more quickly.

Start with the zucchini. Heat a large, deep saucepan over low heat and melt the butter. Add the garlic, zucchini, fennel, lemon zest, a really generous pinch of salt, and a few turns of the pepper mill. Cover and continue to cook over low heat for 1 hour, stirring from time to time.

While the zucchini is cooking, make the batter by whisking the gram flour in a large mixing bowl with 3½ cups (800 ml) of cold water. Set aside for 20 minutes.

Preheat your oven to 425°F (220°C).

When you are ready to cook the pancakes, whisk in ¼ cup (60 ml) of the olive oil, the salt, and half the reserved fennel fronds.

If you have two ovenproof frying pans of a similar size (10 inches/ 25 cm roughly), you can speed up proceedings here by cooking two pancakes at once, but if not, don't worry. Heat your frying pan(s) on the highest heat and add a tablespoon of the oil. →

SERVES 4

FOR THE ZUCCHINI

1 tablespoon butter

1 clove of garlic, finely sliced

6 medium zucchini (about 2 pounds/1 kg), thinly sliced

1 bulb of fennel, finely sliced (keep the fronds)

the zest and juice of 1 unwaxed lemon

3 tablespoons olive oil

a handful of mint

FOR THE FARINATA

4 cups (350 g) gram (chickpea) flour

½ cup (120 ml) olive oil

1 teaspoon flaky sea salt

half the reserved fennel fronds (see above)

TO SERVE

olive oil

2 tablespoons capers

1 cup (100 g) soft goat cheese or goat curd

205

When the oil is so hot it's smoking, pour a quarter of the batter into the hot pan and let it cook for around 30 seconds so that it's bubbling on the sides. Place in the hot oven for 15 minutes, until the top is crisp and deep golden. Carefully remove the farinata from the pan; it should be crisp on both sides but still a little soft in the middle. Put it on a warm plate under foil to keep hot while you cook the others in the same way, adding a tablespoon of oil to the pan each time. You'll easily be able to do them all in the time it takes for the zucchini to cook.

After about 45 minutes, the zucchini should have completely collapsed and softened, almost to a rough purée. Turn the heat off, roughly chop the mint, and add this to the pan with the lemon juice and remaining fennel fronds. Check the seasoning—you will probably need some more salt and perhaps a bit more lemon juice.

Heat 3 tablespoons of oil in the farinata frying pan, and once it's hot, add the capers and cook for about 30 seconds so they are crispy. Scoop out with a slotted spoon and drain on paper towels.

Serve the zucchini over the farinata, with the goat cheese and crispy capers dotted over the top.

Pistachio and ricotta dumplings with peas and herbs

These are light, bright dumplings that are quick and easy to put together. It is a plate that is all about late spring: white, green, and fresh. I use freshly podded peas here, and I don't cook them: I love their pop and sweetness when they haven't been cooked and they work against the softness of the ricotta. If podding peas sounds a bit much or fresh peas are hard to find for you, some briefly boiled frozen ones will work well too.

Chop your pistachios finely; you can do this in a food processor, but be sure that you don't blitz them to a powder, as you still want them to have enough texture, as if they had been finely chopped by hand.

Put the ricotta into a bowl with the pistachios, lemon zest, chopped chile, and the flour. Season well with salt and pepper and mix gently until it comes together as a dough.

Half fill a large saucepan with water and place it over high heat. Roll the ricotta mixture into about 20 little balls, about 1½ inches in diameter. Very lightly dust in a little more flour and place on a cutting board while you wait for the water to boil.

Next, finely chop the herbs, put them into a bowl with the olive oil and the peas, and season with salt and pepper.

Once the water in the saucepan is at a boil, lower the dumplings in and cook them for 4 to 5 minutes, until they all rise and bob to the top. Drain on paper towels and serve about 5 per person, topped with the herby peas and olive oil.

SERVES 4

¾ cup (100 g) shelled pistachios, toasted

2 cups (500 g) ricotta

the zest of 2 unwaxed lemons

1 red chile, finely chopped

½ cup light spelt flour, plus a little extra

sea salt and freshly ground black pepper

a small bunch of spring herbs

10 tablespoons (150 ml) good olive oil

2¾ cups (400 g) freshly podded peas

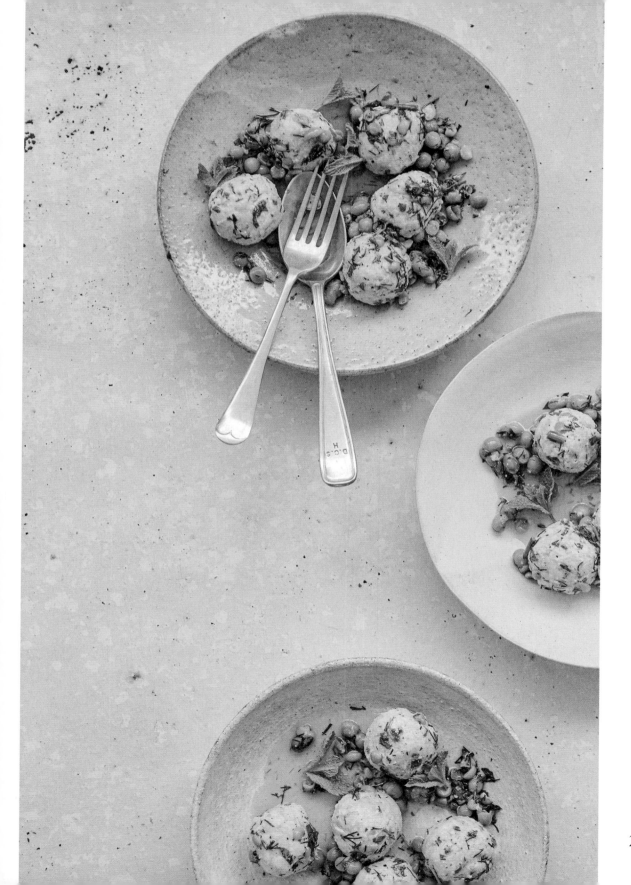

Early-summer gooseberry, elderflower, and almond sponge

MAKES AN 8-INCH
(20-CM) CAKE

14 tablespoons unsalted
    butter, softened, plus extra
    for greasing

½ cup (100 g) superfine or
    caster sugar

½ cup (100 g) light
    muscovado sugar

2 cups (250 g) light spelt
    flour

2 teaspoons baking powder

1 cup (100 g) ground almonds

10 tablespoons (150 ml) milk
    (I use whole or oat milk)

3 organic eggs

the seeds from 1 vanilla pod

the zest of 1 unwaxed lemon

FOR THE GOOSEBERRY COMPOTE

10½ ounces (300 g)
    gooseberries, topped and
    tailed

2 tablespoons elderflower
    and rose cordial
    (see page 221)

¼ cup (50 g) superfine or
    caster sugar

FOR THE WHIPPED YOGURT ICING

¾ cup (200 g) Greek yogurt

¼ cup (50 g) golden icing
    sugar

TO FINISH

fresh elderflowers (if you can
    get them)

This is a favorite cake. The moment when elderflowers and gooseberries cross over is one of my favorite times of the year; everything is still verdant from spring but the bounty of the summer has started to arrive—it's a great time for food.

The sponge is quite a traditional one, spiked with almond, lemon, and vanilla and then doused in elderflower and sandwiched with an easy gooseberry compote and a yogurt icing. It is everything I love about summer cakes. It's not very fancy but this is on purpose, as unless it's a big occasion, I like my cakes simple and natural, gently frosted, so that they tell the story of what's in them rather than hiding the ingredients behind a thick layer of butter and sugar.

If I make this for a special occasion I finish it with some elderflowers if I can get my hands on them, or some other fresh seasonal blooms (see page 296). If they aren't edible flowers, be sure to take them off before eating.

If you plan to eat this over a few days, I suggest keeping the filling and sponge separate and icing each slice as you go, as the cake keeps better out of the fridge, but the icing does need refrigerating. This cake can easily be made with frozen gooseberries if you want a hit of early summer at another time of year—who wouldn't?

Preheat the oven to 300°F (150°C). Grease a deep 8-inch (20-cm) springform cake pan and line it with parchment paper.

In the bowl of an electric mixer, or with an electric hand whisk, cream the soft butter and sugars together until almost white and fluffy.

In a separate bowl, whisk together the flour, baking powder, and ground almonds to get rid of any lumps.

Add half the dry mixture to the butter and mix well; add the milk, eggs, vanilla, and lemon zest, then mix in the remaining dry ingredients. Scrape around the bottom of the bowl and mix again. →

Pour the batter into the pan, using the back of a spoon or a spatula to level out the top, then bake for 1 hour, until the top of the cake springs back and is soft to the touch. Cool for 15 minutes in the pan, then move to a rack to cool completely.

While the cake is in the oven, get on with the compote and icing. To make the compote, place the gooseberries in a saucepan with the cordial and sugar. Place the saucepan over medium heat, bring to a simmer, and turn the heat down to low. Continue to cook gently for 20 to 30 minutes, until the gooseberries are completely soft, have burst to release their juices, and have started to turn jammy. Leave to cool completely.

To make the icing, stir together the yogurt and icing sugar until you have a spoonable icing, and store in the fridge until needed.

Once the cake has cooled completely, use a long serrated knife to slice it horizontally through the middle. I find the best way to do this is to gently skirt around the edge of the cake with your knife, cutting just ⅜ inch (1 cm) into the cake exactly halfway down so that you have a line to follow, then go all the way through following the line you have cut—this will give you a more even result.

Lift the whole cake onto a serving plate, then carefully lift off the top layer—you can slide it onto a plate to do this if you feel happier—and spread the bottom with the yogurt mixture and then the gooseberry compote. Cover with the top of the cake and sprinkle over some elderflowers to finish.

How to use less plastic

The tide is finally beginning to turn and more and more of us are looking to reduce the amount of plastic we use in our daily lives and in our kitchens. As the full realization of what we are doing to our oceans begins to hit us, it's time to look at the wealth of alternatives out there, which often actually work better (and look nicer) than their plastic counterparts.

I appreciate that some of the suggestions here might be things you have already made part of your life, but, if you are anything like me, it's always good to have a gentle reminder.

In the kitchen

Buy in bulk: Wherever you can, buy dry goods and spices in bulk. Save your old glass jars to refill with loose grains, lentils, nuts, and seeds. If you can take them with you to the store and fill from there, all the better.

Bottled water: I fill glass bottles with water from the tap, which I then keep in the fridge to save running the tap if I want cold water to drink. I use a charcoal filter inside the bottle to make the water taste better.

Straws: Try straws actually made from straw (which is what they were named after in the first place) or stainless-steel straws—both are easily found online. Refuse plastic straws when out and about.

Buy unpackaged fruit and veg: Use canvas tote bags to store vegetables in the fridge or freezer. This stops freezer burn and helps keeps veg moist.

Storage containers: Swap your plastic for glass storage containers, or try some enamel storage pots, which can go straight from the oven into the fridge. I'm partial to the ovenware by Chabatree.

Replace plastic wrap: Use wax wraps instead. Health food stores and some grocery stores carry them, and they are easy to find online. There are some great blogs that detail how to make your own, too, which is easy and cheaper. Use a clean, damp tea towel to wrap things like pastry and dough.

Bowl covers: Linen bowl covers are a great way to avoid plastic wrap, too. These are readily available online.

Cleaning cloths: You can buy reusable cloths, which go in the washing machine, rather than paper towels and sponges. Cloths made of natural fabrics and not plastic-derived are obviously the ones to go for. Use wooden-handled brushes for pans and veg scrubbing; I keep one for each. Norwex makes a collection of chemical-free cleaning products I like.

Make your own all-purpose spray: I use an old spray bottle and make a kitchen spray with some boiled water, ¼ cup (50 ml) of white vinegar, a couple of tablespoons of ecological dishwashing liquid (which you can refill at the store), and a few drops of essential oils, which I adjust depending on the season.

Out and about

Coffee cups: This is a very obvious one, but use a reusable coffee cup. Mine is made from old recycled coffee cups, but there are some good glass options, too. I keep one in my handbag and one in my car. My new rule is, if I don't have it I don't buy a coffee. That makes me remember it much more often.

Water bottles: I use a steel bottle for water instead of buying bottled water, an obvious but vital step we should all be taking. If you forget yours, most coffee shops and restaurants will give you a glassful if you ask.

Grocery shopping: Lots of stores now let you bring your own containers to fill with veg or cheese from the deli counter or dry goods if they sell them in bulk.

Plastic cutlery: I try to avoid using this. There are lots of affordable wooden options; I keep a set of reusable wooden cutlery in my handbag and one in my car. Pack your kitchen cutlery for picnics.

Homemade lunches: Making your own lunch will always mean using less plastic. If you buy a daily breakfast, lunch, or dinner, try to eat in for less packaging, or, better yet, take your own in reusable containers.

Strawberry and anise galette

Strawberries are a regular fixture in grocery stores all year. I tend not to buy them in winter; I wait for the local varieties to arrive. They taste infinitely sweeter.

This galette is quick and easy to make, and buttery and flaky to eat. The strawberries roast and melt to a pool of molten scarlet jam in the middle, some still holding their shape, but all of them releasing their juices to create a seriously good jammy center.

What I love most about this, though, is that it uses very little sugar; the natural sweetness of the strawberries shines through. I have given an approximate amount for the sugar I use to sweeten the strawberries, as the amount you need will depend on the strawberries as well as your own tastes (I usually end up using about ¼ cup/60 g).

The surprising element is anise seed, a sweet fennel-like seed that I love. The seeds can be harder to come by than other spices, but if you like, you could replace them with fennel seeds or even just a grind of black pepper (you won't need as much as a tablespoon).

When you take the galette out of the oven it will look a little runny in the center, but it will set within minutes as it cools.

SERVES 4–6

FOR THE FLAKY SPELT PASTRY

1¼ cups (160 g) spelt flour, plus a little extra for dusting

a pinch of flaky sea salt

1 tablespoon superfine or caster sugar

7 tablespoons cold unsalted butter, cut into cubes

a glass of iced water

1 organic egg, beaten

2 tablespoons ground almonds

5 cups (740 g) strawberries

1 tablespoon anise seed (see note above)

¼–½ cup (50–100 g) superfine or caster sugar

TO SERVE

coconut yogurt, whipped with a little honey and vanilla, or thick Greek yogurt, cream, or ice cream

For the pastry, combine the flour, salt, and sugar in a bowl. Add the butter and use the back of a fork or a food processor to cut the butter into the flour, until you have a rough scruffy mixture, still with some bigger chunks of butter.

Add the ice-cold water bit by bit, until the pastry comes together—you will only need 4 to 5 tablespoons. Bring it together into a ball with your hands, or pulse a few times in the food processor. Handle it as little as possible, then wrap it and put it in the fridge to cool and rest for at least 45 minutes or so. →

Meanwhile, hull the strawberries and cut them in half, or any larger ones into quarters. Put them in a bowl with the spice and half the sugar and leave to sit.

Once the pastry has rested, take it out of the fridge to soften a bit and preheat the oven to 355°F (180°C).

Flour your work surface and, once the pastry has warmed slightly, roll it out quite thinly into roughly a 12-inch (30-cm) round, then lift it onto a baking sheet lined with parchment paper.

Sprinkle the ground almonds over the center of the pastry, leaving the edge of the pastry clean.

Pile the strawberries in the middle of the pastry, leaving about a 1½-inch (4-cm) border of pastry to fold over. There's no need to be too precise with the strawberries, as they will shrink and change as they cook.

Next fold the edges of the pastry over the strawberries to hold them in. Brush the edge of the pastry with the beaten egg, then sprinkle the strawberries and pastry edges with the remaining sugar.

Bake in the hot oven for 55 minutes, until the strawberries are soft and bubbling and the pastry is golden and crisp. Serve with my choice of some coconut yogurt stirred with a little honey and vanilla, or with ice cream, cream, or thick Greek yogurt.

Elderflower and rose cordial

Making cordial is actually much easier than you might think, and elderflower grows everywhere in May and June. Even in Hackney, in the middle of one of the world's biggest cities, I could probably show you 100 bushes near our house that bloom into floaty, starry blossoms.

Old wisdom suggests you should pick the flowers on a sunny day and only pick flowers that face the sun. I'm not sure I've been able to taste the difference, but it does make the picking nicer.

It's best to use a rose from the garden; store-bought ones tend to be sprayed, so aren't good to use in cooking. And don't worry that the infused liquid doesn't look very appealing: When the lemon juice is added, the rose's intense color will return like magic. The cordial keeps in a sterilized bottle in the fridge for at least a month.

Fill the kettle with water and boil. Peel the zest from the lemons in long strips. Put the elderflowers into a large bowl with the lemon peel and rose petals. Pour over 2 cups (500 ml) of boiling water and press down the florets, making sure they're submerged. Leave to cool, then cover the bowl and leave to infuse at room temperature for about 36 hours.

Strain the infusion into a medium saucepan, pressing the flowers with the back of a spoon, to release all the liquid, then discard the flowers, branches, peel, and rose petals. Add the sugar and lemon juice to the infusion, then turn the heat to high and cook for 3 to 4 minutes, stirring until the sugar has dissolved and the liquid is starting to simmer. Take off the heat, leave to cool, then pour into a sterilized 1-quart (960-ml) bottle. Seal and store in the fridge for up to a month.

MAKES 28 FLUID OUNCES (800 ML)

2 unwaxed lemons

3½ ounces (100 g) elderflower heads (about 12 heads)

1 small red rose (see note above), petals picked

11½ ounces (325 g) superfine sugar

½ cup (125 ml) lemon juice (3–4 lemons)

221

Herbal infusions

Herbs hold a special magic for me in the kitchen. As a young chef I remember listening to a talk by the amazing Jekka McVicar, the queen of herbs, a guardian of rare herb varieties and an expert on all thing herbal; she talked at length about the healing properties of herbs. She discussed how in days gone by basil would be infused into warm milk and given to infants to calm them before bed. I was totally charmed by this and went on to make a basil panna cotta, which I still make and love serving after a meal. It is soothing and gentle and a perfect end to a meal. I am sure I sleep better after eating it too.

I use herbs in almost everything I cook, picking bay leaves and rosemary and lavender from the garden and softer herbs from my windowsill or from the herbs I store in a little water in glasses in my fridge door.

I make infusions and tisanes with herbs. Their fresh verdant nature is amplified when they come into contact with hot water—the oils are released and gently flavor the water. It's a great way of making sure that you drink enough water too, as while I often forget to sip my water I'll always drink my tea before it's cold. It also a good way of making sure those bunches of herbs are used to their full potential and don't wither unused in the fridge.

It can be lovely to blend a spice with a fresh herb too: the grassy green top notes coming from the herbs and the warmer base notes from the spice, e.g., rose petals with cinnamon, lemon verbena with fennel seed.

Brewing herbal infusions

— Pick herbs as you need them to keep them fresh.

— Two or three leaves or six to eight flowers per person is a good amount.

— Use heatproof glasses for maximum prettiness.

— Don't brew in the same teapot as caffeinated tea, as the tannins can affect the taste.

— To preserve herbs, dry them slowly out of direct sunlight. Either hang from the ceiling with string, or lay them flat in a paper bag, turning them every few days or whenever you remember.

— Infusions can be cooled and stored in the fridge and served over ice for amazing iced tea.

— For another way to make herbal teas, see page 86 for how to juice their essence.

Favorite herbs

Wild fennel: great for digestion; pairs well with lemon zest.

Lemon balm and lemon verbena: good for digestion too; pairs well with fennel seeds.

Basil: green or purple; good for digestion; can be infused into milk for bedtime.

Lavender: calming and centering; strong, so go lightly; good infused with milk.

Lemon thyme: the best of the thymes to infuse; pairs well with black pepper and honey.

Chamomile: good for sleep and to settle a stomach, as well as for cramps; pairs well with vanilla and honey.

Mint: easy to grow, good for after meals; pairs well with orange blossom flowers or water and honey.

Elderflower: brew on its own or with another herb; needs some honey to sweeten.

Sage: needs only a short brew; good with honey and orange.

Nettle: grows everywhere; I like it paired with lemon.

Rosemary: good for digestion; also add to a bath to help with muscle or back pain; very good with honey and squashed blackberries.

Rosehip: vibrant red tea high in vitamin C; you can dry these yourself in a low oven or buy them dried.

Dandelion flowers: use the yellow flowers—one per person; can be bitter, which I love, but sweeten with honey if you need to.

Favorite herbal infusion blends

Rose and cinnamon: fresh or dried rose petals and a crumbled cinnamon stick.

Spiced mint: mint leaves, lemon, bashed fresh ginger, cilantro (coriander) seeds, and black peppercorns.

Ruby vitamin C: dried hibiscus, dried rosehips, lemon zest, and rose petals.

Hedgerow winter herbs: sage, rosemary, blackberries, and lemon slices.

Moroccan mint: mint, orange blossom water, orange zest, and honey.

Herbs can also be infused in water with fruit for extra depth and flavor and poured over ice in the summer. Add the herbs and fruit (see below) to a pitcher and leave to sit for at least half an hour before adding ice and drinking. You can infuse the water several times with one batch of herbs and fruit.

Favorite iced water infusions

— a couple of sprigs of sage and a handful of blackberries.

— a sprig of rosemary and a sliced apple.

— a few sprigs of mint, half a sliced cucumber, and a sliced lime.

— a few sprigs of thyme and a sliced peach.

— a few sprigs of basil and a sliced lime.

— a couple of sprigs of marjoram and a sliced lemon or bergamot.

223

Summer

Best of the season
- Tomatoes
- Zucchini
- Corn
- Eggplant
- Peppers
- Chard
- Baby carrots and beets
- Radishes
- String beans
- Green beans
- Yellow beans
- Cauliflower
- Strawberries
- Cherries
- Black currants
- White currants
- Raspberries
- Huckleberries
- Edible flowers
- Peaches
- Nectarines
- Greengage plums
- Blueberries

Flowers
- Hydrangea
- Yarrow
- Veronica
- Delphinium
- Dahlia
- Rose

Overnight summer birchers

EACH SERVES 2

PEACH AND RYE

⅔ cup (60 g) oats

2 ounces (40 g) rye flakes

1 apple, grated

1 tablespoon barley malt extract

1½ cups (350 ml) oat milk

TO TOP

1 peach, pitted and roughly chopped

4 tablespoons plain yogurt

the zest of 1 unwaxed lemon

RASPBERRY AND HAZELNUT

1 cup (100 g) oats

⅓ cup (50 g) raspberries

3½ tablespoons orange juice

1 cup (250 ml) hazelnut milk

TO TOP

¼ cup (25 g) hazelnuts, toasted

⅓ cup (50 g) raspberries

4 tablespoons oat or coconut yogurt →

On summer mornings I try to eat my breakfast outside. I sit in our garden and eat one of these bowls of bircher with my little boy running around me. I am not a morning person, and since Dylan's arrival, there is even less time in the morning to focus on eating something good, so making this the night before has become a ritual for me and John so that all three of us start the day well.

These are my four favorite flavors for summer. They all work on roughly the same principle but you'll need varying amounts of liquid depending on the fruit you add. I encourage experimenting with your favorite flavors. And if by the morning the bircher is too thin, you could stir in a little yogurt; too thick, a little more milk. I have also made a savory version with almond milk and sesame seeds topped with flaked nori.

PEACH AND RYE

In a large screw-top jar, mix the oats, rye, apple, and barley malt. Pour over the oat milk, cover with the lid, and shake to combine evenly. Put in the fridge overnight.

The next morning, serve topped with the peach, yogurt, and lemon zest.

RASPBERRY AND HAZELNUT

Put the oats into a large screw-top jar. Roughly mash the raspberries and place them in the jar too, along with the orange juice and hazelnut milk. Cover with a lid and leave in the fridge overnight.

The next morning, roughly chop the hazelnuts and spoon the bircher into bowls. Top with the hazelnuts, raspberries, and yogurt. →

CHERRY AND POPPY SEED

1 cup (80 g) oats

2 tablespoons (20 g) millet

2 tablespoons poppy seeds

¾ cup (200 ml) almond milk
(I use unsweetened)

1 pear

1 tablespoon maple syrup

TO TOP

⅓ cup (50 g) pitted cherries
(frozen are fine)

the zest of 1 unwaxed lemon

poppy seeds

MANGO AND VANILLA

1 cup (100 g) oats

the seeds from 1 vanilla pod,
or 1 tablespoon vanilla
paste

7 fluid ounces (200 ml) ready-
to-drink coconut milk

½ a mango, peeled and
roughly chopped

¼ teaspoon ground cardamom

TO TOP

½ a mango, peeled and
roughly chopped

4 tablespoons plain or
coconut yogurt

the zest of 1 unwaxed lime

2 tablespoons coconut chips

CHERRY AND POPPY SEED

Put the oats, millet, and poppy seeds in a large jar and pour over the almond milk. Grate the pear on the thickest setting on your box grater and mix it with the other ingredients, along with the maple syrup. Cover and leave in the fridge overnight.

Spoon into two bowls and divide the cherries and lemon zest between them, then scatter over some extra poppy seeds.

MANGO AND VANILLA

Put the oats into a large jar with the vanilla seeds or paste and pour over the coconut milk. Quickly blitz the mango in a food processor with the cardamom, then mix it with the oats. Cover and leave in the fridge overnight.

Spoon into two bowls and top with the mango, yogurt, lime zest, and coconut.

Cherry and almond breakfast smoothie

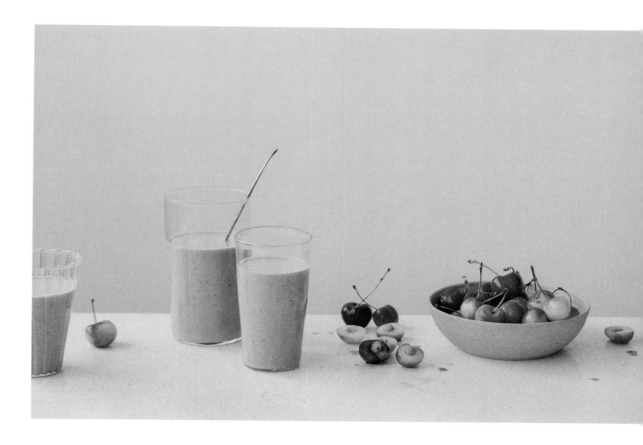

For the few weeks cherries are at their best I eat them all day long. Straight from the paper bag on the way home from the store, baked into cakes and brownies (see page 293), to top pancakes (see page 290), or laid over a bowl of ice for a quick dessert on a hot day. This is how I get cherries into my mornings, and their cheery color never fails to lift my spirits. Almond butter works here to give this smoothie an almost marzipan note; it works with frozen cherries too, once summer is gone.

Place all the ingredients in a blender with a little ice if you'd like it really cold. Blitz until you have a thick, deep red smoothie. Divide between two glasses.

SERVES 2

⅔ cup (100 g) cherries, pitted

2 pears, cored and roughly chopped

1 orange, peeled

½ cup (125 ml) coconut water or cool herbal tea

6 tablespoons (100 ml) almond milk (I use unsweetened)

1 tablespoon almond or other nut butter

Summer morning bowl

1½ cups (200 g) berries

the cheek of 1 medium mango

2 tablespoons chia seeds

2 tablespoons thick Greek or
    coconut yogurt

2 ice cubes

TOPPINGS

more berries

toasted coconut flakes

bee pollen

granola

toasted buckwheat

puffed rice or quinoa

chopped nuts

more yogurt

This is a quick breezy summer breakfast for when porridge is a distant memory. I first ate a breakfast like this in Brazil, where icy açai bowls are the breakfast of choice in the juice bars that line the streets off Rio's beaches. This is my British summer version. It's essentially a thin frozen yogurt, the right consistency for spooning, with some chia seeds for texture and energy. I have left the toppings up to you; use what you have on hand to add texture, flavor and some prettiness. You can use frozen berries if you like, in which case, I'd recommend leaving out the ice cubes. I use a mixture of summer berries (e.g., raspberries, strawberries, and red currants).

Wash the berries and scoop the flesh out of the mango cheek to remove the peel. Put all the ingredients into a blender and blitz for 30 seconds, until everything is combined. I like mine to have some texture from the chia seeds, but you may prefer yours completely smooth.

Top with any of the additional toppings, if you're using them.

Beet borani

There is something a bit 1980s about the word "dip." It makes me think of my parents' dinner parties, Mum in her turquoise and silver lapeled jumpsuit, passing around a bowl of tortilla chips and a layered Mexican creation we called "The Dip."

But a dip, spread, or hummus is a very useful thing to have in your fridge. I make up a batch of some kind at least once a week. It means I have something on hand to dip a carrot in to fill the gap before dinner, or something flavorful to spoon into a bowl of greens and grains, or to spread on a sandwich with a sprinkling of feta and some peppery leaves.

This Iranian dip is a summer favorite. It's usually made with eggplant, but its flavors work with lots of different vegetables. I use different colored beets here, sometimes the deep purple ones, sometimes the golden ones, or even the candy-cane ones, which give the borani a dusky pink hue; on the day we took the pictures, I made all three. You can use vacuum-packed cooked beets here too if you want to make this in a hurry. If your dates are not soft, soak them in a little hot water first.

SERVES 4

3¾ cups (500 g) raw or cooked beets

extra-virgin olive oil

2 soft, pitted Medjool dates

sea salt

1 small clove of garlic, finely chopped

4 tablespoons Greek yogurt

a small bunch of dill, chopped

2 tablespoons red wine vinegar

⅔ cup (100 g) feta cheese

a small handful of walnuts, roughly crushed

½ teaspoon nigella seeds

TO SERVE

yogurt flatbread (see page 456)

crunchy vegetables

If you are cooking your beets, wash them, leaving the skins on, then cover with boiling water and simmer for about 40 minutes, or until they are tender to the tip of a knife. Top off the water when needed. Drain the beets, then leave them to cool.

Once cool, peel the beets and blend in a food processor with 4 tablespoons of olive oil, the dates, and a pinch of salt, until you have a totally smooth purée.

Transfer to a bowl and add the garlic, yogurt, most of the dill, the vinegar, and a pinch of salt if you think it needs it.

To serve, sprinkle over the feta, walnuts, nigella seeds, and remaining dill, then drizzle with a little olive oil. Serve with the yogurt flatbread and crunchy vegetables, for dipping.

Tomatoes with whipped feta

Feta is often used in my kitchen, whether baked with lemon and spice to a crisp top or simply broken into brave pieces on a salad. It brings a welcome creaminess, saltiness, and acidity. Here I whip the feta with a little yogurt, which gives it lightness. It works perfectly against the sweet succulence of summer tomatoes and the crunch of breadcrumbs.

Preheat your oven to 425°F (220°C). Roughly tear the sourdough into pieces and pulse in a food processor until you have rough bread crumbs. A bit of texture is good here, so try not to go too far, otherwise your crumb will be too fine and sandy.

Toss the bread crumbs on a baking sheet with a drizzle of olive oil, a pinch of salt, and some black pepper. Place in the center of the warmed oven for 4 to 5 minutes, or until the bread crumbs have turned toasty and golden.

Meanwhile, cut the tomatoes into slices and wedges, keeping them quite irregular and making the most of the shape of each tomato. Place them in a bowl with the tablespoon of olive oil, sherry vinegar, lemon zest, and a couple of generous pinches of salt and some black pepper. Leave to one side while you move on to the feta.

In a food processor, whip the feta and yogurt together until the cheese is completely smooth and creamy. Taste and add salt, if necessary, pepper, and some of the lemon juice. Scoop into a bowl and top with the nigella seeds.

Spoon the tomatoes with their olive oil and vinegar onto plates and dot the whipped feta around the tomatoes to fill in any empty spaces. Sprinkle over the bread crumbs, scatter over the marjoram, and drizzle with a little more oil.

SERVES 2

1¾ ounces (50 g) stale sourdough bread

1 tablespoon of the best quality extra-virgin olive oil you can find, plus a little extra

sea salt and freshly ground black pepper

4½ cups (800 g) tomatoes

½ tablespoon sherry vinegar

the zest and juice of 1 unwaxed lemon

1⅓ cups (200 g) feta cheese

2 tablespoons thick Greek yogurt

1 teaspoon nigella seeds

4 sprigs of marjoram or oregano, leaves picked

Corn on the cob with mustard-seed butter

There is something about corn and warm days that sits just right. Every single summer holiday I have been on has memories of corn; maybe I seek it out. Crunched straight off the cob, bathed in lime and butter, eaten with sandy feet on the beaches of Indonesia; little plastic cups piled with elote corn, trimmed from its kernels, topped with sour cream, mayonnaise, cayenne, and a squeeze of lemon from stands that line Mexican beaches and roadsides; and tamales—little patties of fluffy cornmeal wrapped in their husks and steamed over fires on the Native American reservations of Arizona.

There is something about the sweet pop of a kernel of corn that makes it OK to eat when it's searingly hot, when almost nothing else (apart from an ice cream or an ice-cold coconut) will do. This is how I've been eating corn the last few summers: grilled and rolled in South Indian spiced butter, then topped with a punchy but fresh green chutney (see page 36 for the recipe). If you don't have time to grill the corn, this still works well on simply boiled corn; boil it for 8 to 10 minutes, until the kernels are tender.

MAKES 4

4 ears of corn

7 tablespoons butter or ghee

1 tablespoon mustard seeds

1 teaspoon cumin seeds

a sprinkling of red pepper flakes

TO SERVE

green chutney (see page 36)

Heat a griddle or grill.

Pull the husks from the corn cobs, and when the griddle is hot, cook the corn, turning regularly, until the kernels are deep gold, brown here and there, and tender—this will take about 10 minutes.

Warm the butter or ghee in a small pan, and once it's hot, add the mustard and cumin seeds. Cook for a minute or so until the mustard seeds pop, then take the pan off the heat and add the red pepper flakes.

When the corn is ready, place it on a baking sheet and pour over the warm spiced butter, then turn the cobs on the baking sheet, anointing every last kernel. Take it to the table, spoon over the green chutney, and eat hot.

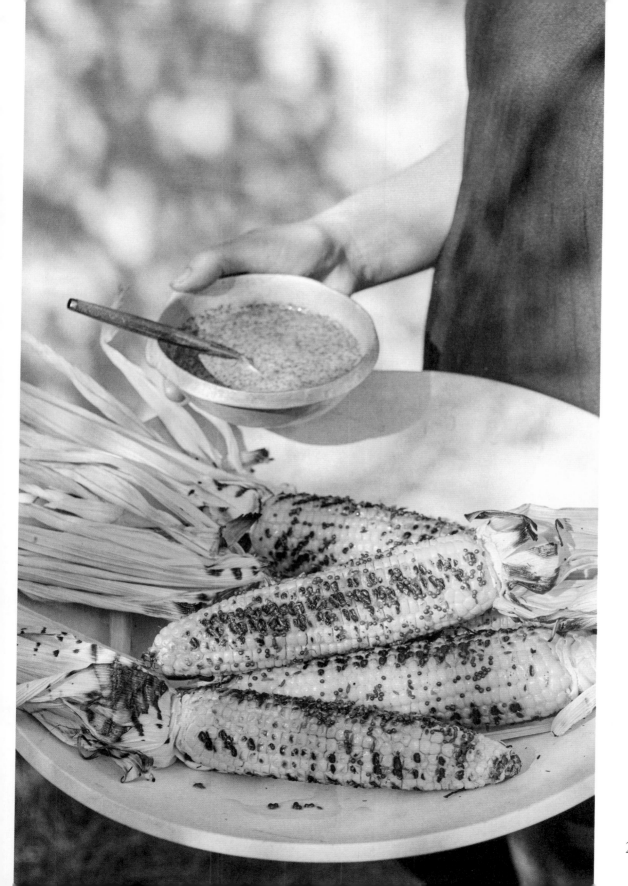

Ajo blanco

I first tried this soup in a very hot kitchen during my first summer as a chef. It was made by one of my all-time favorite cooks, Steve Pooley. There are few people who have taught me more about cooking and the unbridled joy of eating. This soup is just that—a joy. Refreshing and richly satisfying all at once, with a perfect balance of mellow creaminess from the almonds, punch from the sherry vinegar—soaked bread, and sweetness from the grapes.

If you don't have sherry vinegar, red wine vinegar will work in its place, though you might need a little less.

Put the almonds in a frying pan and place over low heat. Shake them around for a minute or two, allowing the almonds to toast very slightly—just the very palest tinge, to accentuate the taste of the nut. Put on a plate and leave to cool.

Put the bread in a large bowl and cover with ½ cup (100 ml) of cold water. Leave to soak for 10 minutes. Once the almonds have cooled and the bread has soaked, tear the bread into your food processor in little pieces, then pour away any water left in the bowl. Add all but a little handful of the almonds to the bread, then add the garlic, cucumber, and ½ cup (75 g) of the grapes. Add a little of the iced water and whizz until smooth.

Now, with the motor running slowly, add the rest of the water, the oil, and vinegar and blitz until really smooth. If you have a powerful blender, your soup may be smooth enough to eat without sieving. If not, use the back of a ladle to press the soup through a sieve into a bowl, forcing out every last drop of liquid.

Season your soup with a little salt and pepper, then taste and add more seasoning, vinegar, or oil until it tastes good to you. Cover and chill in the fridge for at least 2 hours, along with four soup bowls.

Chop the remaining almonds into little shards, and slice the remaining grapes. Once cooled, divide the soup among the bowls, drizzle with a little good olive oil, and top with the almonds, grapes, and dill fronds.

SERVES 4

- 1½ cups (220 g) blanched almonds
- 3½ ounces (100 g) good stale bread (I use sourdough)
- 2–4 cloves of garlic, depending on taste
- 1 small cucumber, peeled and roughly chopped
- ⅔ cup (100 g) green grapes
- 2½ cups (600 ml) ice-cold water
- 14 tablespoons olive oil
- 3 tablespoons sherry vinegar (see note above)
- sea salt and freshly ground black pepper

TO FINISH

- good olive oil
- dill or fennel fronds

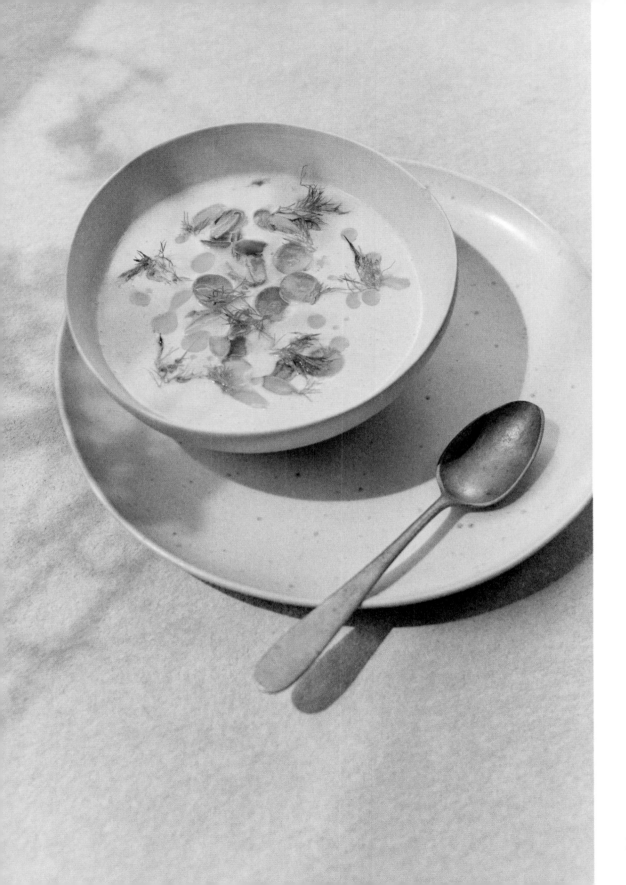

Corn, zucchini, and cilantro soup

While cold soups win the day when it's blistering, most of the soups I eat in summer are hot, but with a steer toward crunch and freshness. This one makes the most of the hero of the hour, papery husked corn on the cob, teaming it with chile, squash, and yellow zucchini and crisp lettuce. The result: a soup layered with texture and freshness that cooks instantly. It's good cold too.

Coarsely grate 1½ zucchini and/or squash; you will use the remaining half later. Heat 1 tablespoon of the butter or oil in a large, deep pan, then add the grated zucchini/squash with a pinch of salt and cook for a few minutes, until they are soft and beginning to color. Place in a blender and pulse a little, keeping a bit of texture. Put to one side.

Heat 2 more tablespoons of oil or butter over medium heat and fry the onion for about 5 minute until beginning to soften, then add the garlic and cook for another couple of minutes without browning. Add the zucchini and squash mixture, and cook for another couple of minutes.

Take a handful of the corn kernels and put to one side for later. Blitz the remaining raw kernels in the blender with up to 4½ cups (1 liter) of water (depending on what consistency you like your soup to be), adding most of the cilantro leaves (saving a few to finish) and all the stalks, the chile and most of the shredded lettuce. Blitz until smooth.

Add the corn mixture to the pan with the zucchini, squash, and onions, then cook over medium heat for another few minutes, stirring and scraping the bottom of the pan to prevent the mixture from sticking. Meanwhile, cut the remaining half zucchini or squash into thin coins. Heat a frying pan with the remaining tablespoon of oil or butter and fry the zucchini or squash, stirring frequently, for 5 minutes, until they start to brown on both sides. Push the zucchini or squash to the side of the pan and add the handful of corn kernels. Continue to cook over high heat until the corn starts to pop and blister. Remove from the heat and grate over the lime zest.

To serve, squeeze over the lime juice and season with more salt and pepper to taste. Ladle into bowls and finish with the remaining lettuce, cilantro, and the golden zucchini, squash, and corn.

SERVES 4

2 medium zucchini and/or yellow squash, or a few baby ones (1 pound/about 500 g)

4 tablespoons butter or olive oil

sea salt

1 onion, finely chopped

2 cloves of garlic, finely chopped

4 ears of corn, kernels only

a small bunch of fresh cilantro, plus more to serve

1 green chile

2 Little Gem lettuce bunches, washed and shredded

1 unwaxed lime

freshly ground black pepper

Tarragon-blistered tomatoes with green oil

This recipe calls for quite a lot of tomatoes because they shrink as they cook, so make it when the season is in full swing and they are at their most affordable and tastiest. I serve these with the little summer herb cheeses on page 246; they would be amazing in a tart too. I often make a double batch and keep half in a jar in the fridge under some olive oil; that way they will keep for a few weeks and are an incredible and speedy way to boost the flavor of a quick dinner.

Preheat your oven to 340°F (170°C). First, prepare your tomatoes. Cut larger ones into quarters, medium ones in half, and leave the smaller ones whole, then place them all on a baking sheet, keeping any cut sides up. Tuck the garlic cloves in around them.

Divide your tarragon into two. Put half to one side, then pick the leaves from the tough stems of the other half and scatter these over the tomatoes. Drizzle with a good amount of olive oil (about 3 tablespoons) and season well with salt and pepper.

Place in the hot oven for 1½ hours, until the tomatoes have shrunk and are sticky and caramelized. Check them after an hour, as some of the smaller tomatoes may be done sooner; if they are, you can scoop these out and put the rest back in.

While the tomatoes are in the oven, make the green oil. Have ready a bowl of iced water. Put a small saucepan of water on to boil. Blanch the parsley for 15 seconds, then take the pan off the heat and immerse the herb in the ice-cold water to keep your parsley green. Strain the parsley using a sieve and use the back of a spoon to squeeze out as much moisture as you can; you can do this using a clean tea towel too—you don't want any moisture left. Use a good blender to whizz the herbs with the oil until they have broken down and the oil is bright green, then strain through a fine sieve. If you are particularly keen on a very smooth green oil, you could strain it through a sieve lined with muslin.

Toast your bread and spread it with the cooked garlic cloves. Pile the roasted tomatoes on top, with some herb oil drizzled over.

SERVES 4

FOR THE TOMATOES

2½ pounds (1 kg) tomatoes on the vine (I use a mixture in all colors)

6 cloves of garlic, peeled

a bunch of tarragon

olive oil

sea salt and freshly ground black pepper

FOR THE GREEN OIL

a small bunch of flat-leaf parsley

7 tablespoons canola oil

TO SERVE

4 generous slices of bread

little yogurt and herb cheeses (see page 246)

Little yogurt and herb cheeses

I make these in summer when I have people coming for lunch. I like them with the tarragon-blistered tomatoes on page 244.

For the herbs I use tarragon, parsley, chervil, or chives. You can add garlic—a grated clove is popular—but personally I find it too overpowering. I often add it to half the mixture to keep everyone happy.

Line a large sieve with a square of muslin and spoon in the yogurt. Sit the sieve over a large mixing bowl and make space for it in the fridge, then let it sit overnight, squeezing out the bag to encourage it to drain before you go to bed and when you wake up. If you have space to suspend the sieve so that it doesn't sit on the bottom of the bowl, all the better.

MAKES 6

4 cups (1 kg) thick Greek yogurt

the zest of 1 unwaxed lemon

a bunch of soft herbs, leaves picked and finely chopped

flaky sea salt

TO SERVE

more soft herbs and edible flowers

good olive oil

Tip the strained yogurt from the muslin into a bowl. Add the lemon zest and herbs and a big pinch of salt.

Line six little ramekins with some more muslin squares that are generous enough to overhang the edges. Spoon the yogurt cheese into the ramekins and use a spoon to smooth out the surfaces. Fold the muslin back over the tops and use something heavy to weigh them down—a can or a jar should work—then leave them in a cool place to firm up. You can leave them for anywhere from an hour to overnight, depending on how firm you would like them.

To serve, unwrap them from their little wrappers, scatter with the herbs and flowers, and drizzle with a little good oil.

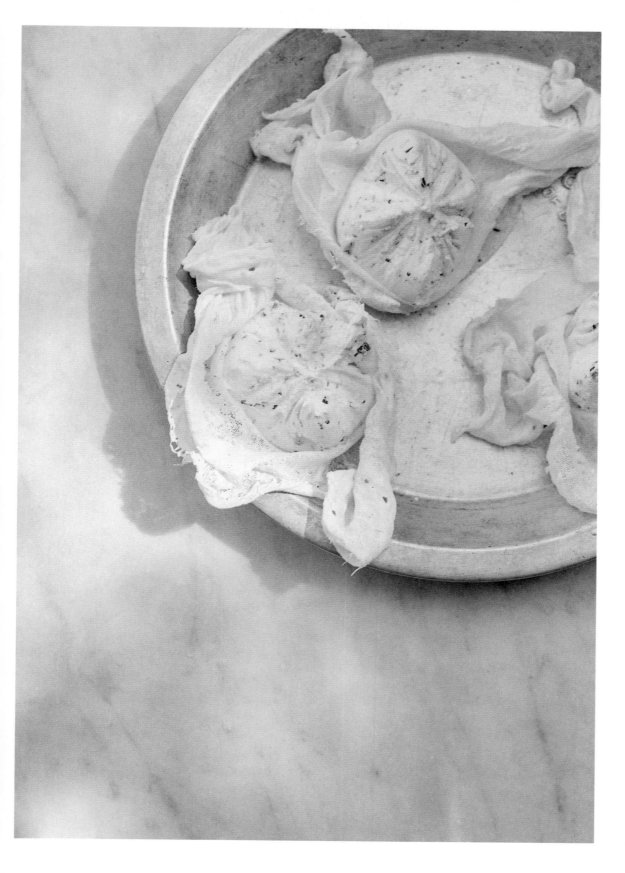

Grilled Caesar salad with crispy chickpeas

A childhood spent in America meant a lot of Caesar salads: the clean crunch of Cos lettuce, the serious hit of flavor from the garlic-kissed dressing, the burnished golden brown of a crouton. This Caesar is a bit different from the ones I ate growing up. The dressing is spiked with tahini, and instead of bread I use crispy chickpeas for croutons (which incidentally are great on their own as a snack or to eat with a few drinks). The lettuce is charred too, adding a pleasing smoky edge to it all, though you could make this just as successfully without grilling the lettuce if you like. I've listed a few other ways of using the dressing, opposite.

SERVES 4

4 Little Gem lettuce heads

1 × 14.5-ounce (400-g) or 10.5-ounce (300-g) can of chickpeas, drained

1 tablespoon canola oil

sea salt and freshly ground black pepper

the zest of 1 unwaxed lemon

FOR THE CAESAR DRESSING

½ a clove of garlic

4 tablespoons light tahini

2 tablespoons Greek yogurt

1 tablespoon olive oil

the juice of 1½ lemons

2 teaspoons Dijon mustard

a scant dash of soy sauce or tamari

TO FINISH

⅓ cup (40 g) Parmesan (I use a vegetarian/rennet-free one)

a small bunch of parsley, leaves picked

freshly ground black pepper

Preheat the oven to 475°F (240°C). Heat a griddle pan over a high heat.

While you're waiting for the oven and griddle to come up to temperature, slice the Little Gems in half lengthways. Toss the chickpeas on a baking sheet with the canola oil and a pinch of salt and pepper, then place in the center of the hot oven for 25 minutes, shaking now and again, until you hear the chickpeas popping and they are blistering and crisp.

Meanwhile, grill the Little Gem halves for a couple of minutes on each side until deep char marks form and they collapse a little. Lay the charred lettuces on a platter and leave to one side.

Next, make the dressing. Finely grate the ½ clove of garlic into your food processor, then add all the other ingredients with 6 tablespoons of water, and blitz until smooth. Taste and adjust the seasoning, adding more lemon/salt/pepper/soy to taste.

When the chickpeas have had their time, scatter over the lemon zest then put them on paper towels to drain and crisp.

To serve, toss the charred lettuce in a few tablespoons of the dressing, then put it onto a platter, scatter the chickpeas over the lettuce, and grate over the Parmesan. Serve with some more dressing, a good grind of black pepper, and a few parsley leaves.

Other ways to use your Caesar dressing

- In a sandwich with smoked
  tofu and lettuce

- To spoon on top of a soup
  or stew

- To dress leftover quinoa
  or grains

- Thickened with a little more
  yogurt for dipping crudités

- To spoon on baked potatoes

Herb, lentil, and lime brown rice salad

Until recently I was never a fan of rice salads—they conjured up memories of 1980s barbecues. But my mother-in-law, Sian, is the queen of them; hers are always packed with flavor and perfectly dressed, so I've been converted. A rice salad is one of those things that gets better after a day in the fridge, making this a good dish to prepare ahead if you have lots of people to feed.

This recipe is now a firm favorite all summer. It's half rice, half lentils, with a spiced dressing that works well with pretty much any pulse or grain.

Soak the raisins in the vinegar and leave to one side.

Fill your kettle with water, and boil. Rinse your rice under cold running water until the water runs clear. Heat a drizzle of oil in a heavy-based pan, then add the rinsed rice and stir to coat in the oil for a couple of minutes. Pour in twice the amount of boiling water. Bring to a boil, then cover with a clean tea towel then the lid (making sure the towel, is tightly secured, away from the heat source), and cook for 8 minutes for white basmati and 25 for brown. Take the pan off the heat and, with the lid on, leave it to sit and steam without peeking.

Heat a pan over medium-high heat. Once hot, add a drizzle of oil and the red onions, and cook for 5 to 8 minutes, until crisp but not burnt. Remove to a plate lined with paper towels to keep them crispy.

Make the dressing. Toast all the seeds in a dry pan for a couple of minutes, until they smell fragrant. Add the ground spices, stir quickly, then take the pan off the heat and place in a mortar. Bash with the pestle until they are broken down a bit. Pour into a pitcher, add all the rest of the dressing ingredients, and mix well.

Take the lid off the rice—it should be light and fluffy and have absorbed all the liquid but if there is any excess water, drain it off. Use a fork to fluff up the rice, then put it in a bowl. Drain and add the lentils, chopped celery, and the dressing. Roughly chop the herbs and add these too, along with the raisins. Season with salt and pepper, mix well and taste, adding more salt, pepper, lime, and oil as needed. Remember it will mellow a little as it sits. When you are ready to eat, scatter over the crispy onions and pile into bowls.

SERVES 4

⅔ cup (100 g) raisins or currants (I use golden raisins)

4 tablespoons red wine vinegar

1⅓ cups (250 g) basmati rice (I use brown basmati)

olive oil

2 red onions, finely sliced

1 × 14.5-ounce (400-g) can of cooked lentils, drained (or 1 cup/250 g home-cooked, see page 461)

4 stalks of celery, finely chopped, any leaves reserved

a large bunch of herbs (e.g., basil, parsley, and cilantro), leaves picked

sea salt and freshly ground black pepper

FOR THE DRESSING

1 tablespoon cumin seeds

1 teaspoon cilantro (coriander) seeds

the seeds from 4 cardamom pods

¼ teaspoon ground cloves

a few gratings of fresh nutmeg

4 tablespoons olive oil

2 tablespoons cider vinegar

the zest and juice of 2 unwaxed limes

1 tablespoon maple syrup

1 tablespoon Dijon mustard

Summer taco salad

I love tacos more than I love salad, and putting taco flavors into a salad makes me love salad a bit more. This is an all-in-one salad; it's a meal on its own, with slow-roasted tomatoes, crumbled tofu, black beans, and a crumbling of crispy tortilla chips. The sweet notes of the tomatoes and the tomato-rich dressing seem to make this a hit with people of all ages, even small ones.

If you want to make this more quickly you can skip cooking the tomatoes and use 3½ cups (200 g) of sun-dried in their place.

Preheat your oven to 340°F (170°C).

First, put the tomatoes on a baking sheet, cut side up, and roast in the oven for 30 minutes. Use your hands to crumble the tofu into small bite-size pieces. Heat a medium frying pan over medium heat and pour in a little olive oil. Add the tofu and a good pinch of salt and pepper, and cook until it is crisp on all sides. While this is happening mix together the chile powder, paprika, cumin, garlic, and lime zest. Add to the pan for the last minute of cooking and stir a couple of times to take the rawness out of the spices and garlic, then take off the heat and cover to keep warm.

Combine all the dressing ingredients in a bowl and mix well.

Thinly shred the heads of lettuce and put them in a large salad bowl. Toss with half the salad dressing, then quarter and pit the avocados, scoop them from their skins, and slice into little pieces. Add them to the bowl with the black beans, scallions, and cilantro leaves. Crumble in the tortilla chips and feta, then toss in along with the tofu. Serve in the middle of the table with the rest of the dressing on the side for spooning over.

SERVES 4

2¾ cups (100 g) cherry tomatoes, halved

7 ounces (200 g) firm tofu

sea salt and freshly ground black pepper

olive oil

a pinch of chile powder

¼ teaspoon sweet smoked paprika

¼ teaspoon ground cumin

1 clove of garlic, finely chopped

the zest of 1 unwaxed lime

2 heads of romaine lettuce

2 avocados

1x 14.5-ounce (400-g) can of black beans, drained (or 1½ cups/300 g home-cooked, see page 461)

4 scallions, thinly sliced

a small bunch of cilantro, leaves picked

2 handfuls of tortilla chips

crumbled feta or Manchego (optional)

FOR THE DRESSING

4 tablespoons passata, or canned crushed tomatoes, puréed then strained to remove seeds

4 tablespoons cider vinegar

3 tablespoons canola or mild olive oil

2 tablespoons maple syrup

½ teaspoon chipotle paste or smoked paprika

Smacked cucumbers with orange and Sichuan pepper

SERVES 4–6

2 cucumbers (about
   1¼ pounds/600 g in total)

2 tablespoons flaky sea salt

FOR THE DRESSING

3 cloves of garlic, finely
   chopped

3 tablespoons tamari or
   soy sauce

2 tablespoons brown rice
   vinegar

1 tablespoon toasted sesame
   oil

1 tablespoon golden honey

a pinch of red pepper flakes

½ teaspoon ground, toasted
   Sichuan pepper

the zest and juice of
   1 unwaxed orange

TO SERVE

½ cup (50 g) peanuts, toasted
   and roughly chopped

Cucumber has been a staple in our house this past year. It's been chopped into batons and devoured by my son, the cooling crispness soothing his little teething gums. Dylan's onto something, as when the weather heats up, cucumber is what I crave: crunchy, refreshing, and altogether a summer food. Seek out the knobbly home-grown cucumbers if you can, as their flavor is much more intense.

This salad is my take on a Fuchsia Dunlop classic: orange and Sichuan pepper provide top notes and interest. It goes well with a bowl of simple honey and soy-dressed noodles and a bit of crisped tofu, if you are after something more filling.

———————————————————

Lay the whole cucumbers flat on a cutting board and bash them with a rolling pin all over (about 10 firm whacks should do the trick).

Cut each cucumber into quarters lengthways, then cut each quarter into roughly ⅜-inch (1-cm) diagonal slices. Place the slices in a bowl with the salt and toss to coat. Set aside for 15 to 20 minutes.

Mix all the dressing ingredients in a bowl with a fork.

Drain the cucumber in a sieve to remove the excess liquid that may have been released, then toss in the dressing and scatter with the peanuts.

Corn, tomatoes, and crispy bread

This is everything I love about late summer. I keep the corn and tomatoes raw here, countering their natural sweetness with a good hit of red wine vinegar. The golden on the outside, chewy on the inside croutons make this summer salad more of a meal. It's finished with some pistachios and pecorino, but feta or Parmesan would work too.

I eat this as a lunch or light supper, and to make it even more substantial, I often pair it with some avocado smashed with a little lime juice and some chopped green chile. You could also roughly chop a couple of avocados through the salad if you like.

Preheat your oven to 425°F (220°C).

SERVES 4

2 slices of good bread (I use sourdough)

olive oil

sea salt and freshly ground pepper

2 ears of corn

1 pound (500 g) tomatoes (all shapes, sizes and colors)

4 scallions

sea salt and freshly ground black pepper

2 tablespoons red wine vinegar

¾ cup (100 g) shelled pistachios

½ cup (50 g) pecorino (I use a vegetarian/rennet-free one)

a small bunch of mint, leaves picked

a small bunch of basil, leaves picked

extra-virgin olive oil

Tear your bread into small rough chunks and lay on a baking sheet. Drizzle generously with olive oil (about 4 tablespoons) and sprinkle with salt and pepper. Roast in the hot oven for 10 to 15 minutes: How long you cook them for will be dependent on the density of your bread. You want the croutons to be crisp on the outside but chewy on the inside, so try to take them out before they are hard all the way through.

Next, onto the salad. Cut the corn kernels from the ears; I do this by resting the end of the corn in a large mixing bowl, which prevents the corn from flying everywhere. Cut the tomatoes into bite-sized chunks—it's nice to keep the shapes and cuts different here—and add them to the bowl. Finely slice the scallions and add these too. Add a good pinch of salt and pepper and the vinegar, and leave it to sit for a while.

When the croutons are ready, take them out of the oven. Roughly chop the pistachios and finely crumble or coarsely grate the pecorino—I like mine crumbled into pieces about the size of a grain of rice. Tear the herbs into the bowl, then add the pistachios and cheese and about 3½ tablespoons of extra-virgin olive oil and toss everything together. Finish by tossing the croutons in just before you serve.

Peppery green salad with apricots and curd cheese

SERVES 4

FOR THE SALAD

1 large head of fennel

4 big handfuls of peppery salad leaves, (arugula, watercress, mizuna, mustard leaf), washed

4 apricots, pitted and cut into eighths

1 cup (100 g) goat curd or soft goat cheese

a handful of hazelnuts, toasted

FOR THE DRESSING

juice of 1 lemon

olive oil

salt and black pepper

a little runny honey

This is all about the balance between peppery leaves and the icy, cleansing flavor of fennel, the sweet, custardy apricots, and some clean creaminess and acidity from the goat curd. Search out more unusual leaves if you can, but arugula and watercress will do fine. Peaches or plums would work well in place of the apricots. A simple, but perfectly balanced, salad.

First, finely slice the fennel, then immerse in a bowl of cold water to stop it browning. Iced water will make the fennel curl and twist into interesting shapes, if you have ice on hand.

Next, make the dressing. Squeeze the lemon juice into a jam jar and top up with twice the amount of olive oil, a pinch of salt and pepper, and a tiny squeeze of honey. Shake well. Taste for balance. Add more lemon, oil, honey, and salt as needed—but remember it'll taste a little mellower on the leaves.

Drain and dry the fennel, then put in a bowl with the washed leaves and apricot slices. Add a little dressing and toss to coat. Tumble into a serving bowl or platter. Crumble over the cheese and hazelnuts.

Quick summer stew with saffron and poached eggs

This is one of the quickest, most flavorful suppers I know. A rich, deeply spiced broth surrounds buttery chickpeas, some sautéed zucchini, caramelly dates, and just-cooked green beans, all topped off with perfectly sunny eggs poached in the broth.

Here I use a spice blend called ras el hanout, a sort of North African garam masala. It's traditionally a blend of cardamom, cumin, clove, cinnamon, nutmeg, mace, allspice, ginger, coriander seed, peppercorn, sweet and hot paprika, fenugreek, and turmeric. It imparts a heady, very slightly sweet note into anything it touches. You can, of course, make your own with a pestle and mortar and a bit of determination. I add a generous pinch of saffron too for that sunshine warmth it gives. Some ras el hanout blends include salt, so check and bear this in mind as you season.

Heat a good glug of canola or olive oil in a pan, add the leeks and garlic, and cook on medium heat for 5 minutes, until the leeks have started to soften. Then sprinkle over the saffron and ras el hanout.

Next add the chickpeas and the stock. Bring to a steady simmer and cook for 15 minutes, until the broth has thickened a little.

Meanwhile, heat a pan with a little olive oil and add the sliced zucchini and the dates. Sauté until the zucchini are browned on both sides and the dates have begun to harden a little and caramelize. You may need to do this in two batches if your pan is small.

Next add the green beans—if you like your beans well cooked, simmer them for a couple of minutes; if you like them with some bite, then straightaway make four little wells in the stew and crack in the eggs one by one, top with a lid, and cook until the eggs are cooked to your liking. I like the yolks just set and the whites firm, which takes about 4 to 5 minutes.

Meanwhile, mix the yogurt with the chile and lemon zest and juice, with a good pinch of sea salt and pepper.

Once the eggs are cooked, spoon an egg into each bowl, ladle over the vegetables and thickened broth, and top with the caramelized dates, sesame seeds, a squeeze more lemon juice, herbs, and the yogurt to spoon over.

SERVES 4

olive oil

2 leeks, finely chopped

2 cloves of garlic, thinly sliced

a generous pinch of saffron

2 teaspoons ras el hanout spice mix

1 14.5-ounce (400 g) can of chickpeas, drained

2 cups (500 ml) vegetable stock

2 zucchini, thickly sliced (about ½ inch [1½ cm])

5 dates, pitted and roughly chopped

1¾ cups (200 g) green beans, chopped into bite-sized lengths

4 organic eggs

½ cup (100 ml) yogurt

a pinch of dried chile

the juice and zest of 1 lemon

a couple of tablespoons of toasted sesame seeds

a few sprigs of fresh mint or basil

How to make the perfect green salad

Each week, a small unassuming bag arrives in my vegetable box, labeled 'Hackney salad'. The leaves are piercing greens, acid yellows, deep emeralds, and rich purples. Each leaf has a unique flavor and is so full of personality. Small salad growers are cropping up all over the U.K. and the U.S., growing interesting leaves, micro salad, salad herbs, and flowers—seek them out when you can.

But even leaves from a supermarket bring the possibility of a really good bowl of salad. I like to buy whole lettuce, cutting and washing them at one time, filling the fridge with a few days' worth of leaves. There is a lot to choose from on the supermarket shelves: the bitter crunch of chicory, the soft frill of lamb's lettuce, spiky arugula as hot as peppercorns, sweet and crisp Little Gems, and red-fringed Cos.

A good salad is all about the balance of the leaves, the perfect dressing, and each mouthful being unique: a pop of lemon, a crunchy leaf, the frond of a delicate herb. I favor cooling, calm leaves to make up most of the plate, with a scattering of hot, peppery, earthy, or citrus notes. For me this is what makes a simple green salad one of the most pleasing things to eat.

1	2	3	4
Choose a base leaf	**Add a bitter note**	**Add a peppery note**	**Add a bright fresh note**
butter lettuce (soft round lettuce)	chicory	watercress	sorrel
Cos lettuce	treviso	arugula	mizuna
Little Gem	escarole	turnip tops	spinach
Reines de glaces lettuce	radicchio	mustard leaf	lamb's lettuce
oak leaf	frisée	nasturtium	pea shoots

How to wash salad well

This may be totally obvious to some, but washing and storing salad well will extend its life and crispness. I like to wash my lettuce as soon as I can after buying, in a big sink full of very cold water, running my hands gently through the leaves. Drain then spin it dry. If you are using it immediately, spin it totally dry; if you are keeping it in the fridge, then leave a little water on the leaves and store it in a bag or the salad drawer, lined with a clean tea towel until needed. This way it will last for over a week.

5

Add a soft
herby note

|

chives

|

mint

|

chervil

|

parsley

|

cilantro

6

Dress carefully
with two parts of
something rich

|

olive oil

|

hazelnut oil

|

canola oil

|

avocado oil

|

plain yogurt

7

And one
part acid

|

lemon juice

|

lime juice

|

wine vinegar

|

balsamic vinegar

|

rice wine vinegar

8

And add a
good seasoning
of sea salt and
freshly ground
black pepper

Summer beet salad with orange blossom water and curd cheese

In this salad I use every color of beets I can get my hands on: the deep pinky-purple beets of my childhood, next to the candy-cane-striped Chioggia beets and the paint-pot yellow ones. It makes for the most beautiful plate of food.

I use orange blossom water here, which I think works particularly well with the earthy flavor of beets; however, its delicate fragrant flavor can split opinion, so if you are not a fan, just stick to the orange zest.

Scrub or peel the beets; if the skin is thin and tender, as it should be at this time of year, a good scrub should do. Use a mandoline or your very good knife skills to slice the beets into ⅜-inch- (1-cm-) thick rounds and place them in a bowl.

Make the dressing by combining all the ingredients and seasoning with salt and pepper to taste. Pour half the dressing over the raw beets and leave to rest for 15 minutes so the flavors can meld and mingle.

Toss the beets with the cilantro, then arrange in a bowl or on a platter and top with the rest of the dressing. Dot the goat curd over the top and scatter over the walnuts.

SERVES 4 AS A STARTER OR A SIDE

1¾ pounds (800 g) raw beets (see note at right)

a small bunch of cilantro, leaves picked and roughly chopped

4½ ounces (125 g) soft, rindless goat's cheese or goat's curd

½ cup (50 g) walnuts, toasted and lightly chopped

FOR THE DRESSING

juice of 1 orange

2 teaspoons orange blossom water or rose water

2 tablespoons extra-virgin olive oil

1 teaspoon golden honey

sea salt and freshly ground black pepper

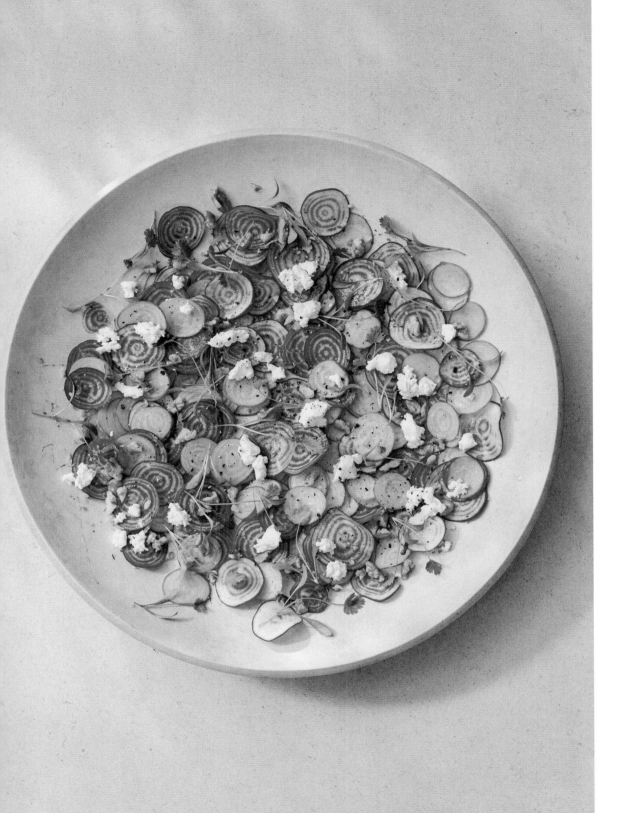

Black sesame noodle bowl

7 ounces (200 g) rice noodles (I use brown rice noodles)

¾ cup (100 g) unsalted cashews

4 tablespoons black sesame seeds

4 tablespoons unsweetened desiccated coconut

a small bunch of cilantro, leaves picked, stalks finely chopped

a small bunch of mint, leaves picked

a few large handfuls of mixed greens

2 scallions, very finely sliced

½ a red chile, finely sliced

2½ cups (150 g) sugar snap peas, sliced in half lengthways

FOR THE DRESSING

3 tablespoons tamari or soy sauce

2 tablespoons toasted sesame oil

2 tablespoons golden honey

2 tablespoons brown rice vinegar

the zest and juice of 1 unwaxed lime

1 small clove of garlic, grated

a thumb-size piece of ginger, peeled and grated

I first made this noodle bowl for a picnic, and it's been made many times since. The dressing is a favorite for summer noodles; I finish it with lots of shredded greens and some final crunch from cashews and black sesame seeds (regular sesame seeds, well toasted, would work just as well), which elevates this from a one-textured noodle salad to something much more interesting. I use brown rice noodles here, as I prefer their depth of flavor and find them more filling and satisfying, but use what you can get your hands on. Swiss chard, kale or spinach will all work here. The salad is great served just warm or cold.

———————————

Preheat the oven to 425°F (220°C). Cook the noodles in a medium saucepan according to the package instructions, breaking them up with chopsticks or a fork from time to time to ensure they don't stick together. Drain and refresh under cold water, then transfer to a large bowl.

Put the cashews on a baking sheet in the oven for 4 minutes, then, once they have toasted for 4 minutes, add the sesame seeds and the coconut. Cook for another 4 to 5 minutes, or until golden.

Meanwhile, whisk the dressing ingredients together. Pour half the dressing over the noodles and toss well to coat, then stir in the chopped cilantro stalks.

Finely chop the cilantro leaves and mint leaves and set aside. Wash the greens, then spin them dry. Remove any tough stalks, stack the leaves, roll up and slice into thin ribbons, then add to the noodles with the scallions and the chile.

Once the nuts, seeds, and coconut are golden, allow them to cool, and roughly chop the cashew nuts.

Toss the herbs, sugar snap peas, and the toasted mixture with your noodles and serve with the rest of the dressing for spooning over.

Ricotta gnocchi with brown-butter tomato sauce

This is another favorite recipe from my *Guardian* column. We made it at the photo shoot and that night I made it again for dinner—that's when you know something is really tasty. These are forgiving ricotta dumplings; they use a little flour and sit in a cherry tomato sauce spiked with the toastiness of brown butter. I use cherry tomatoes, as I find they make the sauce perfectly sweet, but you can use larger ones; you may just need to cook the sauce for a little longer.

The ricotta you use here is important: the watery ricotta that you can buy in most supermarkets is a lot wetter than the strained ricotta that I prefer to use for these dumplings, as well as for dishes such as baked ricotta and desserts. You can buy it in good Italian delis, or you can strain supermarket ricotta yourself. Simply wrap it in muslin and hang it over a mixing bowl for 4 hours or overnight (2 cups/500 g fresh ricotta yields about 1½ cups/400 g strained).

SERVES 6

1¼ cup (150 g) pasta flour (tipo "00")

2 cups (500 g) strained ricotta (see note above)

1 teaspoon flaky sea salt

¼ of a whole nutmeg

1 organic egg, beaten

FOR THE TOMATO SAUCE

3 tablespoons extra-virgin olive oil

2 cloves of garlic, thinly sliced

5 cups (750 g) cherry tomatoes

a generous pinch of flaky sea salt

a small bunch of basil, leaves picked

TO FINISH

3½ tablespoons butter

Parmesan (I use a vegetarian/rennet-free one)

a few basil leaves

To make the gnocchi, spread half the flour out on a work surface in a rough circle and crumble the ricotta on top. Sprinkle over the salt and grate the nutmeg on top. Use your fingers to delicately gather the ricotta into a mound, picking up the flour as you do. Make a well in the middle of the mound big enough to house the beaten egg. Pour the egg in and use a fork to work it carefully into the flour and ricotta until it has become a rough dough. Gently knead the dough, adding a little more flour if needed, until you have a smooth dough (you may not need to use all the flour). Try to be delicate here, as being rough will develop the gluten in the flour and make your gnocchi tough. Once smooth, wrap the dough and put it in the fridge for 1 hour.

While the dough is resting, you can get on with the sauce. Put the oil in a large frying pan with the garlic and place over medium heat for a couple of minutes. Add the cherry tomatoes and salt and cook for 30 minutes, pushing down on the tomatoes occasionally with the back of a wooden spoon until they have all burst and you have a bright red sauce. Add the basil leaves and put to one side. →

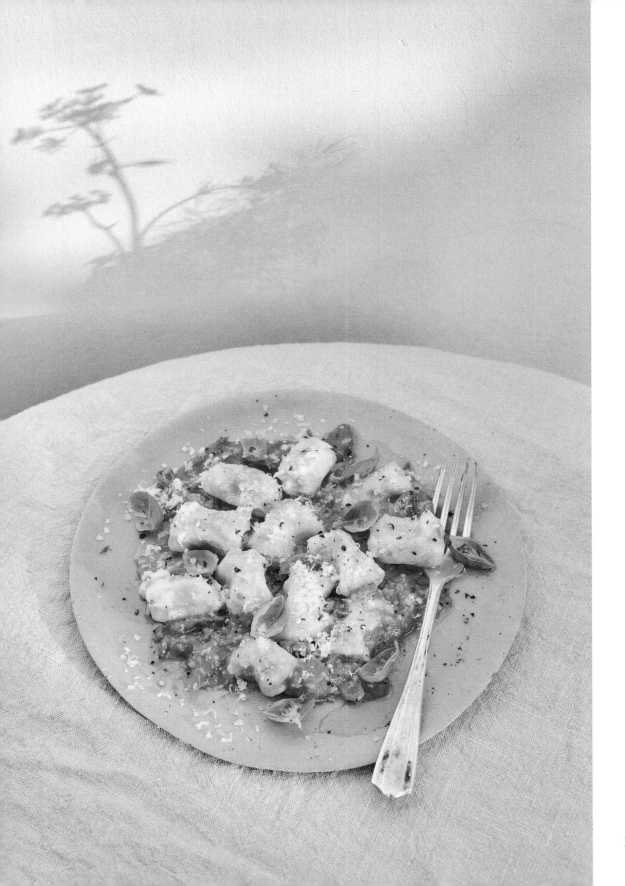

When you are ready to roll your gnocchi, lightly flour your work surface and have a lightly floured large tray nearby. Unwrap the dough and shape it into a 1-inch- (2.5-cm-) thick circle, then divide this into quarters. Take one quarter, and roll it into a log about ½-inch (1.5-cm) thick, rolling it back and forth with both hands until it is even. Be delicate, touching the dough lightly; the lighter the hand the lighter the dumplings. Cut this log into 1-inch (2.5-cm) pieces and transfer them to the flour-dusted tray. Repeat with the remaining three quarters of dough. You can keep the gnocchi in the fridge until you are ready to cook them.

When you are ready to serve, put a large pan of salted water to boil, and warm the tomato sauce gently. In a small frying pan, cook the butter over medium heat until it turns a couple of shades darker and smells nutty, then take off the heat and stir it into the tomato sauce.

Drop the gnocchi into the boiling water and cook until they rise to the surface—this should take about 2 minutes. You may need to cook the gnocchi in batches, or have two pans going if they are small. Toss the drained gnocchi in the tomato sauce. Add a grating of Parmesan and more basil leaves before serving.

Quick orzo with fennel, almonds, capers, and olives

This is a fresh and clean pasta dish with a super-quick sauce made from caramelized slices of fennel, almonds, buttery green olives, and fragrant dill with some cilantro seeds, which may seem a little off track, but trust me, they work amazingly. I serve this just warm, as I think the flavors come out better that way.

This recipe should come together in 15 to 20 minutes, so it's perfect for weeknight dinners and quick lunches. It also keeps really well; I often make a batch of it to take on long journeys as it's good cold.

You can make the olive sauce in advance and it will sit well in the fridge—just cover the top with a layer of olive oil. It's also great spread on toast, next to some roasted vegetables, or spooned on top of mozzarella.

First, bring a large pot of salted water to a boil and cook the orzo according to the package instructions. Heat a large pan over medium heat and add a good glug of olive oil and the fennel. Season with a little salt and cook for 10 minutes, until starting to brown and caramelize.

Put the bread into a bowl and pour over the vinegar and a couple of tablespoons of cold water to soften it. Pound the garlic to a paste with a tiny pinch of salt in the mortar and pestle, then add the cilantro seeds and bash to a coarse powder.

You can continue to make the sauce in a mortar and pestle or switch to a food processor. Either way, add the capers, almonds, most of the dill, and olives one by one, bashing or blitzing as you go. Rip up and add the soaked bread, and finally the olive oil little by little, until the sauce comes together to a nice dropping consistency.

By now the pasta should be cooked; drain it well and add it to the fennel. Take off the heat and stir in the olive sauce. Taste for salt, vinegar, and balance and add a little more of whatever is needed. Serve with a little lemon zest for a final sherbety punch, grated pecorino, and the rest of the dill.

SERVES 4

9 ounces (250 g) orzo pasta (I use whole-wheat)

olive oil

2 bulbs of fennel, trimmed and finely sliced (save any fronds)

sea salt

a thick slice of good bread (I use sourdough)

1 tablespoon white wine vinegar

1 clove of garlic, peeled

1 tablespoon cilantro (coriander) seeds

4 tablespoons baby capers

½ cup (50 g) almonds, skin on, toasted (see page 459)

a bunch of dill or fennel tops

1¼ cups (200 g) green olives, pitted

4 tablespoons extra-virgin olive oil

TO SERVE

1 unwaxed lemon

pecorino (I use a vegetarian/rennet-free one), for grating

Creamy spiced chickpeas, burnt lemon, and string beans

As a light but filling summer dinner, these chickpeas get an outing at least once a week in my house; they take under 15 minutes to cook but the layers of flavor that are imparted would suggest they took much longer.

Often I eat these with a fried egg or some steamed greens and yogurt, but this is my favorite way to serve them in the summer, with some lemon that's been charred on the grill, which adds some mellow acid and sweetness, and green beans cooked in the same way, which lends a pleasing smokiness to things. You could do the lemons and beans on the grill if you like.

Warm the olive oil in a large pan over medium heat, add the cumin seeds, nigella, and red pepper flakes and cook for a couple of minutes until they smell fragrant. Add the turmeric, sliced garlic, and onion and a good pinch of salt and pepper. Cook slowly for 10 minutes, until the onion is soft and sweet. Put a griddle on to heat.

Add the chickpeas to the pan of spices, along with all their liquid (about 1¼ cups/300 ml if using home-cooked), and cook for 30 minutes or until most of the liquid has evaporated.

Peel the strings from the sides of the beans using a speed peeler. When the griddle is smoking hot, add the string beans and char for about 4 minutes on each side, until they are blistered and blackened in places. Squeeze a little of the juice from half a lemon into a bowl, then grill all the lemon halves cut side down until well charred.

Put the yogurt, crushed garlic, a couple of tablespoons of extra-virgin olive oil, and some salt and pepper into a bowl with the lemon juice and mix well. Spoon out a tablespoon of the yogurt mixture into another mixing bowl and whisk with a tablespoon of olive oil.

Once the string beans and lemons are all cooked and the chickpeas are creamy, you are ready to eat. Cut the string beans into long widths at an angle, then mix them with the smaller amount of yogurt and oil. Pile onto plates next to some chickpeas, yogurt, and half a burnt lemon.

SERVES 4

3½ tablespoons olive oil

1 tablespoon cumin seeds

½ tablespoon nigella seeds

a good pinch of red pepper flakes

1 tablespoon ground turmeric

2 cloves of garlic, finely sliced, plus an extra clove, crushed

1 white onion, finely chopped

sea salt and freshly ground black pepper

1½ pounds (700 g) jarred or home-cooked chickpeas (see page 461) or 2 × 14.5-ounce (400-g) cans

1¼ pounds (600 g) string beans, tops trimmed

2 lemons, cut in half

½ cup (150 g) Greek yogurt

extra-virgin olive oil

All-summer salad

This is a salad I make from May to September, while the days are warm. I start making it as the asparagus and new potatoes arrive, and stop when the nights begin to draw in, varying the vegetables with the seasons. This midsummer version, which makes the most of the best tomatoes and string beans, is my favorite.

First put your new potatoes a medium saucepan with a good pinch of sea salt and cover with cold water—you want a good amount of water here, as you will be adding other things to the pan later. Bring the potatoes to a boil, then allow to simmer for 12 to 20 minutes depending on their size.

In another small pan bring some salted water to a rolling boil, add the eggs, and boil for 6 minutes, so that the middles are only just set. If you'd like them hard-boiled, go for a minute more. Crack the shells on a hard surface then run them under cold water for 30 seconds to stop them cooking, then leave to cool.

While the eggs are cooking, whisk together all the dressing ingredients, then taste and season. You want it to be quite punchy, as it will mellow when it hits everything else.

Pit your olives and rip them in half. Peel the cucumber and halve it down the middle, use a teaspoon to scoop out the watery seeds in the middle, then cut it into chunky slices. Roughly chop the tomatoes into different-size pieces. Put them all into a large bowl.

When your potatoes are nearly cooked, add the beans to the pan and cook for the final 3 to 4 minutes. Drain everything and leave to steam dry. Once the potatoes have steamed away all of their moisture, add them to the bowl while they are still warm, along with the beans, and pour over the dressing. Use the back of a spoon to lightly crush the potatoes and allow them to split and soak up some of the dressing.

Peel the eggs, half or quarter them, then dot over the bowl and finish with some chopped herbs or lemon zest if you have some on hand.

SERVES 4

1 pound (500 g) new
   potatoes

sea salt

4 organic eggs

⅔ cup (100 g) Kalamata olives

1 small cucumber

1⅔ cups (300 g) ripe
   tomatoes

7 ounces (200 g) green or
   string beans, topped and
   tailed

FOR THE DRESSING

3 teaspoons Dijon mustard

2 teaspoons whole-grain
   mustard

4 tablespoons olive oil

3 tablespoons white wine
   vinegar

1 teaspoon golden honey

TO FINISH

chopped soft herbs

lemon zest

Lemon poha

I first ate poha on a yoga course in London. It was cooked by an incredible cook from the ashram of Isha Yoga in Tamil Nadu, which I long to visit. Poha, or pawa, is flattened rice that really needs no cooking, just a quick soak to soften it. Poha can be bought easily from any Asian shop, and there are different types, according to thickness; for this recipe you are looking for the thick poha—if you can't find it you could use cooked basmati rice instead. Poha is often eaten for breakfast in India, but I like it any time of day and often make it to sit next to curries instead of normal rice, or eat it on its own as a summer supper.

Soak your peanuts in cold water for at least 30 minutes but ideally overnight. Put the poha into a sieve and wash under running water for a few minutes, moving it around in the sieve—you want the running water to touch it all.

Put a large frying pan with a lid over medium heat and add the oil, cumin, and mustard seeds, chile, and curry leaves. Once the mustard seeds pop, add the scallions and cook for 5 minutes, until soft and sweet.

Next, add the potatoes and cook for a minute, until the edges begin to crisp, then add 3½ ounces (100 ml) of water, cover with the lid, bring to a boil, and cook for 6 minutes, or until the potatoes are cooked through.

Add the turmeric to the pan and stir with a wooden spoon to distribute it evenly. Add the soaked poha, lemon juice, and a good pinch of salt and mix well, then cook for 3 minutes to warm through.

Take the pan off the heat and add the soaked, drained peanuts and the cilantro, tasting and adding more lemon juice and salt if needed.

SERVES 4

5 tablespoons unsalted red-skinned peanuts

8½ ounces (240 g) thick poha

3 tablespoons canola oil

1 teaspoon cumin seeds

1 tablespoon black mustard seeds

1 green chile, finely chopped

2 small handfuls of fresh curry leaves (about 25)

a bunch of scallions, finely sliced at an angle

8¾ ounces (250 g) potatoes, peeled and cut into small cubes

½ teaspoon ground turmeric

the juice of 2 lemons

a small bunch of cilantro, roughly chopped

Harissa, lime, and halloumi with flatbread

Halloumi is a real crowd-pleaser. I have never understood the blanket fascination with it, but I do like its texture when it's cooked just right, charred and crisped a little on the outside and perfectly melting inside.

Here, the halloumi has a quick dip in a rose harissa and lime marinade, which is backed up by a grilled relish that combines smoke from charred red onions, some piquancy from a good drizzle of pomegranate molasses, sweetness from red peppers and a salty olive kick. A cooling yogurt tempers the chile a little as well as providing a pleasing temperature contrast for the grill-hot halloumi.

This is a perfect recipe for the grill. The relish is also great on burgers and toasted sandwiches.

SERVES 6

2 × 8¾-ounces (250 g) packs of halloumi, cut into ¾-inch- (2-cm-) thick slices

the zest and juice of 1 unwaxed lime

1 tablespoon rose harissa

a handful of dried rose petals, crushed (optional)

FOR THE RELISH

2 red onions, cut into 6 wedges, root intact

2 red peppers

a handful of pitted green olives

2 tablespoons pomegranate molasses

sea salt and freshly ground black pepper

FOR THE HARISSA YOGURT

6 tablespoons Greek yogurt

1 tablespoon rose harissa

2 tablespoons light tahini

the juice of 1 lime

1 tablespoon sumac

TO SERVE

6 yogurt flatbreads (see page 456) or wraps

2 tablespoons sesame seeds, toasted

a few sprigs of mint, leaves picked

a few handfuls of salad leaves

Combine the halloumi, lime zest and juice, and harissa in a bowl and use your hands to mix everything and coat the halloumi. Set aside.

Light your grill (or heat a griddle over medium-high heat). Let the flames die down a little, then grill the onions, turning them occasionally, for 10 minutes, or until soft and sweet (they will crisp and blacken on the outside). Char the peppers alongside until black all over, then put both into a bowl and cover with a tea towel while they cool.

Meanwhile, ripple the yogurt with the harissa, tahini, and lime juice, season, then sprinkle with the sumac and refrigerate.

To finish the relish, peel the skins from the peppers and deseed them, then peel the papery outsides from the onions. Chop the peppers with the onions and green olives, then add 1 tablespoon of the pomegranate molasses and mix well. Taste and add more pomegranate molasses, if needed, and a good pinch of salt and pepper.

Stoke the grill or put the griddle back over medium-high heat. Cook the halloumi for 2 to 3 minutes on each side, or until just charred and a little blistered, and softly melting inside. Meanwhile, warm the flatbread on the other side of the grill or griddle for a minute or so on each side.

Pile the halloumi on the flatbread, top with the relish and yogurt, and scatter with sesame seeds, mint, and a few salad leaves.

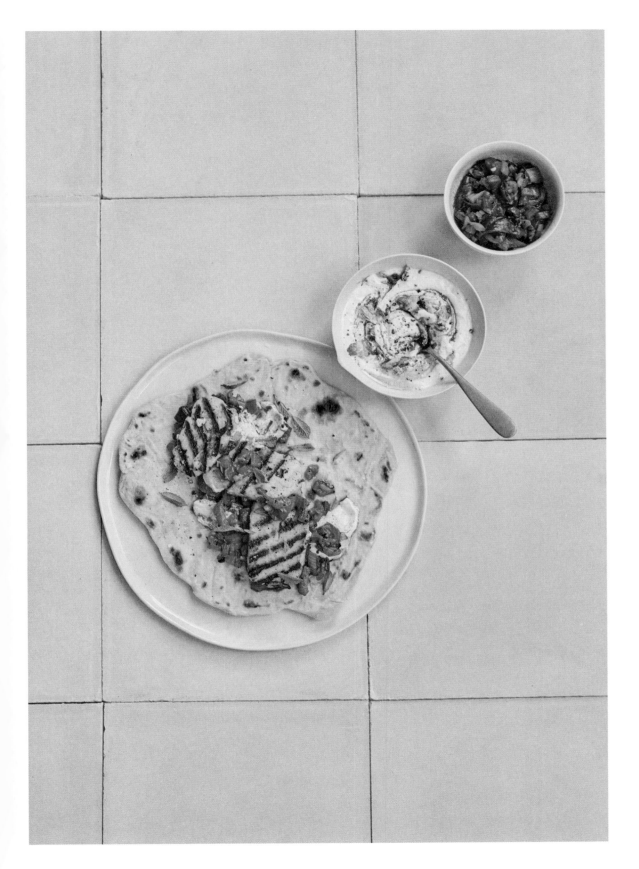

Vegetable-centered barbecues

We've moved quite happily toward eating less meat in our kitchens, but the barbecue hasn't quite kept up, and traditionally vegetarians are ill considered where charred food is concerned—a limp vegetable kebab or an incinerated pepper being the standard token offerings. In restaurants, though, this caveman-esque style of cooking is not all about meat; in fact, vegetables sit center stage in many fire-led chefs' kitchens.

A bit of char and smoke can complement a beloved vegetable or boost a neutral cheese, such as halloumi or feta. An eggplant is an obvious pairing with a bit of smoke—baba ganoush is a friendly blend of vegetables and smolder, as is a halved eggplant grilled and basted in white miso. Onions, too, work well grilled slowly then tossed through plump pearl barley grains. Even halved Little Gems are transformed when quickly charred and simply dressed in oil, vinegar, and chopped herbs.

This charring is, of course, possible on a griddle pan or even a good heavy-based frying pan, but its natural habitat is the grill. The resolution to cook outside to me seems most welcome on a weeknight, when taking the kitchen into the fresh air brings a holiday feeling to an otherwise normal Tuesday or Wednesday.

Tips for barbecuing vegetables

— Cook on charcoal or wood if you can, as it will impart that smoky flavor that gas barbecues won't.

— Use lumpwood charcoal. It's more expensive but will hold heat longer so you will use less. Avoid fire lighters if you can.

— Wait for the right moment to cook. This may sound basic, but wait for the flames to properly die down. You want the coals white hot, gray, and glowing, as they give the most even heat then.

— Control the heat just as you would if you were using a gas stovetop. If things are too hot, then take your food off and let the coals cool down.

— If you are cooking more than one thing, it might be useful to have two temperatures on your grill. To do this, once the coals are hot, pile most of them to one side which will be hot for grilling, and a few on the other side for warming bread and gentler cooking.

— Don't oil your vegetables before they hit the grill. Instead, dress them carefully in good olive oil, citrus, or vinegar after grilling, while they are still warm.

Vegetables and other things that work on the barbecue

All of these can be eaten on their own or mixed into a warm salad with crumbled cheese and chickpeas or beans to make a meal.

Avocado: peel and pit halved avocados, season, and grill until well charred on the outside. Dress with soft herbs, lime, and chile.

Beets: wrap in foil with some woody herbs and whole garlic cloves and bake in the embers as you would a potato for 30 to 40 minutes. Or cut into thin slices and grill until soft and charred, turning every couple of minutes. Dress with orange juice and chopped thyme or marjoram

Cabbage: grill summer cabbages in wedges with the root still attached so they stay together and char until soft and crisp on the outside. Dress with a mustard, honey, and cider vinegar dressing (see page 40).

Carrots: cut into thick strips and cook until soft and charred. Dress with toasted cumin seeds, lemon, oil, cilantro, and pomegranate seeds.

Chicory and radicchio: cut in half down the middle and grill until softened and well charred. Dress with orange zest, whole-grain mustard, vinegar, and good oil. Great with grilled pear too.

Zucchini: cut into thin slices or peel into thin strips and grill until soft and charred (see page 170), then dress in lemon, mint, and herbs. Good with milky soft cheese.

Eggplant: grill whole until soft and blackened all over (see page 286), then cut open and season or mash into baba ganoush; or halve and grill cut side down, turning every so often and basting with white miso throughout the grilling.

Potatoes: wrap in foil with some whole garlic cloves and lemon and bake in the embers for 40 minutes to 1 hour, or slice and grill until soft and charred, turning all the time. Serve with chopped soft herbs, capers, oil, and lemon zest.

Sweet potatoes: cut into long ⅜-inch (1-cm) slices, cook until soft throughout and well charred, turning all the time. Serve with chopped cilantro, yogurt, chile, and lots of lime zest and juice.

Tofu: press to get rid of any excess liquid, then slice thickly and marinate in citrus zest and harissa, or miso and soy. Grill, turning and basting as you go, until crisp. Or marinate in lemon, thyme, and honey and grill until crisp, then eat crumbled into flatbread (see page 236) or over a salad or barbecued veg.

Peaches: cut in half and remove the pit, then grill until charred on both sides. Serve with tomatoes, mozzarella, and torn basil or mint.

Pineapples: peel, cut into wedges, then toss with honey or brown sugar and grill until charred on the outside and soft inside. Serve with ice cream or yogurt.

Lime leaf and cashew tofu cakes

SERVES 4

¾ cup (100 g) cashew nuts

a large thumb-size piece of ginger, peeled and grated

1 clove of garlic, peeled and grated

2 stalks of lemongrass, outer layer removed, finely chopped

1 red chile, roughly chopped

2 lime leaves, roughly sliced

14 ounces (400 g) firm tofu

3 tablespoons nut butter (cashew or peanut)

7 ounces (200 g) green beans, topped, tailed and finely chopped

canola or olive oil

steamed rice, to serve (optional)

FOR THE SALAD

3⅓ cups (200 g) sugar snap peas, cut in half lengthways

8 radishes, finely sliced

3 medium carrots, peeled

a small bunch of cilantro and/or mint, leaves picked and chopped

FOR THE DRESSING

the zest and juice of 1 unwaxed lime

2 tablespoons tamari or soy sauce

a squeeze of golden honey

1 tablespoon white miso paste

These little cakes are packed with freshness and flavor. They also go with a lot of things: brown rice; soy and lime-dressed noodles; or next to a salad. They are great both hot and cold, so are a good thing to take to a barbecue or on a journey. I make a batch on a Sunday for quick lunches and dinners.

Use firm tofu here; if yours feels spongy and full of liquid, you can put a plate on top of it, then place a can on top of that and leave it for 30 minutes for some of the moisture to drain off.

I buy a load of lemongrass stalks and lime leaves when I am in an Asian supermarket and store them in my freezer so I always have them on hand; they really elevate the flavor.

Soak your cashew nuts in cold water to soften them a minimum of 10 minutes but as long as you have.

Put the ginger, garlic, lemongrass, chile, and lime leaves in a food processor and blitz until you have a fine paste; you could do this in a mortar and pestle too. Add the tofu and blitz again until you have a rough paste. Transfer the mixture to a bowl, then add the nut butter and the green beans. Drain and roughly chop the cashews and add these too. Mix well, working the mixture together with the back of a spoon. Shape into about twelve 2-inch (5-cm) cakes and put them in the fridge to firm up a little.

For the salad, put the sugar snap peas into a bowl with the radishes. Use a speed peeler to shave the carrot into ribbons, add them to the bowl along with the herbs, and keep in the fridge until needed. Mix the dressing ingredients in a small jar and put to one side.

Heat your oven on its lowest setting. When you are ready to eat, put a large frying pan over medium heat, add a little oil, and fry as many cakes as will fit into the pan, cooking them for 2 to 3 minutes on each side until burnished and golden brown. Keep them warm on a plate in the low oven while you cook the rest.

Dress the salad and serve it next to the cakes, with a little steamed rice if you are really hungry.

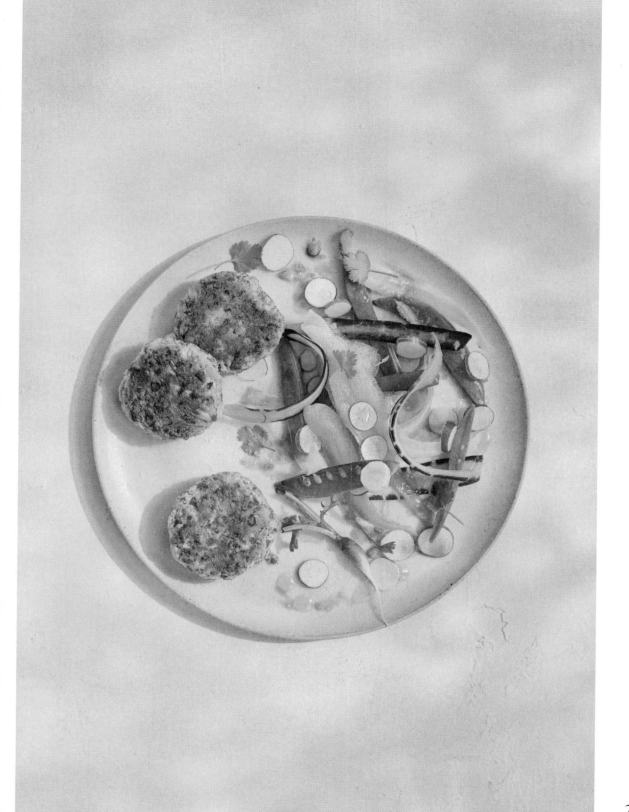

Beet tops tart

SERVES 6–8

FOR THE PASTRY

½ cup (50 g) rolled oats

¾ cup (100 g) white spelt flour

½ cup (50 g) ground almonds

sea salt

10½ tablespoons (150 g) cold unsalted butter or coconut oil, plus extra for greasing

4–6 tablespoons ice-cold water

coconut oil or butter

1 red onion, finely sliced

2 cloves of garlic, finely chopped

a few sprigs of fresh thyme or oregano

2–3 raw beets (about 9 ounces/250 g)

7 ounces (200 g) beet tops or leafy spinach, shredded

1–2 tablespoons cider vinegar (or lemon juice)

sea salt and freshly ground black pepper

3 medium organic eggs

a small bunch of mint, leaves picked and roughly chopped

1 cup (125 g) soft goat cheese

½ cup (50 g) walnuts

about 2 tablespoons golden honey

TO SERVE

peppery green leaves (arugula, lamb's lettuce, mizuna)

Beets are beginning to show up this time of year in all their sweet-shop colors. First come the smaller, sweeter ones with deep green and magenta-veined stems. I adore them and the fuchsia kiss they give everything they touch. This tart is a riot of pink and makes the most of the often forgotten minerally tops too.

There is such a beauty to a really good tart or quiche: crisp pastry and a just-set, quivering filling; for me, they have to be handled with a lightness of touch and put vegetables at the center. Here beets are the heroes, grated and paired with some slow-cooked onion, thyme, a little soft goat cheese, fresh mint, some walnuts (which toast as the tart cooks), and a final drizzle of honey.

I use oats and almonds here to make my pastry, and a slimmer amount of butter than you might expect; the result is a deeply flavored buttery crust with back notes of toasted oats and almonds. It means that I'll just as happily eat this on a Monday as I would as part of a Sunday lunch.

Don't worry if you can't find beets with their tops; you could use some spring greens or spinach on its stem instead. In a pinch, you can use store-bought short-crust pastry here if time is tight.

Preheat your oven to 395°F (200°C). Grease a 10-inch (25-cm) loose-bottomed tart pan.

First, make the pastry. Put the oats into a food processor and blitz until you have a scruffy flour, then add the spelt flour and ground almonds, and a good pinch of salt and blitz again, until everything is mixed together. Cube and add the butter and pulse until the mixture looks like bread crumbs. Add the water a tablespoon at a time, pulsing after each addition, until the pastry comes together in a rough ball. You may not need all the water.

Form the pastry into a ball with your hands, wrap and chill in the fridge for about 30 minutes. →

Next, place the pastry between two sheets of parchment paper and use a rolling pin to roll it out until you have a rough circle about ¼ inch (0.5 cm) thick. Remove one layer of paper and lay the pastry over the tart pan then push it down, making sure it is snug and there are no air bubbles. Take off the other piece of paper and trim off any excess. Alternatively, if the pastry is really cold, you could grate it into the tart pan using the coarse setting on your grater, then push down to fix up any gaps with your fingers.

Now blind-bake your pastry. Use a fork to prick the base a few times, scrunch up a bit of parchment paper, smooth it out, and place over the pastry. Fill with baking beans (or uncooked rice) and bake for 10 minutes. Lift out the paper and beans then put the pastry back into the oven for another 5 minutes. Leave to cool.

Place a large frying pan over medium heat. Add a bit of coconut oil or butter and fry the onion for 10 minutes, until soft and sweet, then add the garlic and thyme and cook for another couple of minutes.

Meanwhile, peel the beets and grate them coarsely on a box grater or in a food processor, which is less messy (and won't stain your fingers). Add the grated beets to the pan of onions and fry for about 30 seconds before adding the beet tops or spinach—you may need to add half first and allow it to wilt down before adding the other half.

Cook for 5 minutes, until everything has dried out a little and there is no liquid left in the pan. Next, add the vinegar and season well with salt and pepper. Transfer to a bowl to cool.

Beat the eggs with the mint, then add to the beet mixture and crumble in half of the goat cheese. Spoon the mixture into the tart case, crumble over the remaining cheese, break over the walnuts, and drizzle a little honey on top, adding as much as is to your taste. Bake for 30 to 35 minutes, or until the filling is golden on top and firm. Serve in generous slices with a shock of peppery green salad.

Roasted avocado tacos with charred tomato salsa

Tacos are summer food. I spend every trip to see my sister in Los Angeles seeking out the best that California has to offer; that means a lot of tacos. These avocado tacos are, if you like, a greatest hits of all the things I have loved about tacos in L.A.: charred corn tortillas, a smoky chile-spiked salsa, pickled jalapeños, and some polenta-crusted avocado. It might seem a little out of the ordinary to cook avocados, but it brings out a totally different character in them, still grassy and buttery but crisp on the outside—do give it a try. These tacos take me back to the palo santo–scented boutiques and the brightly painted stairs that lead up to my sister's house on the hill.

If you can get your hands on tomatillos all the better—they make a great salsa; if not, vine tomatoes will do just fine. I encourage you to seek out corn tortillas made from 100 percent corn masa (dough). They have a totally different texture and flavor from the softer corn and wheat tortillas.

Preheat your oven to 395°F (200°C).

Cut the avocados in half and take out the pits. Cut them in half again lengthways and remove the skins. Put in a bowl and sprinkle with the lime zest, juice, and chile. Toss well to coat. In a separate bowl, mix the polenta with the smoked paprika, cheese, chipotle, and a generous pinch of salt and pepper.

Put the polenta mix on a plate and roll the avocados in it, then transfer to a baking sheet, drizzle with olive oil, and bake for 25 minutes. Alternatively, shallow-fry them in a good bit of olive oil. →

SERVES 4

FOR THE ROASTED AVOCADO

4 just-ripe avocados

the zest and juice of 1 unwaxed lime

1 green chile, chopped

½ cup (50 g) fine polenta

½ teaspoon hot smoked paprika

¼ cup (25 g) hard cheese (Manchego or pecorino work well), grated

a pinch of dried chipotle or red pepper flakes

sea salt and freshly ground black pepper

olive oil

FOR THE PICKLED CHILES

10 tablespoons (150 ml) cider vinegar

2 cloves of garlic

1 tablespoon cilantro (coriander) seeds, bashed in a mortar and pestle

2 tablespoons agave nectar

1 tablespoon flaky sea salt

6 jalapeños or other green chiles →

281

FOR THE CHARRED SALSA

4 ripe, vine tomatoes or tomatillos (unripe green tomatoes)

4 scallions

2 red chiles

2 cloves of garlic

1 tablespoon red wine vinegar

sea salt

lime juice (optional)

agave syrup or golden honey (optional)

TO ASSEMBLE

12 small corn tortillas (see note above)

1 spring cabbage, shredded

a handful of cilantro, roughly chopped

1 cup (100 g) Manchego or feta cheese, crumbled

limes, to serve

While the avocados are baking, make the pickled chiles. Place the cider vinegar in a saucepan with 10 tablespoons (150 ml) water. Bash the garlic cloves and place them in the pan with the cilantro seeds, agave, and salt. Bring to a boil. Slice the chiles into rounds ¼ inch (0.5 cm) thick, leaving the seeds in. When the liquid has boiled, stir in the chiles and remove the pan from the heat. Leave to sit for at least 15 minutes. Any leftovers can be stored in the fridge, covered in the liquid, for up to 3 weeks.

Meanwhile, make the salsa. Put a griddle over high heat. Once hot, char the tomatoes, scallions, and chiles until soft and blackened all over, turning with tongs every 30 seconds or so. You may need to remove the chiles and scallions before the tomatoes. Once everything looks good, cut off the chile stems and scallion roots and transfer the charred veg to a blender with the garlic, the red wine vinegar, and a generous pinch of salt and blitz until you have a punchy salsa. Taste and check that it is nicely balanced: Add more vinegar, lime, or a little agave nectar or honey if it needs sweetness (depending on the sweetness and ripeness of your tomatoes). Put the salsa into a big bowl.

Drain the chiles. Warm the tortillas in a dry frying pan over medium heat or over an open flame, turning them with tongs. Once they are warm and a little charred around the edges, pile them onto a plate. Put them in the middle of the table with the avocado, salsa, cabbage, pickled chiles, cilantro, cheese, and limes for squeezing over, and let everyone make their own tacos.

A wedding-worthy tomato tarte Tatin

Last year on a balmy July day, John and I got married in a tiny church on an island off the Anglesey coast; a little tidal island 100 feet (30 meters) across, separated from the beach by a rocky path that you can only tread at low tide. That morning I walked across the island in my wedding dress, in sea mist that made me feel like I was in a Gothic novel. The tiny church held just 40 people and was lit only by candles. When we came out, the sun was shining and we drove to the reception in my dad's old soft-top and, surrounded by our friends, we ate this tart. I don't think I could be more fond of a recipe.

This is the simplified version—a perfect summer offering. Roasting the tomatoes takes a few hours but requires very little effort, so don't be put off. The tart can also be assembled ahead of time and kept in the fridge. Tomatoes are the star of the show here, so buy beautiful different colors and shapes if you can. A special mention to Sarah and Stuart who cooked our wedding feast with such grace and care; nothing I make will ever taste as sweet.

SERVES 4–6

2¼ pounds (1 kg) good, ripe tomatoes

sea salt and freshly ground black pepper

olive oil

3 red onions, freshly sliced

1 tablespoon red wine vinegar

1 teaspoon brown sugar or golden honey

a small bunch of thyme or oregano

2 tablespoons butter, for greasing

flour, for dusting

1 × 13¼-ounce (375 g) package of all-butter puff pastry

1 organic egg, beaten

½ cup (50 g) baby capers, drained and dried on paper towels

Preheat your oven to 250°F (120°C). Cut the tomatoes in half and put them cut side up on a baking sheet with a little salt, pepper, and a couple of tablespoons of olive oil. Put them in the oven for 3 to 4 hours to slowly roast and sweeten. You may need to take some of the smaller tomatoes out a bit earlier, so keep an eye on them. Once cooked, remove and allow to cool a little. (Sometimes I find it easier to cook the tomatoes overnight: I roast them for 1 hour, then turn off the oven and leave them until the morning.)

Next make the caramelized onions. Heat a tablespoon of olive oil over medium heat and add the sliced onions. Cook for 10 minutes to sweeten and soften before adding the vinegar, sugar, the leaves from a few sprigs of the thyme or oregano (saving the rest for later), and a good pinch of salt and pepper. Cook on a low heat for 30 to 40 minutes, until really soft and sticky. →

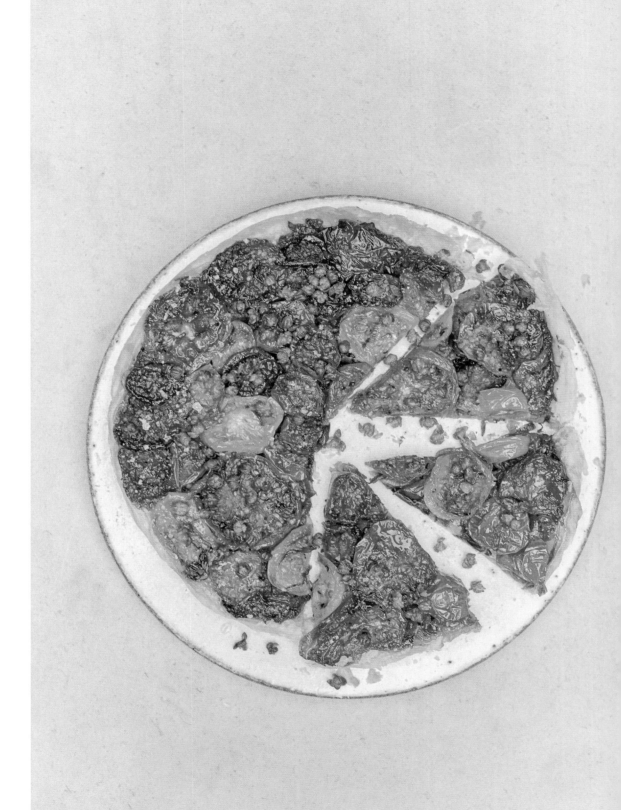

284

Butter a cast-iron or heavy ovenproof frying pan (about 9½ inches/ 24 cm in diameter)—a well-buttered pan will mean the tart comes out easily. Lay the tomatoes cut side down in a kind of mosaic, fitting them all together; don't worry if there is a little bit of overlap. Once they are all squeezed in, scatter the onions over the top.

Lightly dust a work surface with flour and roll out the pastry until it's about ⅜ inch (1 cm) thick, then cut out a circle just bigger than your pan. Lay it over the onion mixture and tuck the sides around the onion inside the pan. You can stop here and put the tart into the fridge if you like.

Once you are ready to cook, preheat the oven to 425°F (220°C). Brush the pastry with a little of the beaten egg and put it in the oven for 25 to 30 minutes, until golden all over and bubbling around the edges.

While the tart is cooking, heat a few tablespoons of olive oil in a frying pan. Have a plate lined with paper towels and a slotted spoon on hand. Once the oil is good and hot, add the capers. They will bloom into little flowers and crisp in just 30 seconds or so. Lift them out and quickly drain them on paper towels.

Once the tart is ready, take it out of the oven and allow it to sit for 5 minutes before running a knife around the edge and carefully turning it out onto a plate. Scatter the capers over the tart before serving.

Buttery eggplants with toasted couscous

SERVES 4

FOR THE PEPPERS

4 red peppers, deseeded
    and cut into thin strips

2 tablespoons olive oil

4 cloves of garlic, finely sliced

1 red onion, finely sliced

2 tablespoons sherry vinegar

½ teaspoon smoked sweet
    paprika

FOR THE EGGPLANT

1 teaspoon ground cumin

1 teaspoon ground cilantro

sea salt

1 tablespoon olive oil

4 long, thin eggplants

plain yogurt, to serve
    (optional)

FOR THE COUSCOUS

1½ cups (300 g) whole-
    wheat giant couscous
    (mograbieh)

1 heaping teaspoon vegetable
    stock powder

small bunches of mint,
    parsley, basil, leaves
    picked and roughly
    chopped, stems reserved

the zest and juice of
    1 unwaxed lemon

6 tablespoons extra-virgin
    olive oil, plus extra to
    serve

1 teaspoon sumac

This is a perfect recipe for a crowd and works brilliantly on the barbecue rather than the broiler if you like. One thing to ensure here is that your eggplants are buttery and soft; raw eggplant has to be one of the worst things to eat. Eggplants is a pretty resilient vegetable, so be brave when you cook it, and give it long enough to make sure it's cooked through. Try to get your hands on the longer thin eggplants, as short fat ones will take much longer to cook through.

_____

First, the peppers. Put the peppers in a frying pan with the olive oil, garlic, and red onion and cook for 20 minutes over low to medium heat, until softened and sweeter and the edges are beginning to pick up some golden color. Add the vinegar and paprika and cook for another 20 minutes, then season well and take off the heat.

While the peppers are cooking, heat your broiler or barbecue to medium. Mix the cumin and cilantro with the oil and a good pinch of salt. Prick the eggplants all over and rub them with the oil. Put them under the broiler or on the barbecue for about 25 minutes, turning them a couple of times. You are aiming for the eggplants to almost completely collapse, so be brave.

Fill the kettle with water and bring to a boil. Toast the couscous in a dry frying pan over medium-high heat for a couple of minutes, until it smells toasty but before it colors. Cover with 4½ cups (1 liter) of boiling water and add the stock powder and herb stems. Turn the heat down to medium and let the couscous simmer for 8 to 10 minutes.

Put the lemon zest and juice in a small bowl with the olive oil. Add the chopped herb leaves and sumac and mix well. Once the couscous is cooked, drain well, remove the herb stems, and dress with half the dressing while still warm.

Place an eggplant on each plate, cut lengthways with a sharp knife, and season the insides well with olive oil, salt and pepper. Serve with a heaping spoonful of the couscous and peppers on the side. Finish with the remaining dressing and some yogurt, if you like.

Smoky roasted carrot burgers

Summer barbecues are often when I feel a bit short-changed as a vegetarian; these burgers are an attempt to remedy that. They are flavor-packed, with umami from the smoked tofu and smoky paprika, and some buttery sweetness from the mashed roasted carrots. These burgers hold up well on the barbecue—just be sure to make them in advance and give them some time in the fridge to firm up.

I roast the carrots in the oven, as I usually like to make these in advance, but if you were so inclined, you could roast them wrapped in foil in the embers of the barbecue. Vegans can replace the Parmesan with a teaspoon of nutritional yeast and the mayo with a vegan mayo.

First, roast your carrots. Place the carrots on a baking sheet with the smoked paprika, cumin, some salt and pepper, and a good drizzle of olive oil. Cover with foil and roast for 20 minutes, then remove the foil and roast for another 10 minutes, until completely soft and starting to brown.

While these are roasting, finely crumble half the tofu into a bowl and add the bread crumbs, parsley, lemon zest, Parmesan, and sesame seeds.

Once the carrots are ready, take them out of the oven (leave the oven on if you want to bake your burgers) and allow them to cool a little before blitzing in a food processor with the remaining tofu, until everything is evenly distributed and the mixture is pretty smooth. Allow to cool a little, then add this to the bread crumb mixture and mix well, using a spoon to mash and persuade everything to come together. If your mixture looks a little dry, add a couple of tablespoons of olive oil or water until it comes together nicely.

Shape the mixture into 6 patties, lay them on a plate, and put them in the fridge for 20 minutes. →

SERVES 6

1¼ pounds (600 g) carrots, peeled and cut into ⅜- to ¾-inch (1–2-cm) rounds

1 teaspoon smoked sweet paprika

1 teaspoon cumin seeds, roughly bashed in a mortar with pestle

sea salt and freshly ground black pepper

olive oil

¾ cup (200 g) smoked tofu

1 cup (100 g) rye bread crumbs

a small bunch of flat-leaf parsley, chopped

the zest of 1 unwaxed lemon

½ cup (50 g) grated Parmesan (I use a vegetarian/rennet-free one)

⅓ cup (50 g) sesame seeds, toasted (see page 459)

TO SERVE

6 good burger buns or slices of rye bread

6 tablespoons good mayonnaise

smoked paprika

12 small lettuce leaves

2 avocados

a bunch of watercress

Once you are ready to cook, put a large frying pan over medium heat and add a little olive oil, swirling it to coat the pan. Add the burgers and cook for 3 to 4 minutes on each side, flipping them once they are well colored. Alternatively, you could cook them in the hot oven for 25 to 30 minutes. If you are barbecuing the burgers, brush them with oil before cooking on one side, flipping only when they are colored and crisp enough to come away from the grates easily.

While the burgers are cooking, split and toast your buns, slice your avocados and snip your cress.

Spread the bottom of each bun with a spoonful of mayonnaise, add a pinch of paprika, then top with the lettuce leaves, avocado, the burger, and a crown of cress. Cover with the lid of the bun and eat immediately.

Supper pancakes with pickled cherries

Cherries are hands down my favorite fruit. They are as much a part of my summers as barbecues and flip-flops. When they start filling my shopping basket, they are all I eat for breakfast, and often dessert, until they are gone again. Accept nothing but the best: glossy deep cerise exteriors and bright green stems. For me, they are the taste of pure summer.

This is a savory take on cherries: They are quickly pickled and wrapped in warm buff-colored buckwheat galettes, topped with a good spoonful of goat cheese and a shock of greens.

The buckwheat grain comes from a leafy plant, not like the grass from which wheat is made, and has a deep distinctive flavor; it is also naturally free of gluten. If you have time, leave the batter overnight as it makes a softer, silkier, and more tender pancake; if not, as long as you have will do.

SERVES 4

2¼ cups (265 g) buckwheat flour

2 medium organic eggs

2½ cups (600 ml) milk (unsweetened almond or cow's milk works best)

sea salt

3 cups (300 g) cherries, pitted

5 ounces (150 ml) red wine vinegar

a good squeeze of golden honey

3 sprigs of tarragon, leaves picked and roughly chopped

2 tablespoons melted butter or ghee

1¾ cups (200 g) soft, rindless goat cheese or goat curd

4 handfuls of peppery green leaves (watercress, lamb's lettuce, arugula)

You can make the batter as much as 24 hours in advance—the longer it sits, the better your pancakes will be—but 30 minutes' sitting time will do if you are in a rush.

Whisk together the flour, eggs, milk, and a good pinch of salt, then put the batter in the fridge for as long as you have.

Next, get your cherries going. Put them in a deep bowl and pour over the vinegar and honey, then throw in the tarragon. Season with a little salt and leave to one side.

Preheat your oven to 225°F (110°C). Once you are ready to cook, heat a large frying pan (about 10 inches/25 cm in diameter) over medium heat. Using a paper towel, rub a little of the melted butter around the pan, then add a small ladleful of batter. Let the galette brown on one side, then flip it over. Once cooked, remove the galette from the pan to a plate and place in the low oven to keep warm while you cook the remainder.

Fill each galette with a little goat cheese, a few cherries, a sprinkle of pickling juice and some peppery greens. Wrap up and devour.

Rigatoni with eggplants and tomatoes

I grew up eating this simple Sicilian pasta dish. There was a little Italian restaurant down the road from our house that made this classic; they called it "penne Siciliana" but it's also often called "penne alla Norma." They added mozzarella to theirs, which gave it all a pleasing creaminess; I prefer to use ricotta salata, which is aged salted ricotta, but if you can't get this, you could use some feta; just crumble it over at the end.

Slice your eggplants into ⅜-inch- (1-cm-) thick rounds. If you have a big seedy one, you might want to salt the slices first; I find that most firm small eggplants don't need salting, but the bigger ones with more seeds do. To salt them, lay them in a colander, sprinkle both sides with salt and leave for an hour. Pat dry with paper towels.

Next, heat a drizzle of olive oil in a large frying pan, add the garlic, and cook for a few minutes until golden at the edges but not burnt. Scoop it out and put the pan back on the heat. Add a little more oil to the pan and cook the eggplants over high heat in a single layer, until they are browned on each side and soft in the middle—you can do this in a few batches. Once they are all cooked, put back into the pan.

Add the tomatoes with the oregano and red pepper flakes, a good pinch of salt, and a grind of pepper. Cook the lot for about 10 minutes, scraping the goodness off the bottom, until you have a nice soft juicy sauce—the veg will still hold its shape a little.

While this is happening, bring a large pot of salted water to a boil and cook the pasta until it is al dente. Follow the instructions on the back of the package, though I usually cook it for a minute or so less. Scoop out a mugful of the cooking water.

Drain the pasta and add it to the pan of eggplants and tomatoes. Stir everything together and add a little of the pasta water to loosen the mixture to a generous sauce, remembering that the pasta will keep absorbing liquid as it sits. Taste and add more salt, pepper, and red pepper flakes as you like, then top with a grating of ricotta, some pistachios, and more olive oil.

SERVES 4–6

1 pound (500 g) eggplants (2 small ones)

extra-virgin olive oil

2 cloves of garlic, finely sliced

3½ cups (500 g) small or cherry tomatoes

a few sprigs of fresh oregano or marjoram

a pinch of red pepper flakes

sea salt and freshly ground black pepper

14 ounces (400 g) whole-wheat penne or rigatoni

¼ cup (50 g) ricotta salata or feta (see note above)

⅓ cup (50 g) shelled pistachios, toasted (page 459) and roughly chopped

Strawberry and rose thumbprint cookies

Childishly simple to make but very good to eat, these little cookies are made of the good stuff: oats, dates, coconut oil, and a quick jam sweetened with coconut sugar. While they are still a treat, this lineup of whole ingredients means I eat these with even more of a smile on my face. They are also great for little ones.

I love rose geranium and use it to infuse berries and rhubarb. I have a little pot of it on my windowsill and tear off a few leaves to add to a pan every few weeks. If rose geranium is a bridge too far for you, you could mimic the fragrant rose notes with a tiny splash of rose water or orange blossom water, or leave it out altogether.

I make these cookies year-round, with apricots or peaches in summer, pears in autumn, and frozen berries in the winter.

MAKES ABOUT 24

FOR THE JAM

3½ cups (500 g) strawberries

5 rose geranium leaves or rose water (optional)

1 vanilla pod, split in half lengthways

3 tablespoons coconut sugar

the juice of 1 lemon

FOR THE COOKIES

½ cup (100 g) coconut oil

1¾ cups (150 g) rolled oats

⅔ cup (100 g) pitted Medjool dates (about 8)

1½ cups (150 g) ground almonds

a pinch of flaky sea salt

the zest and juice of 1 unwaxed orange

Wash and hull the strawberries. If they are really large, cut them in half. Place in a pan with the rose geranium leaves, vanilla pod, sugar, and lemon juice. If you're using rose water instead of rose geranium leaves, add it in small quantities after the jam is cooked and cooled, tasting after each addition to get the right balance. Cook the strawberries over low heat for 30 minutes, until they have completely softened and gone jammy.

Meanwhile, make the cookie dough. Preheat the oven to 335°F (170°C). Melt the coconut oil in a small saucepan and take off the heat. Blitz the oats in a food processor, until you have a scruffy flour. Add the dates and blitz again, until the dough is pinchable between your fingers. Add the almonds and pour the coconut oil in slowly, until the dough is starting to come together, then add the salt, orange juice, and zest.

Line a baking sheet with waxed paper—you may need two baking sheets if yours are small. Take a tablespoon of cookie dough and shape it into disks about ½ inch (1½ cm) deep with your hands. Place the discs on the baking sheet, then stamp an indent into each one with your thumb. Remove the rose geranium leaves from the jam and spoon a teaspoon of jam into each little indent.

Bake for 30 minutes until golden around the edges and jammy and dark in the middle, then transfer to a wire rack to cool.

Cherry and black pepper streusel muffins

Not too sweet and filled with good things, these are muffins I can happily eat for breakfast. I love them studded with cherries, so I make them most in summer, but in truth they could be made with other berries—frozen or fresh—or slices of summer stone fruits. The tops are crumbly and crunchy with their little hats of streusel topping flecked with black pepper and orange zest. These flavors are more subtle than you might expect and add a pleasing warmth and fragrance. The muffins will last for a couple of days in an airtight container.

I use raw cane sugar in these muffins, also called rapadura sugar. It is less processed than lots of commercial sugars, and while a little more expensive, I think it tastes much better too. I use it where recipes call for brown sugar, so you can use light brown sugar here instead. Vegans can use coconut oil and aquafaba (see page 459).

Preheat the oven to 395°F (200°C). Grease a 12-hole muffin pan or line with muffin liners.

First, make the streusel topping by placing all the ingredients in a bowl and rubbing with your fingers until it resembles rough crumbs. Set aside for later.

Melt the butter in a saucepan. Pour it into a bowl and set aside to cool slightly. In a large mixing bowl, combine the flour, baking powder, ground almonds, and salt and use a balloon whisk to break up any lumps.

In another bowl, whisk together the eggs and sugar until it turns a smooth, light caramel color. Slowly pour in the milk, whisking gently as you pour, then add the melted butter, the vanilla, and the orange juice. Gently whisk the wet ingredients into the flour mixture. Toss the cherries in the teaspoon of flour (this stops the juice from "bleeding" into the batter as it bakes) and fold them into the batter.

Fill the muffin liners or holes with the batter to just below the top. Sprinkle the topping over the muffins and bake for 30 minutes, until the tops of the muffins are golden and a skewer inserted in the center comes out clean. Leave the muffins to cool for about 15 minutes before removing them from the pan.

MAKES 12

FOR THE STREUSEL TOPPING

- 3½ tablespoons unsalted butter, cut into ⅜-inch (1-cm) cubes
- ½ cup (70 g) white spelt flour
- ¼ cup (40 g) raw cane sugar (see note at left)
- the zest from 1 unwaxed orange
- a pinch of flaky sea salt
- 1 teaspoon freshly ground black pepper

FOR THE MUFFINS

- 10½ tablespoons (150 g) unsalted butter or coconut oil, plus extra to grease
- 2¼ cups (300 g) white spelt flour, plus 1 teaspoon
- 2 teaspoons baking powder
- 1 cup (100 g) ground almonds
- a generous pinch of flaky sea salt
- 3 medium organic eggs
- 1 cup (200 g) raw cane sugar (see note above)
- 7 ounces (200 ml) milk (I use oat or unsweetened almond)
- 1½ teaspoons vanilla paste
- the juice from 1 orange
- 2 cups (350 g) pitted cherries, cut into quarters

Coconut raspberry cakes for Mum

Since becoming a mother, the love and respect I have for my own mum has grown and grown. Not only was my mum the most incredible mother to me, my brother, and sister, but now she and my dad are helping me raise my son. Sometimes things in life are so huge and far-reaching that it's hard even to know where to start to say thank you. I started with these cakes: two of Mum's favorite flavors—raspberry and coconut, perfectly light, and not too sweet.

These are topped with a whipped coconut frosting that I use a lot. You can use 4 tablespoons of golden icing sugar in place of the honey if you want a more traditional-style vegan buttercream finish. Vegans can use coconut oil and aquafaba here (see page 459).

MAKES 12 LITTLE CAKES

1 × 14.5-ounce (400-g) can of coconut milk

14 tablespoons softened unsalted butter, plus extra for greasing

⅔ cup (150 g) coconut sugar or light brown sugar

4 medium organic eggs

1 teaspoon vanilla extract

a pinch of flaky sea salt

the zest of 1 unwaxed lemon

1 cup (150 g) white spelt flour

1¾ cups (175 g) ground almonds

2 teaspoons baking powder

1¼ cups (150 g) raspberries

2 tablespoons set honey

a handful of coconut flakes, toasted

First, put your can of coconut milk into the freezer for 20 minutes to cool. Once cool, open it carefully, without disturbing the contents. Scoop out the set cream on the top and put it back in the fridge. Keep the more watery coconut milk for later in the recipe.

Preheat the oven to 395°F (200°C). Butter a 12-hole muffin pan.

Beat the butter and sugar until light and fluffy, then add the eggs one by one, beating as you add each one. Add the vanilla, salt, lemon zest, flour, almonds, baking powder, and 4 tablespoons of the watery coconut milk from the bottom of the can and mix until you have a thick batter.

Fold in the raspberries, then divide the mixture among the holes of the buttered muffin tin. Bake for 25 minutes, until risen and golden brown.

To make the icing, use an electric whisk to beat the set coconut cream with the honey in a metal bowl at full speed. Put it straight back into the fridge to cool.

Allow your cakes to cool completely before generously icing them with the coconut cream and scattering them with the coconut flakes.

Flowers in the kitchen

Flowers are part of how I cook in the summer months. Even in the middle of the city where I live there are flowers we can eat everywhere. Outside my house, a little 3-foot (1-meter) bit of earth is full of nasturtiums and marigolds. Greengrocers and even supermarkets have started selling edible flowers and mixing them into their salad blends.

I am a sucker for the color and prettiness flowers add, but most add flavor too, from the punch of chive flowers to the subtle perfumed notes of a viola. I know I verge on sounding a little niche here, but I pick and buy flowers to put on my table, so why not put them on my plate too, particularly as they are often free and easy to find.

A note of caution: Some flowers are poisonous and cause real problems if you eat them, so please stick to the flowers suggested below. If you are unsure whether something is edible, do not go near it. Even decorating a cake with a flower and then taking it off before eating can be harmful if the flower isn't edible.

Borage: vivid, blue star-shaped flowers that are delicious in gin and tonics and Pimm's as well as to top cakes; they freeze into pretty ice cubes.

Fava bean flowers: look like little irises; white and velvety black, sometimes with lilac hues. Delicately flavored, lovely in salads.

Chives and allium flowers: vibrant purple and shaped like little stars, these have a strong chive flavor so use sparingly; they're delicious with scrambled eggs, spring stews (see page 196), and in salads.

Cilantro flowers: these delicate white frond-like flowers are amazing—their flavor mimics the leaves and can be used wherever you might use cilantro.

Cornflowers: beautiful blue in color with a sweet, almost spicy, taste, they're great for adding to teas (see page 222) and decorating cakes.

Zucchini flowers: sunshine yellow and bigger than most edible flowers, they have a sweet nutty flavor and can be stuffed and pan-fried or even battered and deep-fried; you can also tear them over salads.

Elderflower: delicate blooms of tiny off-white star-shaped flowers famously used to make elderflower cordial (see page 221), they are also delicious in gin and tonics, on salads (see page 298) and to top cakes (see page 210).

Lavender: particularly good in baking and brewed into herbal infusions and hot drinks (see page 222). Go lightly.

Nasturtiums: both the flowers and the flat-topped leaves have a lovely spicy flavor, and the flowers come in a range of fabulous neon colors with soft velvety petals. I like to add them to salads, and their peppery flavor works well in pesto.

Pansies: extremely versatile thanks to their gentle flavor; they have a long flowering period and crystallize beautifully. I use them in salads, to top summer toasts, and to decorate cakes.

Rose: generally the more scented the better the flavor will be. Always use garden roses as most store-bought ones will be sprayed with chemicals, unless you buy organic ones; good in cordial (see page 221), jam, and baking (see page 292).

Sage flowers: these come in blue, purple, and white hues, and their shape can vary from one sage to the next. They are wonderfully savory but have a very strong flavor so are best if cooked quickly; good with tomato dishes and sprinkled on pizzas.

Sunflowers: the petals have a bittersweet nutty flavor and a good crunch; they add an amazing burst of color to salads.

Wild primroses: a delicate fragrant flavor; they look beautiful as a spring garnish.

Ramps: pretty white flowers with a gorgeous texture; a sign of spring.

Ways to use flowers in the kitchen

- Freeze them into ice cubes

- To top a pavlova or meringue (see page 302)

- Stirred into cocktails

- Added to a green salad

- To top cakes

- Infused in cream, frozen yogurt, ice cream, and sorbet

- To make cordials (see page 221)

- Stirred into honey and left to infuse

- Added to pesto (nasturtiums work well here)

Summer fruit and elderflower salad

Hot days call for cooling puddings, refreshing fruits, and everything ice-cold. Most summer nights our pudding will be a few cherries and a snap of dark chocolate. If we have guests I'll put the cherries in a bowl of ice to keep them cool while we pick at them. Other nights it's a ripe peach, cold from the fridge and cut into slices. But sometimes I want something that feels a bit more put together, and this is it. I largely make this in summer, when the peaches and cherries are at their best; that means that in London the elderflowers have all bloomed and gone, but if you live further north you might be lucky enough to have a few blooms left that you can scatter over the top. If not, other edible flowers would be pretty but by no means necessary.

SERVES 4

4 ripe flat peaches

2¼ cups (250 g) cherries

a 1-pound (500-g) piece of watermelon

2 tablespoons elderflower cordial (see page 221)

1 unwaxed lime

TO SERVE

1 head of elderflower, flowers picked (optional)

Start by washing all the fruit. Cut the peaches in half and remove their pits. Slice each half into three or four wedges, depending on the size of your peaches.

Next, halve the cherries and if they're ripe you should be able to wiggle their pits out. Cut the rind away from the watermelon and any white edges too. Cut into ¾-inch (2-cm) bite-size bits.

Combine all the fruit in a bowl and stir in the elderflower cordial. Grate the lime zest into the bowl, then add the juice.

Arrange the fruit on a platter and scatter the elderflowers over the top if you're using them.

Peach and cardamom tart

Summer desserts are tricky territory. They need to be sweet and satisfying but light and bright at the same time. This tart centers around ripe summer peaches, the ones with juice that runs down your chin as you eat them; sweet and custardy inside. You could use nectarines too, or even plums or apricots if you were making this outside the window of time when peaches are at their best.

This is an easy and unusual tart. It's light thanks to a crust made from oats, nuts, and coconut oil, spiked with some heady cardamom, and is topped with a quick peach filling that is set not with eggs, but using the binding power of chia seeds.

Preheat the oven to 395°F (200°C). Grease a 9½-inch (24-cm) loose-bottomed tart pan with a little coconut oil and line the base with parchment paper.

Put all the crust ingredients into a food processor and pulse to mix. Press the crust mix evenly into the bottom of the pan—there's no need to push it up the sides.

Prick the base all over with a fork, then scrunch up a bit of parchment paper, smooth it out, and place it over the pastry and fill the paper with baking beans (or uncooked rice). Bake the base for 20 minutes, or until lightly golden, then remove from the oven, take out the parchment paper and baking beans, then set aside to cool.

Combine the chia seeds with the apple juice or water and set aside until they come together to form a gel.

When the base has cooled a little, mix the peaches with the sugar, vanilla, cinnamon, and zest: stir until well combined, then add the chia gel. Pour the peach filling into the tart crust and spread evenly. Bake for 35 to 45 minutes, until the peaches are jammy and set.

Allow the tart to cool completely before removing it from the pan. Serve with coconut yogurt or whipped cream.

SERVES 8–10

FOR THE CRUST

- 6½ tablespoons (100 g) coconut oil or melted butter, plus extra for greasing
- 1½ cups (140 g) rolled oats
- ⅔ cup (75 g) whole-wheat flour
- ½ cup (100 g) pecans, chopped
- 3½ tablespoons (90 g) golden honey
- the seeds from 1 vanilla pod
- 8 cardamom pods, seeds removed and finely ground
- ½ teaspoon ground cinnamon
- a good pinch of flaky sea salt

- ¼ cup (60 g) coconut oil, melted
- 2 tablespoons chia seeds
- 3 ounces (100 ml) apple juice or water
- 6 peaches, cut into ⅜-inch (1-cm) slices
- ¼ cup (60 g) light brown sugar or coconut sugar
- the seeds from 1 vanilla pod
- ½ teaspoon ground cinnamon
- the zest of 1 unwaxed lemon
- coconut yogurt or whipped cream, to serve

Summer pudding

Summer pudding is without doubt my favorite summer dessert and
I wait all year for the black currants to be able to make and eat it.
Black currants apparently aren't a traditional addition, but I love
their tartness. I make my pudding with sourdough, not the sliced
white that even respected chefs favor. This does mean you will
need to patch up any holes in the slices, as the crumb is looser, but
the flavor is worth it. Note: I try to avoid using plastic wrap in my
kitchen, but you really need it here.

Grease a 4½-cup (1-liter) pudding basin or mixing bowl with butter
and lay a sheet of plastic wrap inside, leaving quite a bit of overhang.

Warm the berries in a small saucepan over low heat with the sugar,
vanilla, rose water, and orange juice for about 10 to 12 minutes,
until the fruits start to break down and it all smells fragrant.

Slice the sourdough into ¼-inch (½-cm) thick slices with a very
sharp bread knife and trim away the crusts. Cut a round the size of
the bottom of the mixing bowl and place it inside. Arrange the slices
around the sides of the bowl, leaving some overlap of bread above
the rim of the basin—you will cut this off later. Push the slices into the
sides of the bowl, making sure there are no gaps; patch up any holes
with smaller pieces of bread to make sure it's completely lined.

When the fruit is done, allow it to cool a little, then taste and add a
bit more sugar if it needs it. Strain the fruit through a sieve over a
bowl, and return the strained liquid to the pan. Spoon the fruit into
the bowl on top of the bread. Arrange some more slices of bread
over the top of the fruit to make a lid, again making sure there are
no gaps, then trim off the excess bread.

Pull the plastic wrap over the top and place a snug-fitting saucer on
top of the pudding with a little weight on top (a full jar of jam would
do). Put the bowl, weight and all, into the fridge for at least 3 hours, but
ideally overnight, for the bread to absorb all of the deep purple juices.

When you're ready to eat, simmer the remaining liquid in a saucepan
to reduce it by half and use to pour over the top of the pudding.
Serve with crème fraîche or good pouring cream.

SERVES 6

butter or oil, for greasing

2 cups (300 g) black currants

2 cups (300 g) red currants

2½ cups (300 g) raspberries

4 tablespoons superfine or
caster sugar

1 teaspoon vanilla paste

1 teaspoon rose water

the juice of ½ an orange

½ a loaf of stale sourdough
bread

TO SERVE

crème fraîche or good
pouring cream

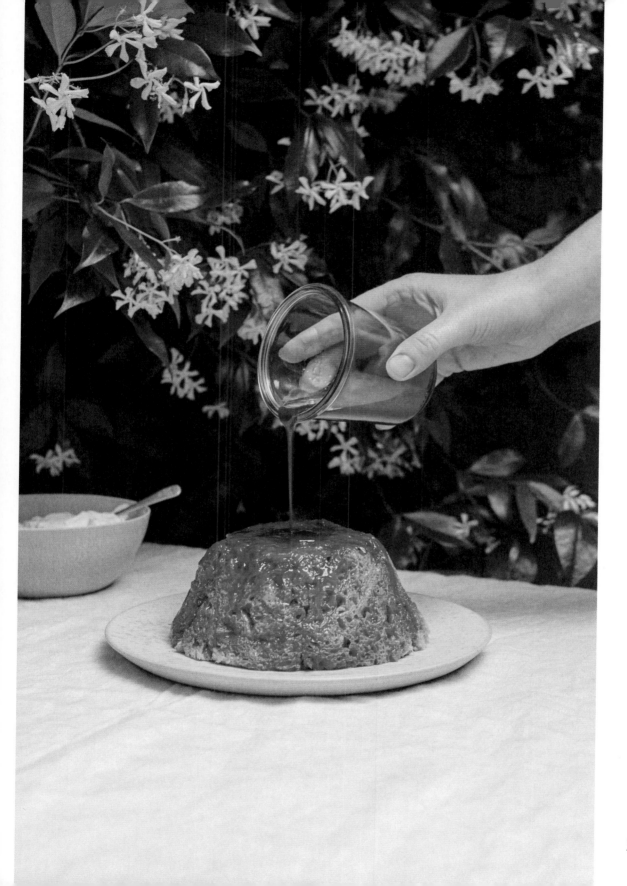

Wedding meringues

This was the dessert I ate on my wedding day. I found it hard to choose what we might eat that day, especially as the end of the meal, the dessert, has always been my favorite part. It happened that we got married in mid-July—prime cherry season—so we decided on this: caramelly brown-sugar meringues, topped with a lemon curd–spiked Chantilly, crème anglaise, and cherries three different ways, as well as a syrup made from fresh myrtle, a symbol of everlasting love, a very sweet touch from the wonderful people who cooked for us. This is a simplified version, no myrtle syrup and only a few simple processes, but well, well worth the bother. A very precious dessert.

Vegans can make the aquafaba meringues on page 459, use coconut yogurt and leave out the curd.

SERVES 8

FOR THE BROWN-SUGAR MERINGUES

½ cup (100 g) soft light brown sugar

½ cup (100 g) white superfine sugar

4 medium organic egg whites

FOR THE TOPPING

4 cups (400 g) cherries, pitted, 8 left whole for serving

2 tablespoons golden honey

1 unwaxed lemon

the seeds from 1 vanilla pod or 2 tablespoons vanilla paste or extract

⅔ cup (150 ml) Greek yogurt

4 tablespoons lemon curd (store-bought is fine) or my grapefruit and honey curd (see page 66)

Preheat the oven to 300°F (150°C) and line a baking sheet.

Put the brown sugar into a bowl, break up any lumps, then add the superfine sugar and mix them together.

Whisk the egg whites until stiff peaks form. Gradually add the sugar while mixing on a high speed, until the mixture is thick and glossy. It's ready when you can pinch it and not feel any granules of sugar.

Spoon the meringue mix into 8 mounds on the baking sheet and bake for 1½ to 2 hours (depending on how chewy you like your meringues—less time means chewier middles). The meringues are ready when they are set and light to pick up. Put to one side to cool.

While the meringues are cooking, put a handful of the pitted cherries into a pan with the honey, lemon juice, and half the vanilla seeds or paste, bring to a boil, then lower the heat and simmer for a few minutes before turning off the heat and letting the cherries macerate.

Mix the rest of the cherries with a little lemon zest—you only want a touch. Mix the yogurt with the remaining vanilla and ripple through the curd.

To serve, I like to make a huge tower for sharing on a big plate, but individual plates work just as well. Layer the meringues with the yogurt and fresh cherries and finish with a whole cherry.

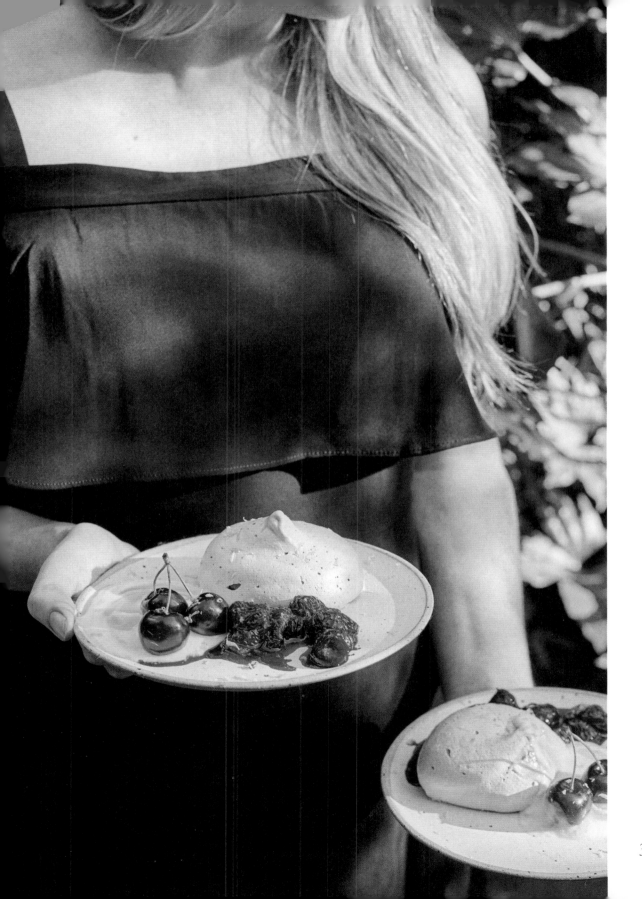

Five summer ice lollies

EACH RECIPE MAKES
8 × 2½-OUNCE (75-ML)
OR 6 × 3½-OUNCE
(100-ML) LOLLIES

SIMPLE VANILLA

1⅓ cups (300 ml) milk (see note)

1¼ cups (300 ml) yogurt (see note)

3 tablespoons golden honey or maple syrup

1 tablespoon vanilla paste or extract

COFFEE AND MAPLE

1⅓ cups (300 ml) milk (see note)

1¼ cups (300 ml) yogurt (see note)

4 shots of espresso or ¼ cup (60 ml) strong coffee

3 tablespoons maple syrup

MATCHA AND HONEY

1⅓ cups (300 ml) milk (see note)

1¼ cups (300 ml) yogurt (see note)

1 tablespoon matcha powder

3 tablespoons golden honey

MANGO, CARDAMOM, AND VANILLA

1⅓ cups (300 ml) milk (see note)

1 ripe mango, peeled and roughly chopped

½ teaspoon ground cardamom

1 teaspoon vanilla paste or extract

2 tablespoons coconut sugar

STRAWBERRY

1⅓ cups (300 ml) milk (see note)

10½ ounces (300 g) strawberries, washed, hulled and roughly chopped

1 teaspoon vanilla paste or extract

2 tablespoons unrefined cane sugar

As a little girl I loved only one ice lolly (Popsicle). I didn't choose the run-of-the-mill orange or the ice-cream truck favorites apple cider or cola, or even the fancy twisted one from the corner shop. For me, it was always the mini milk—vanilla, chocolate, or strawberry, I didn't mind—I just loved its cooling, calming, milky sweetness.

These are some more grown-up versions, though the vanilla and the strawberry go down very well with little people too. I use 2½-ounce (75-ml) molds here, the long round ones that mimic the shape of my beloved mini milks.

I tend to use a creamy oat milk, good organic whole milk, or a homemade nut milk here, and for the yogurt I use good Greek or coconut yogurt. Low-fat milk and yogurt will not work here. You could use store-bought nut milks, but I have found that the lollies end up a little icy, as ready-made nut milks aren't as creamy as homemade; my recipe for how to make your own is on page 458.

For each mini milk recipe, blitz all of the ingredients in a blender (or use an immersion blender) and taste it. Remember that things don't taste as strong when they are very cold, so if your mixture tastes perfect pre-freezing you may like to add a little more flavor or sweetness so that this remains the case when they're frozen. Pour into your ice-lolly molds and freeze for a minimum of 4 hours.

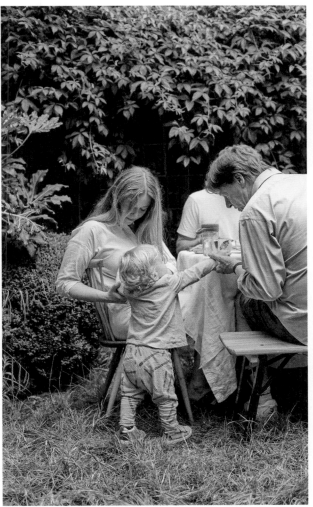

Autumn

Best of the season
    Pumpkins and squashes
    Root vegetables
    Leeks
    Kale
    Lacinato kale
    Chard
    Beets
    Mushrooms
    Borlotti beans
    Blackberries
    Plums
    Apples
    Pears
    Quince
    Elderberries
    Crab apples
    Chestnuts

Flowers
    Cosmos
    Tuberose
    Hypericum

Vanilla and blackberry drop scones

These were a Saturday favorite growing up. We used to make them with blueberries or strawberries on the top of the Aga at home, topping them with too much butter and far too much maple syrup. We'd make a triple batch of batter, as my sister Laura and I would eat eight or ten on the walk.

These are a more grown-up version made with blackberries and vanilla and finished with a saffron-spiked yogurt. Warm from the saffron, sharp and sweet from the blackberries, and comforting from the childhood association. The eight-year-old in me could eat these all day.

MAKES ABOUT 10

1⅓ cups (175 g) white spelt flour

2 teaspoons baking powder

1 tablespoon superfine or caster sugar

a pinch of fine sea salt

1 medium organic egg

1 teaspoon vanilla extract or paste

5 ounces (150 ml) milk (I use unsweetened almond or oat)

1 cup (150 g) ripe blackberries

1–2 tablespoons of unsalted butter

TO SERVE

a small pinch of saffron strands

½ cup (100 g) plain yogurt

2 tablespoons golden honey, plus extra for the table

blackberries (optional)

To make the batter, put the flour, baking powder, sugar, and salt in a large mixing bowl. Use a balloon whisk to stir the dry ingredients and get rid of any lumps of baking powder. Crack in the egg, then add the vanilla and the milk and use the whisk to stir everything into a thick batter. Crush the blackberries slightly, then ripple these through the mixture with a wooden spoon, so you get lovely stains of deep purple as they cook.

Next, soak the saffron in a tablespoon of boiling water. Mix the yogurt with the honey in a separate small bowl.

You can fry the drop scones on a hot flat griddle or in a frying pan. Put your oven on at its lowest setting. Heat the butter in a nonstick frying pan over medium heat and allow it to melt and froth. Use a small ladle to scoop 4 small rounds of batter into the pan—you want each one to be about 2 inches (5 cm) wide. Cook for a couple of minutes, until bubbles rise to the top and the bottom looks set and golden. Carefully and quickly flip the rounds over and cook for another minute or so, until golden and cooked through; keep these warm on a plate in the oven while you cook the rest, adding more butter to the pan as you go if you need to.

Mix the saffron liquid into the yogurt and mix until it's buttercup yellow. Serve the drop scones with the yogurt, some more blackberries if you like, and a little more honey for drizzling over.

Dhal-baked eggs

Like many of my recipes, this was an attempt to partner up two of my favorite things. I love this for brunch, and while dhal may seem a stretch for some in the morning, anyone who's been to India will know that dhal and breakfast go hand in hand.

This is a friendly thing to cook on a weekend morning, but it works well for lunch or dinner too. I use split red lentils, so that they cook quickly, and I only have to use one pan. You could up the chile here if that's your thing—in the morning I like to keep it gentle.

SERVES 4

1 tablespoon olive oil

a thumb-size piece of ginger, peeled and finely chopped

2 cloves of garlic, finely chopped

a small bunch of cilantro, leaves picked, stems finely chopped

1 teaspoon cumin seeds

1 teaspoon ground cilantro (coriander)

1 teaspoon ground turmeric, or a small thumb-size piece of fresh root, grated

1½ cups (300 g) split red lentils

sea salt

6⅔ cups (200 g) spinach

the juice of 1 lemon

freshly ground black pepper

4 organic eggs

1 green chile, finely sliced

plain yogurt, to serve

Fill the kettle with water and boil. Heat the oil in a large wide pan with a lid. Add the ginger and garlic, then the cilantro stems, stirring frequently until the edges of the garlic pick up a little color.

Add the spices and cook for a minute or so to let them toast and release their oils. Add the lentils and stir to coat in the oil. Add 4½ cups (1 liter) of water from the kettle and a good pinch of salt, then stir well. Cook on a low heat for 20 to 30 minutes, or until the lentils are well cooked and the mixture has thickened. You want it to be thick enough so that it just about holds its shape when you make a little well for your eggs.

Add the spinach and put the lid on for 2 minutes, or until the leaves have wilted, then stir well.

When you are almost ready to eat, add the lemon juice and taste the lentils, adding a little more salt and pepper if you need to.

Make four wells in the lentils, then crack an egg into each one and pop the lid back on until the egg whites are firm and the yolks are still runny—this should take about 5 minutes.

To serve, scatter the eggs with the chile and cilantro stems, and have the yogurt on the side for everyone to help themselves.

Mustardy mushrooms on toast

Autumn on a piece of bread. This is what we eat for a quick dinner, sometimes topped with a poached egg. I am very particular about how I cook mushrooms: in a large pan with lots of space for any moisture to escape and a very high heat so the mushrooms crisp and brown around the edges. If you are making this for more than two people I would suggest cooking them in two batches.

I have been lucky enough to go on lots of mushroom-picking trips with one of my mentors and food heroes, Gennaro Contaldo; the mushrooms I tasted with him, cooked on a simple fire in the woods, are unmatched. My autumnal favorites are chanterelles, and porcini (or ceps), as well as black trompette and lamb's foot. Use a mixture of what you can get—even some portobellos would work if wild ones are hard to find.

Set your griddle or grill to the highest heat possible and leave to warm up while you prepare the mushrooms. Use a pastry brush or a piece of damp paper towel to wipe away any dirt from the mushrooms, gently brushing the underside too. If you are lucky enough to have Chanterelle mushrooms you can use a small knife to peel away the outer layer of the stalks to clean them. Tear the mushrooms into bite-sized pieces.

Heat your largest frying pan over high heat and arrange the mushrooms in the pan—you don't want any oil or butter in the pan at this stage. Sprinkle a pinch of salt over the mushrooms and fry them in the dry pan for about 8 minutes, stirring regularly, until the mushrooms have reduced in size by half and any water has evaporated.

Put the bread on the griddle or under the grill to char on each side. Next, add the butter to the pan and allow it to melt and sizzle. Add the garlic and thyme and stir them through the mushrooms. Continue to cook for 2 minutes, then add a splash of vinegar and the mustard and stir everything well.

Taste and take off the heat when the sharpness from the vinegar has evaporated. Serve on the charred slices of toast.

SERVES 2

7 ounces (200 g) mushrooms (see above)

sea salt

2 slices of good bread

1–2 tablespoons of butter

1 clove of garlic, finely chopped

a couple of sprigs of thyme

a splash of cider vinegar

1 heaping teaspoon Dijon mustard

Quick squash piadinas

**SERVES 2 AS A MEAL,
4 AS A SNACK**

olive oil

¼ of a butternut squash
(about 7 ounces/200 g),
peeled, seeds removed
and grated

sea salt and freshly ground
black pepper

10 black olives, pitted and
roughly chopped

1 red chile, finely chopped

1 × 14.5-ounce (400-g) can
of white beans, drained
(or 1 cup/250 g home-
cooked, see page 461)

½ cup (50 g) Parmesan (I use
a vegetarian/rennet-free
one; optional)

the zest and juice of
1 unwaxed lemon

4 medium piadina flatbreads
or flour tortillas

FOR THE TOMATO SALSA

1⅓ cups (200 g) ripe vine or
cherry tomatoes

a small bunch of basil

1 teaspoon balsamic vinegar

1 tablespoon extra-virgin
olive oil

sea salt and freshly ground
black pepper

If you haven't come across them before, piadinas are filled Italian flatbread. These are filled with squash, black olives, chile, and white beans, which add creaminess and substance, and I make a quick basil and tomato salsa to sit next to them. They make a perfect quick lunch or dinner with some salad on the side. They're a great way to use up a leftover bit of squash, though sweet potatoes would work just as well if those are what you have. The Parmesan is optional—I often make these without any cheese at all.

Heat a dash of olive oil in a large frying pan over medium heat, add the squash, and season with salt and pepper. Add the olives and chile, then cook for 8 to 10 minutes, until the squash has softened and lost its rawness.

Transfer to a bowl and add the beans, then gently mash everything—you still want to have some flecks of unmashed squash. Grate in the Parmesan, if using, add the lemon zest and juice, then taste and season if needed. Set aside.

Chop the tomatoes into a salsa consistency, add the basil and chop again, then transfer to a bowl, add the balsamic and olive oil, and season with salt and pepper.

Warm a frying pan big enough for your flatbread over medium heat. Lay a flatbread flat in the pan, quickly spoon half the squash mixture over it, and even it out. Put another flatbread on top and dry-fry, until it is blistered and golden brown, then use a spatula to flip it over and do the same on the other side. Keep the piadina warm while you make the next one.

Serve straight from the pan with the tomato salsa and a little salad, if you are making a meal of it.

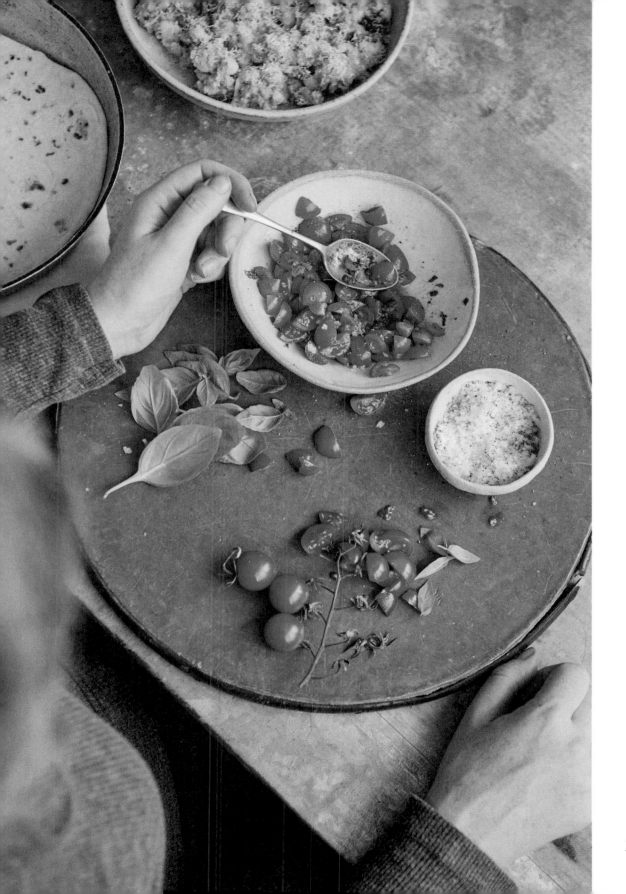

Butter bean, roasted lemon, and caramelized-onion hummus

This really is much more than hummus. I use plump butter beans instead of chickpeas and pan-roasted lemons to bring a spike of mellow acidity, which is nicely balanced out by sweet, slow-cooked onions. I happily eat this with some cooked grains and some steamed veg on the side for a simple dinner.

Heat a medium frying pan with a little olive oil. Once hot, add the sliced onions and cook over medium heat for 10 to 15 minutes, until browned and beginning to crisp a little. Push to one side of the pan. Put the lemons, cut side down, on one half of the pan. Cook for 4 to 5 minutes, until softened, sticky, and brown on the undersides, all the while stirring the onions. Transfer the onions and lemons to a bowl to cool a little.

Put the cilantro seeds in the pan and toast for a few minutes until they are starting to brown and smell toasty. Scrape them into a mortar with all the goodness from the bottom of the pan and bash with the pestle until quite fine.

Put the beans into a food processor with the tahini, a good pinch of salt, and 1 tablespoon of extra-virgin olive oil. Blitz well, until cloudy and creamy. Squeeze in the juice from all the lemon halves and scrape in some of the roasted middles, taking care to pick out any seeds. Add half the onions and pulse a couple of times—try to keep a bit of texture here.

Serve with the rest of the onions scattered on top and a drizzle more extra-virgin olive oil. Serve piled on flatbread, with baby vegetables, or next to some warm cooked grains and veg.

SERVES 4

olive oil

4 onions, finely sliced

2 unwaxed lemons, halved

1 teaspoon cilantro (coriander) seeds

2 × 14.5-ounce (400-g) cans or 1 × 1½-pound (660-g) jar of cooked butter beans, drained

1 tablespoon light tahini

a pinch of flaky sea salt

extra-virgin olive oil

yogurt flatbread (see page 456), to serve

Roasted cauliflower, mustard, and Cheddar soup

This soup is based on the flavors of piccalilli, though it's mellower and less fiery than the stuff you might spoon out of a jar. It's a perky bowl of soup with a subtle kick from a bit of cider vinegar and some mellow spice. I use the brassicas that are starting to show up as the leaves begin to turn.

This is great served with cheese on toast, with a good dash of Worcestershire sauce.

SERVES 4

Preheat your oven to 425°F (220°C). Heat a little oil in a heavy-based soup-size saucepan. Once hot, add the onion and fennel and a pinch of salt and cook for 10 to 15 minutes, until soft and sweet.

Meanwhile, cut the cauliflower into little florets and do the same with the broccoli. Put them on a baking sheet with some salt, pepper, half the cumin seeds, and a good drizzle of olive oil and roast for 20 to 30 minutes, until crisp and golden.

Back to the onions and fennel. Once they are soft and sweet, turn the heat up a little and add the rest of the cumin seeds, the mustard seeds, turmeric, and mustard powder. Allow the mustard seeds to pop as you stir the spices for a couple of minutes to toast them. Next, add the apples, chiles, bay leaves, vinegar, and the bread and cook for another minute, then add the vegetable stock. Bring to a boil and simmer for 15 minutes.

Ladle the soup into a high-speed blender and blitz for a minute until smooth. Taste and add more salt and pepper, if you like.

Once the soup is ready and the brassicas are nicely golden and roasted, ladle the soup into bowls, top with the roasted cauliflower and broccoli, and add a good grating of Cheddar.

olive oil

1 onion, finely chopped

1 bulb of fennel, finely sliced

sea salt

1 medium cauliflower (about 1¾ pounds/800 g)

7 ounces (200 g) broccoli

freshly ground black pepper

1 tablespoon cumin seeds

1 tablespoon black mustard seeds

1 teaspoon ground turmeric

1 heaping teaspoon English mustard powder

2 good eating apples, grated

2 green chiles, roughly chopped

2 bay leaves

1 tablespoon cider vinegar

2 slices of good bread

4½ cups (1 liter) hot vegetable stock

½ cup (50 g) Cheddar, grated or crumbled, to serve

319

Smoky corn chowder

I eat this on early autumn days, when the cold starts to set in, when the sweaters come out of storage and the fire gets lit for the first time, but there is still some papery husked sweet corn around. This is a dish that feels filling and warming while still having crunch and freshness. The first time I made it, John ate three bowls.

If you can get your hands on it, flaky smoked sea salt is a perfect way to finish this dish.

———————————

Bring a small pan of water to a boil, add the eggs and cook for 6 minutes so the yolk is still soft but not runny. Once they are cooked, crack their shells on the work surface so they are easy to peel, then run them under cold water for a minute.

Next put a drizzle of the oil into a large heavy-based saucepan. Once it's hot, add the leek and garlic and cook for 10 to 12 minutes, until the leeks are soft and sweet but not browned.

SERVES 4

4 organic eggs

olive oil

1 large leek, finely sliced

2 cloves of garlic, finely sliced

2 large Russet potatoes, peeled

3 ears of corn, husks removed

1⅔ cups (400 ml) vegetable stock

2 tablespoons smoked water (optional; see note above)

a large bunch of cilantro

5 ounces (150 ml) crème fraîche

the juice of ½ a lemon

Meanwhile, chop the potatoes into rough ⅜-inch (1-cm) pieces. Cut the corn from its cobs; I do this by resting the base of the corn in a bowl so it catches the kernels as they are cut. Once the leeks have had their time, add the potatoes and corn to the pan with the stock and smoked water, if you are using it, then bring to a simmer and cook for 15 minutes or until the potatoes are cooked through and their edges are almost collapsing.

Use this time to peel your eggs and cut them in half, and pick the cilantro leaves from their stems. Roughly chop the cilantro leaves.

Once the potatoes are cooked, stir in the crème fraîche and lemon juice and half of the cilantro and stir to warm them through, then take the pan off the heat.

Serve the chowder in bowls, with the halved egg on top and more cilantro scattered over.

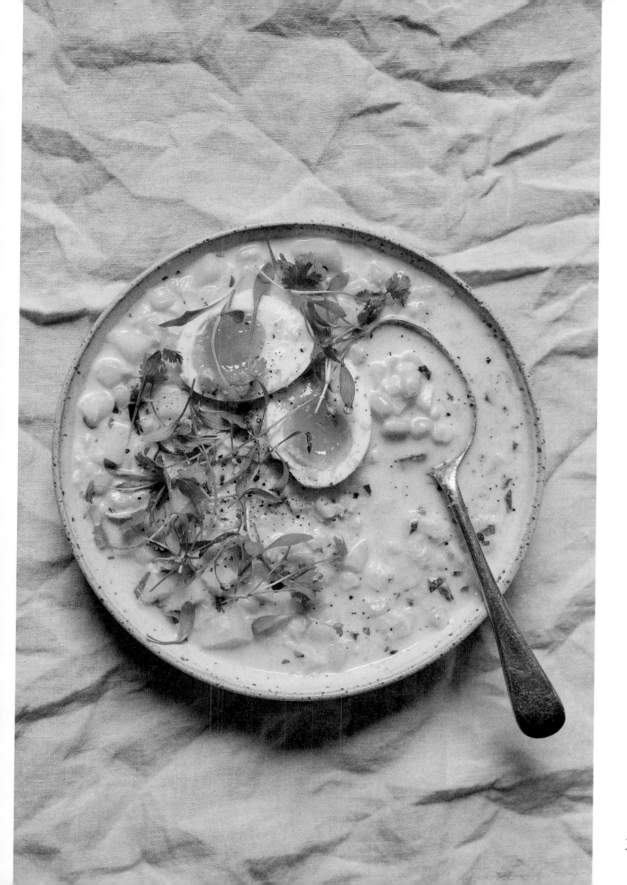

Simple yellow split pea soup with green olives

This is a comforting buttery bowl topped with a quick punch of flavor. This soup celebrates split peas, which seem to have fallen off our cooking radar somewhat but are such good value and cook down to a satisfying yellow, creamy mess. It's simple and quick and mostly made with pantry staples, topped and finished with a flurry of flavors. This is a soup that will sustain.

The protein we get from beans is not a complete protein like those found in eggs, dairy, or quinoa. Pulses have only eight of the nine essential amino acids that make up protein, but the missing piece of the jigsaw can be filled with grains or sesame seeds, which contain the ninth. So eating your pulses with a little bread, or hummus made with tahini, will form a complete protein, providing more energy and nourishment.

SERVES 4–6

15¾ ounces (450 g) dried yellow split peas

2 tablespoons sesame seeds, toasted

1 tablespoon extra-virgin olive oil, plus extra to finish

2 onions, finely chopped

sea salt

the zest and juice of 2 unwaxed lemons (use the zest for topping)

FOR THE TOPPING

½ a cucumber

1 clove of garlic, finely chopped

¾ cup (200 g) Greek yogurt

a handful of green olives, pitted and chopped

a small bunch of mint leaves, chopped

Soak the split peas in cold water overnight. This isn't essential but will halve the cooking time.

Put the drained peas in a large saucepan and cover with cold water. Bring to a rapid boil for 10 minutes, then reduce the heat and simmer for 20 to 30 minutes or until tender. Drain, season, then stir in the toasted sesame seeds and set aside.

Put a large pot over medium heat. Add the oil, onions, and a large pinch of salt. Cook for 5 minutes or so, until soft. Add the cooked split peas and 1½ cups (350 ml) of cold water. Bring to a simmer for a few minutes, then remove from the heat. Ladle half the soup into a bowl and set aside. Use an immersion blender to purée the rest of the soup in the pan. Stir the chunky soup back into the purée. You can thin the soup with more water (or stock) a bit at a time. Add the lemon juice. Taste and adjust the seasoning.

While the soup is cooking, prepare the toppings. Slice the cucumber lengthways, then scoop out and discard the seeds. Coarsely grate it into a bowl. Add the lemon zest and garlic, and season with a big pinch of salt.

Ladle the soup into bowls. Top each with a generous dollop of the yogurt, a spoonful of the chopped olives, some mint, a spoonful of cucumber, and a drizzle of olive oil.

Squash and pink peppercorn salad

This is a salad for bridging the gap between the warm late-summer days and the abundance of autumn. I use a speed peeler to peel the squash into thin ribbons—they aren't cooked but they soften and mellow once dressed with the lime juice. The simple dressing is made with lime and pink peppercorns, with no oil, to keep it fresh.

I serve this with tofu, crisped in the frying pan with honey and soy, and some steamed brown rice if I want to make a meal of it.

**SERVES 2 AS MAIN,
4 AS A SIDE**

1-pound (500-g) piece of butternut squash, peeled and deseeded

1 unwaxed lime

sea salt

1 tablespoon pink peppercorns

½ a bunch of mint, leaves picked

Peel the squash into thin ribbons with a speed peeler or mandoline. Use quite a light touch here, as you want the squash to be delicate and thin; applying too much force will give you thicker pieces.

Place the squash in a large bowl with the lime zest and juice and some salt, then toss to coat.

Roughly bash the pink peppercorns in a mortar with pestle and add them to the bowl. Toss again to mix in the peppercorns. Next, roughly chop the mint leaves and toss them in the squash. Taste and add more salt, pepper, or lime if you think it needs it.

Serve on its own for a refreshing salad, or with rice and tofu (see above) for a more substantial supper.

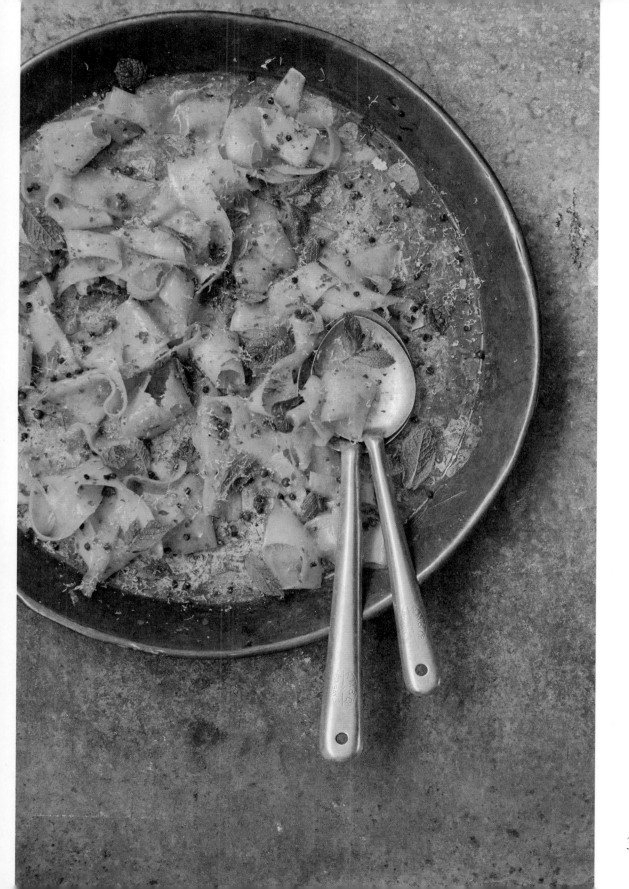

Chard, leek, and walnut crostata

This forgiving tart comes together pretty quickly. The star here is the flaky walnut-spiked pastry. It sits around a center of sweet buttery leeks, chard and some verdant green herbs. It's quite a crumbly pastry, thanks to the walnuts, but they make it so toasty and flaky it's worth it. The tart is free-form, so if the pastry cracks you can pinch it back together with your finger easily—just be sure to do a final check around the outside of the pastry once it's filled to make sure all holes are pinched and no filling can escape. I serve this with some simple boiled potatoes and a lemon-dressed salad.

SERVES 4–6

FOR THE PASTRY

½ cup (50 g) walnuts

1½ cups (200 g) white spelt flour

½ teaspoon flaky sea salt

7 tablespoons very cold butter, cut into cubes

2 tablespoons ice-cold water

olive oil

2 leeks, outer leaves removed, washed and finely shredded

sea salt

a bunch of chard (about 7 ounces/200 g)

2 cloves of garlic, chopped

a pinch of red pepper flakes

1 teaspoon fennel seeds

1 tablespoon red wine vinegar

a large mixed bunch of soft herbs, leaves picked

freshly ground black pepper

¼ cup (25 g) Parmesan (I use a vegetarian/rennet-free one)

3 medium organic eggs

First, make the pastry. Put the walnuts into a food processor and blitz until you have fine, uniform crumbs, but keep an eye on it—if you go too far, they will start to come together as a nut butter. Add the flour and salt and pulse a few times to mix everything evenly.

Next, add the butter and pulse a few times until you have a rough-looking dough. With the motor running, add a tablespoon of the very cold water and pulse again for four turns of the blade. Take the lid off and pinch the dough with your fingers. Add a little more water if it feels dry and keep blitzing until the dough comes together in a ball; it should be a buttery pastry and not feel crumbly. Wrap the dough in waxed paper and put it into the fridge.

Next, warm a frying pan over medium heat, pour in a drizzle of olive oil, and add the leeks and a pinch of salt. Fry for 5 to 7 minutes, until the leeks are soft and sweet.

While this is happening, wash the chard and strip the leaves from their stalks. Slice the stalks into ¾-inch (2-cm) lengths, then roll up the leaves and slice across the middle into ⅜-inch- (1-cm-) wide ribbons. →

Back to the leeks. Add the garlic, red pepper flakes, and fennel seeds and fry in the pan for a couple of minutes to toast the spices. When the pan is smelling aromatic, add the chard stalks and stir. Cook for 5 minutes until the stalks lose their rawness, then stir in the leaves and add the vinegar. Cook until the leaves have wilted, about 4 minutes.

Put the vegetables on a plate to cool and preheat your oven to 425°F (220°C).

Finely chop the herbs and place them in a large mixing bowl. Grate in the Parmesan and whisk in the eggs with a fork. Season with salt and pepper.

Take the walnut pastry out of the fridge and line a large baking sheet with parchment paper. Drizzle some olive oil in the center of the paper. If your baking sheet is quite flat, you should be able to roll the pastry out to a round about 12 inches (30 cm) across and ⅜ inch (1 cm) deep. If you have a standard deep baking sheet, flip it over and place the paper on the underside instead.

Mix the cooled vegetables with the egg mixture. Arrange the vegetables in the center of the pastry, leaving about 1 inch (3 cm) around the edge. Gently fold the pastry border back over the vegetables, pleating a little as you go. It will be crumbly and more difficult to handle than other doughs and may break at its edges, but it will be worth it for the flaky short pastry at the end.

Place the crostata in the center of the hot oven and bake for 35 minutes, until the edges are deep golden and the filling is starting to bubble, then turn the heat down to 395°F (200°C) and bake for another 15 minutes, until the pastry is cooked through.

Cool on the baking sheet for 10 minutes, then slide onto a wire rack to cool and let the pastry crisp up.

Turmeric and quinoa bowl with quick pickled cabbage

A meal in a bowl, this is quick enough to put together any night of the week and is bright, filling autumn eating. If you have a jar of sauerkraut in your fridge (a recipe for my favorite is on page 381), you could skip the quick pickled cabbage and use a couple of tablespoons in its place.

I love the subtle curry tones of shiso leaves, which are available in most Asian supermarkets, but if you can't get them, cilantro—though a different flavor—will also work well.

Finely shred the white cabbage, then put it into a bowl with a good pinch of sea salt, the vinegar, honey, cilantro, caraway seeds, ginger, and green chile. Scrunch it all together with your hands in the bowl to get the pickling process happening.

I like to start by dry-toasting my quinoa in the saucepan until it makes a popping sound—this adds a deeper, toasty flavor to the dish. Add 2 cups (500 ml) of water, a good pinch of sea salt, the turmeric, and lemon halves, and cook for about 10 to 15 minutes, or until all the water has been absorbed and the little curly grain has popped out. I keep the pan on the heat until all the water has gone and I can hear the popping again. Drain any excess water, then squeeze the lemon juice into the pan, reserving a little; add a little olive oil, and more salt, if needed, and a little twist of black pepper.

Meanwhile, bring a saucepan of water to a boil, lower in your eggs, and boil them for 6 minutes. Drain, crack the shells, and run under cold water until they are cool.

Peel and remove the pit from the avocado; slice and squeeze over a little lemon juice. Once the eggs are cool enough to handle, peel them, then roll them in the sesame seeds and cut in half—your yolks should be just set but still soft.

Put your quinoa into a bowl, top with the pickled cabbage, avocado, egg, herbs, and some more sesame seeds.

SERVES 2

FOR THE PICKLED CABBAGE

½ a small white cabbage

sea salt

2 tablespoons white wine vinegar

1 teaspoon golden honey

1 teaspoon cilantro (coriander) seeds

a pinch of caraway seeds

a ⅜-inch (1-cm) piece of ginger, peeled and finely grated

1 green chile, finely sliced

1 cup (200 g) quinoa (a mugful)

sea salt

½ teaspoon ground turmeric or a small thumb of fresh turmeric, grated

1 lemon, cut in half

olive oil

freshly ground black pepper

2 organic eggs

1 ripe avocado

2 tablespoons black sesame seeds, plus more for sprinkling

a handful of shiso or cilantro leaves

Figs, pistachios, and labneh

This is a simple thing to make on an autumn day. Its success relies purely on the figs you use—they need to be ripe, soft and jammy, as they are the star of the show. I use fenugreek here to add some spice—the seeds have a subtle but pleasantly bitter note and taste a little like burnt sugar or maple syrup. Fenugreek is not as well used as lots of other spices but I would urge you to buy some if you don't have it already; it's a great spice to add to curries—toasted and bashed, or to sprinkle over yogurt or hummus. It's widely used in Middle Eastern cooking, so it goes very well here with figs.

To make the labneh yourself, turn to the recipe on page 456. I find it incredibly satisfying to make: a little cradle of muslin with pure sheet-white yogurt hanging, getting thicker and more delicious. If you don't want to make it, use a very thick Greek yogurt.

SERVES 4

¾ cup (200 g) labneh (see page 456) or thick Greek yogurt

2½ tablespoons (25 g) sesame seeds

⅓ cup (50 g) shelled pistachios, roughly chopped

1 teaspoon fenugreek seeds

sea salt

8 ripe figs

a couple of handfuls of peppery leaves (mizuna, arugula, watercress)

the zest of 1 unwaxed lemon

freshly ground black pepper

extra-virgin olive oil

If you want to make your labneh, you'll need to start the night before, following the recipe on page 456.

Toast the sesame seeds, pistachios, and fenugreek in a dry pan over medium heat, until the sesame seeds are beginning to brown, the fenugreek begins to smell sugary and toasty, and the pistachios are warmed and their oils have released—they won't pick up any color. Transfer to a bowl and, once cool, bash in a mortar with pestle—not too much—just enough so the fenugreek is cracked and the pistachios have broken up a little.

Mix a pinch of salt into the labneh or yogurt, then spoon it into the middle of a big serving plate and use the back of a spoon to spread it out a bit, creating undulating waves and ups and downs for everything to fall into.

Make a cross in the top of the figs, then tear them into halves and quarters and scatter them over the yogurt. Scatter over the nuts, leaves and lemon zest, season with a good pinch of salt and pepper, and drizzle with a slick of olive oil.

Sri Lankan squash dhal

This is often on our table in autumn. It's warming and is the sort of thing you can sit on your lap on the sofa and eat with a spoon. I roast butternut squash to pile on top, along with some crispy, minerally kale, which adds a bit more interest to the usually one-textured dhal. I eat this with some roti or chapatis and yogurt.

Here I use a Sri Lankan curry powder, one of my new obsessions. My recipe is on page 189 but you could use the same amount of a good store-bought garam masala plus ¼ teaspoon of ground cloves.

SERVES 6

1 cup (200 g) red lentils

1 medium butternut squash (about 1¾ pounds/150 g), peeled

coconut or canola oil

sea salt and freshly ground black pepper

3 tablespoons Sri Lankan curry powder (see note above)

1 onion, finely chopped

2 cloves of garlic, finely sliced

2 green chiles, chopped (deseeded if you like)

1 cinnamon stick

1 heaping teaspoon ground turmeric or a small thumb of fresh turmeric, grated

1 × 14.5-ounce (400-g) can of coconut milk

1 teaspoon vegetable stock powder or ½ a stock cube

FOR THE KALE

7 ounces (200 g) kale, leaves stripped, stalks reserved

coconut or canola oil

the zest and juice of 1 unwaxed lime

TO SERVE

rotis or chapatis

plain yogurt

Preheat the oven to 425°F (220°C). Wash the lentils in cold running water until the water runs clear, then put them in a bowl of cold water to soak while you get on with everything else.

Cut the squash into rough ⅜-inch (1-cm) pieces, then place on a baking sheet with a little oil, salt, pepper, and a teaspoon of curry powder and toss so everything is coated in the spices and oil. Cover with foil and roast in the hot oven for 20 minutes, then another 10 with the foil off.

Heat a splash of oil in a deep, lidded saucepan and, once hot, add the onion, garlic, chiles, and the cinnamon stick and cook for 10 minutes, until soft and sweet. Fill the kettle with water and boil.

Add the rest of the curry powder with the turmeric to the pan, then take out 1 tablespoon of the mixture and keep in a bowl for later. Drain and add the lentils, the coconut milk, stock powder, and 7 ounces (200 ml) of hot water and bring to a boil, then turn the heat down and simmer for 10 minutes until it has thickened and most of the water has evaporated.

Tear the kale leaves into bite-size pieces, discard any particularly tough stalks, and finely chop the rest. Heat a little oil in a frying pan over medium heat, and add the reserved spiced onions and the kale stalks. Cook for 3 to 4 minutes, until the stalks soften a bit, then add the leaves and stir for a couple of minutes. Once wilted, take the pan off the heat and add the lime zest and juice and a pinch of salt.

Once the squash is cooked, take it out of the oven and stir three-quarters of it into the dhal. Serve in deep bowls with the last of the squash and the kale, the chapatis, and the yogurt.

Smoky mushroom and roasted kale lasagna

This is based on the delicious Vincisgrassi, a mushroom lasagna that hails from the Le Marche region in Italy. The authentic Vincisgrassi uses the smokiness of Parma ham. I didn't want to stop eating this dish, one of my most craved, when I stopped eating meat, so this is topped with some oven-roasted kale instead and an optional dash of smoked water. If you like it you can also add truffle oil; personally I am not a fan, but I know it is well loved so I will leave that decision up to you. I use a mixture of wild mushrooms like chanterelles and porcini, along with some more substantial ones like chestnut or portobellos.

Vegans can make this using dried pasta sheets, which are usually made without eggs, and almond milk, a dairy-free butter, and vegan Parmesan. This may sound like a lot of changes, but it works well, and I make it this way for the vegans in my family often.

Cover the porcini with 7 ounces (200 ml) of boiling water. Clean your mushrooms, using a brush or damp paper towel to dust off any dirt, then tear or slice them into bite-size pieces.

For the béchamel, heat the milk in a pan with the onion, bay leaves, and peppercorns until boiling. Remove from the heat and leave to infuse for 30 minutes. Strain through a fine sieve into a pitcher and set aside for later.

Next cook your mushrooms—you will need to do this in a couple of batches. Melt half the butter in a large frying pan over very high heat and add a splash of olive oil. Let the pan get nice and hot, then add half the fresh mushrooms and cook, moving them around the pan, until they are browned and crisp (about 5 to 7 minutes). Season with a pinch of salt and pepper and remove the first batch to a large bowl. Put the pan back on the heat, add the rest of the butter and a bit more oil, and cook the rest of the mushrooms.

Once the second batch is golden, drain the porcini, keeping the soaking liquid, then roughly chop and add them to the pan of mushrooms, along with the parsley. Stir together and pour into the bowl with the rest of the mushrooms. →

SERVES 4–6

1 ounce (30 g) dried porcini

15¾ ounces (450 g) mushrooms (see note at left)

2 tablespoons butter, plus more for greasing

olive oil

sea salt and freshly ground black pepper

2 tablespoons chopped flat-leaf parsley

5 ounces (150 g) kale, stalks removed, leaves torn into bite-size pieces (2⅓ cups)

10½ ounces (300 g) fresh lasagna sheets

1½ cups (150 g) grated Parmesan (I use a vegetarian one), plus a little extra

truffle oil (optional)

FOR THE BÉCHAMEL

4½ cups (1 liter) whole milk or almond milk

½ small onion

2 bay leaves

8 black peppercorns

4 tablespoons (50 g) butter

⅔ cup (75 g) plain flour

1 tablespoon smoked water (optional; see page 320)

Now back to your sauce. Melt the butter in a heavy-bottom pan, add the flour, and mix well, allowing it to cook for a couple of minutes so the flour loses its rawness. Take the pan off the heat and add the milk bit by bit, starting with small drops and stirring well with a balloon whisk to prevent lumps from forming. Once you have mixed in all the milk, stir in the porcini soaking liquid and put the pan back on the heat. Bring to boil, stirring constantly—the mixture will thicken. Simmer for 3 minutes, then stir in the smoked water (if using) and the parsley and mushroom mixture, and heat gently. Taste and season with more salt and pepper if it's needed.

In a bowl, scrunch the kale with a tablespoon of olive oil and some salt and pepper and mix through the sauce too.

Preheat the oven to 425°F (220°C). Butter an ovenproof dish (about 8-by-12 inches/20-by-30 cm). If you are using dried pasta sheets, boil the pasta in salted water according to the package instructions. If you are using fresh, cook the sheets in boiling water for 2 minutes, cooking 4 squares at a time and assembling the dish as you go.

Start with a layer of pasta, then sauce, then a sprinkling of Parmesan and keep going, building up the layers until you have used all the pasta sheets, and finishing with a layer of sauce and Parmesan. Bake in the oven for 25 to 30 minutes, until golden brown on top and bubbling. Drizzle with truffle oil if you like, and serve with more Parmesan and some green salad.

Roasted cauliflower steaks with Taleggio and pickled peppers

I have a difficult relationship with cauliflower. Despite its recent renaissance it's not something I get excited about often. But roasted to within an inch of its life, soft and buttery in the center, it can be a thing of beauty. These steaks are now the only way I want to eat cauliflower. Topped with capers, pickled red chile, olives, and Taleggio, they are elevated to the main event. When I first came up with the recipe I made it three times in one week. I eat the steaks with lemon-dressed greens or salad and not much else. Preheating the baking sheet makes sure they brown and cook evenly on both sides.

———————————————

Preheat your oven to 425°F (220°C) and place a baking sheet in the oven to heat up for 10 minutes (you may need two); this is so the bottom of the steaks browns nicely.

Put the sliced chile into a small bowl with the vinegar and maple syrup, mix well, and leave to sit.

Cut the root off the bottom of each cauliflower so it sits flat on the board, then cut ⅜ inch (1 cm) off all sides of the cauliflower heads and reserve. Cut the cauliflowers into ¾-inch- (2-cm-) thick steaks (how many steaks you get depends on the size and shape of your cauliflowers). Season each side of the steak with salt and pepper and drizzle with the oil. Put on the hot baking sheet and place in the oven for about 20 minutes, until golden on both sides.

While the steaks are in the oven, make your topping. Roughly chop 1 cup (150 g) of the remaining cauliflower offcuts (any left over can be blitzed up and used for the cauliflower rice on page 36) and place in a bowl with the chiles, bread crumbs, capers, sundried tomatoes, and almonds. Finely grate in the zest of the lemon, then coarsely grate in the cheese and mix well.

Once the cauliflower steaks have had their time in the oven, take them out and divide the topping among them. Gently press the topping down so it sticks to the steaks. Put back in the oven for 10 minutes, until the cheese is melting and golden.

Serve with a bright green salad and perhaps a few boiled new potatoes if you are hungry. Any leftovers are great chopped up and tossed in some pasta.

SERVES 4–6

2 red chiles, sliced

2 tablespoons vinegar

1 teaspoon maple syrup

2 large heads of cauliflower (about 1¾ pounds/800 g each)

sea salt and freshly ground black pepper

2 tablespoons olive oil

6 small pickled red chile peppers (about ¼ cup/ 30 g), roughly chopped

1 cup (100 g) bread crumbs

4 tablespoons baby capers

1 tablespoon sundried tomatoes, roughly chopped

a small handful of almonds, roughly chopped

1 unwaxed lemon

1⅓ cups (150 g) Taleggio cheese, fridge cold

TO SERVE

green salad

boiled new potatoes

Pumpkin and red lentil kofte with smoky tomato sauce

SERVES 4 (MAKES ABOUT 18 LITTLE KOFTE)

1¼ pounds (550 g) pumpkin or butternut squash, cut into small cubes

olive oil

sea salt and freshly ground black pepper

1 red onion, finely chopped

¾ cup (150 g) red lentils

a good pinch of red pepper flakes

1 teaspoon ground cinnamon

the seeds from 2 cardamom pods, ground to a powder

1 teaspoon ground turmeric

1 tablespoon tomato purée

¾ cup (100 g) dried apricots (I use the unsulphured ones), roughly chopped

1 cup (100 g) unsalted shelled pistachios, or almonds, roughly chopped

1 organic egg

olive oil

mint and parsley leaves, to serve

FOR THE SMOKY TOMATO SAUCE

2 red onions

2½ pounds (1 kg) ripe vine tomatoes, halved

sea salt and freshly ground black pepper

1 teaspoon smoked hot paprika

olive oil

1 green chile

1 teaspoon golden honey

This is an outrageously good combination of gently spiced squash-and-lentil kofte and a smoky green-chile-spiked tomato sauce. It's one of the dishes I often make when I have a mixed table of diners, some sold on eating mostly vegetables, and others still skeptical—it shouts with deliciousness.

This is quite satisfying as it is, but if you wanted something to sit beside it, some giant couscous, orzo, or quinoa dressed with lemon and oil would be great.

Preheat your oven to 425°F (220°C).

Put the chopped pumpkin on a baking sheet, drizzle over some olive oil, season with salt and pepper, and cover the sheet with foil. Roast in the hot oven for 20 minutes with the foil on, then remove the foil and roast for another 10 minutes.

For your sauce, put the onions and tomatoes in a roasting pan, add the smoked paprika and a little olive oil, and season well with salt and pepper. Toss to make sure everything is coated, then roast in the hot oven for about 45 minutes, or until the tomatoes have shriveled and lost a lot of their moisture. Fill your kettle with water and boil.

Meanwhile, put a large frying pan over medium heat, add a drizzle of olive oil and the onion and cook for 10 minutes, until soft and sweet.

At the same time, put the lentils into plenty of boiling water and cook for about 12 minutes until they are tender, then drain and allow to sit in the sieve to steam dry.

Once the onion in the pan is soft and sweet, add the spices and cook for a couple of minutes to toast them, then take the pan off the heat, scoop the onions into a large mixing bowl, and leave to cool.

Once cool, add the tomato purée and the chopped dried fruit and nuts. Once the lentils are cool, add those too along with the egg. →

Once the squash is ready, allow it to cool a little, then use a fork to mash it up on the baking sheet and scoop into the kofte mixture. Mash everything together, until you have a rough mixture that will come together in a ball when you squeeze it in your hand. Season with salt and pepper and put into the fridge for 20 minutes to rest.

Line a baking sheet with parchment paper. Take the bowl out of the oven and shape the mixture into golf ball–size rounds. You may need a bowl of warm water nearby to dip your fingers in as you go, as the kofte mixture can become sticky. Place the shaped kofte on the lined pan and put them back into the fridge for another 15 minutes to firm up.

Meanwhile, take the tomatoes out of the oven and roughly chop the chile. Blitz the tomatoes in a food processor with the chopped chile and taste. Add a little more salt, pepper, and the teaspoon of honey if your tomatoes aren't that sweet, remembering that the dried fruit in the kofte will bring some sweetness to the dish. When you're happy, set aside until you're ready to eat.

Heat a large frying pan over medium heat, add a drizzle of olive oil, and fry the kofte in batches, gingerly rolling them over to brown and crisp on all sides for about 5 to 7 minutes. Meanwhile, gently warm the sauce.

Serve the kofte with the tomato sauce, the herb leaves, and a grain (see note in intro) if you are hungry.

Toasted quinoa, kale, and lemon bake

This bake gets points for wholesome ingredients: kale, quinoa, and almond milk; it tastes anything but wholesome, though. It is generous and sustaining. This works best with a fresh head of kale, which I often find is more delicate, softer, and more full-flavored than the prechopped stuff you buy in bags, but either will work.

Vegans can use coconut oil and replace the cheese with vegan Parmesan or a teaspoon of nutritional yeast. Gluten-free flour works well here too. Leftovers can be sliced once the bake has cooled and set and quickly warmed in a pan with a little olive oil, which yields very good crispy sides.

Preheat the oven to 400°F (210°C). Butter a medium ovenproof gratin dish or baking dish. Fill your kettle with water and boil.

Rinse the quinoa under running water, put it into a pan, and toast it for a couple of minutes with no oil until it smells nutty, stirring all the time to keep it from burning. Next, add a good pinch of salt and 4½ cups (1 liter) of hot water from the kettle, bring to a boil, then simmer for 15 minutes, until tender. When the quinoa is cooked, drain it in a sieve, but use a bowl underneath to catch the liquid; you will use this later.

Half-fill a large saucepan with boiling water and bring it back to a boil. Add a pinch of salt, then add the kale leaves—you may need to press down to immerse them all—and cook until tender; this will take about 3 minutes. Drain the kale well and blend to a purée with 4 tablespoons of its cooking water.

Melt the butter in a saucepan until bubbling, add the flour and cook for a minute, so it loses its raw flour flavor, then add ⅞ cup (200 ml) of the quinoa cooking water and the milk. Stir or whisk over medium heat, until the sauce has thickened; this will take a few minutes. Add the spices, the lemon zest, and some salt and pepper.

Add the puréed kale, lemon juice, thyme, and cooked quinoa and grate in half the cheese. Pour into the greased baking dish and grate over the remaining cheese. Bake for 35 minutes, until crisp on top.

SERVES 4

1 cup (200 g) quinoa

sea salt

2 pounds (1 kg) head of kale, leaves stripped (about 6 cups/400 g without the stalks)

2 tablespoons butter or coconut oil, plus extra for greasing

2 tablespoons white spelt flour

⅔ cup (170 ml) milk (I use unsweetened almond)

½ teaspoon ground allspice

⅛ a fresh nutmeg, grated

the zest and juice of 1 unwaxed lemon

freshly ground black pepper

a few sprigs of thyme, leaves picked

1 cup (100 g) Gruyère (I use a vegetarian/rennet-free one)

Making friends with your freezer

Most evenings I like to cook something fresh from scratch. Having a pan in my hands and hearing the rock of a knife on the board is when I feel at my happiest. But, like anyone, some nights I don't have time for an hour at the stove yet still want to eat something nourishing and full of flavor. Sometimes that's a sourdough pizza from around the corner, or a quick omelette and a couple of rounds of toast, but most often when I don't feel the urge or have the time to cook, I turn to my freezer.

My freezer is stacked with bags and containers of food that are ready to go. A meal can be made in the time it takes to defrost some dhal and prepare a quick shock of lime, cilantro and green chile to go on top. In the days after my son was born I was deeply smug about the few days I had spent cooking and filling my freezer. We relied on it for the first three weeks. And with him still so little it's great to know we have backup dinners if it's been a long day. A freezer full of food for me is like insurance for your taste buds, well-being, and sanity. It's also a great way to cook if you live on your own or as a couple, as most recipes yield four servings, and it's always cheaper and easier to cook for more. Who wants to be left with half an onion?

Batch cooking

I make a big batch of a soup, stew, or dhal every couple of weeks; even little falafels or polpette (see page 366) can be frozen. Every so often I'll make a big lasagna or lentil shepherd's pie and freeze half. Below is a list of recipes that you could freeze. Make the base recipe and leave off any fresh garnishes if you plan to freeze it. If your pans and freezer are big enough, you could even double or triple the recipe.

Finishing touches

One thing I love about making a big batch for the freezer is the opportunity to use a recipe in lots of different ways. As you take each portion out you can be guided by what you feel like that day, adding final flourishes, texture and even some quickly chopped fresh elements. These will bring your once-frozen dinner back to life. Here are a few ideas for freezer staples:

Soup

— Add a swirl of yogurt mixed with a little tahini and some toasted seeds.

— Top with chopped herbs, oil, and chopped toasted almonds (see page 459).

— Swirl in a good spoonful of pesto and some quick olive oil, salt, and pepper croutons.

— Top with crispy kale and a grating of cheese.

Dhal

— Serve with a boiled egg, chopped toasted cashews, chile, and cilantro.

— With a quick chop of cilantro, mint, green chile, and lime.

— With mango chutney, crushed poppadoms, and lots of mint.

— With wilted greens, yogurt, and grated cucumber, and lots of lemon.

Polpette

— Have with spaghetti, chopped cherry tomatoes, oil, and basil.

— Rolled into a flatbread with hummus, pickles, and leaves.

— Squashed into a burger bun or good bread with avocado, gherkins, mayo, and hot sauce.

— With a quick tomato sauce, quinoa, fresh herbs, and lemon zest.

Vegetable stew

— Use as a base for baked eggs.

— Add some cooked chickpeas and a poached egg and top with torn basil.

— Stir in some lentils, top with some mashed veg, and bake in a "shepherds pie."

— With creamy polenta, greens, and some Parmesan (I use a vegetarian/rennet-free one).

Here are recipes from this book most suited to batch cooking and freezing:

— Turmeric and lime-leaf broth with roasted root vegetables (page 402)

— Squash polpette (page 366)

— Gentle potato chowder with toasted chile oil (page 22)

— Green peppercorn and lemongrass coconut broth (page 27)

— Little pea and white-bean polpette (page 43)

— Quick carrot dhal (page 46)

— Butter bean stew with kale and sticky blood oranges (page 50)

— Sri Lankan green bean and tomato curry (page 189)

— Pistachio and ricotta dumplings with peas and herbs (page 208)

— Pumpkin and red lentil kofte with smoky tomato sauce (page 338)

— Boston baked beans for a crowd (page 354)

— Sri Lankan squash dhal (page 332)

— Cauliflower-topped Puy lentil pie (page 422)

— Smoky mushroom and roast kale lasagna (page 333)

Extending the seasons

Autumn is an abundant time of year so as well as being a means of having ready-to-eat food, freezing is a great way of preserving without having to worry about sterilizing jars and getting out the jam pan. It is also a great way to hold on to some of the things we love to eat in summer for a bit longer: the chiles and tomatoes, the blackberries and sloes of autumn. A freezer is a magical kitchen time machine.

Making the most of your freezer

— Portioning: I like to freeze things I will use in small portions in ice cube trays or silicone molds and once frozen, pop them out into a freezer bag (which I wash and reuse). This is great for baby food, herb garnishes, pestos, etc.

— Maximizing space: freeze anything like cooked beans or berries flat on a baking sheet first and then pour them into a bag; that way they will freeze individually and you can use as much as you need rather than having to defrost a whole block.

Herbs

— Juice your herbs (see page 86): they can then be frozen and used in a multitude of dishes.

— Freeze woody herbs whole and use from the freezer.

— Chop leftover soft herbs and pile into ice cube trays; cover with water or olive oil and push down to submerge them.

Fruit

— Avocados: these freeze well; I mash mine with lime first and freeze in ice cube trays.

— Bananas: peel and chop bananas so that they can be broken down by a food processor or blender for smoothies.

— Berries: freeze flat on a baking sheet first, then scoop into bags.

— Citrus: freeze the juice or slices that can be added to drinks like ice cubes.

Grains and pulses

— Make a double batch of hummus; it freezes well.

— Cook a big batch of dried beans or lentils (see page 461) and freeze in portions; they will taste so much better than canned ones.

— Cooked grains freeze well.

Other things I keep in the freezer

— Corn tortillas: you can cook them from frozen.

— Seeded flour tortillas.

— Good sourdough—sliced—for toast.

— Pizza dough: rolled out into rounds after its first proof and frozen between waxed paper.

Kale and butter bean pie

Sometimes I crave crunch and texture from a pie. This one is crisp, with a buttery, rösti-like grated celeriac roof. The flavors beneath are warm and satisfying: the round sweetness of nutmeg, custardy butter beans, toasted walnuts, the minerals of kale, and a sharp punch of cider vinegar. If you are after a really hearty meal, you could even serve this with some mashed potatoes. Use parsnips instead of rutabaga here if you like—they will roast in the same time.

Preheat the oven to 425°F (220°C). Spread the rutabaga out on a baking sheet, drizzle with olive oil, season with salt and pepper, and roast for about 30 minutes, or until golden-edged and tender. Spread the walnuts on a baking sheet and toast in the oven alongside the rutabaga for 6 minutes, or until golden. Roughly chop and set aside.

Heat a little olive oil in a large pan and add the red onion, cook for about 10 minutes or until soft, then add the garlic and cook until it just begins to color at the edges. Quickly add the flour and stir for a minute to cook out its rawness, then add the stock little by little, stirring after each ladleful so the sauce doesn't become lumpy.

Strip the kale leaves from the stalks, slice the stalks really finely and tear any big leaves in half. Add the kale to the pan with the vinegar, put the lid on, and allow the kale to wilt for a couple of minutes. Add the butter beans and use a spoon to mash them a little. Take the pan off the heat and add the mustard, cheese, walnuts, and roasted rutabaga. Stir to combine, taste and season with salt and pepper, then pour into an ovenproof dish (about 8 by 10 inches/20 by 25 cm).

To make the topping, grate the celeriac using the coarse side of a box grater (you could also use a food processor to do this). Place the celeriac into a sieve, sprinkle with salt, and allow to sit for a few minutes to draw some moisture out. You can squeeze the celeriac with your hands to speed the process up a bit. Transfer the celeriac to a bowl, grate the nutmeg over, then add the thyme leaves. Give everything a quick mix with your hands, then scatter it over the pie filling. Dot the butter on top and bake for 20 minutes, or until the filling is bubbling and the topping is golden.

SERVES 4

1 small rutabaga (about 1 pound/500 g), peeled and cut into ⅜-inch (1-cm) chunks

olive oil

sea salt and freshly ground black pepper

1 cup (100 g) walnuts

1 red onion, finely sliced

2 garlic cloves, peeled and finely sliced

2 heaping tablespoons flour (I use buckwheat flour)

1¼ cups (300 ml) vegetable stock

7 ounces (200 g) kale

1 tablespoon cider vinegar

1 × 14.5-ounce (400-g) can of butter beans, drained (or 1 cup/250 g home-cooked see page 461)

1 heaping tablespoon whole-grain mustard

3½ ounces (100 g) Cheddar, crumbled into small pieces (¾ cup)

FOR THE RÖSTI TOPPING

1 large celeriac, peeled

½ a whole nutmeg

a small bunch of thyme, leaves picked

2 tablespoons butter or olive oil

345

Parsnip, butter bean, and blackberry bake

This is a pan full of all that is good about autumn: honey- and mustard-roasted parsnips, cold-weather herbs, butter beans that char and crisp, and blackberries that burst and dye the pale parsnips a deep purple in the heat of the oven. It's a painting of a dish. I finish it off with some buttery toasted rye flakes and hazelnuts. Serve this in the roasting pan in the middle of the table for maximum effect.

―――――――――――――――

Preheat your oven to 395°F (200°C). Cut your parsnips into halves and quarters and put them into your largest roasting pan. Add a good pinch of salt and pepper and most of the thyme and bay. Mix the mustard, vinegar, honey, and 3 tablespoons of oil and pour half of it over the parsnips, saving the other half for later. Toss everything together to coat each parsnip well, then roast in the hot oven for 25 minutes, until the parsnips are beginning to turn golden.

Once the parsnips have had their time, take them out of the oven, add the beans and blackberries, and gently turn the parsnips over to mix them in. Roast for another 20 minutes.

While this cooks, heat the butter in a frying pan with the remaining thyme, and add the rye flakes, chopped hazelnuts, and a good pinch of salt. Move them around in the pan until the flakes are golden and they smell buttery and toasty, then transfer to a bowl.

The bake is ready when the blackberries have burst and painted the golden parsnips, and the beans have crisped and popped out of their skins a little. Pour the rest of the mustard and honey dressing over the pan and turn everything over in it to coat each parsnip and bean. Sprinkle the rye and hazelnuts over the top and serve in the middle of the table with your greens.

SERVES 4–6

1¾ pounds (750 ml) parsnips, peeled

sea salt and freshly ground black pepper

a small bunch of thyme

6 bay leaves

2 tablespoons whole-grain mustard

2 tablespoons cider vinegar

2 tablespoons golden honey

olive oil

1 × 14.5-ounce (400-g) can of butter beans, drained (or 1 cup/250 g home-cooked, see page 461)

1½ cups (200 g) blackberries

2 tablespoons butter or olive oil

½ cup (50 g) rye flakes or rolled oats

¼ cup (25 g) hazelnuts, toasted (see page 459) and roughly chopped

TO SERVE

cooked greens dressed with lemon and olive oil

Chermoula, carrot, and chickpea fritters

SERVES 2

1 × 14.5-ounce (400-g) can
of chickpeas, drained
(or 1 cup/250 g home-
cooked, see page 461)

olive oil

2 carrots (about 8¾
ounces/250 g), peeled

1 clove of garlic, finely
chopped

a small bunch of cilantro,
stems and leaves finely
chopped

1 small preserved lemon, skin
only, finely chopped

2 teaspoons cumin seeds,
toasted

2 teaspoons sweet smoked
paprika

3½ ounces (100 g) cottage
cheese

4 tablespoons chickpea
(gram) flour or plain flour

sea salt and freshly ground
black pepper

FOR THE HERB SALSA

¼ cup (40 g) currants or
golden raisins

1 small preserved lemon,
skin only, finely diced

a small bunch of flat-leaf
parsley, leaves picked

a small bunch of cilantro,
finely chopped

3 tablespoons olive oil

2 teaspoons pomegranate
molasses

TO SERVE

mashed avocado

green salad

These little carrot fritters make use of the much forgotten cottage cheese, the preserve of 1980s dieters, but if you buy a good one made with whole milk, it's a gentle, creamy cheese, with a welcome texture, which deserves more attention. Chermoula is a smoky chile-spiked herb salsa from North Africa—this version uses preserved lemon—a big flavor that pitches in to elevate the grated carrot and chickpeas.

I use chickpea (gram) flour to bind my fritters, but plain flour will do just as well. For a vegan version, leave out the cottage cheese and up the chickpeas by ½ cup (100 g). If you don't have pomegranate molasses, a mixture of honey and balsamic vinegar works in its place.

Put the chickpeas into a blender with 2 tablespoons of olive oil and blitz until you have a rough, crumbly texture. Pour into a large mixing bowl.

Grate the carrots into the bowl, add the garlic, cilantro, preserved lemon, spices, cottage cheese and flour, then mix together lightly. You don't want to over-mix the batter—there should still be flecks of cottage cheese visible. Lightly season with salt (as the preserved lemons are salty) and plenty of freshly ground black pepper.

Now for the salsa. If you are using raisins, chop them up a little. Mix all the ingredients, including the currants or chopped raisins, together in a small bowl, then taste and adjust to your liking, adding a little more pomegranate molasses if needed.

Divide the fritter mixture into 8 and use your hands to shape into small patties. Put a large nonstick frying pan over medium heat, adding a couple of tablespoons of olive oil. Once hot, lower in the fritters and leave to cook for 3 to 4 minutes, until golden brown on one side, then flip them over to cook the other side.

Serve the fritters with generous spoonfuls of the salsa, mashed avocado, and a shock of green salad.

Chard, lentil, and bay leaf gratin

This gratin tastes greater and more indulgent than the sum of its parts; it's also very easy to throw together. It is one of the rare occasions I use heavy cream, but in this instance it is well worth it. The flavors are firmly rooted in Italy, though I use Cheddar to top it, as I like the sharpness it adds. We eat this with some steamed broccoli or greens on the side and nothing more. I have made this using a thin cashew cream for vegans (see page 110 for the recipe).

SERVES 4

1 cup (250 ml) vegetable stock

1 × 14.5-ounce (400-g) can of chopped tomatoes

3 bay leaves

1 cup (250 ml) heavy cream

1 × 14.5-ounce (400-g) can of green Puy lentils, drained (or 1 cup/250 g) home-cooked, see page 461)

14 ounces (400 g) chard (Swiss or rainbow)

butter or olive oil

2 cloves of garlic, finely chopped

a whole nutmeg

⅓ cup (50 g) aged Cheddar, grated (optional)

Preheat your oven to 395°F (200°C). Put the stock into a saucepan with the tomatoes and bay leaves and bring to a simmer. Cook for 10 to 15 minutes until the mixture has reduced by about a third, then pour in the cream and the lentils and cover to keep warm.

Cut the chard stalks from their leaves and shred the leaves into ⅜-inch- (1-cm-) wide ribbons, then cut the stems into ¾-inch (2-cm) lengths, keeping them separate.

Heat a shallow ovenproof pan with a lid over medium heat, add a couple of tablespoons of butter or drizzle of oil and add the garlic, cook for a minute or two before adding the chard stalks, then cover and cook for 5 minutes, until they have lost their rawness. Take the lid off and stir in the leaves, then take the pan off the heat.

Pour in the lentil mixture, add a good grating of nutmeg, and use a spoon to turn everything over until it is well mixed. If you don't have an ovenproof pan, you could transfer the mixture to a gratin dish at this point. Dot over the cheese, if you are using it, then bake in the hot oven for 25 minutes, until golden and bubbling.

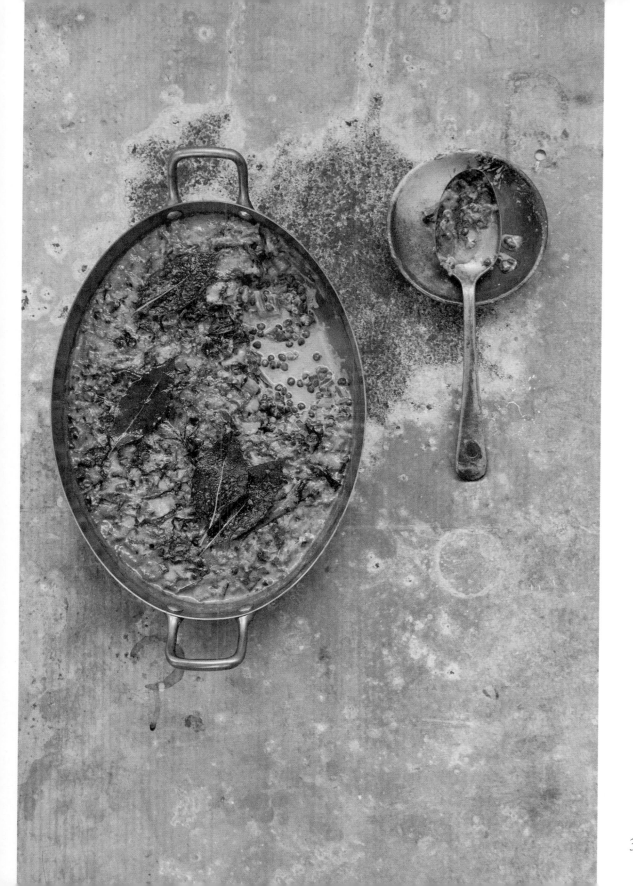

Roasting pan dinners

The principle of the roasting-pan dinner outlined below works well with almost anything. I follow a basic formula of one or two vegetables, an herb, an accent flavor, such as chile or lemon, and then something hearty–a pulse or some torn-up bread. Bear in mind that you need a vegetable that softens when it cooks–such as sweet potato or zucchini–to add a little stickiness and to prevent things from burning. If you are roasting something (such as potatoes) that won't do that, you might want to add a little stock or wine to make sure everything cooks evenly and so the flavors mingle in the best way possible.

Try this with whatever takes your fancy; here I've given a few suggestions. Use a deep, approximately 8½-by-11-inch (A4-size) baking sheet here. Bake for 30 to 55 minutes at 425°F (220°C) until the vegetables are soft and golden. Each serves about 4.

1	2
A main vegetable	**A soft vegetable**
1 butternut squash, roughly chopped	3 red onions, peeled and cut into wedges
3 medium sweet potatoes, roughly chopped	1 jar of roasted red peppers, roughly chopped
1 celeriac, thickly peeled and chopped into bite-size pieces	2 leeks, shredded
3 bulbs of fennel, cut into 8 wedges	1 small head of savoy cabbage, cut into thin wedges
2½ pounds (1 kg) parsnips, peeled and cut in half and into quarters	2 handfuls of roughly chopped late tomatoes

3

A hearty
add-on

1 × 14.5-ounce
(400-g) can of butter
beans, drained

1 × 14.5-ounce
(400-g) can of
chickpeas, drained

1 × 7-ounce (200-g)
package of ricotta (see
page 364 for method)

1 × 7-ounce (200-g)
block of feta cheese

2 slices of
good bread, torn

4

Liquid

3½ ounces
(100 ml) vegetable
stock

3½ ounces
(100 ml) cider

3½ ounces (100 ml) red
or white wine

5

Herbs

a small bunch of any
woody herb, such
as thyme, rosemary,
oregano, sage, or bay
leaves, leaves picked

a large bunch of a
soft herb, such as
mint, basil, or tarragon,
roughly chopped

6

A flavor
boost

the zest of 1 lemon

a teaspoon of hot
smoked paprika

the zest of 1 orange

a handful of fruit:
blackberries or chopped
plums or pears

a tablespoon of spice:
cumin, cilantro, mustard
seeds

Boston baked beans for a crowd

I made these for Dylan's first birthday. There were about twenty of us, and we put a huge pot in the middle of the table and ate them with baked potatoes and a lime-spiked red cabbage slaw (see the recipe on page 381). They seem to be popular with people of all ages and are particularly good around bonfire night. Indeed, you could cook them in a big cast-iron pan in the embers of the fire, if that's your kind of thing. This makes a big batch of beans that will feed a crowd; leftovers can be frozen or will keep in the fridge for 4 to 5 days, and in my opinion, the beans are best the day after they are cooked.

This is one instance where I would encourage you to cook your own beans, or to use canned. I regularly talk about jarred beans being superior to canned, but here they will be too soft and break down too much while cooking.

SERVES 8

2 red onions, peeled and halved

4 tomatoes, stalks and all

2 carrots, scrubbed

1 large leek, washed and cut into a few big pieces

2 bay leaves

1 whole chipotle chile or 1 heaping teaspoon chipotle flakes

1 cup (250 g) home-cooked navy beans (see page 461), cooking water reserved, or 2 × 14.5-ounce (400-g) cans of navy beans or butter beans, liquid reserved

3 tablespoons English mustard powder

4 tablespoons molasses

3 tablespoons Worcestershire sauce (I use a vegetarian one)

sea salt

Put a large cast-iron pot or deep saucepan over low heat, then add the vegetables, bay leaves, and chile to the pot, followed by the beans and their liquid. Add the mustard powder, molasses, and Worcestershire sauce. Give it a good stir, using a folding rather than a mixing motion—you don't want to break up the beans.

Bring to a gentle simmer, then turn the heat down and cook uncovered on very low heat for 1½ hours without stirring (stirring will break up the beans), until the sauce is thick and sticky. Carefully remove the onion, tomato, carrots, leek, chile (if using a whole chile), and bay leaves. Discard the bay leaves, then set the rest aside for a few minutes to cool slightly before spooning into a food processor and blitzing until smooth. Once smooth, stir this mixture back into the beans.

Next, add a good amount of salt to the beans, stir well and taste. Balance with a little Worcestershire sauce, molasses, mustard, or salt, if needed. Serve your beans simply on toast, topped with a poached egg, on a baked potato, or with my sweet potato mash (see page 357).

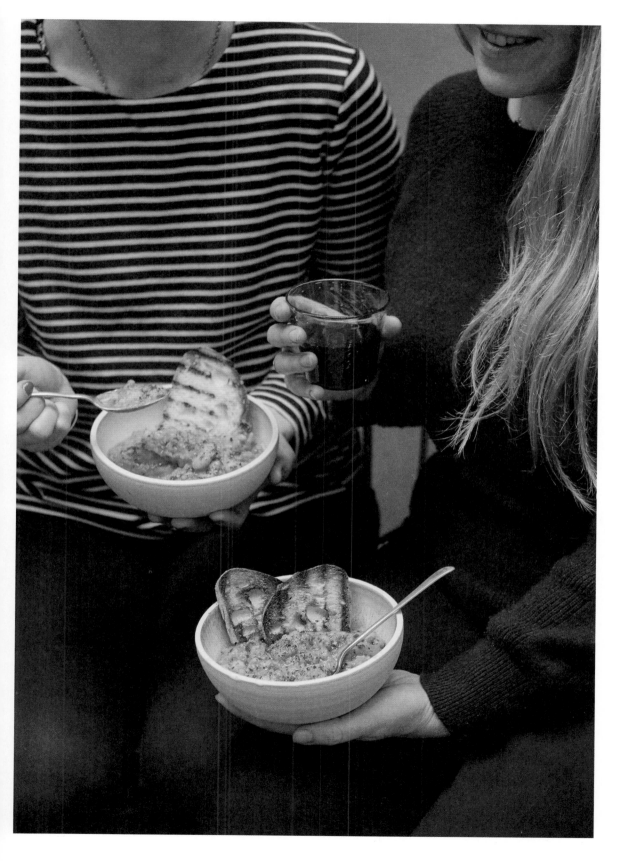

Angel hair with lemon and cold-weather herbs

This pasta is as simple as they get, dressed with oil, herbs, and a little garlic and lemon; it is the kind of pasta I like best. I ate this on a rare day off from the white tableclothed restaurant I worked at in a tiny village in the wilds of Tuscany. I sat and ate this in a simple trattoria in Florence, an hour's bus ride away, where there were plastic tablecloths and wine straight out of a barrel.

I still remember this as one of the best bowls of pasta I have ever eaten, and each time I have it it's like resetting my cooking clock, a reminder that simple is pretty much always best.

———————————————

Bring a large pan of well-salted water to a boil; you want enough water for the pasta to really swim around in it and enough salt that the water tastes like the sea. Add the pasta and cook at a rolling boil for 4 minutes.

Meanwhile, strip the rosemary and thyme leaves from their stems and discard the stems.

Place a frying pan over medium heat, add the olive oil, garlic, and all the herbs and allow the oil to heat and cook the herbs gently. Be careful: You don't want the herbs to crisp, just to release their fragrance into the oil. Take them off the heat before they crisp.

Drain your cooked pasta, keeping a mugful of the pasta water. Use tongs to scoop the pasta into the frying pan with the herbs, and toss it in the oil over the heat for a minute or so, adding a little of the starchy pasta water to loosen the sauce and allow it to coat the pasta better.

Take the pan off the heat and grate in the zest of the lemons and the Parmesan. Use tongs to toss and make sure that each little angel hair is coated in the herbs, oil, cheese, and zest. Taste and season with a little salt and pepper if you like, twirl onto four plates, and serve with more Parmesan for grating over the top.

SERVES 4

sea salt

12¼ ounces (350 g) angel hair pasta

4 sprigs of rosemary

4 sprigs of thyme

⅞ cup (200 ml) extra-virgin olive oil

2 cloves of garlic, finely sliced

12 sage leaves

2 unwaxed lemons

⅓ cup (30 g) Parmesan (I use a vegetarian/rennet-free one), plus extra to serve

sea salt and freshly ground black pepper

Sweet potato mash with cilantro and chile

This is a recipe for the most delicious sweet potato mash I can remember eating. It's not a meal in itself, but it has so much flavor and depth that I find myself making it and then building meals around it, not the other way around. It's based on a recipe by one of my favorite cooks, Skye Gyngell.

This mash has so much going on that it can be paired with quite simple things. Try topping it with crispy halloumi, serving it with peppery greens and a poached egg, or piling it into tortillas with black beans and avocados for quick tacos.

Peel the sweet potatoes and cut them roughly into ¾-inch (2-cm) cubes, then put them into a large saucepan and add the chile. Pour in enough cold water to cover, add a good pinch of salt, and bring to a boil over medium heat.

Once they have come to a boil, lower the heat and simmer for about 15 minutes, until the potatoes are really cooked through, then drain in a colander and leave them to steam dry for 5 minutes.

Take a handful of the sweet potatoes and put it in the food processor. Slice the stem off the chile, roughly chop the rest of it, and add this too. Add the cilantro leaves and stems, butter or coconut oil, tamari, and maple syrup and blitz until very smooth. Meanwhile, mash the rest of the sweet potato with a potato masher. Mix the whizzed potato into the mash, then taste and adjust the seasoning if needs be.

MAKES ENOUGH FOR 4

2¼ pounds (1 kg) sweet potatoes

sea salt

1 red chile

a small bunch of cilantro

3½ tablespoons butter or coconut oil

2 tablespoons tamari or soy sauce

2 tablespoons maple syrup

357

Chard and ricotta pasta for Dylan

Food has taken on a new meaning for me in the last couple of years. It's an everyday miracle and this is what I try to remind myself when I am inevitably reaching for a cinnamon bun or a bar of chocolate. But over the last year, when I was pregnant and beyond, the food I ate was actually helping me create another human—another total miracle.

As the son of a food writer, I imagined Dylan would be sipping spirulina smoothies by now, but that's not the case. In fact his palate is quite delicate: He's a pasta lover. What I have begun to understand even more deeply is that we each have our own journey in food, and that eating is learning. Just because I offer him food it doesn't mean he will eat it; he's surrounded by food all day long but he still wants pasta and that's OK—it's a lifelong journey and an adventure. This one is for you, my little guy.

Pull the chard leaves away from the stalks. Warm a couple of tablespoons of olive oil in a deep frying pan over medium heat. Finely shred the chard stalks and add them to the pan with the garlic and a pinch of salt. Allow the stalks to cook like this for a couple of minutes, then grate in the zest of the lemon. Cook for another 3 minutes, until the stalks have lost their rawness and toughness.

Put a large pan of salted water on to boil, and when it's at a rolling boil, add the spaghetti and cook according to the package instructions.

Back to the chard. Finely shred the leaves and add them to the pan of stalks. Spoon in a dash of pasta water (no more than about 3 tablespoons) to help the leaves steam and wilt as they cook.

Mix the ricotta with the juice of half the lemon, and season well with salt and pepper.

Drain the pasta, reserving a mugful of pasta water. Add the pasta, ricotta, and reserved pasta water to the pan of chard and mix well. Finish with a good grating of nutmeg and serve in warm bowls.

SERVES 2

5¼ ounces (150 g) chard

olive oil

1 clove of garlic, finely chopped

sea salt

1 unwaxed lemon

7 ounces (200 g) spaghetti

3½ ounces (100 g) ricotta

whole nutmeg, for grating

Autumn bowl

I love how gentle and nurturing eating from a bowl feels. A reminder, perhaps, of childhood meals spooned from a bowl—but it's also unfussy, quick, and adaptable. It requires food that's sufficiently soft to tackle without a knife. Bowl food, as I see it, is a meal that's built around a subtly flavored grain or pulse. Food that is simultaneously soothing, bolstering, undemanding, and sustaining. And it's easy to tweak favorite combinations as the seasons change.

This is my version of a bowl I ate in California. Autumn is peppered with warmer days that feel like the end of summer, and this is what I eat on those days. Filling and warming but punchy and fresh, thanks to a quick chile sauce. This makes more than you need and will keep in the fridge for a week or so.

SERVES 2

¾ cup (150 g) brown rice (about a mugful)

sea salt

1 teaspoon coconut oil

1 head of spring greens

olive oil

7 ounces (200 g) mushrooms

freshly ground black paper

butter, for frying

the juice and zest of 1 unwaxed lemon

2 organic eggs

a small bunch of basil, leaves picked

FOR THE SAUCE

6 red chiles

2 jarred roasted red peppers, roughly chopped

1 clove of garlic, chopped

1 tablespoon white wine vinegar

1 tablespoon golden honey

2 teaspoons light olive oil

Preheat the oven to 395°F (200°C). First, cook your brown rice—put it in a saucepan with twice its volume of cold water, a good pinch of salt, and the coconut oil. Turn the heat to high, bring to a boil and boil for 20 to 25 minutes. Keep an eye on it to make sure it doesn't boil dry. You can add a bit more boiling water, if needed.

Cut your head of spring greens into slim wedges (how many will depend on the size and shape), place on a baking sheet, and toss them in a little olive oil. Season the greens with salt and pepper, then put in the oven to roast for about 25 minutes.

Meanwhile, make your sauce. If you like things hot, keep the seeds in; otherwise deseed the chiles. Put the chiles, red peppers, and a pinch of salt into a mortar with pestle or a blender and bash or blitz until you have a coarsely textured paste. Add the other ingredients and mix well.

Sauté the mushrooms in a large, hot pan with a little butter, until starting to crisp and caramelize around the edges. Once they are cooked, season, add the juice of half the lemon, and keep warm.

Fry your eggs to your liking; dress the rice with the lemon zest and juice from the other half of the lemon and a little olive oil. Add salt and pepper, and pile all the elements into the bowl in the order you prefer—I like to keep things separate so I can make up each forkful as I choose—and finish with a scattering of basil.

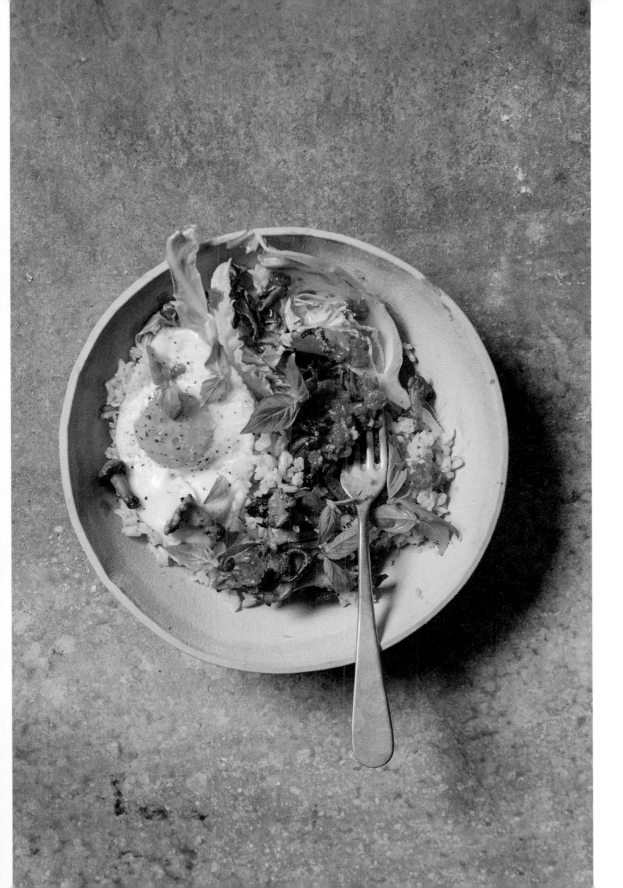

Orzo with spiced tomato sauce and feta

This is our new weeknight staple. It's much more than it looks; the toasted spices give the tomato sauce another dimension, and while I love simple pasta pomodoro, it's nice to have something else that's easily on hand to mix up a quick weeknight pasta. I keep all these spices at home, and most of the fresh things can be bought at my (in fairness, pretty good) corner shop. Dried oregano will stand in for fresh if you don't have it.

SERVES 4

1¾ pounds (800 g) fresh tomatoes or 2 × 14.5-ounce (400-g) cans of chopped tomatoes

1 teaspoon cumin seeds

1 teaspoon cilantro (coriander) seeds

1 tablespoon nigella seeds

olive oil

1 onion, finely chopped

2 cloves of garlic, finely sliced

a pinch of chile powder

sea salt and freshly ground black pepper

a small bunch of oregano or a good pinch of dried

7 ounces (200 g) orzo

good extra-virgin olive oil, to finish

7 ounces (200 g) feta cheese

If you are using fresh tomatoes, roughly chop them, discarding the cores. Heat a frying pan over medium heat and add the cumin, cilantro, and nigella seeds. Toast for a minute or so, until they release their fragrance.

Add a splash of oil to the pan, then add the onion, garlic, and chile powder and cook on a low heat for 10 minutes, until the onions are soft and sweet. Then add the tomatoes and a good pinch of salt and pepper, stir, and cook for about 20 minutes until they have broken down and formed a sweet soupy tomato sauce; you can add a little water here to loosen the sauce if necessary. Pick the oregano leaves from their stems and add them to the pan. Season well with salt and pepper, remembering that you will be adding salty feta at the end.

Meanwhile, cook the orzo in boiling salted water for about 10 minutes, or a couple of minutes less than the package instructions—you'll cook the pasta for a minute or two in the sauce, so you want it to be just less than al dente. Once the orzo is ready, drain it, keeping a mugful of the pasta water.

Add the orzo to the tomato sauce and let everything cook for a minute or two, adding a little of the pasta water to loosen everything—you are looking for a gentle, thick, souplike consistency.

Serve the pasta with lots of good olive oil (be generous here) and crumble over the feta. Eat right away.

Figs, ricotta, radicchio, almonds

This last year or so, since my son, Dylan, arrived, I've been learning a new way to cook. No more long evenings in the kitchen: For now, my cooking is sandwiched into a neat window of time before baths and stories, so I've rediscovered the joy of one-pan or one-pot meals. While I love the feeling of a pan over a flame, there is something very pleasing about knowing your dinner is cooking while you sit down and do something else.

Though the method may be simple, I still want flavors and textures that excite me, as well as bringing some balance. Here figs, almonds, radicchio, and plump cannellini make a complete meal.

If your ricotta is very wet, put it in a small sieve lined with muslin set over a bowl in the fridge for a few hours. You will probably get a couple of tablespoons of liquid in the bowl, which you can discard.

Preheat the oven to 425°F (220°C) and get a large lipped roasting pan. Scatter the beans into the pan, making a little space in the middle for the ricotta, then turn the cheese out into it.

Scatter the quartered figs on top of the beans. Grate the zest of the lemon all over the pan, focusing particularly on the ricotta. Sprinkle over some of the thyme leaves and red pepper flakes and season. Drizzle a little olive oil over then roast for 45 minutes, or until the ricotta has shrunk a little and is beginning to brown, and the beans have softened and their skins crisped.

Meanwhile, make the herb oil: Bash the rest of the thyme leaves until you have a deep green paste, add 4 tablespoons of olive oil, the chopped fresh chile, and season with salt and pepper.

When your mixture has had 35 minutes, put the almonds on a separate baking sheet, season and roast for the last 10 minutes of the time.

Remove the two baking sheets from the oven, roughly chop the almonds, and sprinkle the radicchio over the mixture. Drizzle over the herb oil and serve in the middle of the table for everyone to dig in.

SERVES 4

7 ounces (200 g) ricotta

1 × 14.5-ounce (400-g) can or jar of cannellini beans, drained

4 figs, tough stems removed, quartered

1 unwaxed lemon

a small bunch of thyme or oregano, leaves picked

a pinch of red pepper flakes

extra-virgin olive oil

1 red chile, finely chopped

sea salt and freshly ground black pepper

1 cup (100 g) almonds, skin on

1 head of radicchio, shredded

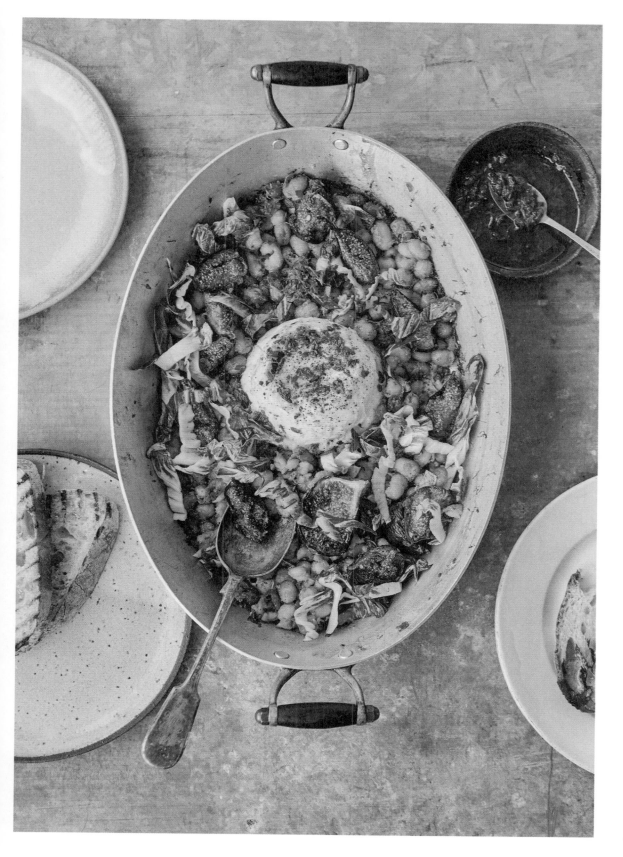

Spaghetti with squash polpette

SERVES 4

12¼ ounces (350 g) spaghetti

sea salt

a few basil leaves, to serve

FOR THE POLPETTE

olive oil

1 small fennel bulb, finely
chopped

½ a red onion, thinly sliced

1 clove of garlic, crushed

1 cup (100 g) butternut
squash, peeled and grated

¾ cup (150 g) cooked Puy
lentils (about half a
drained can)

½ cup (50 g) bread crumbs
(I use whole-wheat)

⅓ cup (100 g) ricotta cheese

the zest of 1 unwaxed lemon

¼ cup (25 g) pecorino or
Parmesan cheese (I use
a vegetarian/rennet-free
one), finely grated, plus
extra to serve

1 red chile, chopped, or a
pinch of red pepper flakes

a few sprigs of parsley, leaves
picked and roughly chopped

sea salt and freshly ground
black pepper

FOR THE PISTACHIO
PESTO

a small handful of shelled
pistachio nuts (about
¼ cup/25 g)

a small bunch of basil, leaves
picked

4 tablespoons olive oil

juice of ½ a lemon

a handful of grated pecorino
or Parmesan cheese

This is my comfort food. Little polpette made from squash and fennel, speckled with lentils, and light from the ricotta, tossed with spaghetti that's had the bright green kiss of some pistachio pesto.

Once rolled, the polpette freeze well and can be slowly fried from frozen in some olive oil. Here, I bake them for ease and to make their load a little lighter.

———————————

Put a pan over medium heat, add a drizzle of olive oil, then the fennel and onion. Fry for 10 minutes, until soft and sweet, then add the garlic and cook for a few more minutes. Take the pan off the heat and allow to cool.

Put the fried vegetables in a mixing bowl, add the grated squash with the other polpette ingredients, and mix well. Season generously and leave to sit for 20 minutes. Meanwhile, preheat the oven to 475°F (240°C).

Divide the mixture into 12 portions and roll into little balls. Place them on a baking sheet and drizzle well with olive oil, or, if you want to be precise, brush them all over for a perfectly crisp outside. Bake for 20 minutes, until they have a golden crust. You can also fry them in a little olive oil for 3 to 4 minutes on each side until golden brown.

While the polpette are baking, pop all the pesto ingredients into a food processor with a little salt and pepper. Add 2 tablespoons of water and blitz to a chunky paste. If you prefer a little more oil in your pesto, add some more here, but I like the freshness of it the way it is. Taste and adjust the amount of lemon, cheese, and seasoning if you need to.

When the polpette have had 10 minutes in the oven, fill a large saucepan with boiling water, add salt, and once at a rolling boil, add the spaghetti and cook according to the package instructions.

Drain the spaghetti, reserving some of the cooking water. Add the pesto and mix it in well, adding a little of the reserved pasta water to loosen if needed. Put the spaghetti on a big platter, then top with the polpette, a bit more cheese, and some basil leaves.

Plum, sloe gin, and hazelnut cobbler

Plums and sloe gin are such a great pairing; add a crumbly hazelnut cobbler topping, and you know it's going to taste pretty good, but when this came out of the oven, the plums a deep magenta and the cobbler golden and puffed up, it looked and tasted even better than I had imagined. It's taken over from crumble as my go-to autumn dessert. The plums are great too just stewed with the sloe gin and eaten with yogurt.

_____

Preheat the oven to 475°F (240°C). Cut the plums in half and remove their pits. Put the plums in a saucepan with the sloe gin and vanilla and cover with a lid. Cook over low heat for 20 to 30 minutes, until the plums are soft and the liquid has thickened.

Meanwhile, make the cobbler topping. Blitz the hazelnuts in the food processor until they resemble fine bread crumbs, then add the flour, baking powder, and sugar and pulse a couple of times to combine everything. Cut the butter into cubes and add to the food processor with the thyme and salt. Blitz again until the mixture resembles rough bread crumbs. Add a tablespoon of water and pulse again, until it comes together as a firm dough.

Butter an 8-inch (20-cm) baking dish and spoon the plums into the bottom. Drizzle over the honey and use a tablespoon to dollop the dough on top, leaving a few gaps in the topping so the juices can bubble through.

Bake in the hot oven for 15 minutes, until the cobbler topping has risen and is deep golden. Top with a few more hazelnuts if you like, and serve with crème fraîche and a swirl of honey or some ice cream.

SERVES 4

2 pounds (900 g) plums

¼ cup (60 ml) sloe gin

the seeds from 1 vanilla pod or 1 teaspoon vanilla paste

2–4 tablespoons honey, to taste

FOR THE TOPPING

⅓ cup (50 g) hazelnuts (skin on or off)

¾ cup (100 g) white spelt flour

1 teaspoon baking powder

¼ cup (50 g) raw cane sugar (rapadura, see page 293)

7 tablespoons unsalted butter, chilled

a few sprigs of thyme, leaves picked

a pinch of flaky sea salt

TO SERVE

crème fraîche, yogurt, or ice cream

Honey cake with lemon and cilantro seeds

I would put cilantro (coriander) seeds in everything I made if I could get away with it. I love their clean citrus notes backed up by a heady spiced floral back note. I add them to gin and tonics, to soups and stews, to top dips and to scatter over tomato salads. In my mind they are good wherever you might think to use lemon. So here one of my favorite cakes has had a reinvention. For the picture, I poured a syrup made with the juice of half a lemon, half a tablespoon of honey, and a tablespoon of cilantro seeds over the top. It's sweet, heady, and not at all savory. Give it a try.

SERVES 8–10

14 tablespoons unsalted butter, at room temperature

1 cup (200 g) superfine or caster sugar

4 medium organic eggs

1 cup (150 g) white spelt flour

the zest and juice of 2 unwaxed lemons

6 tablespoons golden honey

1 tablespoon cilantro (coriander) seeds, toasted and crushed to a fine powder

1½ teaspoons baking powder

1½ cup (150 g) ground almonds

Preheat your oven to 375°F (190°C). Grease a 9½-inch (24-cm) cake pan and line with waxed paper.

First, beat the butter and sugar in a large mixing bowl until light and fluffy—you can do this in a stand mixer or with a hand-held whisk if you like. Crack in one egg, add a tablespoon of flour and beat until mixed in, then do the same with the other 3 eggs. Add the lemon zest and juice and the honey and mix.

In a bowl, mix the ground cilantro seeds, remaining flour, baking powder, and almonds and whisk so that there are no lumps.

Mix the dry ingredients into the honey mixture, until everything is combined. Spoon into the lined pan and smooth out the top. Bake in the hot oven for 50 minutes, until golden brown on top. The honey will make it brown quicker than a normal cake, so if need be, cover the pan with foil to stop it browning any further. Remove from the oven and leave to cool in the pan.

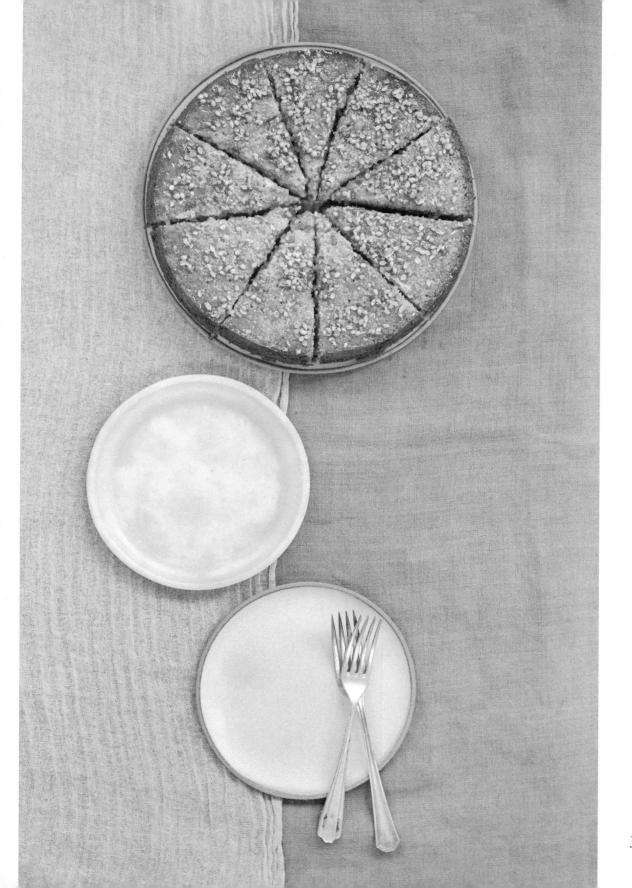

Malt loaf with prunes and black tea

Malt loaf is pure nostalgia to me. I remember eating it in my grandma's flat—high up in a 1970s tower block. Inside it was perfect and spotless, well turned out like her. I'd eat this after sitting at her dressing table and putting on all her make-up, the smell of pressed powder and lipstick wafting around the bedroom. The one we ate was from the shop, spread with margarine, though this homemade one deserves some good salted butter.

Malt extract is easy enough to buy, though you may have to go to a large supermarket or whole-food shop for it. If the surface of the loaf browns more quickly than you'd like it to, cover with foil for the last few minutes of cooking. Vegans can replace the eggs with aquafaba (see page 459).

I brush the outside of the loaf with a little extra malt extract, which gives it that telltale tackiness. I then wrap it up and let it sit for a few days, as it is much better with age: The crumb softens, the fruit mellows, and the shiny malty exterior soaks in. A gentle recipe, for my grandma; how I wish we could still share a slice.

MAKES A GOOD LOAF

1 cup (125 g) prunes, pitted

1 cup (125 g) raisins

5 ounces (150 ml) hot strong black tea

butter or oil, for greasing

5 ounces (150 ml) malt extract (see note above), plus 2 tablespoons to finish

⅔ cup (100 g) light muscovado sugar

1 cup (125 g) whole-wheat spelt flour

1 cup (125 g) white spelt flour

1 teaspoon baking powder

a pinch of fine salt

2 medium organic eggs

Put the prunes and raisins in a shallow bowl, cover with the hot tea and leave to soak overnight (or as long as you can manage). Preheat the oven to 355°F (180°C). Butter a deep loaf pan measuring 8 by 3½ inches (20 by 9 cm) and line it with parchment paper.

Put the malt extract and muscovado sugar in a small saucepan and warm, without stirring, over medium heat, until the sugar has dissolved, then take off the heat.

Put the flours, baking powder, and salt into a large mixing bowl and use a whisk to get rid of any lumps.

Using an immersion blender, purée 2 tablespoons of the soaked fruit so that you have a chunky paste. Pour the warm malt and sugar mixture into the flour, and add the fruit paste and whole fruits. Break the eggs into a small bowl, beat lightly with a fork, and fold into the mixture.

Scoop the mixture—it is quite soft—into the lined loaf pan and gently smooth the surface. Bake for 50 minutes to 1 hour, until lightly springy, then remove from the oven and leave to cool in the pan. While the cake cools, brush the surface with a little more malt extract.

Blackberry, bay leaf, and honey tart

SERVES 8

FOR THE PASTRY

1½ cup (300 g) white spelt
flour, plus extra for dusting

a pinch of flaky sea salt

½ cup (50 g) ground blanched
almonds

2 teaspoons golden honey

9 tablespoons cold unsalted
butter, cut into small
pieces

1 large organic egg yolk,
beaten

10½ tablespoons unsalted
butter, at room
temperature, plus extra for
greasing

6 tablespoons golden honey

3 medium organic eggs

1½ cups (150 g) ground
blanched almonds

3 tablespoons plain flour
(I use white spelt)

the zest of 1 unwaxed lemon

the zest of 1 unwaxed
clementine

the seeds from 1 vanilla pod

2½ cups (350 g) blackberries

4–6 bay leaves

TO SERVE

4 heaping tablespoons Greek
yogurt

1 unwaxed lime

a squeeze of golden honey

Here an easy almond-and-spelt pastry hugs honey-sweetened almond frangipane, a generous layer of quick blackberry compote, and a scattering of blackberries. If your blackberries are particularly tart, you can toss them in a little sugar or honey to sweeten.

The bay leaf here is subtle, and unlike when it cooks in stews, it imparts a gentle flavor, so you can be quite bold with the amount of leaves you use. Damsons would work really well here too.

You can make your pastry by hand or in a food processor. Put the flour, salt, almonds, and honey in a large mixing bowl. Using your fingertips, rub the butter in the flour until the mixture looks like coarse bread crumbs. Add the egg and gently work everything together using your hands, until you have a ball of dough. Remember not to work the pastry too much at this stage, or it will be chewy. Wrap the dough and pop it into the fridge to rest for at least 30 minutes.

Butter a 9-inch (22-cm) nonstick loose-bottomed tart pan. On a lightly floured surface, roll out your pastry, turning it every so often, until it's about ¼-inch (½-cm) thick. Carefully roll your pastry around the rolling pin, then unroll it carefully over the pan. Ease the pastry into the pan, making sure you push it into all the sides. Trim off any excess, then prick the base of the pastry case all over with a fork and pop it into the freezer for 30 minutes.

Preheat your oven to 395°F (200°C). Get yourself a large square piece of waxed paper, scrunch it up, then unwrap it and use it to line your pastry crust. Fill the case right up to the top with uncooked rice or ceramic baking beans, and blind bake for 10 minutes in the hot oven. Take the crust out, carefully remove the rice and waxed paper (you can save the rice to use for blind baking another time), then return the crust to the oven to cook for another 5 to 10 minutes, until it's firm and almost biscuit-like. Leave to cool. →

While the pastry crust is cooling, make your frangipane. Mix the butter and honey until soft, then add the eggs one by one and stir well. Mix in the almonds, flour, citrus zests, and vanilla, and mix until you have a smooth thick paste.

Purée half the blackberries with an immersion blender and pour over the cooled tart base, then top with the frangipane. Scatter over the remaining blackberries and push them into the frangipane a little, then lay the bay leaves on top and push these in too. Bake in the oven for 30 to 40 minutes, until the frangipane is set and golden brown. If the edges of the pastry or the top of the tart look as if they are browning too fast, you can cover them with foil.

Mix the yogurt with the zest of the lime, a little of its juice, and the honey and keep in the fridge until needed.

Allow the baked tart to cool before taking it out of the pan and removing the bay leaves. Serve just warm in generous slices, with spoonfuls of the lime yogurt.

Maple toffee apple and pear crisp

This is everything I want in an autumn dessert. Melting orchard fruits spiked with ginger and cardamom and a topping that's half-crisp and half-crumble, which reminds me of oatmeal cookies eaten as a child. I eat this with thick Greek yogurt mixed with a little honey and vanilla or, if it's really cold, good hot vanilla custard.

———————————————

Preheat your oven to 395°F (200°C).

Peel the apples and pears and roughly slice them. Toss them with the maple syrup on a baking sheet and cover another with foil. Roast for 15 minutes in the hot oven, then remove the foil and roast for another 10 minutes, until the edges catch and caramelize.

Meanwhile, roughly chop ⅓ cup (50 g) of the prunes and all the figs, finely chop the ginger, and place it all into the bottom of a 9½-inch (24-cm) round baking dish. Grate over the zest and add the juice of ½ the lemon, add the vanilla and spices, and mix everything together. Cover the dish with a clean tea towel and leave to one side.

Make the topping by rubbing the oats, almonds, butter, sugar, flour, and salt together with your fingers. It will feel wetter than a crumble topping and you'll be left with larger pieces of butter, but you should have a very rough crumbly dough after about 4 minutes. Chop the remaining prunes roughly and mix them in too.

When your apples are ready, mix them with the fruit and spices in the baking dish, then sprinkle over the topping. Bake in the oven for 25 minutes, until deep golden.

I serve mine with some Greek or coconut yogurt, whipped with a little vanilla and honey.

SERVES 4–6

3 apples

3 pears

2 tablespoons maple syrup

⅔ cup (50 g) prunes

⅓ cup (50 g) dried figs

2 pieces of candied ginger, finely chopped

1 unwaxed lemon

the seeds from 1 vanilla pod or 1 teaspoon vanilla paste

½ teaspoon ground cinnamon

½ teaspoon ground cardamom

FOR THE TOPPING

1 cup (100 g) rolled oats

½ cup (50 g) ground almonds

7 tablespoons butter or coconut oil

⅓ cup (75 g) light brown sugar

¾ cup (100 g) white spelt flour

a small pinch of salt

TO SERVE

Greek or coconut yogurt, whipped with a little vanilla and honey

Flavored spirits

Pretty much my favorite holiday ever was one spent with John on a small deserted island off the coast of north Wales, only accessible by boat if the seas are on your side. We were there for a week and there was very little to do apart from watch the birds and the sea, climb the hill and jump from the rocks into the crashing waves. Every night we watched the sunset and sipped our own sloe whisky. That was the first year I made it, and it's a ritual I've kept up, so we now have sloe gin, whisky, and brandy for Christmas. I've begun experimenting with other flavors too. This is a rough guide but if you'd like something more exact, try the Bergamot gin on page 452.

Flavors

Fruit

You can use a huge range to flavor your spirit. I like to extend the life of autumn berries and fruits; try damsons, blackberries, and sloes. Rhubarb, late cherries, cranberries, and black currants also work well, and citrus is amazing—see page 452 for more on that.

Use 7–14 ounces (200–400 g) of fruit per 4½ cups (1 liter) of spirit, depending on how strong the flavor of the fruit is.

Herbs

Adding a few sprigs of herb will help infuse your spirit with a botanical note, but go easy as they can be strong. Use 1–2 sprigs or leaves depending on how strong the herb is. I love rosemary, thyme, basil, sage, and bay leaves. Mint and elderflower work well in the early summer too.

Spices

Spice will add depth and warmth to your spirit. I prefer to use fresher-tasting spices like cardamom, vanilla, and cilantro (coriander), but cloves, nutmeg, fresh ginger, and juniper work well too. Use anything from a pinch to a heaping teaspoon, depending on the potency of the spice and how spiced you want it to be.

Sweetness

I like to add some sugar to all my flavored spirits (I do have quite a sweet tooth). How much will depend on the sweetness of the fruit I'm adding. Sloes, for instance need a lot of sugar—I add about 6 tablespoons to each liter bottle, less for sweeter fruits. Once it's been infusing for a couple of days, taste your spirit, and if it is too tart, you can always add a little extra.

Choose your spirit

White spirits such as white rum, vodka, or gin are more neutral. Whisky or brandy work too, but you might need to think more carefully about the flavors you add to them, as it's harder to complement the deeper flavors of dark spirits; autumn fruits and spices work well. The better the quality of the spirit, the nicer your finished drink will taste; you don't need to buy the very best, but equally you'll taste it if you use firewater.

To make your spirit

Put your flavorings into a wide-topped bottle or jar with a lid and pour over your spirit.

How long to infuse

Different flavorings will take varying amounts of time to infuse. You need to trust your taste buds here and taste every day or so, until it tastes good to you. Here is a rough guide:

— Leave strong flavorings, such as chile, vanilla, and citrus, for about a day.

— Woody herbs and spices need 5 to 7 days.

— Berries and strong-flavored fruit can take around 3 to 4 weeks to fully impart their flavor.

— Milder fruits and florals will take up to a month.

When it's ready, pass it through a sieve to remove all the flavorings and then through a sieve lined with muslin to get rid of any leftover bits that might make it turn sour. The spirit will keep in a cool, dark place for about a year.

To serve

Serve mixed with tonic, fruit juice, or seltzer over ice with lots of citrus slices and/or cucumber. I like a tiny sloe whisky or sloe brandy around the fire on a camping trip.

Honey and tahini halva

Growing up we always had little boxes of halva at home, tucked away in a corner of the bread bin. My mum adores it; she'd buy it by the ounce from our local deli. It was one of the things I could never make my mind up about, loving the buttery sweetness of each mouthful but being slightly disarmed by the gentle but present back note of tahini. Now, I love the stuff, but it's hard to find any that's good and not packed with glucose syrup, so I have taken to making it myself. I am definitely becoming more and more like my mum and I couldn't be happier about it.

Grease a small container, roughly 5 by 2 inches (12 by 5 cm), and line it with waxed paper.

In a heavy-bottom saucepan, heat the honey over medium heat and keep an eye on the pan—as soon as bubbles start to form around the sides, set your timer for 5 minutes.

Fill a small bowl with very cold water. At the end of the 5 minutes, use a clean spoon to drop a small amount of the honey (about half a teaspoon) into the bowl; do not touch it while it is hot. The honey will drop to the bottom, and once it has sat there and cooled for 30 seconds or so you can test it—it should come together as a tacky ball between your fingers. If it's too soft, put the pan back on the heat but for no more than a minute, as the honey changes very quickly once hot, and you don't want it to go past the tacky ball stage.

MAKES 20 SMALL PIECES

flavorless oil, for greasing
½ cup (200 g) golden honey
½ cup (150 g) light tahini

Set the honey aside for 3 minutes to cool, then add the tahini and beat with a wooden spoon to combine.

Pour the mixture into the lined pan and chill for at least 36 hours, then cut into small squares. It will keep in the fridge for up to a month.

Red cabbage and juniper sauerkraut

You can eat this two ways: either raw as a quick slaw, or you can leave it for a few weeks to ferment into a bright fuchsia sauerkraut.

It makes a clean-tasting autumnal slaw; but a little time and fermentation sharpens the flavors and turns it into a different offering altogether. If you want to eat it in its crunchy slaw stage, you'll only need to add a good pinch of salt.

There are so many virtues to sauerkraut. We have been making and eating ferments—kombucha (see page 56)—for the last few years and I have to say that as well as being good to eat, I do think they have had a positive overall effect on how I feel. I am not a fan of the super-fermented style, so I keep my fermentation times quite short (up to one week in the summer, perhaps two in the winter), but I'll leave that up to you and your taste buds.

While there are a lot of great things about fermented foods, filling your house with wonderful smells is not one, so find a nice cool spot where this can sit, and leave it be until you are ready to jar it up and put it in the fridge.

If you are planning to ferment your cabbage you will need 1 to 3 weeks and a large bowl, a ceramic crock, or a large, deep container with a lid, a plate that fits inside the crock, a heavy weight (a jar with water in it, a heavy stone, a pestle), and a tea towel.

Put the cabbage and fennel into a large bowl as you prepare it and sprinkle with the 2 tablespoons of salt total as you go, layer by layer (if you plan to eat this as a slaw, just sprinkle the whole lot with the pinch). Bash the juniper and fennel seeds in a mortar with pestle to a coarse powder. Add the apple and spices to the vegetables and massage together for a few minutes. The cabbage should start letting out water, helped along by the salt.

If you are eating this as a slaw, stop at this stage and serve. →

MAKES ABOUT 4 JARS OR SERVES 8

- 2½ (1 kg) red cabbage, finely chopped or sliced on a mandoline
- 1¾ pounds (800 g) fennel, finely chopped or sliced on a mandoline
- a good pinch of flaky sea salt or 2 tablespoons fine sea salt
- 1 tablespoon juniper berries
- 1 tablespoon fennel seeds
- 7 ounces (200 g) crisp eating apples, grated

To ferment, pack everything, including all the juices, into your crock or container and press down firmly so that it is covered by the liquid. Place a plate on top of this and use the weight to add pressure. Cover with the tea towel. You may not have much liquid at this point, but check it every few hours for the first day, removing the cloth, weight, and plate and applying pressure with clean hands—this will help extract more liquid. By the end of the day you should have about an inch of liquid above the top of the cabbage. Replace the plate, weight, and cloth each time. You want the natural yeasts in the atmosphere to get into the container while keeping out flies and dust. Keep in a cool, darkish part of your kitchen.

The sauerkraut will start to taste good within a few days but improves greatly by the second week. Check it every couple of days to make sure it is still submerged, pressing down if not. If a little surface growth appears, simply scrape it off—it is not a problem. When your kraut is ready, press it into sterilized jars with some of the liquid and a tight-fitting lid. Store in the fridge for up to 3 weeks.

Winter

Best of the season
    Turnips
    Jerusalem artichoke
    Savoy cabbage
    Red cabbage
    Carrots
    Beets
    Parsnips
    Kale
    Leeks
    Potatoes
    Celeriac
    Red cabbage
    Brussels sprouts
    Cauliflower
    Rutabaga
    Blood oranges
    Quince
    Chestnuts
    Apples
    Clementines
    Tangerines
    Pomegranate

Flowers
    Winter jasmine
    Dogwood
    Honeysuckle
    Poinsetta

Chocolate rye porridge with quick honey pears

I have had an up-and-down relationship with porridge my whole life. The ups: its warmth on a cold day, a bowl in my hands like a morning hot-water bottle. The downside: the monotonous texture—I want each spoonful to be different and interesting. I know for some this reliable consistency is the appeal, but not for me.

For me, porridge is as much of an opportunity to get interesting flavor and texture into my day as any other. I know the traditionalists out there might be rolling their eyes, but porridge is personal. My winter morning staples are oats flecked with poppy seeds, cooked in almond milk with lemon zest and vanilla. Another favorite is coconut milk with pinhead oatmeal, a good pinch of cardamom and a little honey, topped with toasted coconut and ripe vanilla-scented persimmon.

This, though, seems to be my very favorite of winter breakfasts: chocolate, a malty back note from the rye flakes, and a very quick honeyed pear compote. I use 50/50 rye flakes to oats, but it can be made with oats alone if that is what you have. Barley malt works well on top too, if you want an extra hit of sweetness.

First, make the pear topping. Heat the pears and honey in a small pan over medium heat for 5 minutes, or until just warmed through and beginning to soften, adding a tiny splash of water if it's looking too dry.

Meanwhile, put all the porridge ingredients into a pan with 3½ ounces (100 ml) of hot water and cook for 5 to 8 minutes until the oats come together; add more water if it looks too thick.

Spoon the porridge into bowls and top with the pears, almond butter, and almonds.

SERVES 2

FOR THE QUICK HONEY PEARS

2 pears, cored and sliced

1 tablespoon golden honey

⅔ cup (50 g) rolled rye flakes

⅔ cup (50 g) rolled oats

1¼ cups (300 ml) unsweetened almond milk or cow's milk

a pinch of flaky sea salt

2 teaspoons raw cacao or unsweetened cocoa powder

a pinch of ground cinnamon

2 teaspoons golden honey

TO SERVE

2 tablespoons almond butter

a handful of chopped almonds

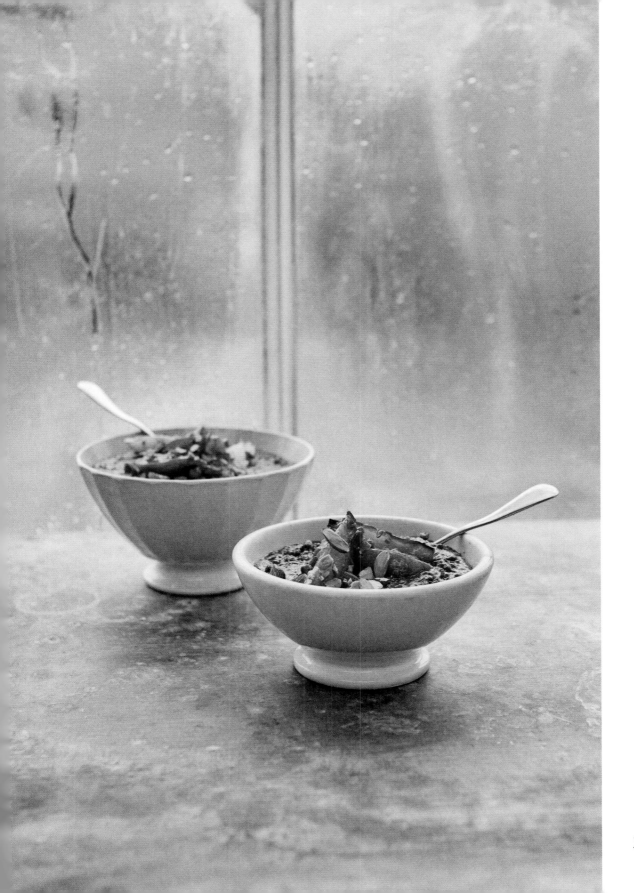

Greens, coconut sambal, and mustard-seed fried eggs

I most often eat this for breakfast, but it would sit happily on the table at any time of day. This kind of breakfast is on every brunch menu when I go to visit my sister in Los Angeles, and is popping up more and more around where I live too. It's really simple to make at home and the gentle Indian flavors make for an enlivening start to the day. I use a few cherry tomatoes here but I know they are far from their best in winter, so if you'd prefer you could use a few canned cherry tomatoes.

SERVES 2

FOR THE SAMBAL

1 red chile, roughly chopped

1 clove of garlic, bashed

4 cherry tomatoes, roughly chopped

3 shallots, finely chopped

sea salt

the zest and juice of 1 unwaxed lime

1 tablespoon coconut oil

1¾ ounces (50 g) creamed coconut

FOR THE GREENS

1 small head of Lacinato kale, curly kale, or winter greens

1 teaspoon coconut oil

1 red chile, finely chopped

the juice of ½ a lemon

FOR THE EGGS

1 teaspoon coconut oil

1 teaspoon mustard seeds

2 organic eggs

toasted chapatis, to serve

First, make the sambal. Put the chile, garlic, tomatoes, and shallots into a mortar with a big pinch of salt and the zest of the lime; bash with the pestle until you have a rough paste.

Heat a frying pan with the coconut oil and fry the paste for a few minutes, until it smells really fragrant and has turned a deep red color. Scrape out into a bowl to cool, and set aside while you get on with the greens.

Tear the leaves of the greens from their stalks and roughly chop the stalks, discarding any particularly tough ones. Put the pan back on the heat, add the coconut oil, then the stalks and the chile, and fry for a couple of minutes to soften a little.

Once the stalks have softened, add the leaves and fry, stirring regularly for 4 to 5 minutes, until they wilt and turn a deep green. Squeeze over the lemon juice, stir, put on two plates, and keep warm, then put the pan back on the heat for the eggs.

Grate the creamed coconut into a bowl and mix in the cooled sambal paste. Add the lime juice, stir, and taste to adjust the seasoning, adding more salt, lime, and even a bit more chile if needed.

To fry the eggs, melt the teaspoon of coconut oil in the pan over medium heat and add the mustard seeds. Leave until they start to pop. Crack in the eggs and cook until the whites are completely set and the mustard seeds gather around the edges. Place the eggs on top of the greens and serve everything with a couple of charred chapatis and the sambal.

Potato and mustard-seed masala omelette

I ate this on repeat on a trip to Kerala a few years ago and it has become one of those recipes that makes its way into my kitchen so often that it feels like a good friend. It makes an amazing quick supper, without compromising on interest and flavor. In the summer I make this with tomatoes in place of the root vegetables—most other vegetables that blend well with a bit of spice would be welcome, too. We also eat it for a weekend brunch, paired with a spoonful of avocado and a cup of coffee or milky chai. Use any cooked root vegetables here; this is a great way to use up leftovers.

SERVES 2

1 teaspoon black mustard seeds

a pinch of cumin seeds

a pinch of ground turmeric

a pinch of garam masala

2 handfuls of leftover cooked root veg, cut into ⅜-inch (1-cm) slices

a bunch of scallions, finely chopped

a small bunch of cilantro, stems finely chopped, leaves roughly chopped

1 green chile, finely chopped

4 organic eggs

sea salt

1–2 tablespoons of butter

1 unwaxed lemon

Heat a nonstick pan over medium heat and add the mustard and cumin seeds. Keep moving them around the pan until they start smelling toasty and the mustard seeds begin to pop. Next, add the turmeric and garam masala and take the pan off the heat.

Pour the spices into a bowl and add the potatoes or other root vegetables, scallions, cilantro, and chile. Mix well, then scoop out a third of the mixture and put to one side.

Break the eggs into the bowl, add a good pinch of salt, and mix everything together with a fork. You can either cook one large omelette or two small ones. Either way, heat a nonstick frying pan over medium heat and add the butter. Swirl it around to make sure the pan is well covered with butter, add all or half the mixture, swirling the eggs around for 30 seconds or so, then use a spatula to pull the eggs away from the side of the pan, tipping the pan to let the still-runny egg fill the gap. Leave it to set for a minute.

Slide the omelette onto a plate and top with the rest of the potato mixture. Finish with a little lemon zest and a squeeze of lemon juice.

Winter root and seaweed fritters

Fritters have become one of the things I cook the most, and these are crisp and moreish, as well as being packed with goodness. There are lots more fritter ideas on page 126. If seaweed is a bridge too far, you can leave it out, but it's a subtle note, not a mouthful of sea. If you are finding seaweed hard to come by, sheets of toasted nori (sushi seaweed) are usually easy to get your hands on and can be crumbled into the mixture. Emerald Cover is a favorite brand for seaweed.

Yuzu is a Japanese citrus fruit that adds a bright zippy note. It's hard to come by fresh, but bottles of juice are now widely available. A mix of lime and clementine would work well too.

————————————

Start by making the sauce. Put the lemon and orange zest into a mortar with the chile, yuzu juice, and a good pinch of salt. Use the pestle to grind the mixture into a thick dipping sauce, then transfer to a bowl and set aside.

Roughly chop the pumpkin seeds, then grate the root veg, using the coarse side of a box grater or the coarse grater attachment of your food processor (this will be much quicker).

Put the onion into a large mixing bowl with a big pinch of salt and the zest of the lemon. Squeeze in a few drops of juice and use your hands to scrunch the onion until it has broken down a bit and is lightly pickled.

Next add the grated veg, seaweed, flour, chile, ginger, and the pumpkin seeds. Season the mix well with a little more salt and a good bit of black pepper, then mix in the eggs.

Pour a little oil into a heavy frying pan and spoon heaping tablespoons of the batter into the pan—you should be able to get about 16 fritters out of the mixture. Press down gently with a spatula to flatten. Cook for 2 to 3 minutes on each side, not moving them much, so a lovely golden crust develops. Keep the fritters warm in a low oven as you cook the next batch. Serve with the yuzukosho and some peppery leaves.

SERVES 4 (MAKES 16 LITTLE FRITTERS)

FOR THE YUZUKOSHO SAUCE

the zest of 1 unwaxed lemon

the zest of 1 unwaxed orange or mandarin

1 red chile, finely chopped

1 tablespoon yuzu juice (see note above)

sea salt

2 tablespoons pumpkin seeds, toasted

1 pound (500 g) root vegetables, peeled

1 red onion, finely sliced

1 unwaxed lemon

2 tablespoons dried seaweed flakes (e.g. dulse, wakame)

1 tablespoon flour (I use chickpea or gram flour)

1 red chile, finely chopped

a small thumb-size piece of ginger, peeled and grated

freshly ground black pepper

4 organic or free-range eggs, lightly beaten

olive oil or coconut oil

peppery leaves, to serve

Fennel and lemon Scotch eggs with tomato chutney

MAKES 4

6 medium organic eggs

1 tablepoon sweet smoked
   paprika

olive oil

1 red onion, finely chopped

2 cloves of garlic, finely sliced

1 tablespoon fennel seeds

sea salt and freshly ground
   black pepper

1 × 14.5-ounce (400-g) can of
   butter beans, drained

1 small sweet potato (about
   4¼ ounces/120 g), grated

½ cup (50 g) grated cheese
   (I usually use Cheddar)

the zest of 1 unwaxed lemon

1 red chile, finely chopped
   (or a good pinch of red
   pepper flakes)

a small bunch of flat-leaf
   parsley, leaves picked and
   roughly chopped

1 cup (100 g) mixed small
   seeds (e.g., sesame,
   sunflower)

Dijon mustard, to serve
   (optional)

mayonnaise, to serve
   (optional)

FOR THE TOMATO
   CHUTNEY

1 × 14.5-ounce (400-g) can of
   chopped tomatoes

1 small stick of cinnamon

2 tablespoons capers

1 tablespoon red wine vinegar

My husband, John, loves Scotch eggs. I have to say I've always thought they were a little bit suspicious, but I've been persuaded that they do have an appeal. These are delicious. They are a great portable snack, the perfect size for lunch with a few leaves. They are also a great thing to make ahead, as they sit well and are good cold. I make these with a quick tomato chutney but a store-bought one would work just as well.

The size of egg is important here, as the timing is based on medium ones. I use seeds to coat the eggs, which is much less fuss than the usual flour, egg, and bread crumbs. If you want a runny yolk you can deep-fry the eggs until golden on the outside, for 3 to 4 minutes, but I opt for oven baking to keep them a little lighter; it does give you a hard-boiled center but that's OK by me.

First, put 4 of the eggs into a pan of cold water and bring to a boil. Once the water is boiling, start a timer and boil for 3 minutes. Crack the cooked eggs just to break the shell, then sit them in cold water until they are cool enough to handle. Carefully peel them, then roll them in the smoked paprika until they are covered in dusty bright red.

Preheat the oven to 395°F (200°C).

Meanwhile, put a frying pan over medium heat and add a little olive oil. Fry the onion and garlic for 5 minutes, until soft and sweet, then take out half of the onion and put in a bowl with the leftover smoked paprika, the fennel seeds, and a good pinch of salt and pepper.

For the chutney, put the pan with the rest of the onion back onto the heat. Add the tomatoes, cinnamon, capers, and the red wine vinegar, then cook for 20 minutes until reduced and thick—a chutney consistency. →

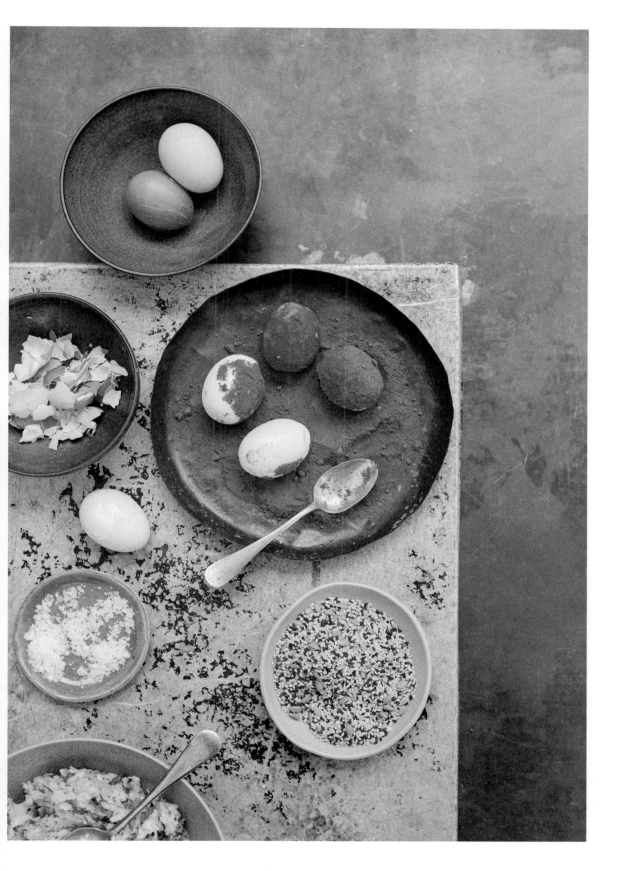

In another bowl, mash the beans with a potato masher until pretty smooth. Add the sweet potato, cheese, lemon zest, chile, and parsley, along with the onion and garlic mixture, and crack in one of the remaining eggs. Mix well, season with salt and pepper, and divide into four equal portions.

In the palm of one hand, flatten one-quarter of the bean mixture into an oval-shaped pattie. Pop a paprika-dusted egg into the middle of the pattie. Gently and quickly shape the mixture around the egg evenly, molding it with your hands (almost like you're handling a hot potato), making sure the egg is snugly wrapped with no air gaps.

Crack the remaining egg into a shallow dish and beat well. Put the seeds on a plate with a good pinch of salt.

Roll the wrapped eggs in the beaten egg, then in the seeds, and place on a baking sheet lined with parchment paper. Repeat with the other 3 eggs.

Put into the hot oven for 30 to 40 minutes, until golden. Rest for a few minutes before eating with the cooled chutney, as well as some Dijon mustard and mayonnaise, if that's your thing.

Mini squash and chive dumplings

I make these dumplings year-round, but I find them especially pleasing in the winter when the party season hits, as they are the perfect thing to have with a glass of something sparkling. Or I make a batch for dinner and freeze the rest; they are a brilliant travel or plane snack as they hold up to being carried around.

These do take time to put together; I enlist a couple of helpers for the dumpling folding. The finished dumplings will be more than worth the effort, and the process is social if done with friends, meditative if done on your own. They can be made ahead and frozen if you like.

You can make gyoza pastry yourself, but I always buy it. You'll find packages of fresh or frozen in most Asian supermarkets, and they are readily available online and in bigger supermarkets. If you are using frozen gyoza wrappers, make sure they are defrosted before you use them: It will take 30 minutes. Cover them with a slightly damp paper towel to keep them from drying out and be gentle when pulling them apart. You will find lots of videos online, if you are struggling to figure out exactly how to fold your gyozas.

To make the filling, put the chile, garlic, ginger, and scallions into a food processor and blitz until finely chopped (or pound by hand in a mortar with pestle, if you like).

Add the cabbage and squash to the food processor, along with the sesame oil and soy sauce, and blitz again until you have a coarse paste (you can finely chop the cabbage and grate the squash if you don't have a food processor). Scrape the mixture into a bowl and mix in the chives.

To assemble the dumplings, you'll need the filling, the gyoza wrappers, a bowl of cold water, and a clean baking sheet. Take one of the wrappers from the pile and put it in the palm of your hand: You will need to do this slowly and carefully. Keep the rest of the wrappers covered with damp paper towels to keep them from drying out. Spoon a heaping teaspoon of the filling into the middle of the wrapper—don't be tempted to overfill it, or it will be hard to seal. Use your finger to dampen the edge of the wrapper with a little water. →

MAKES ABOUT 30

½ a red chile, seeded and roughly chopped

2 cloves of garlic, peeled

a 1-inch (3-cm) piece of ginger, peeled and chopped

2 scallions, trimmed and chopped

7 ounces (200 g) white cabbage, roughly chopped

7 ounces (200 g) butternut squash, peeled, deseeded and roughly chopped

1 teaspoon sesame oil

½ tablespoon soy sauce

a small bunch of chives, chopped

30 gyoza wrappers, defrosted if frozen

peanut or vegetable oil

FOR THE DIPPING SAUCE

½ cup soy sauce or tamari

½ cup brown rice vinegar

4 tablespoons golden honey

2 tablespoons chile sauce

1 tablespoon toasted sesame seeds

Fold the wrapper in half, then fold the edge into little pleats, working from one side to the other, until the whole open edge is sealed. Press down firmly along the edge to seal completely. Keep going until you've used up all the filling. The dumplings can be stored in the fridge for a couple of days or in the freezer for a few months.

When you are ready to cook the dumplings, make your dipping sauce by whisking all the ingredients together in a small bowl. Fill the kettle with water and boil.

Pour a little oil into a nonstick frying pan (for which you have a lid) big enough to hold at least 8 dumplings, and put it over medium heat, remembering that you need to cook them in a single layer. As the pan starts to warm, put the dumplings in, with their flat bottoms in contact with the pan. Fry them until they are golden underneath. →

As soon as the bottoms are crisp, pour in hot water from the kettle to come halfway up the side of the dumplings. Turn the heat up, bring the water to a boil, and cover with a lid. Once boiling, reduce the heat to medium and cook for 8 minutes.

When the dumplings are cooked, remove the lid and turn the heat up to high. The water should almost have evaporated. You now want to cook them for a final minute or so, until the bottoms get nice and crisp. Serve warm with the dipping sauce.

Roasted onion and miso soup with a rarebit top

This is one of the most comforting things that I can remember cooking. The slow sweet onions and miso make a deeply flavored soup with just the right blend of mellow sweetness and savory punch. The soup is good on its own, but it's taken to a new level of comfort and deliciousness with a quick rarebit top. Cheese, mustard, and crème fraîche (though you could use good thick Greek yogurt too) melt on toasted bread for a burnished golden roof—the top stays crisp and the bottom soaks up the soup, like a good dumpling. Here I cook the onions without oil, as the salt encourages them to release their liquid and cook to a pleasing butteriness.

I've not tried a vegan version, but I'm guessing that swapping the cheese for a tablespoon of nutritional yeast and the crème fraîche for some nondairy yogurt might work well, though you'd only need to grill it for a minute or two.

Put the onions into a pan over low heat and sprinkle with a generous pinch of salt. Stir and cover, leaving the pan on the heat, until the onions are totally soft and have reduced in size by about half—you don't want too much color here. You may need to add a splash of water occasionally if the onions look like they're sticking. This will take about 20 minutes.

Next, add the oil and the flour and stir constantly for about 3 minutes to help the flour cook out, then add the wine and let it bubble for a minute. Add the veg stock and the thyme sprigs and cook for 1 hour, until deep, rich, and golden.

Once the soup has had its time simmering, add the miso and stir in. Taste for seasoning, adding some black pepper; you shouldn't need more salt as the miso is quite salty. Remove the thyme sprigs.

Preheat your broiler. Mix the cheese, mustard, Worcestershire sauce, and crème fraîche and spread liberally over the 4 pieces of bread. Ladle the soup into heatproof bowls, top each with a slice of the bread, and put under the broiler until the cheese is bubbling.

SERVES 4

4 medium onions, finely sliced

sea salt

1 tablespoon canola oil

2 tablespoons flour (I use spelt)

an 8-ounce (250 ml) glass of white wine

6½ cups (1.5 liters) good vegetable stock

a few sprigs of thyme

1 tablespoon dark miso

freshly ground black pepper

FOR THE RAREBIT TOPPING

1 cup (100 g) Cheddar cheese

1 teaspoon whole-grain mustard

a good dash of Worcestershire sauce (I use a vegetarian one)

6 tablespoons crème fraîche

4 slices of good sourdough bread

Velvet squash broth with miso and soba

A blanket of a soup for a cold day. I first made this on a bitterly cold morning, mist creeping up the garden, and every breath visible as I walked to the store for a piece of ginger. This soup is loosely rooted in Japan—I use sake here, but white wine would work too.

The miso stirred into a paste with bashed toasted walnuts is a great addition to noodle soups or to a sandwich, and I just spoon it out of the bowl too. I use 100 percent buckwheat soba noodles, but any soba or thin rice noodles would work.

First, heat a large pan over medium heat and add a good drizzle of oil, then add the leeks with a pinch of salt. Cook for 10 to 15 minutes, until soft and sweet, adding a little water if they stick.

Next, peel the butternut squash (I do this for a really velvety soup, but you can leave the skin on—it just might not be quite as smooth) and cut into small pieces (about ¾ inches/2 cm). Once the leeks are cooked, add the sesame seeds and ginger to the pan, turn up the heat, and cook until the sesame seeds are starting to brown and toast.

Now add the squash, sake or wine, and stock and allow to simmer for about 20 to 25 minutes, or until the squash is well cooked through. Squeeze in the juice of the lime. Blend the soup until velvety smooth, then put it back in the pan.

While the soup is cooking, toast the walnuts in a dry pan over low heat, then bash them in a mortar and pestle until they look like rough bread crumbs, and mix with the miso, honey, tamari, and vinegar.

Cook the soba noodles according to the package instructions, refresh them under cold water until cold, then leave them to one side.

Taste the soup and add more salt and lime if it needs it, remembering it is quite neutral, and flavor will be added by the walnut miso.

To serve, put the noodles into four deep bowls and ladle over the broth. Finish with a spoonful of the miso, and some sesame seeds and herbs if you want.

SERVES 4

peanut or canola oil

2 leeks, trimmed and shredded

1 butternut squash (about 1¾ pounds/800 g)

2 tablespoons sesame seeds

a small piece of ginger, peeled and chopped

6½ cups (1.5 liters) sake or white wine

1.5 liters good vegetable stock

1 lime

1 cup (100 g) walnuts

2 tablespoons white miso

2 tablespoons golden honey

1 tablespoon tamari or soy sauce

a tablespoon of rice wine vinegar

10½ ounces (300 g) soba noodles

TO SERVE (OPTIONAL)

toasted sesame seeds

Asian herbs (I use cilantro and shiso)

Turmeric and lime-leaf broth with roasted root vegetables

A combination of lifting aromatics and wintry earthy root vegetables, roasted until crisp around the edges and sweet. A broth for cold days and especially good if you are feeling the chill of the day or need some perking up from feeling under the weather. You could use whatever root vegetables you have on hand; potatoes and beets work well too, but I like the flavor of the sweeter root vegetables against the heady turmeric and lime leaves. I particularly love using rutabaga here; it's an underrated root vegetable that should, in my opinion, be used as much as in-vogue sweet potatoes or the ever-present parsnips.

SERVES 4

8 small carrots (7 ounces/ 200 g), halved if big

4 small parsnips (12¼ ounces/ 350 g), quartered or halved

1 small rutabaga (1 pound/ 500 g), peeled and roughly chopped

sea salt

coconut oil

a small thumb-size piece of ginger, peeled

a small thumb-size piece of turmeric, peeled

a bunch of cilantro

2 banana shallots, finely sliced

1 clove of garlic, finely sliced

1 tablespoon cilantro (coriander) seeds, bashed

1 red chile, finely chopped

1 × 14.5-ounce (400-g) can of coconut milk

4 lime leaves

TO SERVE

1 cup (200 g) cooked quinoa or wild rice (about ½ cup/75 g uncooked)

1 lemon or lime, cut into wedges

Preheat the oven to 425°F (220°C).

Place the chopped vegetables on a baking sheet with a big pinch of salt and a tablespoon of coconut oil. Put in the oven and remove after 5 minutes to toss everything in the oil. Return to the oven for about 35 minutes, until everything is golden, tossing from time to time.

Grate the ginger and turmeric, pick the cilantro leaves from the stems, roughly chop the stems, and set the leaves aside.

Put another tablespoon of oil into a small saucepan, add half the shallots, and cook for about 5 minutes over medium heat, until beginning to brown. Next, add the cilantro stems, garlic, cilantro seeds, red chile, turmeric, and ginger and cook for a few minutes before adding the coconut milk and lime leaves. Fill the emptied coconut milk can with water and pour it into the pan. Season well with salt and pepper and simmer for 10 minutes.

Meanwhile, heat a pan over high heat with another tablespoon of coconut oil, and once it's melted and really hot, add the remaining shallots and cook until crisp and golden, taking care not to let them get too dark—there is a sweet spot when they are just brown, but they will darken quickly, so be ready to scoop them out with a slotted spoon, then drain on paper towels to keep their crispness.

Once the vegetables are ready, spoon the cooked quinoa or rice into four bowls, top with the vegetables, ladle over the soup and top with the cilantro leaves and crispy shallots. Serve with the lime or lemon wedges.

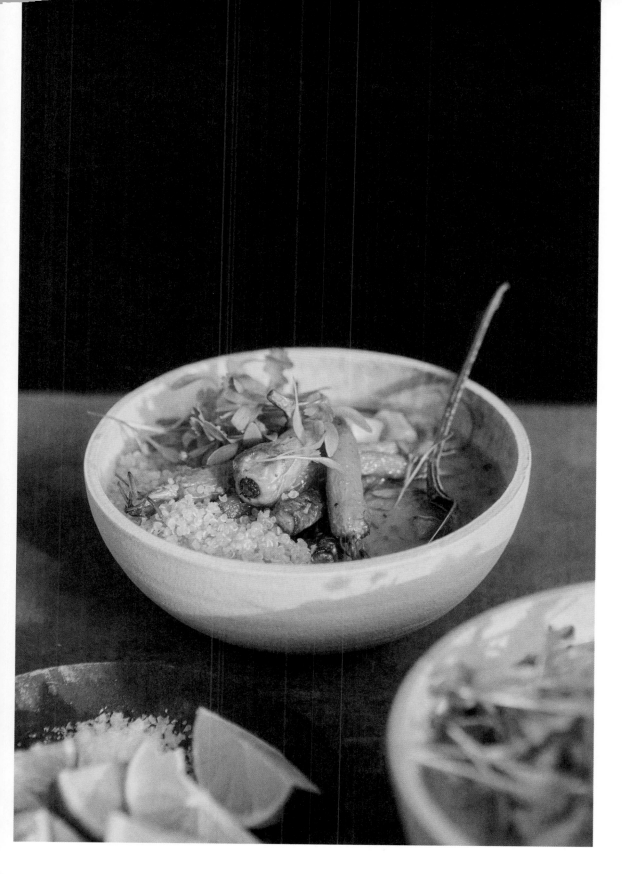

Kale and Brussels sprouts Caesar slaw

This is a staple winter salad, fresh but generous in flavor all at once. The dressing is based on the rich flavors of a Caesar salad dressing but using soaked nuts and seeds as a base, which adds creaminess without adding too much oil and is a filling addition to the salad. I am sure a few more toasted seeds or nuts scattered over the top would be good.

You can use pretty much any winter greens or cabbage, but be sure to shred them quite thinly. The cheese can be left out or swapped for whatever you have (any blue or hard cheese) and any soft herbs you have (a mixture of a couple works best).

The slaw is better after sitting for a couple of hours, as the dressing softens the greens a little, and the flavors will come together. Seed and nut butters work instead of the soaked seeds and nuts, if that's easier, but choose a gentle, ideally untoasted one. This is a great way to use up leftover Christmas greens and cheese.

SERVES 6–8

FOR THE DRESSING

⅓ cup (50 g) sunflower seeds

½ cup (50 g) nuts (I use blanched almonds)

1 clove of garlic, peeled

1 tablespoon Dijon mustard

the juice of ½ a lemon

about 14 ounces (400 g) kale or other winter greens, stalks removed

4 cups (350 g) raw Brussels sprouts

a small bunch of soft herbs

about 1 cup (150 g) blue cheese or hard cheese (optional)

First, soak your seeds and nuts for the dressing in cold water: 15 minutes will do, but you could leave them as long as overnight—this helps the dressing become creamier.

Once soaked, drain the seeds and nuts and put them in a blender (a high-speed blender works best here) with all the other dressing ingredients, then blend until smooth. Add ⅞ cup (200 ml) of water and blend again to a creamy dressing (how long you need to blitz it for will depend on the speed of your blender). Keep in the fridge until you are ready to dress the salad.

Slice the greens and sprouts as finely as you can, then put them all in a big bowl. Roughly chop the herbs and add these to the bowl, then pour over the dressing and mix well. I do this with clean hands to make sure that the dressing coats every little bit of green. When you are ready to serve, crumble over some leftover cheese, if using.

Miso roasted squash and potatoes with almonds and kale

A centerpiece of a dish: squash, potatoes, and greens cooked together on one baking sheet. The harissa, miso, and lemon combo is a great foil for some of the richer dishes that show up at this time of year. I eat this on its own; sometimes we cut some tofu into little pieces and add it to the pan, tossing it in the dressing for the last 10 minutes of cooking too.

I have served this on Christmas Day for the last few years; the ease of cooking vegetables together helps with time and oven space.

Preheat the oven to 425°F (220°C).

Cut the potatoes into halves or quarters no larger than your thumb. Cut the squash in half lengthways (no need to peel), use a spoon to scoop out the seeds, then cut it into ¾-inch (2-cm) slices.

In a small bowl mix together the olive oil, miso, harissa, and lemon juice.

Put the potatoes and squash on a baking sheet with half the harissa mixture. Toss well, using your hands, to make sure everything is coated. Roast for 40 to 45 minutes, until everything is cooked through and browning at the edges. Turn everything once or twice to make sure it browns evenly, and keep a close eye on it, as it can burn in a flash.

Add the shredded kale and roast for a final 10 minutes. It should crisp up a little. Transfer to a serving dish, spoon over the remaining dressing, and scatter with the toasted almonds.

SERVES 8

1 pound (500 g) small Yukon Gold potatoes, scrubbed clean,

1½ pounds (700 g) butternut or other squash

4 tablespoons olive oil

3 tablespoons white miso

2 tablespoons harissa

the juice of 1 lemon

1½ cups (100 g) shredded kale leaves

1 cup (100 g) almonds, skin on, toasted (see page 459)

Homemade curry pastes

	Malaysian rendang	Lemon and harissa tagine
Spices	a few gratings of nutmeg the seeds from 3 cardamom pods 1 small cinnamon stick white peppercorns	1 tablespoon cilantro seeds a small cinnamon stick a good pinch of saffron threads
Aromatics	4 lime leaves or the zest of 1 unwaxed lime 2 shallots, roughly chopped 2 stalks of lemongrass, bashed and roughly chopped a thumb-size piece of ginger, peeled	4 preserved lemons, flesh discarded, pith finely sliced 2 small red onions and 4 cloves of garlic, roughly chopped and cooked until soft and sweet
Chile	4 dried red chiles, soaked in warm water to soften	2 tablespoons harissa
Base	1 × 13.5-ounce (400-ml) can of coconut milk	1 × 14.5-ounce (400-g) can of chopped tomatoes
Oil	1 tablespoon peanut oil	1 tablespoon olive oil
Top note	a small bunch of cilantro	a small bunch of mint

South Indian curry leaf	Smoky Thai massaman	Method
a small handful of curry leaves 1 tablespoon mustard seeds 1 tablespoon cumin seeds 1 teaspoon cilantro seeds	½ teaspoon cloves 2 tablespoons cumin seeds 1 teaspoon cilantro seeds a small cinnamon stick	**1** Toast the spices (for smoky Thai massaman, toast the aromatics too).
a thumb-size piece of ginger 2 cloves of garlic, peeled a ¾-inch (2-cm) piece of turmeric (or ½ teaspoon dried)	3 shallots, roughly chopped 5 cloves of garlic, peeled 2 stalks of lemongrass, bashed and roughly chopped a thumb-size piece of ginger, peeled	**2** Blend the spices and aromatics to a paste.
2 fresh green chiles	5 dried red chiles	
1 × 7-ounce (200-g) block of creamed coconut	1 × 14.5-ounce (400-ml) can of coconut milk 2 tablespoons tamarind paste	**3** Add the base, oil, and top note to the mixture and blend again to form a loose paste.
2 tablespoons coconut oil	2 tablespoons peanut oil	
a small bunch of cilantro	1 tablespoon golden honey	

Party bao with sweet potatoes and pickled cucumbers

MAKES 20

FOR THE BAO

8½ tablespoons unsalted butter

2 × ¼-ounce (7-g) sachets of dried yeast

2½ pounds (1 kg) strong white bread flour, plus extra for rolling

1 teaspoon baking powder

¾ teaspoon baking soda

2 tablespoons flaky sea salt

olive oil

FOR THE FILLING

3½ pounds (1.5 kg) sweet potatoes, sliced lengthways and chopped into ¾-inch (2-cm) slices

4 tablespoons tamari or dark soy sauce

2 tablespoons golden honey

2 tablespoons finely grated ginger

1 tablespoon five-spice powder

2 good pinches of red pepper flakes

6 tablespoons toasted sesame oil

1 large cucumber

2 tablespoons mirin

1 tablespoon honey or maple syrup

3 tablespoons rice wine vinegar

a pinch of freshly ground white pepper →

I love bao. If you've not come across them, they are light but pleasingly chewy little steamed buns stuffed with flavorful fillings. Not so long ago, while I was pregnant, I got into a habit of buying them, and every Saturday, without fail, I walked to the little bao stand at Broadway Market, a short stroll from my house, to get one of their daikon bao. There is something so pleasing about the cloudlike little dumplings, always packed with flavorful stuffings and piquant lime and chile.

These are a bit of an undertaking. I tend to make them when I am having a few people over. I think they suit being eaten with a drink. As a snack I'd suggest two; three to make a meal of them. I double this for a party. Leftover buns make a great vehicle for some scrambled eggs the next morning too, with the leftover sauce and some scallions and chile—an idea stolen from my lovely friend Georgie.

This recipe makes 20 bao, perfect for a party. You can easily halve the recipe if you're just cooking for a few friends.

You can make the bao a day in advance (re-steaming them before serving).

Melt the butter in a saucepan over a low heat. Put the yeast into a large bowl with 15 ounces (450 ml) of warm water and leave for a few minutes, until tiny bubbles begin to form.

Now mix in the flour, baking powder, baking soda, sea salt, and the melted butter until it all comes together, then knead for 10 minutes to form a silky dough. Place in an oiled bowl, cover, and leave in a warm place to prove for a couple of hours.

Once the dough has doubled in size, knock it back by kneading it for a few seconds on a floured surface. Split it in half, then, using your hands, roll each half into equal-size logs.

Cut each log into 20 small, equal pieces (I find it easiest to cut each into 4, then cut those smaller pieces into 5). Roll each piece of dough into a ball and place on baking sheets lined with waxed paper. Cover and leave to prove again for 30 to 45 minutes. →

Knock each risen bun back with the palm of your hand, then, using a rolling pin, roll into oval shapes about 5 by 3½ inches (12 by 9 cm). Coat a chopstick with a little oil, place it across the width of each bun, and fold the dough over, then gently remove the chopstick.

Set a large steamer (preferably with two tiers) over medium heat, and get the water boiling. Place a layer of parchment paper in each steamer basket, then arrange the buns on top, spaced at least 1½ inches (3 cm) apart, then leave them to steam, not too fiercely, for 10 to 12 minutes, until they have puffed up and are light and fluffy and cooked through. Leave to cool, then cover and chill overnight if you are preparing them in advance. You could make them even further in advance and freeze them until needed.

Preheat the oven to 475°F (240°C).

FOR THE DIPPING SAUCE

3 tablespoons white miso

3 tablespoons golden honey

1 tablespoon brown rice vinegar

1 green chile, finely chopped

a large piece of ginger

TO FINISH

a bunch of scallions, finely sliced

a large handful of cilantro, leaves picked

2 cups (250 g) salted roasted cashews, crushed

For the filling, toss the sweet potatoes on a baking sheet with the tamari, honey, ginger, five-spice, half the red pepper flakes, and 4 tablespoons of the sesame oil. Roast for 20 to 30 minutes, turning halfway, until glazed and soft.

Shred or slice the cucumber into a bowl with the other pinch of red pepper flakes, the mirin, honey, rice vinegar, white pepper, and the remaining 2 tablespoons sesame oil. Toss to coat and set aside for 10 minutes before eating, or chill for up to 5 days.

Make the dipping sauce by whisking all the ingredients together until you have a thick, rich sauce.

Split the buns open and fill with the roasted sweet potato, drained cucumber, scallions, cilantro, and lots of crushed cashews for texture.

Creamy polenta with radicchio and charred mushrooms

The earthiness of the mushrooms and bitter notes of the radicchio make this recipe the perfect thing to eat with naturally sweet polenta.

Fill the kettle with water and boil. Cut the radicchio or chicory into quarters, then put the pieces into a large, shallow dish. Chop or tear your mushrooms in half and add them to the dish.

In a small bowl, combine the red wine vinegar, garlic, marjoram, olive oil, and a big pinch of salt. Mix well, then pour over the radicchio and mushrooms and leave to marinate for at least 40 minutes.

Get on with your polenta. Pour 4½ cups (1 liter) of boiling water from the kettle into a large pan over medium heat. Slowly add the polenta in a steady stream, whisking as you go. Cook for 5 minutes, or until the polenta thickens a little, then turn the heat down and simmer for 10 minutes, until cooked, stirring frequently (at least every 5 minutes) to make sure that it doesn't stick or get lumpy. The polenta is cooked when it has lost its grainy texture and feels smooth.

Add the butter and Parmesan to the cooked polenta, then season to taste with salt and black pepper. Set aside until the mushrooms have had their marinating time.

Heat a griddle over medium heat. Remove the mushrooms and radicchio from the marinade, allowing any excess to drip off back into the shallow dish. Reserve the marinade.

Grill the mushrooms and radicchio until they have become charred and soft throughout, about 3–4 minutes on each side. Once cooked, chop them very roughly and put them back into the marinade. Meanwhile, gently heat the polenta over low heat to warm it through.

When everything is ready, ladle the polenta into bowls and top with the radicchio and mushrooms, another grating of Parmesan, and a small pile of watercress.

SERVES 4

2 heads of radicchio or 4 of chicory

6 large portobello mushrooms

4 tablespoons red wine vinegar

4 cloves of garlic, finely sliced

a small bunch of marjoram or oregano, leaves picked

6 tablespoons olive oil

sea salt

FOR THE POLENTA

1 cup (150 g) of polenta or cornmeal (about a mugful)

2 tablespoons good butter

½–¾ cup (50–75 g) freshly grated Parmesan (I use a vegetarian/rennet-free one), plus extra to serve

sea salt and freshly ground black pepper

a big handful of watercress

Roast celeriac, fennel, clementine, and almond aïoli

I made this on a bleak winter's day, a wash of gray with little going for it other than that it encouraged me to stay inside, light a fire, and cook. I decided to use the celeriac that had arrived in our veg bag that week, but I wanted something filling and warming and bright too. I decided to fry the celeriac in butter until it was just brown, adding a deep caramel toastiness to the gentle veg. I did the same with a couple of heads of fennel and then boosted its freshness with some charred clementine. It was all topped off with an easy almond aïoli.

You could make a traditional aïoli if you like, but this one, made with deeply toasted almonds, backs up the brown butter. It is best made in a good high-speed blender—that way it will be super creamy and smooth; a little texture won't be the end of the world, though. I make a larger quantity than I need, as it will keep in the fridge for up to a week. I use it for sandwiches or as a dip, but if you'd prefer to keep a tight ship, you can halve the ingredients.

I serve this with some spelt or quinoa and a peppery salad, dressed with a little clementine juice and good olive oil with a generous grating of black pepper.

SERVES 4

1 celeriac (about 1¼ pounds/600 g)

butter or olive oil

2 heads of fennel, cut into ⅜-inch (1-cm) wedges

2 clementines, peel on and cut in half

a good pinch of red pepper flakes

the zest of 1 unwaxed lemon

flaky sea salt and freshly ground black pepper

FOR THE ALMOND AÏOLI

1½ cups (150 g) blanched almonds

1 lemon

¼ cup (60 ml) extra-virgin olive oil

1 teaspoon Dijon mustard

1 small clove of garlic

sea salt and freshly ground black pepper

Start by soaking 1 cup (100 g) of the almonds for the aïoli in ½ cup (125 ml) of cold water. Preheat the oven to 425°F (220°C).

Thickly peel the celeriac with a knife, then cut it into irregular medium pieces about the size of a coin.

Meanwhile, make the aïoli. Put the remaining ½ cup (50 g) of almonds on a baking sheet and toast in the oven for 8 minutes. You want them to be deeply toasted and dark golden but in a matter of minutes they can go from well toasted to burned, so keep an eye on them. Once toasted, pour into a bowl and leave to cool. →

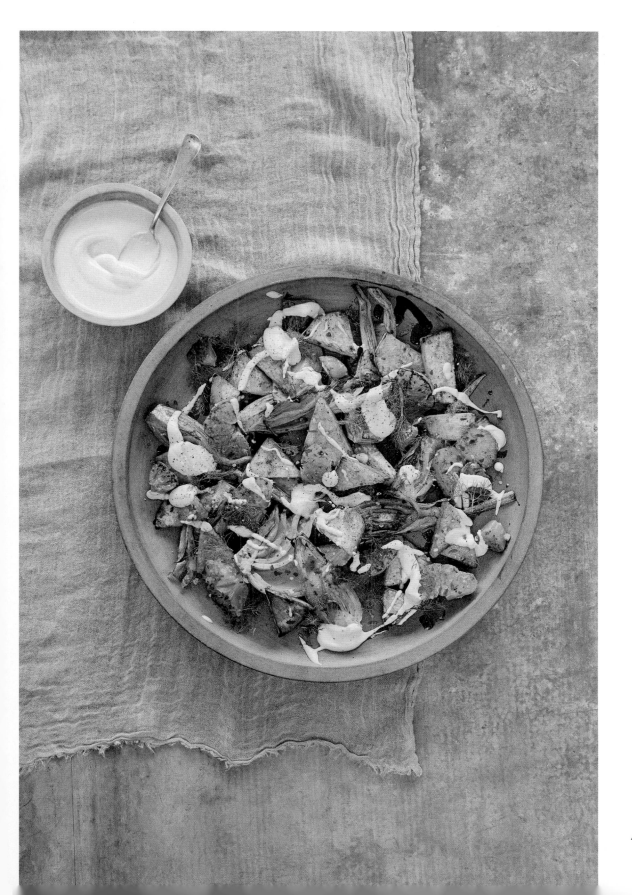

Drain the soaked almonds and put them into a high-speed blender with a generous ½ cup (125 ml) of fresh cold water, the juice of half the lemon, the oil, and mustard. Blitz on high speed until you have a very smooth mayonnaise-like paste. Add the garlic and toasted nuts and blitz in the blender, until it's smooth again. Season with salt and pepper and taste, adding a little more lemon, oil, or salt if needed.

Heat a large frying pan over medium heat and add a couple of tablespoons of butter and the celeriac. Season well and cook until browned all over, then scoop the celeriac onto a baking sheet and put the pan back on the heat.

Add the fennel wedges and cook in the same manner until well browned—you may need to add some more butter as you go if anything looks like it's sticking—then add the clementines, cut side down, and cook for 5 minutes, until charred. Transfer the clementines and the fennel to the baking sheet, and sprinkle with the red pepper flakes and lemon zest. Roast in the oven for 10 minutes, until cooked through and charring at the edges.

Once all the veg are cooked, carefully peel the clementines, scatter over the baking sheet, then serve with generous spoonfuls of the aïoli.

Golden saffron mash with winter greens and poached eggs

This is as sunny as winter food gets. Cloudlike, buttery mash with the warm glow of saffron in the background. I top this with a poached egg, which bathes the mash, thanks to its runny yolk. Greens add some minerally depth and toasted almonds some crunch. This feels sophisticated, thanks to the saffron, but it's an easy dinner and as soothing as a meal can be.

In a large saucepan, cover the potatoes with cold water, add a pinch of salt, and bring to a boil over medium heat. Allow to bubble away for 20 to 30 minutes, until the potatoes are tender.

Meanwhile, melt the butter in a frying pan over a medium-low heat, and when it starts to bubble add half the garlic, the soaked saffron, and its water. Allow to cook for 1 to 2 minutes, until the garlic starts to look golden. Take off the heat.

Once the potatoes are ready, drain them, then return to the saucepan. Mash well, then add the saffron butter and mash again. Taste and season with salt and pepper.

De-stalk the Lacinato kale, then chop the stalks into ⅜-inch (1-cm) pieces and roughly tear the leaves. In the frying pan you used for the garlic and saffron butter, heat a glug of olive oil and add the remaining garlic. Allow the garlic to cook in the oil for a minute, then add the chopped Lacinato kale stalks and the nutmeg. Cook over medium heat for 3 to 4 minutes until the stalks start to soften.

Half-fill a large saucepan with boiling water, add 2 tablespoons of vinegar, then bring to a simmer. Break each egg into a cup and drop it gently into the simmering water. Set a timer for 3 minutes.

While the eggs are poaching, add the Lacinato kale leaves to the stalks in the frying pan and sauté with the remaining tablespoon of cider vinegar. Add a pinch of salt and stir until the leaves wilt.

Carefully lift the eggs out of the water with a slotted spoon and drain on paper towels. Spoon the mash onto warm plates, top with the eggs, sprinkle over the almonds, and serve the greens on the side.

SERVES 4

2½ pounds (1 kg) Russet potatoes, peeled and cut into even-size chunks

sea salt

3½ tablespoons butter

2 cloves of garlic, finely chopped

2 pinches of saffron, soaked in 1 cup (250 ml) boiling water

freshly ground black pepper

1 pound (500 g) Lacinato kale, or spinach

olive oil

¼ teaspoon grated nutmeg

3 tablespoons cider vinegar

4 organic eggs, at room temperature

1 cup (100 g) almonds, skin on, toasted (see page 459)

Whole roasted squash

Roasted squash is something that I have returned to after a few years of avoiding it. Along with the other vegetarian stalwarts of mushroom risotto and stuffed peppers, there was a time when roasted squash was the offering of choice and it got a bit boring. This recipe has me welcoming it back with open arms, thanks to two things: firstly its very British flavors—there's not a pomegranate in sight—and secondly, how it's cooked. I roast the squash until it's completely cooked before stuffing it, making sure that it is crisp inside and out and the filling is well seasoned and light.

This is a wonderful way to use some of the more unusual varieties of squash. I use onion and kabocha squash here, filled with plump grains and sweet roasted fennel, some good sharp Cheddar, and topped with toasted buttery oats. A butternut would work too, though you won't get quite as much of a hollow for stuffing. If you are using a butternut, cut it in half lengthways before roasting to make it easier to fill. Most squashes will roast in roughly the same time, with the exception of the thick-walled pumpkins; I'd avoid those.

SERVES 4

a mixture of round whole squashes, about 1¾ pounds (750 g) squash per person

4 bulbs of fennel

1 bulb of garlic

olive oil

sea salt and freshly ground black pepper

1¼ cups (250 g) freekeh or pearl barley

4½ ounces (125 g) sharp Cheddar or other cheese, grated (1 1/4 cups)

the zest of 1 unwaxed lemon

a bunch of fennel tops or dill

1 red chile, deseeded if you like

a knob of butter

generous ½ cup (50 g) rolled oats or barley flakes

1 teaspoon fennel seeds

Preheat the oven to 395°F (200°C).

Use a big, heavy knife to cut off the base of each squash, so they sit upright on a baking sheet. Cleanly cut about 1½ inches (3–4 cm) off the top of each one in a single piece (you are going to put the tops back on). Use a metal spoon to scoop out the seeds and the fibers until you have a neat hole.

Trim the fennel, removing any tough outer leaves, then cut the bulbs into a few big wedges.

Put the squash on a large baking sheet or two. Scatter the fennel wedges around and put the bulb of garlic in too. Drizzle with olive oil, making sure you get inside the squash, and season with salt and pepper. Pop the tops back on the squash. Roast for 45 to 60 minutes, or until the squash are tender and the fennel has started to soften and brown. If your squash take a little longer, you can remove the fennel once it's nicely soft and brown, as you don't want it to overcook. →

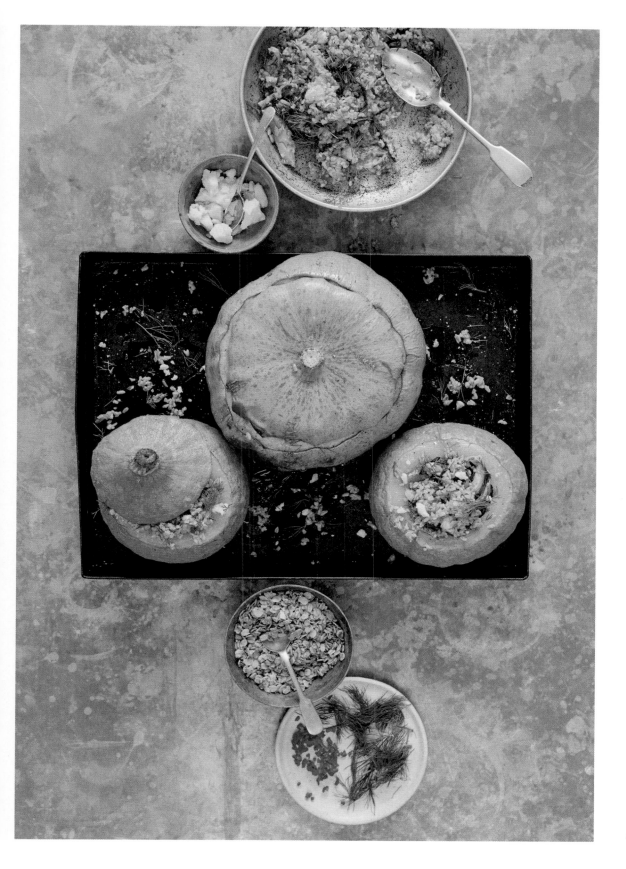

Meanwhile, put the freekeh or pearl barley in a medium pan and cover with cold water. Add a big pinch of salt, then bring to a boil and simmer until al dente (about 12 minutes for freekeh and 25 minutes for pearl barley). Drain and transfer to a large bowl.

Remove the garlic and fennel from the baking sheet. When cool enough to handle, squeeze the roasted garlic from its papery skins into the freekeh. Roughly chop the fennel and add it to the bowl along with the cheese, lemon zest, and some salt and pepper. Chop the fennel tops and chile and add these too. Taste the mixture and adjust the seasoning, if you like. Divide the filling mixture among the squash and return them to the oven for 10 minutes.

Meanwhile, heat the butter in a small pan, and add the oats, fennel seeds, and a little salt and pepper. Stir to coat in the butter, then toast the flakes until golden (this will take about 5 minutes). Drain on a plate lined with paper towels.

Once the squash and freekeh are out of the oven, take the tops off the squash and sprinkle over the toasted oats. Place in the middle of the table for everyone to dig in.

Baked celeriac macaroni with a crispy olive top

This is a take on a classic mac and cheese, but the sauce comes from some sweet roasted celeriac and plump butter beans. It's lighter and way less cloying than a straight-up mac and cheese, but still creamy, satisfying, and full of flavor. I top it off with some Lacinato kale (or kale), a few walnuts and black olives, which crisps to form a colorful textured crown that elevates this to another level. I add a little Parmesan to the sauce, but nutritional yeast works really well here if you'd prefer to keep it completely free of cheese.

Preheat the oven to 425°F (220°C).

Thickly peel and cube the celeriac and place it on a baking sheet along with the garlic, a little olive oil, and a pinch of salt. Toss everything together, then roast for 20 minutes, until blistered and tender. Turn the oven down to 395°F (200°C).

Transfer the roasted celeriac and garlic to a food processor with all the remaining ingredients except for the milk and pasta and blitz until you have a completely smooth, thick sauce. With the motor running, add the milk until you have a smooth and creamy sauce—the consistency of a thick béchamel—adding a little more if you need to.

Put a large pot of water on to boil with plenty of salt. Once boiling, cook the pasta for 4 minutes less than the package instructions. Drain and return to the pot, drizzle with a little olive oil, and toss to coat.

Next pour the celeriac sauce over the pasta bit by bit and keep stirring so that it folds into all the tubes. You should be able to use up all the sauce, but if you have any left over, it will keep in the fridge for up to 3 days.

Transfer the pasta to an ovenproof pan or baking dish. Pour the topping ingredients into a bowl and toss so that everything is mixed evenly, then scatter over the top of the creamy pasta. Bake for about 20 to 25 minutes, until the pasta and sauce are warmed through, the kale is crispy, and the olives blistering.

SERVES 6

1 celeriac (about 1¼ pounds/600 g)

3 cloves of garlic, peeled

1 tablespoon olive oil

sea salt

1 × 14.5-ounce (400-g) can of butter beans, drained (or 1 cup/250 g home-cooked, see page 461)

½ cup (50 g) freshly grated Parmesan or nutritional yeast

1 teaspoon whole-grain mustard

a good pinch of cayenne pepper

2 tablespoons olive oil

1 teaspoon cider vinegar

1⅔ cups (400 ml) milk, or as needed

12¼ ounces (350 g) whole-wheat macaroni or rigatoni

FOR THE TOPPING

8¾ ounces (250 g) Lacinato kale, leaves stripped and roughly torn

¾ cup (75 g) walnuts, roughly chopped

⅔ cup (100 g) pitted black olives, such as Kalamata

¼ cup (25 g) grated Parmesan or nutritional yeast

421

Cauliflower-topped Puy lentil pie

I made this pie after a bracing walk on a wintry Welsh beach, a long stretch of sand lined with pines on one side and tempting glistening sea on the other. Icy cold, we dipped our toes in, then ran to the car. On the drive home I became fixated on pie, and an hour or so later we were eating a comforting crust of mashed cauliflower on top of a rich lentil ragu, cooked until the lentils were almost soft. Its warmth spread all the way to our feet. I use cauliflower, but you could also use potato or a mix of root vegetables.

SERVES 4

olive oil

2 tablespoons mustard seeds

about 20 curry leaves, fresh if possible

2 carrots, peeled and finely chopped

1 onion, finely chopped

1 tablespoon cumin seeds, bashed

1 tablespoon cilantro (coriander) seeds

2 cloves of garlic, peeled and finely sliced

a thumb-size piece of ginger, peeled and finely chopped

1 × 14.5-ounce (400-g) can of Puy lentils, drained (or 1 cup/250 g home-cooked, see page 461)

1 × 14.5-ounce (400-g) can of chopped tomatoes

1 teaspoon vegetable stock powder or ½ a stock cube

2 pitted dates (I use Medjool)

1 red chile, seeded and chopped

juice of 1 unwaxed lemon

2 medium heads cauliflower (about 2¼ pounds/1 kg with leaves removed)

sea salt

1 tablespoon coconut or olive oil

Preheat the oven to 425°F (220°C).

Put a good glug of oil into a large, heavy pan. Get it nice and hot, add the mustard seeds and curry leaves, and cook until the seeds pop. Take the pan off the heat, reserve half the seeds and leaves, then put the pan with the remaining mixture back on the heat.

Add the carrots and onion to the pan and cook for another 10 to 15 minutes, or until soft, sweet, and nicely browned. Add the cumin, cilantro, garlic, and ginger and cook for 3 to 4 minutes, to toast the spices and allow the garlic and ginger to release their oils. Take care that the garlic doesn't burn.

Add the lentils, tomatoes, stock, and half a can of boiling water. Roughly chop the dates and add them to the pan with the chile and the zest of half the lemon. Season with salt and simmer over medium heat for 15 to 20 minutes, or until thick, rich, and flavorful.

Meanwhile, make the mash. Break the cauliflower into florets, slice the stalk, and put into a lidded pan with about ¾ inch (2 cm) of boiling water. Put over high heat and steam until tender. Drain, put back in the pan, and put over the heat for a minute to dry out the cauliflower.

Allow it to cool a little, then blitz in a food processor with the coconut oil and a big pinch of salt. When you have a silky-smooth mash, fold in the reserved mustard seeds and curry leaves.

Once the lentils are ready, add the lemon juice and mix well. Spoon into an ovenproof dish, top with the mash, and bake for 20 minutes, or until golden and bubbling.

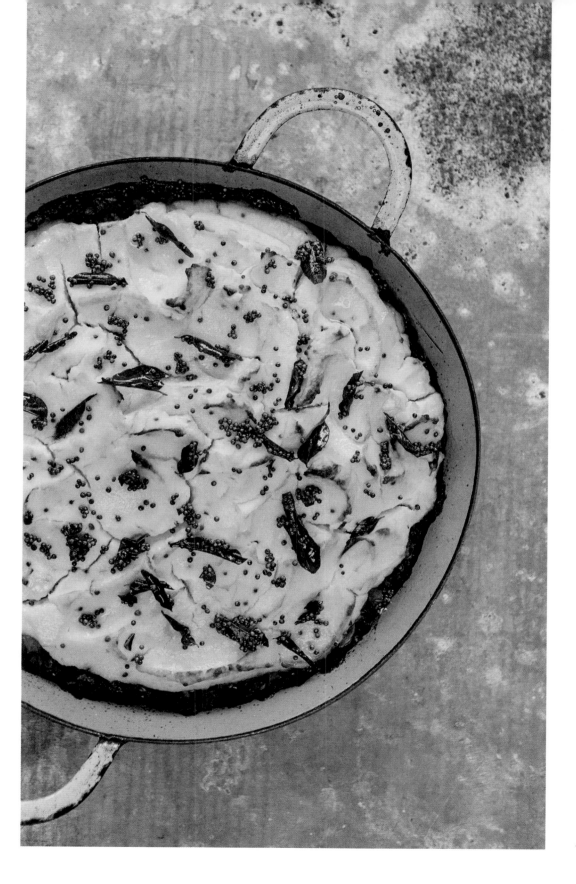

How to make a
green holiday wreath

On my wedding day a simple eucalyptus wreath hung on the door, the only decoration in the sixteenth-century church on the island halfway out to sea where we married. There is something so pleasing about the flow of a wreath—all the leaves and flowers trailing in a round after each other. Holiday decorations in our house are centered around flowers and foliage.

I made this wreath with the help of brilliant London florist Alex Whitmore, who filled our wedding with flowers and built an arch for us to get married under. We made the wreath by first wrapping little bunches, which made things look much more thoughtful. The house smelled of Christmas for days afterward. This wreath is made from the things I love—foliage, subtle berries, and different shades of green. I prefer to keep it tonal and simple, but if you like you could use brighter colors, red berries, and dried things like nigella pods or cinnamon sticks.

What you need

— Thin floristry wire, green is best

— Good sturdy scissors or pruning shears

— A round grapevine or wicker wreath, or a wire wreath frame—you can make your own with sturdy wire, too

— Ribbon for hanging

— Moss (optional)—you can buy this from a florist

— Lots of foliage—you will need more then you think, as you will have to strip the stems and you'll only want to use the nice bushy bits. You can buy this at a florist or forage for it in your garden or in local parks. Be sure to ask first, if it's not yours, and only take a little from each tree. We used juniper branches, lots of different types of eucalyptus, olive branches, mimosa, and privet.

1. Get everything together

Get all your equipment together and make sure you have enough space to work in. You will inevitably make a mess, so set up somewhere you can sweep up easily.

2. Attach the moss, if using

If you are using a metal or homemade wire frame, I'd recommend getting some moss. If you are using a wicker one, then you can skip this stage. Tear your moss up into pieces small enough to wrap around the frame. Attach it to the frame by wrapping the wire around it continuously. Make sure it's sturdy, as it is the foundation of the wreath. You don't want the wreath to be entirely flat, so use a good amount of moss to get a good round shape from the start.

3. Make bunches of foliage

Snip off little branches from your foliage. Whether you keep like foliage with like or not is up to you. If you're going for a tidier-looking wreath, try to make each clipping of a similar size. For a more organic look, use different lengths of foliage in each small bunch.

Use short pieces of wire to attach about four or five little branches together. You may need to strip a few leaves from the lower parts of stems to make it easier to bind them together.

4. Attach the bunches

One by one, attach the little bunches to the frame, tucking the stems into the moss, if using. Use the wire to secure the bundles firmly. You can keep the spool of wire continuously attached for ease.

5. Keep adding and turning

Keep adding the bunches in the same direction, turning the wreath as you go. Each bunch should overlap with the previous one, so no ends are showing.

6. Tweak

Have a look at your wreath and tweak if needed—snipping bits off or adding bits in if any of the foundational elements are showing.

Use some beautiful ribbon to hang on your door.

Tips

— Moss is a great foundation for this wreath. It gives depth, and also enables your foliage to last longer if you spray it every couple of days to keep it damp.

— Try to get as much texture and interest into the wreath as possible by using a variety of leaf shapes, tones, and sizes.

— If you want to make your wreath look symmetrical, try to keep your bunches similarly sized.

— If you desire a more architectural wreath, you can leave some of the wire frame exposed or strategically use color to give it an ombré look.

With thanks to Alex Whitmore, @ae_whitmore.

Apple, rye, and walnut Bundt

It's rare that I eat a cake without frosting, but this cake has everything going for it just as it is. It's light and generous due to the apple; the back note of the rye adds depth and the walnuts a buttery crunch. It's the kind of cake that is just the right wintry side of stodgy. You can use aquafaba (see page 459), to make it vegan.

This cake is also good with a little Greek or coconut yogurt whisked with some vanilla seeds or paste and a touch of honey.

SERVES 8–10

⅔ cup (190 g) canola oil or melted butter, plus extra for greasing

1½ cups (200 g) whole-wheat spelt flour, plus extra for the tin

14 ounces (400 g) apples, peeled, cored and roughly chopped (I use Cox's)

the zest and juice of 1 unwaxed lemon

½ teaspoon ground ginger

14 tablespoons (200 g) packed soft light brown sugar (such as Wholesome Foods)

⅓ cup (50 g) rye flour

2 teaspoons baking powder

a good pinch of flaky salt

1 cup (100 g) walnuts, roughly chopped

2 teaspoons vanilla paste

3 medium organic eggs

Preheat the oven to 375°F (190°C). Grease a 10-cup Bundt pan or Kugelhopf pan with canola oil or butter, then lightly dust the inside with flour and tap out any excess.

Put the apples in a bowl, add the lemon zest, and squeeze over a few drops of the lemon juice and toss well, then add the ginger and a tablespoon of the sugar. Toss to coat, then leave to one side to allow the flavors to mix and meld.

In another bowl combine the flours, baking powder, and salt and whisk to get rid of any lumps, then stir in the chopped walnuts.

Put the oil or butter into a pitcher with the rest of the sugar, the vanilla, eggs, and the lemon juice and mix to combine.

Stir the butter and sugar mixture into the dry mixture and mix well. Then stir in the apples and pour into the mold. Bake in the hot oven for 45 to 55 minutes, or until a skewer inserted in the center comes out clean.

Pull the cake out of the oven and leave the pan on a baking rack to cool for at least 30 minutes or until the pan feels cool. Turn the cake out onto a plate.

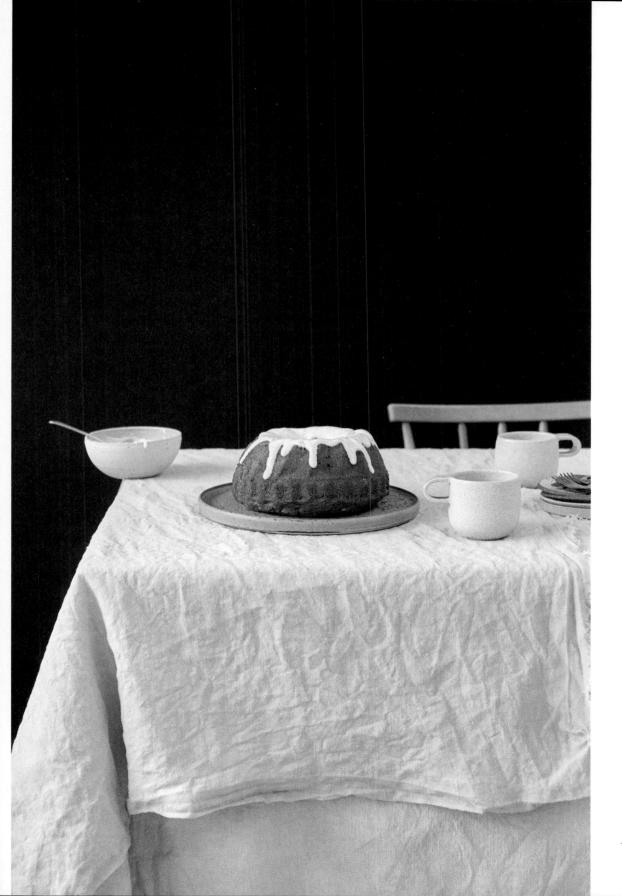

Almond and smoked-salt blondies

These blondies are somewhat bottle blonde. Though they don't have the cocoa or hefty amount of chocolate that a brownie would (which makes them a blondie), I do use muscovado sugar, which turns them a deep dark brunette. If you like, you could use a lighter sugar, though the deep maltiness of muscovado works so well. The topping is blonde, however—it's a quick, fudgy meringue-like almond topping that keeps them looking a bit blonder.

Sometimes I make these with a blend of spelt and rye flour, as I like the deep rich back note that the rye brings. The smoked salt adds something and works so well with the almonds and chocolate, but if you can't get hold of it, normal flaky salt will work just fine. These can also be made with coconut sugar and aquafaba (see page 459), which would make them vegan.

SERVES 8–10

2 teaspoons baking powder

½ teaspoon flaky smoked sea salt, plus a pinch

2 cups (250 g) white spelt flour

⅔ cup (190 g) coconut oil or unsalted butter

⅔ cup (125 g) lightly packed dark muscovado sugar

⅔ cup (125 g) superfine or caster sugar, plus an extra ¼ cup (50 g)

3 medium organic eggs

2 teaspoons good vanilla extract or paste

4½ ounces (125 g) dark chocolate (at least 70% cocoa solids), chopped into large pieces

¾ cup (100 g) almonds, skin on, roughly chopped

Preheat the oven to 395°F (200°C). Grease an 8-inch (20-cm) square baking pan and line with waxed paper.

Place the baking powder, salt, and flour in a bowl and mix together with a whisk to get rid of any lumps.

Place the coconut oil or butter in a pan and melt it. Add the sugars and whisk until they have mostly dissolved, then pour into a bowl. Set aside to cool for 15 minutes.

Separate one of the eggs and keep back about 1 tablespoon of the white, then put the rest into the bowl with the yolk and the rest of the eggs. Beat the eggs, coconut oil, and vanilla extract together with a whisk. Fold in the flour mixture and chocolate. Once everything is incorporated, pour the mixture into the lined tin.

Whisk the tablespoon of egg white until fluffy, then add the almonds, the extra ¼ cup (50 g) of superfine or caster sugar, and a pinch of salt. Spread over the top of the blondie mixture with a spatula. Bake in the oven for 30 minutes, until crisp on top and still a little gooey inside.

Leave to cool for 10 minutes, then remove from the pan, slice into squares, and try not to eat them all.

Toasted coconut rice pudding with sticky prunes

I make my own toasted coconut milk here, which is a genius idea that I got from my friend Heidi Swanson. I make a bigger batch than you will need, but it is a brilliant thing to have on hand for curries and soups, as well as to pour on cereal or add to porridge. You could also just use canned coconut milk and perhaps top the pudding with some toasted coconut. I toast the coconut for the milk so that it's deep golden but not burnt—this makes the milk very different in flavor to the calmer, more neutral flavor of regular coconut milk.

I make a quick topping with Pedro Ximénez sherry, which is gloriously thick and raisin-y, but you could also use some dark sherry with a couple of tablespoons of dark brown sugar. These prunes sit well with vanilla ice cream, whipped coconut yogurt or cream, or on the side of a simple tart.

SERVES 6

FOR THE TOASTED COCONUT MILK (MAKES 4½ CUPS/ 1 LITER)

2⅓ cups (200 g) coconut flakes

a pinch of flaky sea salt

FOR THE RICE PUDDING

butter or coconut oil, for greasing

½ cup (100 g) short-grain rice

⅓ cup (70 g) coconut sugar

1 teaspoon vanilla paste or the seeds of 1 vanilla pod

FOR THE PRUNES

1¼ cups (150 g) prunes, pitted

3 ounces (90 ml) Pedro Ximénez sherry

3½ tablespoons water

Preheat the oven to 425°F (220°C).

Spread out the coconut in a large roasting tray and place in the center of the oven. Toast for 5 to 10 minutes, until deeply golden all over, really brown but not burnt.

Put 4½ cups (1 liter) of cold water (preferably filtered) into your blender. Add the toasted coconut and salt and blitz on the highest setting for a couple of minutes, until as smooth as possible. Strain through a nut milk bag or a muslin cloth set over a bowl.

Turn the oven temperature down to 335°F (170°C) and lightly grease a 8-inch (20-cm) square pan with butter or coconut oil. Mix the rice, sugar, vanilla, 2 cups (500 ml) of the coconut milk (the rest can go into a jar in the fridge to use when you like) and 1¼ cups (300 ml) of water and stir well. Put the rice in the pan and bake for 90 minutes, stirring it three or four times to ensure it cooks evenly.

About 20 minutes before the rice is due to come out of the oven, place the prunes in a small, lidded saucepan with the sherry and water over low heat. Stew gently until the rice is done, and serve with 3 to 4 prunes per person.

Sea-salted chocolate and lemon mousse

This is a pretty maverick way of making a chocolate mousse, which was brought to my attention by a great chef friend. It's based on a technique by the French chemist Hervé This. Don't worry, it's really quite easy, though you do have to follow the recipe to the tee. It uses water, not cream, and the mousse is whipped over a bowl of ice, which chills the chocolate. The result is a cleaner, less cloying mousse that is unadulterated chocolate, backed up by a little lemon, salt, and vanilla. Lemon is rarely paired with chocolate, but I think it works incredibly well. If you'd prefer, orange or even lime could be added too.

Half-fill a large mixing bowl (or saucepan) with water and ice, then sit another mixing bowl inside it.

Put the chocolate, salt, honey, vanilla, and lemon zest into a saucepan with ¾ cup (175 ml) of cold water. Place on a low heat and stir until it all comes together and the chocolate has just melted.

Use a spatula to scrape the mixture into the mixing bowl set over the ice bath and whisk with a balloon whisk (an electric one will be too powerful). Keep whisking until it looks shiny but isn't yet set (like a thick chocolate sauce). The whisk will make little ribbons of chocolate on the mousse when lifted. You will be whisking for about 3 minutes, but keep an eye on it; as the mousse will thicken really quickly, and will set in the fridge as it cools. Have a taste and check if you're happy with the flavor. If the mousse tastes a little grainy, it is probably because it has been over-whisked. Don't panic, just scrape the mixture back into the original saucepan, melt, and start again.

Once ready, spoon into ramekins and place in the fridge. Chill for at least 3 hours before serving.

To make the brittle, have a plate lined with waxed paper ready. Toast the sesame seeds in a pan over medium heat until well browned, then add the maple syrup and take off the heat. Scoop the seed mixture onto the waxed paper and leave to cool completely.

Serve the mousse topped with sesame seeds and the brittle.

SERVES 4

7 ounces (200 g) dark chocolate (at least 70% cocoa solids)

a good pinch of flaky sea salt

2 tablespoons golden honey

the seeds from 1 vanilla pod

the zest of ½ unwaxed lemon

FOR THE QUICK BRITTLE

½ cup (50 g) sesame seeds, plus extra to finish

2 tablespoons maple syrup

Fig, banana, and dark chocolate cake

SERVES 10–12

⅓ cup (60 g) coconut oil, melted, plus extra for greasing

2 tablespoons milled flax seeds

¾ cup plus 2 tablespoons (200 ml) hazelnut or almond milk (I use unsweetened)

2 teaspoons cider vinegar

2⅔ cups (400 g) dried figs, stalks removed

2½ teaspoons baking soda

2¾ cups (360 g) whole-wheat spelt flour

½ teaspoon baking powder

1 teaspoon coarse sea salt, finely ground

½ teaspoon ground cinnamon

14 ounces (400 g) peeled banana (about 4 large bananas)

3½ ounces (100 g) applesauce

1 teaspoon vanilla extract

7 ounces (200 g) dark chocolate (85% cocoa solids), chopped

FOR THE FROSTING

Generous ¾ cup (190 ml) maple syrup

1⅓ cups (120 g) raw cacao powder

¾ cup (180 g) almond milk (I use unsweetened)

1½ teaspoons vanilla paste

⅔ cup (120 g) coconut oil, melted

a pinch of flaky sea salt

This is the cake I baked for Dylan's first birthday. I wanted a cake with no sugar and filled with good stuff. Dylan ate very little of his piece; instead he rubbed it all over his face and threw it on the floor, which he really enjoyed, so I guess that's the point. The rest of us loved it, and I have made it for almost every celebration since. This cake has got more steps than I would usually go for, but it means you get a light cake with a good crumb and some serious depth of flavor. This is loosely based on a recipe from my friend Henrietta Inman. The recipe makes enough for four-tier cake, but if you want a smaller cake, just halve the quantities.

———————————————

Preheat the oven to 375°F (190°C) and line the base of two 8-inch (18–20-cm) round loose-bottom cake pans with parchment paper. Grease the sides with coconut oil.

Mix the flax seeds with 3 tablespoons of water and leave for about 15 minutes to form a gel. Combine your chosen nut milk with the cider vinegar and set aside.

Roughly chop the figs, then put them in a medium saucepan with 1⅔ cups (400 ml) of cold water and bring to a boil. Turn down to a medium boil and boil until all the water has evaporated and the figs are soft. Remove from the heat and immediately add 1 teaspoon of the baking soda; the figs will fizz a little. Set aside to cool slightly.

Mix the spelt flour, the rest of the baking soda, baking powder, sea salt, and cinnamon and whisk to get rid of any lumps.

Mash together the bananas, apple purée, coconut oil, and vanilla extract and add the flax seed gel and nut milk mix.

Blitz the figs with an immersion blender to make a figgy paste, leaving a good amount of lumps, and add to the banana, flax, and milk mix. Finally fold in all the dry ingredients and the chocolate until just combined. Transfer to your prepared pan. →

Bake for 30 minutes, then reduce the oven temperature to 355°F (180°C) and bake for another 15 to 20 minutes, or until a skewer inserted in the center comes out almost clean. Leave the cakes to cool in their pans until completely cold.

To make the frosting, put all the ingredients into a blender and whizz until smooth. If it is very runny, you may want to put it in the fridge for 10 to 15 minutes to firm up a little, then take it out and leave at room temperature until you are ready to use it.

Cut each cake in half horizontally so you have four layers in total. Dab a little frosting on the plate you're going to serve the cake on, to keep it still. Place the first layer on top, add a quarter of the frosting, and spread it over the top. Repeat with the following layers, finishing with the last quarter of frosting on the top.

The cake will last a good 3 to 4 days in the fridge in a sealed container.

Mozzarella and citrus with toasted cilantro seeds

This is a very lovely thing to eat at any time but I find it particularly good around Christmas—the citrus is at its best and the freshness it brings really punctuates the rest of the richness in our kitchen at this time of the year. I love the addition of cilantro seeds, toasted to within an inch of their life to bring out a buttery citrus note that makes this little plate sing. Use the best olive oil you can get your hands on.

SERVES 4

1 tablespoon cilantro (coriander) seeds

4 clementines or blood oranges

2 balls of buffalo mozzarella (about 8¾ ounces/250 g)

2 tablespoons crème fraîche

seeds from ½ a pomegranate

4 handfuls of peppery greens

2 tablespoons good extra-virgin olive oil

Toast the cilantro seeds in a dry pan until they smell really fragrant and have turned a deeper brown. Bash them in a mortar with pestle or grind in a spice grinder until you have a fine powder.

Next, using a very sharp knife, slice one end off a clementine so that it sits flat against your cutting board, then cut away the peel and any pith in strips from top to bottom so that no pithy white is visible. Turn the clementine on to its side and slice into thin rounds. Repeat with the other three.

Tear the mozzarella into large pieces, divide among four plates, then spoon the crème fraîche on top. Season well, then add a good pinch of the toasted cilantro. Put the clementine slices on the plates and add the pomegranate seeds. Drizzle over the oil and serve with good bread and lemon and oil-dressed leaves.

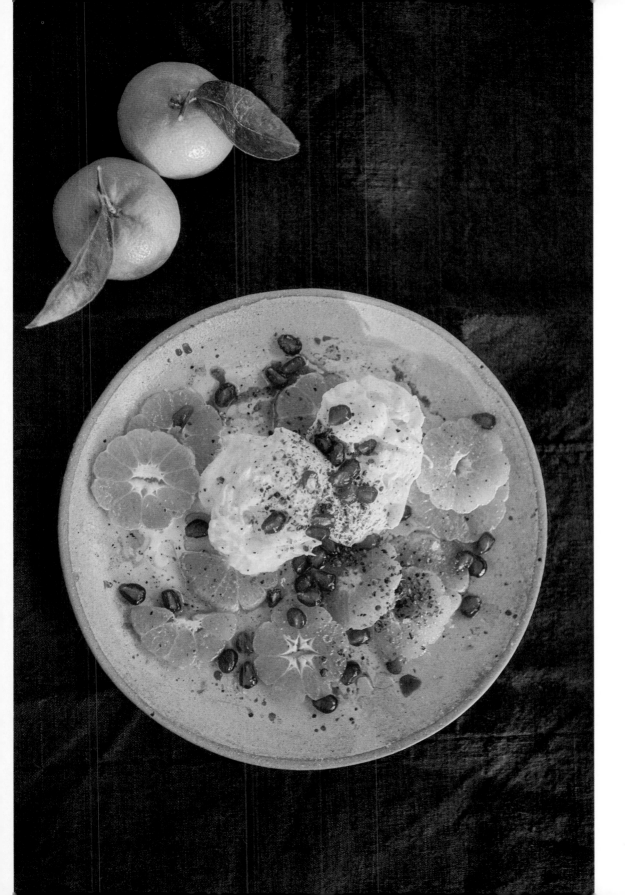

Christmas Eve orecchiette

This pasta is a little more indulgent than my usual weeknight pasta, as sometimes when we are all gathered I veer toward a bit more decadence. I often make this on Christmas Eve; the warming blanket of cheesy pasta in a bowl can be eaten from laps while last presents are wrapped. It suits pretty much any winter evening, though. You can use almost any good melting cheese you have on hand or a mixture—fontina is my favorite, but Cheddar or soft goat cheese would work too. You could also use kale or greens instead of broccoli.

Bring a large pan of salted water to a boil; meanwhile, chop the stalks of the broccoli into ⅜-inch (1-cm) pieces, leaving the florets intact.

Put the broccoli into the water and cook for 3 minutes, until tender and still bright green. Remove with a slotted spoon (don't drain it—you need the hot water) and leave in a colander to steam dry.

Reduce the heat to low and place a large heatproof bowl on top of the pan, making sure it doesn't touch the water. Add the crème fraîche to the bowl, along with the fontina and lemon zest, then stir. Once the cheese has melted, carefully remove the bowl from the heat and set aside, then turn the heat up to high.

Add the pasta to the water and cook according to the package instructions. Meanwhile, mix the hazelnuts with the thyme, lemon zest, olive oil, and a good pinch of salt. Heat a frying pan over medium heat, then add the nut mixture and cook for 3 to 4 minutes, until crisp and starting to brown.

Once the pasta is ready, put the broccoli back into the pan, leave for 30 seconds, just to warm it through, then drain, reserving a mugful of the cooking water for later.

Put the pasta and broccoli into the bowl of melted cheese and toss to coat, adding a splash of the reserved cooking water to loosen the cheese to a smooth, silky sauce.

Transfer to a serving bowl, sprinkle the nuts on top, and serve.

SERVE 6

FOR THE PASTA

sea salt

14 ounces (400 g) purple sprouting broccoli, trimmed

4 tablespoons crème fraîche

2¼ cups (250 g) fontina (see note above), rind removed

the zest of 1 unwaxed lemon

1 pound (455 g) orecchiette

FOR THE CRISPY HAZELNUTS

1¼ cups (100 g) hazelnuts, skin on, finely chopped

a few sprigs of thyme, leaves picked and finely chopped

the zest of 1 unwaxed lemon

3 tablespoons olive oil

Celebration celeriac and sweet garlic pie

This has been my Christmas centerpiece for the last couple of years. It is everything I want in a pie: a Cheddar and winter herb flaky pastry; a creamy filling, sweet with balsamic garlic and roasted celeriac; and a crisp grated celeriac roof. This high-sided pie takes a little time, but at Christmas I think that's OK.

————————————

Put the flour in a mixing bowl. Add the butter and salt. Rub gently with your fingertips until the mixture is like fine bread crumbs. Stir in the herbs, lemon zest, and Cheddar.

Beat the egg yolk with 1 tablespoon of cold water. Add to the flour and mix until it forms a dough. Add more water, a teaspoon at a time, until it comes together into a smooth dough. Wrap and chill in the fridge while you make the filling.

For the filling, put the cloves of garlic in a saucepan, cover with cold water, and bring to a gentle simmer. Cook for 2 to 3 minutes, then drain.

Wipe the saucepan dry. Add the garlic and 1 tablespoon of olive oil and fry over high heat for 2 minutes. Add the balsamic vinegar and 7 tablespoons (100 ml) water, bring to a boil, and simmer gently for 10 minutes.

Add the honey, most of the rosemary and thyme (reserving the rest, with the sage), and a good pinch of salt. Continue to cook on medium heat for another 5 minutes, or until most of the liquid has evaporated and the garlic cloves are coated in a dark syrup.

Meanwhile, peel the celeriac and cut it into quarters. Set aside 10 ounces (300 g) and slice the rest into ¾-inch- (2-cm-) thick pieces. Put them into a saucepan, cover with hot water and boil for 7 to 10 minutes, until they are soft and have turned slightly translucent. →

SERVES 8–10

FOR THE PASTRY

scant 1 cup (250 g) plain spelt flour, plus a little extra for dusting

9 tablespoons cold unsalted butter, cubed

½ teaspoon fine sea salt

a few sprigs each of rosemary, thyme, and sage, leaves picked and finely chopped

the zest of 1 unwaxed lemon

3½ tablespoons good grated Cheddar

1 medium egg yolk

3 to 5 tablespoons (50–70 ml) cold water

FOR THE FILLING

3 heads of garlic, cloves separated and peeled

olive oil

1 teaspoon balsamic vinegar

1 tablespoon golden honey

2 sprigs each of rosemary, thyme, and sage, leaves picked and finely chopped, plus extra to finish

2¼ pounds (1 kg) celeriac

8 ounces (220 g) Lancashire or good Cheddar cheese, crumbled (2 cups)

½ cup (150 g) crème fraîche

the juice of ½ a lemon

1 tablespoon whole-grain mustard

a small bunch of parsley, chopped

Worcestershire sauce

2 organic eggs, beaten

freshly ground black pepper

Drain and put in a big mixing bowl. Add the cheese, crème fraîche, lemon juice, mustard, parsley, a splash of Worcestershire sauce, and eggs. Add a good pinch of salt and grind of pepper, and gently fold in the garlic cloves.

Preheat the oven to 355°F (180°C). Sprinkle flour onto a work surface and roll out the pastry to ⅛-inch (3–4 mm) thick. Line a 8-inch- (20-cm-) diameter cake pan with the pastry, ensuring a little spills over the edges.

Pour the filling into the pastry crust. Coarsely grate the reserved celeriac and pile it on top. Finish with the reserved rosemary and thyme, all the sage, and a drizzle of olive oil. Bake for 45 minutes, or until the tart filling has set and the top is golden brown.

Remove from the oven, leave to cool a little, then take it out of the pan. Lay a few herbs on top and serve warm.

Setting a celebratory table

Setting a table is a job I love; every task tinged with the anticipation that the table will soon be filled with friends and family. There is something so magical about leading people into a room with a set table, candles, and music. With a mood set you can serve simple food, but everything will feel a bit more considered.

I have a bit of an obsession with tableware; from glasses to napkins, pitchers to platters, every nook of my kitchen is filled. When setting a table, think about using different heights. Glassware, candles, and flowers will all add to the rise and fall. Use one color or fabric as a guide, and then build everything around that. Most of all, though, make it casual and achievable; use what you have for everyday with a few added touches.

Linen

A tablecloth or a linen runner is always where I start, then you can layer up fabrics creating amazing texture. You can buy linen tablecloths now pretty affordably from most homeware shops, or buy a couple of yards off the roll from a crafts store. I like to wash mine and hang it on the cloting line so it has a crumpled texture and isn't too neat. Brown paper is a good substitute if linen feels too much. You can cut place mats from fabric too; the frayed edges look nice. Muted base tones work well for lots of different occasions, then you can use other things to create accents.

Flowers and foliage

Use the season's plants and blooms as decoration. Herbs are amazing; they will make the table smell good too. I put my herbs or flowers in little bottles, jars, and modern stem vases, usually only one or two stems in each vase, and play with height. Here are some ideas of what to use throughout the year.

Winter: bay leaves, rosemary, snowdrops, winter berries and twigs, little bags of homemade truffles. Eucalyptus looks great laid down the middle of the table.

Spring: bunches of primroses, daffodils, painted Easter eggs, chocolate eggs, hyacinths.

Summer: sweet peas, roses, lemons, bunches of aromatic mint, lavender, cherries, lemons.

Autumn: imperfect squashes, rosehips in little pitchers, autumn leaves, skeleton leaves, seed heads, dainty pine cones.

Place settings

Menus are nice mementos for people to take home; I have a shoebox of menus that I love to look at. They can be written on simple cards or paper in your best handwriting.

Place settings are a good idea if you want to choreograph who sits where, written simply on cards or even on little stones with a chalk pen or marker.

If it's a really special dinner, you could think about homemade gifts: teas, little meringues, essential oil blends, homemade truffles, small bottles of sloe gin or cordial. I did this at my wedding but haven't done it since, so I'm talking really special meals here.

Drinks

I like to keep drinks on the table or near it if they're in small ice buckets and pitchers. That way you don't have to top off everyone's drink all night. I always keep a couple of pitchers of flavored water on hand: blackberry and sage; cucumber and mint; bergamot or lemon; rosemary and thyme.

I use a mixture of different glasses: Duralex, fine glass tumblers, and Champagne saucers. Charity shops and garage sales are amazing places to pick up old glassware.

Napkins

Linen napkins are easy to find and quite reasonable, but you can also use fabric pieces. If they have a bold pattern, fold them inside out, or use squares of soft denim or simple white cloth. Tie velvet ribbon, brown string, or brightly colored twine around them; you can also lay leaves, herbs, or even pressed flowers on top, securing them with a nice paper clip or even some bright washi tape.

Lights and candles

Lights are so important. I go for candles: sometimes just one, other times a mixture. Church candles, classic tapered beeswax ones, tea lights in glasses are all cheap. I love to use dark candles in gray, navy, and black. For something more special, festoon lights, fairy lights, or even paper lanterns hanging from the ceiling would all look amazing too.

Serving your food

I don't have matching sets of everything. I do keep plates white and pretty similar, but the rest is a mixture of treasured things: platters for food, bowls for dipping and snacks. My table is a tapestry of everything I love—I almost always put all the food in the middle rather than serving it plated; I love the interaction, the hand crossing and passing around. Shop around for interesting things from antiques and vintage fairs.

Kids' tables

Color and fun are key here. I make my kids' tables every color of the rainbow with party hats, pom-poms, colored napkins. Once I even made biscuits with names on them—admittedly, that was going a bit far.

Membrillo, buttermilk, and poppy-seed cake

This is quite a decadent cake. It uses membrillo, the quince paste that we eat with cheese at Christmas, to make an insanely good festive cake. I bake it in a brownie pan but you could use a standard cake pan too. Membrillo can be quite expensive but any fruit cheese (damson, pear) would work well in its place. There isn't much other sugar in the cake batter, as most of it comes from the membrillo. I have also made a version of this swapping good marzipan for the membrillo, which is equally delicious.

SERVES 15

⅓ cup (75 ml) canola oil or melted butter, plus a little extra

2 cups (250 g) white spelt flour, plus a little extra for the pan

1 tablespoon baking powder

⅓ cup (70 g) superfine or caster sugar

½ teaspoon fine sea salt

½ cup (60 g) poppy seeds

the zest of 2 unwaxed lemons

2 medium organic eggs

1½ cups (350 ml) yogurt or buttermilk

8¾ ounces (250 g) membrillo (quince paste), cut into tiny cubes

2 tablespoons demerara (or coarse brown/turbinado) sugar

¼ cup (20 g) almonds, skin on, lightly toasted and chopped

Preheat the oven to 425°F (220°C). Grease and flour an 8-by-12-inch (20-by-30-cm) baking dish.

Combine the flour, baking powder, superfine or caster sugar, salt, poppy seeds, and lemon zest in a large bowl.

In a separate smaller bowl, whisk together the eggs and the yogurt, then whisk in the oil or melted butter.

Add to the flour mixture and stir briefly, until just combined. Gently fold in two-thirds of the membrillo cubes until they are evenly distributed. Transfer the cake mixture to the prepared dish. Arrange the remaining membrillo across the top in a pleasing pattern. Sprinkle with the demerara sugar, then the almonds.

Bake for 20 to 25 minutes or until a toothpick inserted in the center comes out clean. Serve warm or at room temperature.

Winter

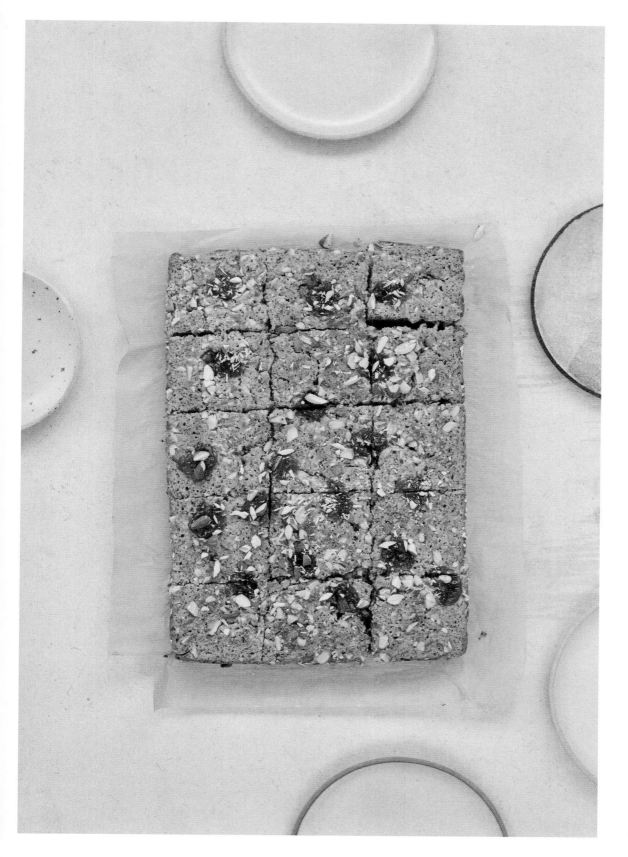

Salted chocolate truffles

MAKES ABOUT 48

⅓ cup (60 g) coconut oil, plus a little extra to grease

2 tablespoons (30 g) coconut sugar or light brown sugar

¾ cup (200 g) raw almond or cashew or hazelnut butter

7 ounces (200 g) dark chocolate (at least 70% cocoa solids)

the seeds from 1 vanilla pod

2 big pinches of flaky sea salt

ADDITIONAL FLAVORS

the zest of 1 unwaxed orange

the zest of 1 unwaxed lemon

the zest of 1 unwaxed lime

swap the salt for smoked sea salt

1 red chile, finely chopped

2 cardamom pods, seeds removed and crushed

½ teaspoon ground cinnamon

TO COAT (USE ONE OR MORE)

⅓ cup (50 g) raw cacao or cocoa powder

finely chopped pistachios, almonds, hazelnuts

finely chopped candied orange peel

finely chopped candied ginger

grated chocolate (dark, milk, or white)

crushed dried rose petals

These are very easy truffles: no tempering chocolate; no rolling or filling; just some simple melting, mixing, and pouring—your own little chocolate factory. This batch makes a lot, and will keep you in truffles for a couple of weeks or can be wrapped up and given as Christmas presents. If you are giving them as a gift, do remember to tell whomever you are giving them to that they need to be kept in the fridge (they will be fine out of the fridge for a few hours, though). These truffles are made with coconut oil, nut butter, and coconut sugar, so they don't give me the crazy sugar high of other chocolates.

I have given you a choice of flavorings and coatings so you can take the basic mixture and make it as flavorful or as colorful as you like.

Grease an 8-inch square brownie pan with coconut oil. Heat the coconut oil and sugar in a saucepan over low heat. Once the oil has melted and the sugar has dissolved into the oil, take the pan off the heat and add the nut butter, chocolate, vanilla, and salt. Stir off the heat until everything has melted. If you're adding another flavor, stir it in now.

Pour the mixture into the pan. Chill for about 2 hours, until set solid. While the truffle mix is cooling, get your chosen coating or coatings ready and put each in a little bowl.

Once set, turn the truffle slab out onto a cool work surface and cut into squares (mine are ½ inch/1–1½ cm), then gently dip each truffle in its coating to cover.

The truffles will keep in the fridge for up to 2 weeks in a sealed container.

Vanilla and lime
mulled wine

This is the mulled wine I have been making for years and it's as delicious as it is offbeat. You make a quick syrup infusion to ensure you get as much flavor as possible out of the spices and aromatics, then add the rest of the wine and warm through so that all the alcohol doesn't boil away.

Strip the zest from the clementines and limes, using a potato peeler to produce large pieces. Juice the fruit.

Put the sugar in a large saucepan over medium heat, then add the pieces of peel and the fruit juice. Add the cloves, cinnamon stick, bay leaves, star anise, and about 10 gratings of nutmeg. Halve the vanilla pods lengthways and add to the pan, then stir in just enough red wine to cover the sugar.

Let this simmer until the sugar has completely dissolved into the red wine, then bring to a boil and simmer for 4 to 5 minutes to allow the heat to bring out the flavors.

Turn the heat down to low and add the rest of the wine. Gently heat without boiling, then cover and leave to sit for about 30 minutes. When you are ready to serve, warm the mulled wine again without boiling and ladle it into heatproof glasses.

SERVE 10

2 clementines

2 limes

½ cup (100 g) light brown sugar or maple syrup

6 cloves

1 cinnamon stick

3 fresh bay leaves, crushed in your hands

2 star anise

1 whole nutmeg

2 vanilla pods

2 bottles of good, full-bodied red wine

Bergamot gin

Winter is the time for citrus in every shade, from lemon chiffon to saffron mandarins, tangerines, Moro blood oranges, kumquats, and tiny key limes. To my delight, I managed to get my hands on some Meyer lemons recently, a less acidic variety, with a sherbet tangerine kick—they hail from California. Any of these citrus fruits would work well in this gin, but I've used my favorite of all, the bergamot.

The heady bergamot orange is a fragrant citrus that grows in France and Italy. It looks like a squat green lemon. Its juice is more acidic than lemon, but its peel is uplifting—it has a deeper, almost woody citrus scent. I adore it. You can also buy bergamot lemons that look like a traditional lemon but taste sweeter, with a more orange skin; I like to use the greener bergamot oranges, as they have more of the floral lemony notes I love, but both work. I have made a pretty pink-tinged blood orange version too.

I make this in a similar way to limoncello, with some added sugar, so it's sweeter than regular gin, meaning you can drink it straight over ice or in a gin and tonic. I made a big batch this year that I'm saving for next year's Christmas presents.

Peel long strips of rind from the bergamots using a vegetable peeler, taking care not to use too much of a heavy hand; otherwise, you'll end up with a lot of bitter pith.

Place the peel in the bottom of a lidded clean glass jar or bottle and add the gin, using a funnel if it's easier. Leave in a dark place for the flavors to develop; this can take from 1 to 3 weeks. Generally, once the peel has turned white, all its flavor has been infused.

Once your gin has had its steeping time you are ready to mix it with the sugar syrup. Put the sugar and 1¼ cups (300 ml) of cold water into a saucepan and bring to a gentle boil, allowing all the sugar to dissolve, then simmer for another 10 minutes. Allow to cool completely.

Strain the gin into a pitcher, then add about the same volume of sugar syrup and taste it, adding a little more to taste—the more sugar, the smoother the flavor.

Pour the gin into sterilized bottles and secure with a top. It will keep for years, although it's unlikely to last that long.

MAKES 2¾ CUPS (650 ML)

6 bergamots (see note above)

2 cups (500 ml) good gin

1⅓ cups (300 g) packed superfine or caster sugar

Grapefruit and bay bitters

Last Christmas was a write-off. We all got ill—a rare occurrence in our family—and Christmas was canceled. Once we were better, we finally managed to get dressed and walk to the local pub. We sat around a table, all a bit overexcited to be outside. We ordered gin and tonics—not the traditional recovery remedy, I guess—and they arrived in huge glasses, with cucumber, elderflower, and spiked with the most delicious grapefruit bitters. The bitters turned a pretty standard gin and tonic into something incredible. I don't drink that much, so when I do have a glass of wine or a gin and tonic, I want it to be the best it can possibly be.

I'd never thought of making bitters before, but after a bit of research I couldn't believe how easy they were—a few flavors left in some alcohol for a few weeks. They make a great present in a nice little bottle too. You could swap in most citrus here.

MAKES 1 CUP (250 ML)

1 grapefruit

1 orange

¼ teaspoon cilantro (coriander) seeds

½ teaspoon black peppercorns

1 bay leaf

⅜-inch (1-cm) piece of cinnamon stick

1 cardamom pod, just split open

1 vanilla pod, split open

1 coffee bean

1 cup (250 ml) vodka

Preheat the oven to 285°F (140°C). Very finely peel the zest from both the grapefruit and the orange, using a vegetable peeler, and spread it out on a baking sheet. Bake for 20 minutes, until dry but not quite brittle, then remove and allow to cool on the tray.

Put the zest with all the other ingredients into a large jar and pour over the vodka. Leave to steep for 2 to 3 weeks. How quickly it steeps will depend on the warmth of the room and the potency of all the ingredients, so once you hit 2 weeks, keep tasting it, and bottle it once you are happy with the flavor.

Strain the vodka through a muslin cloth, squeezing through all the last bits of liquid. Pour into a little bottle and store in a cool place; it should keep for years, as only a dash is used at a time.

To use the bitters, add half a teaspoon to a gin and tonic or to sparkling water.

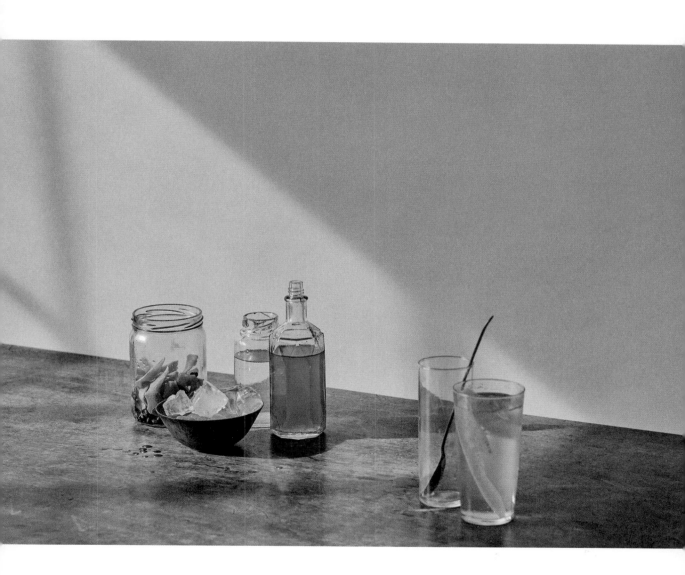

Basics

Labneh

A strained yogurt that is thicker than Greek yogurt. Use it like ricotta in salads or mix with herbs and lemon zest, and drizzle with good oil to use as a dip. You can even roll it into balls and store them under oil in the fridge if you want to keep it a little longer; it will keep for 5 to 6 days. This is a staple in our house and we make about a batch a week. Remember to make it the night before you want to eat it.

MAKES ABOUT 1½ CUPS (350 G)

1 teaspoon flaky sea salt	2 cups (500 g) full-fat Greek yogurt

Whisk the salt into the yogurt. Pour into the middle of a piece of cheesecloth set in a sieve resting over a bowl, tie the corners together, and suspend over the bowl in the fridge overnight. If you don't have cheesecloth, you can strain it through a coffee filter.

The following day, gently remove the labneh from the cheesecloth and store it in the fridge. Bring to room temperature before using.

Yogurt flatbread

There is a corner shop about 100 paces from my house, but I still find myself making these in a fix; they are pleasingly simple and also work brilliantly in a frying pan or on a grill.

MAKES 4

1⅔ cups (200 g) plain flour (I use spelt), plus extra for dusting	¾ cup (200 g) Greek yogurt, or 10 tablespoons (150 ml) warm water
1 teaspoon baking powder	

Put all the ingredients into the bowl of your food processor and pulse until the mixture forms a ball. If you don't have a food processor, this can be done in a bowl using a fork to begin with, followed by your hands; it will just take a little longer.

Turn the dough out onto a clean work surface dusted with flour and knead for a minute or so, to bring it all together. Put the dough into a flour-dusted bowl and cover with a plate. Put to one side to rise a little for 10 to 15 minutes. Don't expect it to rise like normal dough, but it may puff up a tiny bit.

Dust another clean work surface and rolling pin with flour, then divide the dough into four equal pieces. Using your hands, pat and flatten out the dough, then use the rolling pin to roll each piece into a disk roughly 8 inches (20 cm) in diameter and ⅛-inch (2–3-mm) thick.

To cook in a frying pan: Warm a frying pan or griddle that's a bit larger than your flatbread over medium heat. Once your pan is nicely hot, cook each flatbread for 1 to 2 minutes on each side, until nicely puffed up and golden in places, turning it with tongs.

To cook on a barbecue: Once your barbecue flames have died down but it's still good and hot, cook each flatbread for 1 to 2 minutes on each side, turning with tongs, until nicely puffed up, and a little charred (see page 274 for some barbecue tips).

Quick, no-rise frying pan pizza dough

To get a super-crisp base, start your pizza in a thick-based pan on the heat; I use a an 11-inch (28-cm) cast-iron one, but you could use a couple of smaller ones. If you don't have a cast-iron pan, put your dough on a thick baking sheet on the stovetop instead, which will help with the crust.

MAKES 2 MEDIUM PIZZAS

2⅓ cups (300 g) white spelt flour, plus extra for dusting

10 tablespoons (150 ml) tepid water

1 teaspoon baking powder

fine sea salt

1 tablespoon olive oil, plus more for cooking

Preheat your oven to 475°F (240°C) or as hot as it will go. You'll also need a large frying pan for this recipe (it needs to be ovenproof).

Put the flour, water, and baking powder into a food processor with a good pinch of salt and the tablespoon of olive oil and pulse until the dough comes together in a ball. You could also do this in a bowl using a fork to begin with, followed by your hands; it will just take a little longer. Turn it out and bring the dough together in your hands.

Get your frying pan on medium-high heat (if you have two pans about the right size you can do both pizzas at once). Cut the dough into two equal halves and cover one half. Put the other half on to a floured work surface and roll it out into a ⅜-inch- (1-cm-) thick circle, about the size of your frying pan.

Gather all your toppings, drizzle a little oil into the hot pan, then lift the dough into the pan. Leave it on the heat for about 3 minutes, so the base is starting to cook, then quickly top your pizza (see the toppings chart below) and put it into the oven for 8 to 10 minutes. Be careful when taking it out, as the pan handle will be very hot!

Slow sourdough pizza base

To make this recipe you will need an active sourdough starter—this is a mixture of flour and water that has been left to ferment over time. You would normally keep it in your fridge and "feed" it with flour and water once a week. If you don't have a starter, see if you can get a friend to give you one—the best starters are ones that have been alive for years.

Assuming you are going to make the dough in the evening to make pizzas for the next day's lunch or dinner, you will need to feed your sourdough starter using your normal method that morning. Repeat this again at

Base sauce	Cheese	Vegetable	Flourish
pesto	ricotta	blanched purple sprouting broccoli	olives and capers
romesco sauce	Parmesan (I use a vegetarian/ rennet-free one)	grilled zucchini and their flowers	herbs—basil/rosemary/ thyme/oregano
garlic and olive oil	pecorino (I use a vegetarian/ rennet-free one)	wilted greens	fresh red or green chile
tomato sauce	Taleggio	radicchio	an egg cracked in the middle
roasted tomato tomato sauce	mozzarella	thinly sliced new potatoes	a sprinkling of red pepper flakes and fennel seeds

457

lunchtime, then leave the starter at room temperature (it should be nice and bubbly).

Your starter will be active enough to use by the evening.

You can also use this dough to make sourdough loaves (see below).

**MAKES 6 MEDIUM PIZZAS
OR 12 SMALL PIZZETTE**

10½ ounces (300 g)
    sourdough starter

1⅔ cups (300 g)
    whole-wheat flour

2 cups (300 g) white
    spelt flour, plus
    extra for dusting

1¼ cups (300 ml)
    lukewarm water

3 teaspoons (15 g)
    fine sea salt

Combine all the ingredients except the salt in a large mixing bowl. Stir with a large wooden spoon until it comes together then use your hands to bring it together into a ball. Let the dough rest in a floured bowl for 20 minutes, then sprinkle over the salt and mix again. Turn the dough out onto a clean floured work surface and knead for 5 to 10 minutes, until it is no longer sticky (add additional flour if the dough is too sticky or water if it is too dry).

Split the dough into four balls and put them on a floured baking sheet. Cover with a damp kitchen towel and put them in the fridge for 12 to 24 hours.

Take the dough out of the fridge about 2 hours before you plan to make the pizzas.

Follow the instructions on page 457 for how to make pizza.

If you don't want to use all the dough to make pizza immediately, you can freeze the dough. Once the four balls have had their fridge proof, divide each ball into three again and place in the freezer on a baking sheet overnight, and then pop into a freezer bag, where they will keep for 3 months. Defrost the dough fully before using it, then flour a work surface well and stretch out the dough with your hands until you're happy with the shape and size. Add your toppings and bake as usual.

To make a sourdough loaf

This dough can also be baked as a large 2-pound (1-kg) loaf or two smaller 1-pound (500-g) loaves. To do this don't split the dough into four before the first proof, then knock it back after the first proof and shape it in a round or place into two 1-pound (500-g) containers. Allow it to proof overnight in the fridge, covered loosely with a clean cloth, until the dough has doubled in size and doesn't spring back when pressed with a finger. Take the loaves out of the fridge 2 hours before you want to bake them and let them come to room temperature. Preheat your oven to 475°F (240°C), then bake small loaves for 30 minutes and a large one for 45 to 50 minutes, until golden and it sounds hollow when tapped.

Homemade milk from nuts, oats, and seeds

I have a few types of milk in my fridge at any one time, usually a small carton of organic cow's milk, almond milk, and oat milk. I like to vary the kinds of milk I use, to make sure I am getting as much nutrition as possible and to make the most of their individual flavors.

It is easy, more nutritious, and much cheaper to make your own nondairy milk at home. All you need is a decent blender and a nut milk bag (a muslin bag made for draining nut milk), or failing that, a piece of muslin or a thin tea towel.

These milks can be made from most nuts and seeds and some grains. My favorites are almonds, pistachios, walnuts, hazelnuts, macadamia nuts, cashew nuts, sunflower seeds, pumpkin seeds, sesame seeds, hemp seeds, and oats. Here is a universal recipe that can be used for any of these. It works on ratios rather than weight, so I use a U.S. cup measure, but if you don't have one of these don't worry—a mug will work fine.

Take 1 cup of your chosen nut, seed, or oat and place in a bowl. Cover with a cup of cold (ideally filtered) water and leave to soak for 8 hours; this will allow the nut to release all its nutrients and maximize the goodness in your milk.

Once the soaking time is up, drain the nuts and place in a blender, discarding the soaking water. Add 4 cups of fresh cold (ideally filtered) water to the blender and blitz until you have a thin, smooth, cloudy mixture.

You can add any flavorings at this point if you like: a teaspoon of vanilla paste or the seeds from a pod, a few dates, or a tablespoon of golden honey to sweeten. Spices like cinnamon (about a teaspoon) and cardamom (half a teaspoon) also work well. Once added, blitz again.

Put a nut milk bag or cloth over the mouth of a pitcher and pour the nut milk through. Allow it to sit and drip into the pitcher or bowl for 5 to 10 minutes, then use your hands to squeeze out as much moisture from the nuts as you can.

Pour the milk into a clean bottle; it will keep in the fridge for 3 to 4 days. The leftover nut pulp can be added to hummus or can be used in place of ground almonds in baking.

A quick note on toasting nuts

I use toasted nuts in a lot of my recipes. I have assumed that most people know how to toast nuts, but if it's not something you do regularly, here is a quick guide.

To toast in the oven: Put your nuts on a baking sheet in an oven preheated to 390°F (200°C) for 4 to 8 minutes, depending on the size of the nut and how much you want them toasted. Once toasted, pour into a bowl and leave to cool: they will keep cooking if you leave them on the hot baking sheet.

To toast in a pan: heat a frying pan over low heat, add the nuts, then toss every 30 seconds

or so, until they have subtly changed color and smell toasty. Once toasted, pour into a bowl and leave to cool—they will keep cooking if you leave them in the hot pan.

The degree to which you toast your nuts will have a huge effect on the flavor of the finished dish. I usually toast mine to a medium toast—still buttery with a little toasty flavor—but for some dishes you might want to keep the flavor cleaner and toast them less; for richer dishes, toast them more.

Aquafaba

Aquafaba is the water left over from cooking legumes and pulses, such as chickpeas. When whipped, it miraculously transforms into a meringue-like consistency and can be used in place of eggs in baking dishes.

How to use aquafaba in baking

To use aquafaba, first you have to make sure it's thick enough. If you're using canned chickpeas, chances are it will be, although note that it can vary from brand to brand. If you're cooking your pulses from scratch, make sure you discard the soaking water and always cook your beans in fresh water. Cook and cool the beans, then drain, reserving the precious liquid. If the liquid isn't gloopy, reduce it by about a quarter. If you don't want to use the pulses you've cooked immediately, you can freeze them in sandwich bags. Make sure your aquafaba is well sieved; you don't want to end up with pieces of chickpea in your meringue.

The general rule for aquafaba is 1 tablespoon for 1 yolk, 2 tablespoons for 1 white, and 3 tablespoons for a whole egg. So, in a cake that calls for 3 eggs, you would use 9 tablespoons (or 135 ml) of aquafaba. One 14.5-ounce (400-g) can of beans will yield around 5 ounces (150 ml) of aquafaba.

If you have a stand mixer or electric whisk, now is the time to use it, as however it's being used, aquafaba always needs to be whisked. Place the aquafaba in a scrupulously clean bowl and whisk, just as you would with egg whites to make meringue. The aquafaba is ready to use when it's holding its own and forming soft peaks with the whisk.

Aquafaba meringues

These are a revelation. Totally egg-free meringues that have a perfect texture and chew. Ideally this would be done in a stand mixer (because they're the most powerful), but an electric hand whisk will work too.

MAKES 10–12 LARGE MERINGUES

a flavorless oil, such as peanut oil

1 14.5-ounce (400-g) can chickpeas

a pinch of fine sea salt

⅔ cup (150 g) superfine or caster sugar

1½ teaspoons cream of tartar

the seeds from 1 vanilla pod or 1 teaspoon vanilla paste

Preheat your oven to 230°F (110°C). Line two baking sheets with nonstick parchment paper and rub it with a tiny drop of oil.

Using a sieve, drain the chickpeas and measure out 5 ounces (150 ml) of chickpea water. Pop the chickpeas in the fridge or freezer to use later. Pour the chickpea water into the bowl of your stand mixer (or large mixing bowl), add the salt, and whisk on a high speed until the aquafaba is white and very stiff.

In a bowl, combine the sugar and cream of tartar. Turn the mixer speed down a little, then add the sugar to the aquafaba 1 tablespoon at a time, making sure that each spoonful of sugar has dissolved before you add the next—you can check this by rubbing a little of the mixture between your fingers; if it's grainy, keep going.

Continue until all the sugar has gone, then add the vanilla and whisk on high for another

couple of minutes. The meringue should now be looking very thick and glossy; if it's not, keep whisking.

Spoon 10–12 piles of the meringue mixture onto the baking sheets, making sure they have a little space to spread, and bake for 2 hours, until crisp on the outside and caramel-colored. After 2 hours, turn the oven off but leave the meringues inside to cool completely—it's really important that you don't open the door while the meringues are cooking or cooling. The meringues will keep for 2 days in a sealed container.

Easy vegetable stock

This recipe is one from *A Modern Way to Eat*. It's a favorite in my house and still my preferred way to make stock. You'll need two 4½-cup (1-liter) preserving jars that will fit in your fridge. Don't feel tied to the amounts of veg below—the great thing about stock is that you can use up all the trimmings and odds and ends you have in the fridge. Just work to the same ratio, half-filling your jars with veg.

MAKES TWO 4½-CUP (1-LITER) JARS

2 carrots, roughly chopped

1 red onion, cut into wedges

1 leek, cut into rounds

2 stalks of celery, roughly chopped

2 bay leaves, scrunched

a small bunch of thyme

1 teaspoon flaky sea salt

a few black peppercorns

Fill the kettle with water and boil it. Divide the chopped veg and other ingredients between your two jars. Fill the jars with the just-boiled water, leaving an inch gap at the top—each jar should hold about 3 cups (750 ml). Pop the lids on and leave in a safe place to cool down.

When cool, sieve right away for a light veg stock, or put in the fridge for 12 hours and then sieve for a more full-bodied stock.

Once sieved, pour the stock back into the jars and store in the fridge, where it will keep for up to a week.

Perfect home-cooked pulses

I have moved from using canned pulses to cooking my own in big batches and freezing them in portions; they are much more delicious and buttery cooked at home.

The length of time it takes to cook a dried pulse will depend on how long ago it was dried. The older it is, the longer it will take to cook. I encourage you to buy pulses from places where they are less likely to have been sitting around for a long time; supermarkets and anywhere that has loose pulses that you buy by weight are good options.

A note on beans and protein. Pulses have only seven of the essential eight amino acids, which make up a complete protein. But the missing piece of the jigsaw can be filled by grains or sesame seeds, which contain the eighth. So eat your pulses with a little bread or in hummus with tahini.

Soaking

Most beans need an overnight soak in double their volume of fresh cold (ideally filtered) water. Soaking them makes them much easier to digest and reduces their famous side effects as well as their cooking time; it also allows them to cook more evenly. If you don't have time to soak them, don't fret, as there are a couple of other options. Give them a quick soak, for as much time as you have, but ideally for 2 hours, or cook them without soaking—though in my experience the time you save by not soaking them will only be replaced by the extra time they take to cook.

Cooking

Drain the soaked pulses, put them into your largest pan, and cover with cold water to about 1 inch (3 cm) above the level of the pulses. Bring to a boil, then boil steadily for 5 minutes

(10 for kidney beans)—this is important, as it deactivates the toxins in the pulses—and after that, turn down the heat to a very gentle simmer and cook until tender and creamy. Cooking on low heat like this will make sure the skins stay intact and that your pulses cook evenly. It is better to shake your pan rather than stir with a wooden spoon, as stirring will break the skins of the pulse. A cooked pulse should remain intact but should collapse into a buttery, creamy mush when squeezed. Chickpeas will remain a little harder but should still be soft throughout. I season my pulses once they are cooked, as seasoning them while cooking is said to toughen them.

Freezing

You can freeze your cooled pulses in their cooking liquid, in portions as they would come in a can, but I prefer to freeze them without their liquid. I season them well, then drain the liquid and allow the pulses to cool before freezing them in meal-size bags. If I have time, I freeze them on a baking sheet first, to keep them from sticking together, and bag them up once frozen.

Soaking and cooking times for dried pulses

Quick
Soak 30 minutes and cook 30 to 40 minutes.

lentils
moth beans
mung beans
split peas

Short
Soak 2–3 hours and cook 30 to 40 minutes.

aduki beans
black-eyed beans

Medium
Soak 4 hours and cook 1–1½ hours.

borlotti beans
butter beans
cannellini beans
navy beans
kidney beans
pinto beans

Long
Soak 8 hours or overnight and cook 1½–3 hours.

chickpeas
fava beans
soybeans

Index

Acknowledgments

It does indeed take a village to write a book, let alone have a baby and get married all in the same sensational year. None of it would have happened without these people; this book belongs to all of you.

John, no words come close and thank you will never ever be enough. You let this take over our lives; you are the most gentle, loving, and, frankly, incredible dad and husband. This all has new meaning now.

Dylan, my funny, curly-haired little man. I can't believe how lucky I am to spend every day with you. You constantly remind me what life is really all about; no one could give me a greater gift. You are my teacher, my heart, my all.

Mum and Dad, the open-hearted and completely generous way you have supported us all while I wrote this book leaves me speechless. I am so grateful that my little boy gets to spend so much time with you both, my two favorite people. He loves you more than words, Nannan and Nandad, as we all do.

Owen, my brother, you are always a reminder to me to fight hard for what I believe, to be wise, loyal, funny. Thank you for everything you bring to our family and to the world.

Laura, every day I wish you were nearer, but knowing you are truly happy is all I need. Even though you are so far away, you still manage to be my other half, my sounding board, and the greatest friend I'll ever have.

Louise Haines, your kindness, patience, wisdom, and tireless encouragement leave me in awe. Thank you for trusting me and allowing me to be so involved in every part of this book. I can never thank you enough.

Ana, I loved working with you, from your wild creative urges to your sweetness, your warm heart, and moody playlists. This book is so much richer thanks to your images. I am so grateful to you.

Rachel, thank you for adding your friendship, your heartfelt and always original creative force to this book. Thanks for steering me though the wobbles and helping us make a book that I am so very proud of.

Jonny, thank you for your incredible design. The gentle and considered way you looked at each little element made this book what it is. I know how very hard you worked—thank you. Keep fighting the good fight.

Louise Tucker, our savior; thank you for making this book a reality. Without you, I don't think we'd have made it. I so enjoyed working with you.

Sarah Thickett, thank you for all your hard work getting us off the ground—much love.

To Imogen Fortes, thank you for your graceful editing. You were a joy to work with. To Annie Lee, thank you once again. You are so wonderful.

Michelle, thank you for all that's gone before and what's to come. You are amazing.

Matt Clacher, full of great ideas, I look forward to what's in store.

Felicity, thank you for being an incredible friend, agent, and confidante. I feel so very, very lucky to have you on my side.

Jess, you are incredible. I will ever never forget your generosity and unwavering support as I learned how to be a mum. I am incredibly lucky to work with you and call you my friend. Here's to some exciting new adventures ahead.

Anna Shepherd, another generous soul. You cared about the recipes in this book as if it were your own, and in part it is. I love having you around; thank you for everything.

Emily, I wish we could still kick around together every day; thank you for everything you have brought to these shoots and to my life. You are the very best.

Rosie, thank for your incredible skills and bringing your calmness to the kitchen. Kitty, what a babe; thanks for always being 10/10. Nena, I love working with you; thanks for being the most organized cook in history.

Frances, Verity, Issy, thank you for volunteering your time. You were all such lovely ladies to have around.

Mina and everyone at Guardian Cook, thank you for your continued support. I am incredibly proud to write for you.

Issy Croker, thank you for being a wonderful friend, and a brilliant collaborator and a very, very kind soul.

To all the amazing people who tested these recipes in your homes, your time and care mean so much to me; thank you from the bottom of my heart. Nena Foster, Angelique Mercier, Jenny Box, James Gold, Olenka Lawrenson, Priya Thakar, Anja Dunk, Emma Ballinger, Jack Bannochie, Christina Mackenzie, Nick and Anna Probert, Emily Taylor, Carys Williams, Kate Stockdale, Jock Shepherd. Ellie Shepherd, Alison Lea-Wilson, Luke Shaller, Vanessa Fogarty, Alice Lutyens, Tara Al Azzawi, Ellie Matthews, Alisa Stewart, Evie Hone, Josie Hearnden, Matt Clacher, Madeleine Porteous, Holly Wulff Peterson, Philippa Tolmay, Caitlin Scheybeler, Sian Dale, Ceri Tallett.

Thank you to the amazing people whose fruit and vegetables fill these pages: Natoora, Worton Organic Garden, Rushton's The Chef's Greengrocers. And thank you to e5 Bakehouse; without your bread, we'd be in trouble.

To the amazing ceramics collective, Turning Earth, particularly Andrea Roman, Lisa Ommanney, and Ned Davies for lending me their works of art. David Mellor, Sue Pryke, thanks for the loan of your incredible ceramics and homewares.

To de Buyer, Magimix, Stokke, thank you for your generosity.

My incredible family and all my friends, sorry for (once again) disappearing off the face of the earth while I wrote this book. Here's to more adventures ahead.

The Jones Aunties and Uncles, and especially Aunty Avril, for all those years in California and for keeping us in check.

Ged, thank you for your magic.

All The Dales, especially Sian and Roger for stepping in when we needed help most. You are all so kind and generous. Granny Liz, the world's most glamorous great-granny.

And lastly, but by no means least, to you, the people who buy and read and cook from these books. I am still a little shell-shocked that I get to do this as my job. The fact that these books are used and loved in people's kitchens fills me with joy and pride in the very best way. From the bottom of my heart, thank you.